BOWLED OVER

BIG-TIME COLLEGE FOOTBALL

BOWLED OVER

FROM THE SIXTIES TO THE BCS ERA

Michael Oriard

The University of North Carolina Press CHAPEL HILL

This book was published with the assistance of the Thornton H. Brooks Fund of the University of North Carolina Press.

© 2009 THE UNIVERSITY OF NORTH CAROLINA PRESS

Designed by Kimberly Bryant
Set in Arnhem and The Sans by Tseng Information Systems, Inc.
Manufactured in the United States of America

The paper in this book meets the guidelines for permanence and durability of the Committee on Production Guidelines for Book Longevity of the Council on Library Resources.

The University of North Carolina Press has been a member of the Green Press Initiative since 2003.

Library of Congress Cataloging-in-Publication Data
Oriard, Michael, 1948–
Bowled over : big-time college football from the sixties to the BCS era / Michael Oriard.
    p. cm.
Includes bibliographical references and index.
ISBN 978-0-8078-3329-2 (cloth : alk. paper)
1. Football—United States—History. 2. College sports—United States—Marketing. 3. College sports—United States—Management. 4. College athletes—Recruiting—United States. I. Title.
GV950.O7 2009
796.332—dc22   2009016597

cloth   13 12 11 10 09   5 4 3 2 1

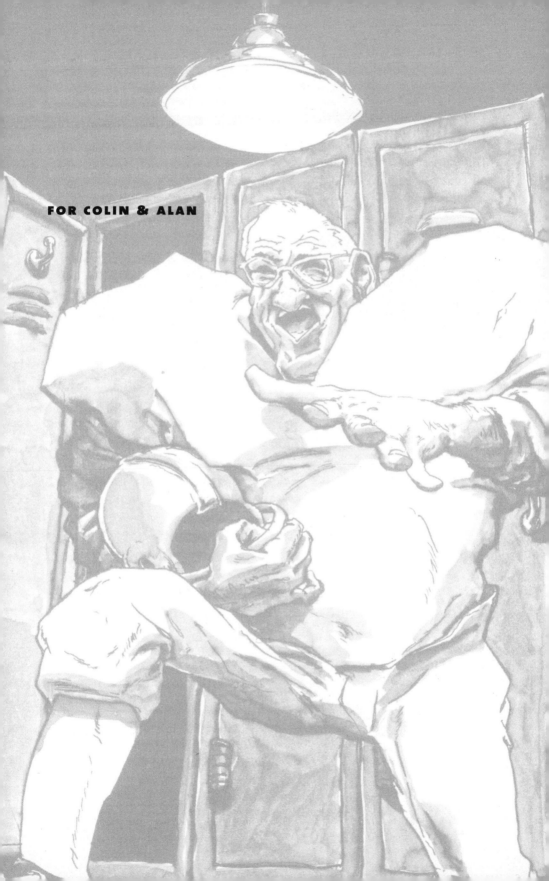

FOR COLIN & ALAN

Contents

Illustrations and Tables

Acknowledgments

This is the third book on which I worked with David Perry at the University of North Carolina Press and the one on which we worked the closest. In addition to David's routine contributions as editor in chief of the press, I am grateful for his good counsel regarding an early draft of my book. Other members of the UNC Press staff—Jay Mazzocchi, Dino Battista, and Gina Mahalek— are becoming like old friends. Thanks to all of them once again for their many and varied contributions.

Phil Thompson, a player from my generation at the University of Kentucky when it integrated its football team, shared his experiences with me in some remarkable e-mails and items from his scrapbooks. I salute him and thank him. At Oregon State University, archivist Karl McCreary located salary information from the 1960s for me, and the former chair of my department, Robert Schwartz, and the successive deans of my college, Kay Schaffer, Larry Roper, and Larry Rodgers, have been uniformly supportive. I am grateful to all.

My greatest debt, as always, is to my wife, Julie, and our two sons, for reasons too numerous to list but which might be reduced to the fact that they keep my priorities straight. I am dedicating this book to our sons, who in different sports and in different ways made their athletic careers as enriching as mine was for me. I salute them for accomplishing this under much more difficult circumstances than I faced.

BOWLED OVER

INTRODUCTION

This book is a companion to my *Brand NFL: Making and Selling America's Favorite Sport* (2007). They began as a single volume, which was itself a hybrid: an account of football in the 1960s, when I myself played, leading into an exploration of how the game at both the college and professional levels has changed since then. There proved to be too many narratives to develop coherently, though the necessary bisection was not all gain. What has happened in the National Football League (NFL) in recent decades has powerfully affected what used to be known as Division I-A college football (now the Football Bowl Subdivision)—think only of the lure of million-dollar NFL salaries for "student-athletes" and the impact on college coaches' salaries as pro coaches began making millions. Many NFL players, in turn, are shaped in part by their college experiences—think here of the sense of entitlement that follows some athletes from college to the pros. In fact, one of the fundamental differences in football today from football in my day is the general sense of a continuous path from youth leagues all the way to the NFL. Boys of my generation knew little about the NFL beyond what they figured out from watching the weekly game on Sunday. Boys today know everything about the NFL that *SportsCenter* and the rest of our 24/7 sports media and entertainment industries show and tell them. Boys of my generation might have dreamed of playing pro football some day. Like-minded boys today might plot a course—through weight rooms, diet supplements, summer camps, personal trainers, recruiting gurus—for getting there.

Seeing the entire American football world as a whole has its advantages, then, but so does a tighter focus on one part of it. This book considers the part of our larger football culture with the longest and richest history, as well as the most profound contradiction at its heart. From the moment that university administrators in the 1890s realized that the new public passion for intercollegiate football provided opportunities for university building, college football has been torn between the competing demands of marketing and educating. Knowing that the contradiction at the heart of big-time college football is more than a century old is useful when the latest "crisis" erupts. That knowledge should also give us pause, however, to wonder why we have failed for so long to resolve the contradiction.

While conflicting priorities in college football are anything but new, they have reached a level that seems qualitatively different from how it played out even in my own youth in the 1950s and 1960s. College football since then has changed in two ways: suddenly and gradually. Suddenly, in "the '60s," that period conveniently dated from November 1963, when John F. Kennedy was shot down in Dallas, to August 1974, when Richard Nixon resigned in disgrace. The '60s peaked around 1967–70—the years when Detroit, Newark, south central Los Angeles, and dozens of other cities exploded in race riots, campuses from Columbia to Berkeley exploded in antiwar protests, and Woodstock, New York, exploded in rock music and free love. Martin Luther King Jr. and Robert F. Kennedy were assassinated, Neil Armstrong walked on the moon, four students at Kent State were killed by National Guardsmen, and hippies became no longer just the kooks in *Life* magazine but also the kid upstairs in his bedroom with a sweetish odor oozing out from behind a locked door. Football, too, was convulsed in these final years of the decade. Black players called their coaches racist and boycotted practice. White players at the University of Maryland got their coach fired for demeaning them. Demeaning them?! That's what coaches had always done to motivate their "boys."

No comparable cataclysm in either college football or American life has occurred since the 1960s, yet the experiences of playing and following the game today are astonishingly different from what they were just a couple of generations ago. The entire history of big-time intercollegiate football since the late nineteenth century has been a tortuous working out of the sport's fundamental contradiction of being, at one and the same time, a commercial spectacle and an extracurricular activity. But sometime in the late 1980s or 1990s, incremental changes reached a tipping point or crossed a boundary beyond which the contradiction has become unsustainable. While the disruptions of the 1960s, particularly the racial protests on northern campuses, were felt as a genuine revolution, this subsequent economic transformation has not. This second revolution played out in slow motion, but at some point many followers of college football awakened to a realization that the game had changed in basic ways. The simplest measure of this transformation would be the million-dollar salary that became the norm for coaches in top programs in the 1990s, three times as much as just a decade earlier and many, many times the $20,000 or $25,000 salaries of the 1960s.

Obviously, more than inflation was at work here, and the amounts of money now flowing in and out of top programs created a new world. For $25,000, a coach was something like a professor (perhaps a dean) of football. For $1 million, he was the impresario of a high-priced commercial entertainment. In college football's long reign as the dominant form of the sport, from the 1870s into the 1950s, potential revenue was largely restricted to gate receipts. Radio broadcasting rights began paying small dividends in the 1930s; the National Collegiate Athletic Association (NCAA) actively restricted television in the 1950s, fearing the potential impact on attendance. Merchandising and fund-raising (beyond the arrangements between boosters and recruits) were nonexistent throughout the entire period. (For a kid in the 1950s to own a sweatshirt imprinted with "Property of USC Football," he had to know someone who knew someone in the University of Southern California football program.) A business plan for athletics amounted to building a large stadium and then selling tickets. The athletic director (or graduate manager of athletics, as he was initially known) was a former coach who got on well with the old boys in the booster club. To oversimplify only slightly, his job was to support his football coach in building a team that could fill the stadium on Saturday afternoons.

Now, those who stage the games are driven by financial concerns to a degree unknown even thirty years ago. As I have attempted in a couple of previous books to understand what football has meant to Americans since we invented our version of the game in the 1870s and 1880s, economics always seemed the backdrop against which the more important stories played out. In recent years, economics have increasingly seemed the story that mattered the most. Generating revenue has been a preoccupation of athletic directors and university presidents since the stadium-building boom of the 1920s, but money was a less powerful driving force when the opportunities for both spending and generating revenue were more restricted.

Criticism of too much commercialism and too little academic emphasis in college football is nearly as old as the game, and so too is public indifference to these perennial "problems." "Everyone" knew that boosters were subsidizing the swift halfbacks and brawny tackles arriving on campus from farms and mill towns in the 1920s and 1930s (after a few decades of less systematic hiring of the occasional "tramp athlete"). But few cared. Big-time college football has always had its faculty critics, joined by disdainful writers in the intellectual journals—the stereotype of the pointy-headed Great Scold is as enduring as the Big Man on Campus and the Dumb Jock—but the vast football public has been largely indifferent to this criticism so long as it did not hurt the prospects for "my team" on Saturday. The most powerful mass media—first the daily newspaper with its bulging sports sections, then radio, then television—have always been more boosterish than critical of big-time football, for the obvious reason that they have depended on enthusiastic fans to be their own readers, listeners, and viewers. Local media have tended to have close relations with the home team, and the major football-playing universities tend to be located in smallish towns, where the local sports editor and beat writers have particularly cozy relationships with the football coach and director of athletics. The national media have faced a different need: appealing to the broadest possible audience. Although *Sports Illustrated* and ESPN issue periodic jeremiads against the abuses in college football, those tend to be overwhelmed by the weekly or daily coverage of the big games and top stars. Local or national, the mass media have operated under conditions that inhibit sustained criticism.

The media played a key role in American universities' two great missed opportunities in the twentieth century to address college football's great contradiction. Had the popular press waged a campaign on behalf of the Carnegie Foundation's report in 1929, it might have generated enough public support to overwhelm boosters and pressure (or free) college administrators to consider genuine reforms. Likewise, when the NCAA went through the throes of reform in the late 1940s and early 1950s, centered around a proposed "Sanity Code," indifference or opposition in the press again assured that the reformist spasm, weak as it already was, would pass. The Carnegie Report prompted a few universities to de-emphasize their football programs but had no broad impact on "commercialism" and "professionalism," the terms commonly used for the twin curses on the game. Intermittent scandals and controversies erupted and subsided until the 1950s, when a cheating ring at West Point, slush funds at West Coast universities that eventually shut down the old Pacific Coast Conference, and continuing rancor in the NCAA between rival factions that viewed themselves as honest and the other side as corrupt or hypocritical seemed to demand drastic action. Instead, out of the wrangling in the NCAA came the athletic scholarship, a solution to the long-standing scandal of "professionalism" by making it legal. (The fact that a scholarship for mere athletic prowess, rather than academic achievement or financial need, was considered a violation of university values until this time points to the very different climate in which college football was once played.)

The establishment of the athletic grant-in-aid in 1956 set the stage for the debates at NCAA conventions in the 1960s that culminated, in 1973, in the one-year scholarship, renewable at the coach's discretion. I will argue that this little-noted and mostly forgotten reinvention of the athletic scholarship marks a crucial turning point for big-time college football. The more obviously consequential events were the College Football Association's successful challenge to the NCAA's television monopoly in 1984, then the succession of bowl alignments in the 1990s, culminating in the Bowl Championship Series in 1998, which consolidated two distinct economic classes for big-time football programs and widened the gap between them. The one-year scholarship, backed by the mindset that it represents, exposed so-called student-athletes to the mounting pressures of an increasingly commercialized sport while denying them a share in its new bounty.

This slow-motion revolution is the subject of the second half of this book. I will propose that the institution of the one-year scholarship in 1973 was in part a response to the upheavals of the 1960s, the subject of the first half. Here, I present my account of football in the 1960s as a story not about my life in football but about football during my lifetime, from the perspective of one who was there but on the periphery of the events that transformed the game. The beginning and end of the "long '60s" coincidentally bracketed my own football career. In November 1963, when President Kennedy was assassinated in Dallas, I was a sophomore at Gonzaga Prep in Spokane, Washington, putting in my fall afternoons on the B-squad and awaiting my chance to be a varsity player. In early April 1968, when Martin Luther King fell in Memphis, I was a sophomore at Notre Dame, a walk-on scrub who had not suited up for a single game the previous fall but was about to be given the opportunity to become an actual Fighting Irish football player. In May 1970, when college-aged kids in National Guard uniforms gunned down four students at Kent State, I was a senior, soon to graduate, not participating in spring practice and therefore not prodded to weigh protest against football. (My subsequent brief NFL career coincided with the end of the era. In September 1974, a month after Nixon left the White House in disgrace, I left the NFL after four seasons, cut by the Kansas City Chiefs at the end of a strike-torn training camp.)

During my four years at Notre Dame, Southeastern Conference schools at last began integrating their football teams, but they did not complete the process until after I had graduated. As a senior in 1969, I played against Georgia Tech and Tulane, then against Texas in the Cotton Bowl, when their teams were still all white. My senior season marked college football's centennial but also became a milestone for other reasons, as major racial protests disrupted football programs at Oregon State, Iowa, Wyoming, Indiana, and Washington. I must have had some awareness of these events at the time—my memory is regrettably spotty—but they were far removed from my own experience at Notre Dame. The extraordinary national and world events of my college years, which changed me and my entire generation forever, in my own mind at the time had nothing to do with my life on football fields. I suspect that in this I was more typical than not. Participants are not necessarily the best witnesses, let alone interpreters, of the history in which they live. I make no claim to a privileged understanding of the 1960s football revolution that I describe. I simply offer, not my own story, but a personal perspective on the story of that larger football world of which I was a part.

I am interested in the personal actors in that story, particularly those who were age nineteen or twenty or twenty-one like I was but whose college football experience was so different from mine. But in line with my previous explorations of the media's role in shaping our football culture, I am more interested in these events as public dramas, staged and scripted by local newspapers and the national media. Football has functioned as a kind of public theater since it was first discovered by the mass-circulation newspapers in New York in the 1880s. Whether or not fans have thought about spectator sports on these terms, they have experienced them in this way. Some dramas are generic to all sporting contests: the Home Team repulsing the Enemy, the various plots for different types of heroes. Others are specific to certain sports: the dual between pitcher and batter, so utterly different from the helmet-rattling collision in football. Others still are dictated by specific circumstances either within or outside the sport; the uproar over steroids in Major

League Baseball and the accusations of rape against lacrosse players at Duke come to mind as recent examples. The racial dramas in college football in the 1960s fall in this last category. How newspapers covered (or did not cover) these events created the public drama.

While the two parts of the narrative that follows address different topics, there are important links between them. One is the relationship between coaches and athletes, and their relative positions in the evolving world of big-time college football. A more fundamental one is the central importance of race. The 1960s saw the end of college football's era of segregation. In the succeeding era of full integration, as black athletes became dominant on the field but lagged behind in the classroom, the key issues facing the NCAA and its member institutions have been racial at their core, though rarely acknowledged as such. (I follow Harry Edwards and others in understanding that African American athletes face more directly and intensely what all athletes face.) As I have noted, I will also explore the strong possibility that the institution of the one-year scholarship in 1973—which transformed "student-athletes" into "athlete-students"—was a response to the racial upheavals of the late 1960s.

I bring a personal perspective not just to the events from my own playing days but also to the developments in college football since I graduated. My bedrock experience that has shaped my outlook is easily described: at Notre Dame in the late 1960s, I not only received the best education that my university offered but also enjoyed a full college experience while playing big-time football at the highest level. Since 1976 I have been an English professor at a Pac-10 university, observing college football's most recent struggles with its fundamental contradiction more or less from the inside; and for the past several years, I have been writing about the cultural history of American football. Expressed personally, my fundamental concern regarding college football today is that my 1960s experience may not even be available to "student-athletes" in our more fully commercialized, higher-pressure football world. At the same time, an athletic scholarship today buys exactly what it bought during my college years. Tuition, board, and housing cost more in real dollars, but they have the same value. Or perhaps less: with less opportunity to receive a real education, athletes today might be taking a cut in real benefits.

Or not. Determining how well big-time college football serves the athletes today is one of two crucial challenges facing the institutions that sponsor it. The other is to determine how well it serves the institutions themselves.

Saturday's spectacles provide Americans with a unique social and cultural experience. A college football game at Michigan or Alabama (like a basketball game at Indiana or Duke), with its bands and cheerleaders, its pregame tailgating, and its postgame partying, is something like a folk festival or a weekly Mardi Gras, providing a sense of community, meaningful ritual, and sheer pleasure for millions of Americans each weekend in the fall.[1] Following the local team, or connecting from afar as alumni, provides passionate involvement in something that deeply matters yet ultimately does not (and so is "safe") and creates a sense of community whose social benefit is hard to measure but nonetheless is real and powerful. But can universities afford to keep providing that social benefit, and can they provide it without exploiting those who do the actual providing—the young men on the field? Those are the urgent questions of the moment.

Fewer than two dozen athletic departments break even in any given year; as few as a half dozen have done so in each of the last several years. But this superelite depends on the rest, on all of the programs that struggle with annual deficits. A superconference comprised only of the very top programs would have a passionate following only in its schools' own states and among their alumni. Although the Big East is conspicuously the weakest Bowl Championship Series (BCS) conference on the field, the other five conferences need it in order to have fully national representation. Without the weaker teams within BCS conferences, the perennially stronger teams would have no one to be perennially stronger than. The superelite even need the non-BCS conferences, if only to throw up a Cinderella challenger each year and provide one of the narratives of which football fans never weary. The superelite need the rest, but whether the rest can afford their role is increasingly uncertain.

The first three chapters of this book, comprising Part I, describe the politicizing of football in the 1960s and the two-part racial revolution of that era, set against my sheltered experience at Notre Dame. Following a brief interlude—in which I lay out the case for seeing the one-year scholarship as a belated response to the political and racial turmoil in athletic departments of the late 1960s—Part II then considers the world of big-time college football as it was remade first by NCAA legislation in the early 1970s and then by the radically uneven distribution of financial resources in the 1980s and 1990s. Chapters 4 and 5 explore college football's fundamental contradiction as it has played out in the NCAA's dual agenda of achieving academic reforms while relentlessly chasing revenues, then tease out the impact of this dual agenda on the athletes in its fostering of both entitlement and exploitation. Chapter 6 considers the possibilities for reform. Instead of offering yet one more set of proposals to be ignored, I suggest that we refocus the conversation. From any reasonably objective perspective, the case for reform seems overwhelming. For a football coach to make several times as much as the university president is obviously crazy. For the nonprofit extracurricular activity of a few dozen students to generate as much as $60 million in revenue is obviously crazy. And expecting the athletes who generate those millions to put in full-time hours, at the equivalent of minimum wage, and also be full-time students like everyone else in their classes is obviously crazy.

Yet if big-time college football is so obviously crazy, why does it survive in our temples of higher learning, overseen by college presidents who are some of the smartest people in the country? The answer is equally obvious: because the sport historically has served vital functions in American higher education, and it is not at all obvious that it no longer does so. That's the crux of the issue. It is not possible to think in any meaningful way about reforming college football without thinking also about the nature and needs of the institutions whose football might need reforming.

For me, the second half of this book is no less personal than the first because writing it has meant wrestling with a subject about which I have felt profoundly ambivalent as a beneficiary of a system that seems to fail too many others. Some readers will dimly remember the revolutions of the 1960s, but for many it will be a surprise to realize how recently these events played out. The tale of distorted priorities, on the other hand, is likely so familiar that it might seem not worth belaboring yet again. I have tried to offer a new way to think about it. These are obviously not the only stories that could be told about college football since the 1960s.[2] They are the stories that most interest me, and I can only hope that they will interest readers, too.

A final note on sources. Getting reliable data on either football finances or athletes' academic performance used to be immensely difficult, if not impossible. Beginning in 1970, the NCAA every few years published the results from surveys of institutional revenues and expenses for athletics, but responses were voluntary, there was little consistency in the reporting, and the organization published only aggregate data. Investigative journalists for major daily newspapers periodically gathered the available information on coaches' salaries, bowl revenues, television-rights fees, or some other aspect of college football finances, but their data were always partial and never wholly reliable.

In the 1990s, when Congress began requiring annual financial reports to document compliance with Title IX, a wealth of data became suddenly available (for each year since 1995). Even here, because accounting procedures varied—including institutional or state support (tuition waivers, student fees, or direct allocations) in football revenue or counting it separately, while treating or not treating indirect costs, capital expenses, and debt service as football expenses—a clear understanding of football finances did not necessarily emerge. However flawed, data for each NCAA institution at least was now available (posted on the U.S. Department of Education's website).

Around the same time, Congress began requiring the publication of graduation rates, which the NCAA later revised with its own Graduation Success Rate (GSR) to account for transfers. (Under federal guidelines, an athlete in good academic standing who transferred to another school and even graduated from that school would count against his original university's graduation rate. GSRs tend to be about ten percentage points higher than federal graduation rates.) Here, too, the accompanying NCAA press releases always reported aggregate rather than individual institutional data—for all of Division I-A, for example—but as with the Department of Education's data on revenues and expenses, a little digging into the NCAA's website could find the figures for individual institutions. Both the federal graduation rate and the NCAA's GSR compared athletes to students overall (who were overwhelmingly not on full scholarship, increasingly had to work in order to afford their tuition, and often left school for financial reasons). Whether or not such comparisons were appropriate, at least the data were now available.

Finally, the NCAA itself, under the leadership of Myles Brand since 2003, has begun publishing various kinds of financial data on its website for the sake of transparency and to encourage institutional responsibility. In this spirit, the organization in 2008 began reporting revenues and expenses in a new way, still in aggregate form rather than for individual institutions but avowedly with consistent accounting methods that made the data more meaningful and reliable. (Several athletics officials immediately challenged the consistency of even this improved method.) In short, there are now mountains of data on both the financial and academic dimensions of big-time football that were not available even two decades ago. (With a December 2008 deadline for my final draft—and minor revisions possible until mid-March—the figures used are the most current ones available as of those dates.)

Yet the data remain partial and what they reveal not always self-evident. Nonetheless, while direct comparisons between specific institutions are still difficult, the available data can reveal the broader outlines of the institutional range in big-time football, today's so-called Football Bowl Subdivision. They can help us think more clearly than used to be possible about the ways that tremendous, and tremendously uneven, financial growth has likely affected college football, the universities that sponsor it, and the young men who play it. The data reveal the *system* of big-time college football more clearly than before, if not the specific institutions and individuals within it.

While care must be taken with the available data, anyone who would understand big-time college football must also be wary of an alternate temptation: to generalize from published anecdotes. Popular sports journalism thrives on compelling personal stories—the famous football player who finishes four years of college still reading at a fourth-grade level, the rash of felonies in a particular football program—which are crafted into morality plays that purport to reveal general truths. There is always an element of truth in these stories, but how representative the individual cases are cannot easily be known, and compelling anecdotes coupled with faulty statistics can be particularly misleading. These media-made morality plays are important for my purposes, not as revelations of broader truths but as themselves an important element in the culture of big-time football. "True" or not, they shape what many people believe. And for institutions engaged in an enterprise so tied to promotion and marketing, public scandal is the worst nightmare.

Neither the personal stories nor the mounds of data can provide the most crucial information of all: clear evidence of whether institutions on the one hand and "student-athletes" on the other continue to receive the benefits from big-time college football that both once did. Knowing with greater certainty whether or not they do is a prerequisite for deciding what, if anything, should be done to change the way we now conduct the game. While this book cannot provide that answer, I hope that it clarifies what is at stake in asking the questions.

PART I FOOTBALL AND THE 1960S

FROM THE SIDELINES OF A
FOOTBALL REVOLUTION

I want it long, straight, curly, fuzzy

Snaggy, shaggy, ratty, matty

—Hair *(Broadway opening, April 29, 1968)*

Looking back, someone today might conclude that to play football in the 1960s was to choose authoritarian discipline over personal freedom, violence over peace and love, the war in Vietnam over the revolution at home. Period photographs seem to tell that story: athletes with square jaws, square crew cuts, and square attitudes over here, wild-eyed protesters and wild-haired hippies over there.[1] Actual confrontations became symbolic dramas, as when UC Berkeley football players heckled the speakers at the rally in October 1964 that inaugurated the Free Speech Movement at Berkeley. Or when athletes at the University of Pennsylvania in 1965 chanted, "Hit 'em again, harder, harder," while their teammates scuffled with protesters. Or when forty "burly 'jocks,'" as *Time* magazine called them, blockaded Low Library on the Columbia University campus in April 1968 to starve out the student protesters occupying the building. In a long insiders' account of the protests at Columbia, *Ramparts* (the anti-*Time* of the era) repeatedly referred to the antiprotesters as "the jocks," while also noting that the dean whose position they supported was "a former crew oar."[2] Jocks were reactionaries. Football players were quintessential jocks. My country, right or wrong—sis boom bah!

Jim Sweeney, the head football coach at Washington State University in the late 1960s, called football "a fortress that has held the wall against radical elements." That was the belief, anyway, and the clean-cut football player indeed looked like the antihippie and antiradical of the era. In a speech in June 1968, Homer Babbidge, the president of the University of Connecticut, described college athletes as "the guys in the white hats—they keep their hair cut short, they're clean, they're orderly, aware

*Protesters (top)
and antiprotesters
(bottom) at Columbia
University, April
1968 (Courtesy of the
Columbia Spectator)*

of the importance of law and order and discipline." Short hair was the visible sign of deeply held traditional values.[3]

So much to-do about hair in the '60s, as if the fate of Western civilization lay in the hands of barbers. At the NCAA convention in January 1969, delegates passed legislation allowing schools to rescind the scholarships of players guilty of "manifest disobedience." Protesters were the target, but as the Associated Press reported, "Several coaches here have expressed concern over long hairdos, beards, and mustaches by players." "Long hair and beards not only defy orderliness," declared the faculty representative from the University of Texas during the floor debate, "but under certain circumstances can be detrimental to performance."[4] Take that, Troy Polamalu!

In another report from the front lines of sport's "mod revolution," the Associated Press's Will Grimsley in 1970 mentioned a freshman defensive back at the University of Minnesota who quit football after he was told to cut his hair, as well as the two long-haired tennis players at the University of Florida who hired an attorney after being suspended. According to Grimsley, football coaches in particular wanted athletes who looked like football players, not a bunch of hippies with "Prince Valiant hair bobs, mutton-chop sideburns, mustaches, beards, candy-striped trousers, frilly cuffs and beads."[5] In the 1960s, buzz-cut nation met long-hair nation and Afro nation at the barricades. The buzz cutters won the battles but obviously lost the war.

Well-barbered football players might have looked like Eisenhower Republicans left over from the 1950s, and some no doubt were, but football players were not necessarily more conservative than their classmates. As a student at Notre Dame from 1966 to 1970, I was not alone in playing football while opposing the war, wearing my hair short for football without intending a political statement—and even doing these things without feeling hypocritical. According to Grimsley, both my college coach and pro coach belonged to the "antihair party." Ara Parseghian at Notre Dame believed that "wearing a beard or a mustache gives empathy or sympathy to a movement that is certainly the direct opposite of what we strive for in college football." Hank Stram, my coach with the Kansas City Chiefs for four years in the early 1970s, professed "discipline, dedication, duty" and backed them up, as Grimsley accurately reported, with the threat of a $500 fine for overly long sideburns. Mustaches and beards were unthinkable. When I showed up for an off-season conditioning session in the spring of 1974 with a Stanford-grown beard—I was a graduate student from January through June—I might have driven a small wedge into my relationship with Hank, who cut me five months later at the end of the players' strike.

In the 1960s "the Big Game" and "the Barricades," terms juxtaposed in the title of a *Sports Illustrated* article in January 1966, became symbols of an unbridgeable political and cultural divide.[6] Football may have been just a game, but it represented "traditional" values cherished by the Right and abhorred by the Left. Routine pregame pageantry, with the national anthem and perhaps an ROTC color guard, took on new meaning in the 1960s. On the other side of the barricades, in our histories and memories of the 1960s, yippies are better known for dressing up in Santa Claus suits and tossing coins to passersby on Wall Street or for nominating Pigasus the Pig for president in 1968, but a yippie wearing a football helmet while demonstrating against the 1968 Democratic Convention in Chicago was similarly waging revolution through symbols.[7] In its October 1968 issue, the avant-garde literary journal *Evergreen Review* published a one-act play titled *Football*, in which the character named Coach (clearly Lyndon Johnson in an overstuffed football uniform) conducts a surreal press conference with a chorus of Reporters after a game that has left thousands of spectators and players crushed, decapitated, or otherwise slaughtered. Jock Lib radicals in Berkeley issued a communiqué before the Big Game in 1970, declaring their "direct opposition to pig Amerika's death culture as epitomized by gladiatorial football clashes."[8] To some, football symbolized the vital force of Western civilization; to others, it was its murderous endgame.

Football in its many forms since the Middle Ages had always been "a mimic game of war,"[9] and American football was understood in that way from nearly its beginning. Walter Camp wrote about "the foot-ball army" and "the kicking or artillery work" in the 1890s, and later coaches, such as Army's Charles Daly and Harvard's Percy Haughton, elaborated on those connections.[10] One of the Left's more curious notions in the 1960s pushed that basic idea in a new direction by denouncing football as a *territorial* game—offenses seizing yardage as they marched down the field—and thus a symbol for American imperialism run amok in Southeast Asia. Insofar as football is territorial, a more apt analogy would be all of that meaningless Russian land seized by Hitler's troops before being repulsed at Leningrad and Moscow in World War II, the original "red zones" I suppose. As any football fan knows, one team can outgain the other by hundreds of yards and still lose. Comparably distorted

Cartoon illustration of "Coach" (Evergreen Review, *October 1968*)

logic came from the Right. More dispassionate folks today might wonder how unquestioning submission to the coach could be an expression of American patriotism, given the fact that the United States was born in 1776 by rejecting tyrannical authority and rugged individualism has long been one of our most cherished national traits.

Behind the symbols and ideological projections lay a messier reality. Whatever short hair and football meant to Ara Parseghian and Hank Stram, or to any number of their coaching colleagues, we players were individual citizens, not a political team. In playing football at Notre Dame as something akin to a private vision quest, then continuing to play less dreamily in the NFL, I could remain oblivious, or at least impervious, to the fact that for much of the country, football embodied a set of values that most in my generation were repudiating. And I was certainly not alone. A cofounder of *Rising Up Angry*, a radical underground newspaper in Chicago, had played football at Lake Forest College.[11] In his memoir of the sixties, a cofounder of the Liberation News Service, the underground's alternative to the Associated Press and United Press International, described meeting a "a two-hundred-pound football player" from New Mexico State "who has managed to turn on the entire team to grass, rock, and Marianne's sandal shop" (the local hippie joint).[12] Football fans over age fifty remember Dave Meggyesy, George Sauer, and Chip Oliver for leaving the NFL in protest or to pursue radical causes or countercultural lifestyles.[13] We should also remind ourselves that these men, before they quit, were football players with radical and countercultural ideas. Beyond a certain point on the spectrum of leftward thinking, there was no longer room for football: the sport in its fundamental nature *is* competitive, rule governed, and physically aggressive, rather than collaborative (with the other team, that is), anarchic, and pacifist. But short of that point, football could coexist with all kinds of countercultural and politically progressive values.

At Columbia the radical students occupying Low Library and the Majority Coalition that opposed them were known to each other, not so affectionately, as "pukes" and "jocks." In their book-length account of the protest, the staff of the *Columbia Daily Spectator* used the terms "Majority Coalition" and "the athletes" interchangeably to describe the antiprotesters and explained that the athletes "were at Columbia primarily because of their skill in sports and had come to feel like outsiders, bystanders to the academic currents of the University. The visceral revulsion they felt for the demonstrators led them to join forces with those conservatives who intellectually repudiated the Left and who formed Columbia's political out-group."[14] In *Life* magazine's account, one Columbia grad student described the counterrebels as "the so-called 'jock faction,' the Majority Coalition of which campus athletes formed the core."[15] Press coverage routinely identified Paul Vilardi, the spokesman and a cofounder of the Majority Coalition, as a former football and baseball player whose athletic career had been cut short by injuries.[16]

On the other side, however, James Simon Kunen, the protester whose own version of the events, *The Strawberry Statement—Notes of a College Revolutionary* (1969), became an instant '60s classic, was a member of the Columbia crew who slipped away from the sit-ins for his daily workouts on the river. A member of the varsity wrestling team organized the kitchen that provided meals for the besieged students. Vilardi himself told the *Daily News* that he and his friends supported the protesters' cause, just not their tactics.[17]

Jocks and pukes, in other words, had more in common than their media stereotypes suggested. One historian of student radicalism has pointed out that, despite the Columbia protesters' description of their foes as "little more than a minority of racist 'jocks,'" two-thirds of Columbia undergraduates opposed the sit-ins.[18] "Jocks," or better yet "burly jocks," were more conspicuous than the rest of their classmates, and they were singled out by reporters because they made for good theater, filling a necessary role for a simple morality play. At UC Berkeley, yes, football players heckled protesters at the Free Speech rally in 1964, but other football players marched against the war at the Vietnam Day protest in 1965.[19] Football in the 1960s symbolized a set of ideas neither inherent in the sport nor necessarily held by those who played it. One might well wonder where that stereotype came from.

AMERICAN FOOTBALL

American football was always American; it was the context for "American" that changed in the 1960s. What most of the world calls football—or *futbol* or *Fußball*—is soccer to us, and we are not entirely alone in going our own way. Gaelic football, Australian Rules football, and Canadian football thrived at least in part due to similar postcolonial or nationalist impulses. The game that evolved into American football was first organized in the 1870s by students at Harvard, Yale, Princeton, and a few other northeastern universities, led by a Yale student, Walter Camp, "the Father of American Football." Elite British secondary schools presented them with two options: the rules governing the Football Association (soc-cer) and the Rugby Union. Harvard alone among the American schools preferred the running to the kicking game, but as the country's leading university, Harvard had the most influence. Once persuaded that rugby-style football was superior, Yale and the other schools took it up. Camp in particular then set about to make the American version less chaotic, devising the rules that put the ball in play from scrimmage, creating offenses and defenses, and assigning each position its special duties. As the dominant figure at Yale, Camp also developed not just particular offensive systems but the very idea of system itself, with Yale grads like himself returning to New Haven each fall to help train the team and de-vise tactics for the season. Unable to match Yale's system, rival schools hired coaches (often Yale grads) in defiance of a fundamental principle of amateur sport. (Paying coaches marked the first step down that long, slippery slope of "professionalism.") Camp made American football a coaches' game. Although he would have been appalled by the prospect, today's "geniuses" on the sidelines owe their multimillion-dollar sal-aries to him. Likewise, the coaching tyrants of the 1960s derived their authority ultimately from Walter Camp.

Camp was also a tireless promoter of the new game, teaching sports-writers and the public alike to think of football as a "scientific" contest of strategy and intricate teamwork overseen by a mastermind coach and coordinated by a "field general" at quarterback. To Camp, a football team was a little like a battalion but more like a corporation run on "scientific" principles. As early as 1891, Camp was declaring in popular magazines that the new American game of football "offered inducements to the man of executive ability," who could hone his instincts for foresight and management on the playing field.[20] It is highly doubtful that all of the players and spectators at the time viewed football as Camp did. Many no doubt preferred thrilling runs or licensed mayhem to intricate team-work. But Camp's ideas were circulated in countless newspapers and popular magazines, the most influential mass media of the day.

In a typical remark in a 1910 essay, Camp declared that "each country seems to have a foot-ball spirit of its own, and that spirit can be satisfied only with a characteristic game."[21] This idea that American football was distinctly American in "spirit" as well as geography echoed a long habit of Americans celebrating the uniqueness of the United States among the world's nations. At the same time, much about American football as it would spread throughout the country over the following decades was indeed unique—not just the game on the field as it evolved away from rugby, but also the pageantry of cheerleaders and pep rallies and pregame bonfires and marching bands, the entire social world of homecoming and the football weekend, the role it played in the American educational system and in binding schools to their local communities. In all of these aspects, football was distinctly American, but by custom, not by ideology. To like football was neither an act of patriotism nor a defense of embattled values.

Ideology hovered around the game, to be sure. Developed by young men at elite institutions of higher education, football from the beginning was marked by its upper-class roots, in sharp contrast to baseball, the more broadly democratic "national pastime." It did not take coaches long, however, to discover that the brawny sons of mill workers and coal miners tended to be hungrier than the offspring of the monied classes for the game and its rewards. Large numbers of these mill workers and coal miners were newly arrived in the country, and by the 1920s, football was becoming an agent of "Americanization" for new immigrants, as Nagurskis and Carideos were displacing Bakers and Mahans in football lineups and on All-America teams. Football was ethnically transformed at the very moment when anxiety over the influx of eastern and southern European immigrants was becoming a national crisis. Notre Dame's go-it-alone stance within the NCAA, which has alienated much of the football public in recent decades, began in necessity at this time, when anti-Catholic bigotry within the Big Ten forced Knute Rockne to schedule games wherever he could find them. "Fighting Irish" was initially an opponents' slur, before Notre Dame embraced the name after many years of being Rockne's "Ramblers" or "Nomads" for their cross-country schedules. Notre Dame was the first America's Team, but the America that Notre Dame represented in the 1920s—working-class, immigrant, Catholic—was the America of outsiders. Over time, these outsiders entered the mainstream, as the national hysteria over immigration in the 1920s gave way after World War II to celebration of the great American melting pot, with the multiethnic football team as one of its most powerful symbols.

JOCKS AT THE BARRICADES

Football has thus been deeply but unconsciously embedded in a collective sense of "the American Way" since the 1920s or even earlier, but it was only when that American Way was under attack that the game acquired any overt ideological resonance. Long before the 1960s, football had its detractors, though not on political or ideological terms. From nearly the game's beginning, the twin evils of college football, for progressive and conservative critics alike, were "commercialism" and "professionalism" in their various forms. No one called the sport capitalist or socialist or fascist or any other–ist, and football was American made but not a symbol of America. Even when student radicalism emerged on college campuses, leftist students tended to object to football chiefly for being at the center of an *apolitical* and anti-intellectual college life that "siphoned off energy that might otherwise have gone into more serious (perhaps even political) activities."[22] The negative stereotype of the football player was the dumb jock, not the reactionary jock.

Nonetheless, an ancestry for the antiprotest "burly jocks" at Columbia in 1968 can be traced back to the beginning of the twentieth century to football players who engaged in strikebreaking. Historian Stephen Norwood has documented numerous episodes in this fascinating story.

- In 1901 football players and other students from the University of California unloaded a freighter during a longshoreman's strike in San Francisco.
- In 1903 football players and track men were among the students from the University of Chicago who replaced striking stokers for Great Lakes shipping companies.
- Later that year, varsity athletes from the University of Minnesota "formed a wedge, and blasted through the picket line at the Pillsbury-Washburn mill" in Minneapolis.
- In 1905 members of the football team, prominently led by their 6´3˝ star Buck Whitwell, joined fellow Columbia students in breaking a strike of subway workers in New York City.
- Also in 1905 Marshall Field & Co. in Chicago hired football players from Northwestern to make deliveries during a teamsters' strike.
- That same year, football players were among the 200 Yale students who made up about 15 percent of the strikebreakers during a railroad strike.
- In 1912 football players from Wesleyan served as sheriffs' deputies guarding a textile mill during a weavers' strike.
- During the "Red Scare" of 1919, "nearly the entire Harvard football team" joined an army of more than 200 students to patrol Boston's streets during a policemen's strike.

This range of incidents could be distilled into one Ed Rush, a Yale foot-ball player from the 1890s who became a professional strikebreaker with a hired army ready to be deployed wherever it was needed during these years.[23]

As Norwood explains, football players were not uniquely drawn to antilabor activism but were part of the broader male student popula-tion that engaged in such activities, motivated not by political convic-tion but by the unconscious privilege of their social and economic class. Their temporary employers valued the student strikebreakers for their wholesome appearance before the public, in contrast to the more typi-cal "menacing, semicriminal element, recruited from the lower class" to be scabs. The labor and socialist press despised students not as re-actionaries but as "rah rah sissies" due to their "enthusiasm for frivolous athletic and social pursuits." What distinguished football players from their classmates was their brawn—this "formidable array of strength and beef," as one newspaper reporter described the footballers from Columbia in 1905—not their politics. The college administrators with their corporate interests were the ones with political views: antagonis-tic to organized labor, they encouraged the strikebreaking. Engineering students were as prominent as football players in strikebreaking during this era because they believed that their future profession was threat-ened by labor unions.[24]

For college students in the early twentieth century, strikebreaking was sometimes a "lark" (more akin to a later generation's panty raids than its antiwar protests), though more often it was a virile adventure, an oppor-tunity for proving one's manhood and as such not so much an extension of football as a comparable experience available to greater numbers. It substituted for the annual "cane rushes" and "Bloody Mondays" in which sophomores had initiated freshmen on nineteenth-century col-lege campuses, but which college authorities had recently banned due to the brutality and mayhem of the practices.[25] (Collections of stories about college life much in vogue in the 1890s and early 1900s—*Harvard Stories*, *Princeton Stories*, *Yale Yarns*, *Cornell Stories*, *Ann Arbor Stories*, *Stanford Stories*, and the like—invariably included a nostalgic tale of the freshman-sophomore "rush," "cane spree," or similar violent ritual of bygone days.) In short, football players were in no way uniquely marked by conservative or antilabor politics.

According to Norwood, student strikebreaking ended around 1923 and never again reached the same level, even during the Depression.[26]

With a great influx of working-class and immigrant students, colleges (particularly urban and state colleges) became less elite over the 1920s and 1930s. Many of these new students had radical political ideas. At the same time, football players increasingly occupied a world apart, as college football expanded into a commercial spectacle packing enormous stadiums around the country. The radical student movement of the 1930s—"when the old left was young," as one historian casts the era—seems virtually a template for the expanded student radicalism of the 1960s. And within that movement in the 1930s were precedents for the jocks-versus-pukes conflict that rocked Columbia in 1968. In fact, Columbia was a key site in this early period, too. In April 1932 football players and other athletes at Columbia attacked the students who were leading a one-day boycott of classes to protest the expulsion of Reed Harris, the muckraking editor of the campus newspaper. The jocks likely cared less about the specific reasons for Harris's expulsion than they did about his editorial the previous November attacking football as a "semi-professional racket."[27] On that occasion, several of them had "threatened to beat [him] up." The left-leaning journalist Heywood Broun responded to the turmoil at Columbia with a joke about the football players' educational priorities, not their politics. Siding with the protesters against President Nicholas Murray Butler "and his football favorites," Broun suggested that this was "the first time in the history of American education [that] football players were observed fighting to get into class."[28]

Accounts of labor strife and political protest at USC, UCLA, and Cal in 1934 and 1935 portrayed football players in similar roles. When West Coast longshoremen went on strike in May 1934, a physics professor at Cal and the employment office at USC recruited football players as strikebreakers. After the longshoremen's walkout expanded into a general strike in San Francisco in July, USC football star Homer Griffith was singled out as "one of the heroes" in breaking it.[29] A few months later, a group of "vigilantes" at UCLA that included police and "brawny athletes" (recruited by an assistant football coach, who told them "to remember where your jobs and eligibility come from") broke up a protest over the suspension of five radical students.[30] "Husky football players" also roamed the campus to ensure that student demonstrators did not persuade others to join the boycott of classes.[31] When students at UC Berkeley organized a sympathy protest, a dean there recruited "conservative undergraduates from the Greek houses and the football team" to break it up. As the caption to a photo in the *Los Angeles Evening Her-*

ald and Examiner put it, "football players ran the protesting students off campus."[32] The following spring, Cal football players, "egged on by the coach," broke up another rally, this one to support a student expelled for having communist affiliations.[33]

Football players at the University of Michigan were also involved in antilabor incidents in the 1930s, though on which side is unclear. In an era before athletic scholarships, when coaches and boosters often arranged employment for the school's athletes, Michigan players routinely received summer jobs at Ford's River Rouge plant in Dearborn, with light duties that allowed plenty of time "for a bit of pre-season" practice. (Outside criticism ended that part of the arrangement.) According to an account in the Communist Party's *Daily Worker*, in the summer of 1937 Michigan coach Harry Kipke instructed his 50–75 players employed at the plant "to 'co-operate' with the office in spying" on their fellow workers. The *Worker* reported with pleasure, however, that "none of them exert themselves in the 'co-operating,' as they have a sense of fair play."[34] I have not been able to corroborate this incident, but another journalist cast at least some Michigan players in a very different light, placing them among "the gangsters, gunmen, pugilists[,] . . . football players, cops and convicts" who made up the plant's Ford Service Department, a private militia under the direction of the sinister Harry Bennett that was deployed in a continuous dirty war against organized labor.[35]

This small handful of documented cases leaves uncertain the extent of such activity,[36] but on their own these cases suggest that football players tended to be reactionary. As one prolabor writer from the time concluded: "The real cure for college radicalism, school officials discovered, was football."[37]

What we know about college football in the 1930s suggests a more complicated picture, however. As American universities became more democratic in the 1920s and 1930s, their football teams became even more thoroughly democratized. Reed Harris could denounce college football as a "semi-professional racket," after all, because football players tended to be those brawny sons of steelworkers and coal miners, many of them recent immigrants to the United States, who were lured to campus by jobs (real or phony) or cash from boosters, as well as by the chance for an education and entry into the great American middle class. The fathers of football players were much more likely to be longshoremen than shipping-company executives and the athletes themselves to feel like paid employees rather than eager schoolboys. During a period when the NCAA had no oversight powers, scholarships were not sanctioned, but "subsidization" was rampant. At the University of Pittsburgh, where players' subsidies were tied to a carefully worked-out system, the football team in 1937 demanded cash payments before they would agree to play in the Rose Bowl at the sacrifice of the income they could earn over the Christmas vacation.[38] Stanford players likewise lobbied successfully for $50 each for playing in the 1940 Rose Bowl.[39] In 1938 two football players quit at Auburn when their demand for higher pay was refused, and a player at Louisiana State University was kicked off the team for trying to organize a players' union.[40] There were likely more such incidents, but these are the only ones that I have found.

There is no reason to assume that football players in the 1930s were disproportionately reactionary or even apolitical. Whether or not they were open to free speech and communism, many working-class athletes would surely have sympathized with striking longshoremen and labor unions. Recall that in the incident at Cal in November 1934, the dean recruited not just any football players but "conservative undergraduates from the Greek houses and the football team."[41] A literal reading of the sentence is likely the sound one: the football players who participated were the conservative members of the team. It would make sense that coaches, as managerial professionals with middle-class salaries, were more likely to be conservative. New York University coach Mal Stevens in 1934 praised football for providing an emotional "safety valve," without which "we might turn to bolshevism, communism or some other form of social unrest." Another coach at an unnamed eastern college "bawled out" a player who spoke out for "the liberal management of the school paper." A player at Harvard got in trouble with his coach for sending a letter of support to a pacifist meeting. (All of these incidents were reported in a radical magazine, the *Student Advocate*, not the mainstream press.)[42] Again, we have no idea how representative these few coaches were. Moreover, civic leaders and university administrators also used football itself for progressive purposes in the early 1930s, when they staged postseason "unemployment games" to raise money for various charities (the long-running College All-Star Game was created as one of these benefit games). Football teams of the 1930s were undoubtedly made up of individuals with varying political views that were not reflected in popular stereotypes.

The 1930s radicals who reported the incidents of strikebreaking and rally busting on campus tended to criticize football players not for their politics but for their anti-intellectualism and condemn the sport for the way it was run and not for its inherently reactionary nature. In *King Football: The Vulgarization of the American College* (1932), Harris accused the players who threw eggs during the strike at Columbia of expressing their opposition to "the forces of intelligence" and not of liberal or leftist ideas. Other progressive commentators such as James Wechsler and Edward Cole were less condescending to athletes. Wechsler described them as young men too wearied by their football labors for politics, who were warned to avoid meetings of the Social Problems Club but were recruited by a coach (responding to his own administrative bosses) "to help 'mop up' the radicals." For Cole, the players were just "the hired hands . . . employed at a new task . . . stamping out this menacing, contagious disease" of student radicalism. Both Wechsler and Cole saw football players essentially as exploited workers who would awaken to the harsh realities of Depression America in due course. Citing a recent article in the *Nation*, Cole noted that some "'ex-football players,' cheated of their expected careers" (the reward for a college education), were now longshoremen, and that "the militancy of West Coast labor is due in great part to the 'awakening' of some college athletes."[43]

The sweeping ideological pronouncements about football in the 1930s came from the Right, not from the Left. In 1935 William Randolph Hearst's *New York Evening Journal* editorialized (on radicalism at Columbia): "For some reason which the psychologists can perhaps explain, football and Communism don't go well together. We never heard of a soap-box orator who made a team. We never heard of a good halfback who cared two straws for Marx or Lenin."[44] In personal letters and public addresses over the 1930s, the commissioner of the Big Ten Conference, John L. Griffith, claimed a direct connection between athletics and "the American Way," which was obviously superior to "the Communist way, the Nazi way or the Fascist way."[45]

Yet what distinguished the American Way from the Communist way suddenly disappeared during World War II, when "self-reliance" and the "quickness of unchanneled wit" learned on football fields became potent weapons against Fascism. According to the sports editor of the *Omaha World-Herald* who used these terms in a 1942 column, our Russian allies shared these sporting traits with us. Football suddenly was no longer anticommunist, only anti-Fascist. From the radicals' side, the American Communist Party in the late 1930s, under the banner of the

Popular Front, softened its criticism of commercialism and exploitation in college football, and its *Daily Worker* began reporting on the sport in more or less the same manner as the mainstream press—a strategy for forging stronger ties to sports-loving American workers. After the war, in a 1946 column, sports editor Lester Rodney celebrated college football as a "democratic game" that is "played hard and honestly and with high team spirit and amateur verve." (Rodney personally preferred pro football because its players—its workers, that is—were openly paid.) Rodney, of course, assumed that American workers and Russians shared a common passion for democracy.[46]

My point is simply this: long before the 1960s, football was recruited for ideological purposes, but it could mean pretty much whatever a writer wanted it to mean as the times demanded. And football players were always more varied and complexly human than their stereotyped images.

FOOTBALL AND THE COLD WAR

In the 1950s the American Way was again threatened from without, and football became more explicitly "American" as "America" itself became more highly charged with the onset of the Cold War and the Atomic Age. In the world of sport, Americans confronted the Soviet Union most dramatically in the quadrennial Olympic Games. According to the Olympic spirit, no one was supposed to keep national scores, but of course everyone did, and Americans collectively cheered—and sighed in relief—when the United States triumphed in Helsinki in 1952 on a burst of gold medals on the final day, despite reports of billion-ruble Soviet investments in state-run athletics for propaganda purposes. When the USSR outmedaled and outpointed the United States in Melbourne in 1956, the American press made much of the Soviet superiority in women's events and obscure sports like Greco-Roman wrestling and rifle shooting, while the red, white, and blue team continued to dominate in men's track and field. After describing Charley Jenkins's upset of his Russian challenger in the 400 meters, *Newsweek* declared the lesson of the 1956 Olympics: "A country can no more train a man to win an Olympic gold medal than it can train him to write a Nobel Prize novel. There is a most un-Marxian creative aspect to Olympic victory."[47]

The contrast was between amateur and state-run sporting systems and not between distinctly American or Soviet sports, but Cold War politics sometimes spilled into the coverage of homegrown sports like baseball and football as well. Football was particularly vulnerable to criticism and ripe for celebration. Wire-service stories in the early 1950s informed American readers that the Soviet press was maligning football as "a carnival of murder and mayhem" and "part of a capitalist plot to whip the toiling masses up into a 'bestial' frame of mind for World War III." Football, we were told, "was designed to brutalize American youth and prepare it to take its place in an 'army of bandits and haters of mankind' under the United States policy of militarization."[48] In the Cold War climate, a sportswriter's tirade over proposals to reform college football could take strange turns. In 1951 Dick Hyland of the *Los Angeles Times* denounced a plan to eliminate the recruiting and subsidizing of football players as "another step along the path to making all individuals faceless creatures of a Socialistic machinelike, humanless state."[49]

That such lunatic notions could appear in a major metropolitan newspaper tells us much about the era. Chicago Bears owner George Halas evoked a similar image during congressional testimony in 1957 in his case to counter the threat to the NFL of antitrust law (another communist plot). Presenting two photos to the members of the House committee—one of mass calisthenics in a stadium emblazoned with a hammer and sickle, the other of football at Chicago's Soldier Field bordered in red, white, and blue—Halas asked the congressmen which of the two they believed the American public wanted.[50] More generally, new sets of symbols and metaphors were simply available in the 1950s to impose on old problems, as when a sportswriter referred to a rebellion of players at the University of Washington as a "Husky Soviet."[51]

Such casual references suggest an emerging mindset that would make football an ideological flash point in the 1960s. Its fullest Cold War elaboration has to be *Dementia Pigskin*, a paean to American football written in 1951 by Francis Wallace, one of the best-known American sports journalists of the day. After a stint as one of Knute Rockne's student press agents at Notre Dame in the early 1920s, Wallace covered sports for several New York dailies (where he broke the story about the "win one for the Gipper" halftime pep talk and helped popularize the nickname "Fighting Irish"). He then became a regular contributor of both fiction and nonfiction to popular magazines (several of his serialized football novels were also made into Hollywood films). In the major phase of his long career, Wallace wrote the annual "Football Preview" for the *Saturday Evening Post* from 1937 through 1947, then for *Collier's* from 1948 until the magazine folded in 1957.

With *Dementia Pigskin*, then, Wallace came before the public not as a crank but as a football expert with credentials spanning three decades. Coincidentally, as a screenwriter he was also one of the founding members of the Motion Picture Alliance for the Preservation of American Ideals (MPA), a group founded in Hollywood in 1944 to defend, as its statement of principles put it, "the American way of life" against "the rising tide of Communism, Fascism and kindred beliefs, that seek by subversive means to undermine and change" it.[52] The little-known MPA began the anticommunist blacklistings in Hollywood that were later taken up by the painfully well-remembered House Un-American Activities Committee (HUAC). Despite calling himself "prominent" in the founding of the organization,[53] Wallace does not appear in the published memoirs and histories of the MPA and anticommunism in Hollywood. Next to Walt Disney, John Wayne, and numerous others, Wallace was a small-time Hollywood player. But he was a big-time sportswriter, and the concluding chapters of *Dementia Pigskin* were his personal contribution to the anticommunist crusade in the name of football.

Chapter 32, "Intangibles," described the lessons taught by football, beginning with reflections on *loyalty* as the finest human quality and the one most "inherently American." In declaring that loyalty "is inculcated in youth by nothing so much as football," Wallace invoked a long tradition of valuing teamwork and school spirit as character building. Now, however, in the context of an America threatened by godless enemies, Wallace translated the loyalty learned on football fields into loyalty to "family, friends and faith . . . to marriage, to country and to God." Football erected a bulwark against the "determined attack against loyalty to fundamental beliefs" that was currently under way, against the new "smart" attitude that laughs at "religion, marital fidelity, individualism as against the master state, and patriotism." Wallace chiefly blamed "a communistic control room" for the present assault on traditional American values, but he also faulted the naïveté of "otherwise good Americans" that made them the communists' unwitting accomplices. Fortunately for them, "football doesn't buy any of that. The football nut still loves his good old American corn. So did the boys who raised the flag at Iwo Jima, and the other boys who still follow the American flag and believe in the American ideas."[54]

Both the bizarre logic and the seamless move from civic virtues like individualism and teamwork, learned through football, into "family, friends, and faith" are breathtaking. Communists' loyalty to their own cause, after all, was presumably what made them frightening. Insofar as football taught loyalty, why would it foster loyalty "to marriage, to country and to God" rather than to cohabitation, internationalism, and dialectical materialism? Wallace's assertion that *individualism* in football was anticommunist appears particularly ironic from the perspective of the 1960s, when conservatives would make submission to the coach's authority football's paramount virtue.

From "Intangibles," Wallace moved to "Tangibles" in the following chapter, where he slipped back into commonplaces. He likened being "in shape" for football to military preparedness—invoking the truism that "games are not won on Saturday afternoons but during the long, punishing pre-season training period, the weekly practices during the season itself, and the psychological treatment during all of this." Likewise, football's combination of "trained personnel, knowhow and teamwork"—Walter Camp redux—modeled the American system of private enterprise, "which has amazed and dominated the world" and "is still the hope of the civilized part."[55]

Dementia Pigskin then concluded with a chapter titled "Analogies," in which Wallace returned to his more extravagant ideological claims. After a section called "Football as a Way of Life," the next one, "Political and Ideological Analogy," began by citing the recent national trend "toward the left—away from individuals toward governmental controls and 'democratic socialism,'" in which some poor dupes slide all the way to "outright socialism" or "eventually communism." Against this threat, Wallace offered "football thinking on current political and ideological systems."

According to Wallace, both football and the American form of government evolved "from the old brutal push-and-pull rugged individualism." In turn, both football and the United States must beware the dangers of a "showy razzle-dazzle offense which leaves itself vulnerable" because it is not grounded in the old fundamentals. (This is only an analogy, of course, but by such reasoning, Woody Hayes's three-yards-and-a-cloud-of-dust offense soon to be developed at Ohio State would express 100 percent Americanism, while trick plays would be akin to a communist plot. The NFL's pass-happy Los Angeles Rams of the 1950s would be dangerous subversives.) Also, the American Revolution rejected a British system in which "a man had to be born a star and never had a chance to work himself up from the reserves to the varsity squad or earn stardom on his own abilities." Today's socialists embraced the opposite heresy, perversely insisting on "an equal share of production" for everyone: "Every man on the squad is entitled to a letter and there shall be no All-Americans."

Neither football nor life worked that way, Wallace reminded his readers. Hitler and Mussolini tried socialism, "and we've seen where they wound up." Fortunately, Americans created a system that "defeated nazism and fascism," "saved communism" despite itself (the Red Army presumably played an incidental role), and "is still financing British socialism." And this system was grounded in the principles at the heart of football:

> We established a new *American system* based upon achievement—a system which emphasized *opportunity*, *incentive*, *initiative*, *hard work*, *competition*; which *rewarded the star* because he provided the margin of victory. The team helped the star and the star helped the team. America was made by the teamwork of ball-carriers and linemen; by the willingness to play on the scrubs while working for the chance to make the varsity. By following the direction of the coach (who had *earned his job*, *too*) this combination produced our *knowhow*. The system emphasized such things as *courage*, *loyalty*, *respect for law*, *sportsmanship* and all our other native virtues.[56]

In this mix of truisms with nonsense, on behalf of American exceptionalism (and American football exceptionalism), the italics are all Wallace's; he needs no help from me. Wallace could have drawn certain elements of his game plan for America from the MPA's 1947 pamphlet cautioning Hollywood filmmakers against "the More Common Devices Used to Turn Non-political Pictures into Carriers of Political Propaganda." Among the warnings were these: "Don't deify the common man" and "Don't glorify the collective."[57] And I was destined to become an offensive lineman. Sigh.

TOUGHNESS

I would certainly not argue for any direct influence of *Dementia Pigskin* on Americans' thinking about football. Rather, I take Wallace's manifesto to be an unusually explicit statement of ideas that remained unspoken, mostly unthought, until a Great Threat called them into play. Like the early 1950s (during the HUAC hearings and the Korean War), the late 1950s (following the launch of Sputnik) were particularly ripe for linking football to anticommunism. Longtime sportscaster Bill Stern, a Francis Wallace of the radio booth, in a 1958 broadcast pointed out that Harvard, Chicago, New York University, and City College—all "hotbeds of communism"—either had no football team or, in Harvard's case, did not fully support it. Stern invited his listeners to consider the connection.[58] In this same spirit, in the occasional public speech or interview, a coach would declare football "our best defense against Communism" or the source of "the toughness necessary to survive the next war" or some similar Cold War tonic—ideas in turn mocked by the game's critics.[59] The men who founded the National Football Foundation and Hall of Fame in 1958 explicitly envisioned an organization for perilous times. *New York Times* sports columnist Allison Danzig described their outlook this way: "They look upon football as a vital force in the life of the nation, developing the rugged virtues and tough leadership qualities indispensable for the survival of a free world menaced by a ruthless and conspiratorial tyranny." The foundation's first president, Chester LaRouche, declared that the Hall of Fame honored football heroes of the past "to remind our youth and all our people through great historical exhibits and through print and over the air, that there shall be no softening of our fiber as we face the task of world leadership." In receiving a gold medal at the foundation's first awards dinner, President Dwight Eisenhower, a former Army player and coach, celebrated football and other sports for instilling the competitive spirit, morale, and fitness needed in the "great contest" with a foe (unnamed but unmistakable) who was "ponderous, persistent, deadly, . . . clever and powerful" and "out to win by whatever means and at whatever cost."[60]

This was the Football Establishment speaking on a formal occasion. I doubt that many ordinary citizens in the 1950s thought about football in such explicitly pro-American, anti-Soviet terms. Rather, with the Cold War as the backdrop against which all of American life played out, such full-blown Cold War rhetoric broke out on occasions of self-conscious pontificating. Interestingly, after the Russians' launch of Sputnik in 1957, there was a distinctively Cold War argument *against* football as well as for it: the game was a distraction from universities' serious business of training scientists and engineers to achieve victory in the space race. As an editorial comment in the *Saturday Evening Post* in 1958 put it: "Many critics of football are crying 'overemphasis' more loudly than ever these days, now that the American educational system stands accused in some quarters of falling behind Soviet Russia's in classroom standards."[61] As both an activity and a symbol, football remained supremely malleable for ideological purposes.

The aspect of Cold War football with the deepest roots was the cult of toughness, a perennial part of American football culture since its beginnings in the late nineteenth century but particularly pronounced in the popular media in the 1950s and 1960s. As at the turn of the twentieth century under Teddy Roosevelt, this obsession emanated even from the White House. In 1956 President Eisenhower established the President's Council on Youth Fitness to address the "muscle gap" that exacerbated the "missile gap" with the Soviet Union; and in 1960 President Kennedy wrote in *Sports Illustrated* that the physical weakness of "The Soft American" (his title) was "a menace to our security." Sportswriters had been assuring anxious parents since the 1930s that football, when properly organized and supervised, was safe for their children. In 1962 *Look* magazine's Tim Cohane once again told parents that high school football was safe but fortunately not *too* safe, because "football teaches a boy to cope with the risks of physical danger and pain, risks often inseparable from the activity of living itself." American technology and material abundance were our national glory but also our potential downfall. As Cohane put it, football "demonstrates the value of work, sacrifice, courage and perseverance. These lessons are especially salutary in our modern society with its delinquency problem, lack of discipline and physical softness."[62] A similar emphasis on stoicism and deferred gratification, struggle and competition, in sports like football marked the 1890s and the 1920s. Promoting these particular virtues had more to do with anxieties about industrialized, bureaucratic, and affluent modern American life than with the Cold War more specifically. (Note that Cohane attached no political coloring to football's character-building traits.) The Soviet Union in the 1950s simply posed the looming threat of the moment.

Toughness has no politics, but it acquired political resonance in the 1950s and 1960s. The cultural rebellion of the 1960s—free love, getting high, doing your own thing—rejected the cult of toughness. Football meant competing rather than sharing, making a kind of war rather than love, working hard rather than having fun, enduring pain rather than pursuing pleasure, deferring gratification rather than demanding it now, hanging in rather than dropping out. Yet as such, football's deepest conservative impulses belonged as much to the Old Left as to the Old Guard.

The ultimate instiller of toughness was the football coach. And the coach as tyrant, who belonged to a long and surprisingly much-honored tradition by the 1950s, became the central figure in the college football rebellions of the 1960s.

Sometime in the 1950s, a story akin to an urban legend spread even to the remote Pacific Northwest where I lived: Bear Bryant, head coach at Texas A&M, had a "pit," a hole in the ground into which he sent two competitors for a starting position to take on each other, no holds barred. Whoever emerged from the pit played that week. The story was a little like the tale, usually whispered at night around a campfire, about the escaped maniac with a hook instead of a hand who prowled Lover's Leap. Bear Bryant was a boogeyman of my football childhood.

Apparently the story was apocryphal, but it was little more brutal than the facts of Bryant's coaching career as Bryant himself and some of his players later described them. At Kentucky in 1946, according to the Bear's own account, when he took over a team of underachieving, pampered stars, "we ran off a few and worked some of them extra hard, and they quit, too, and I probably made more mistakes and mishandled more people than anyone ever has. But we got the rest of them motivated, and they started winning that first year." This is the forgotten episode in Bear Bryant's career; the next one became the basis for his legend. At Texas A&M in 1954, the new coach took two busloads of players to godforsaken Junction, Texas, for preseason training and returned with one bus half full. The survivors became famous, long before they were immortalized as the "Junction Boys" in a book by Jim Dent and Gene Stallings in 1999 and an ESPN movie in 2002. Bryant's own comment in 1966: "Well, you say, what kind of coaching is that when you lose about 100 boys and keep only 27? I have to believe I wouldn't lose that many today, because I'm not the driver I was and I probably don't demand as much, but let me tell you that was the beginning of a change in attitude at A&M."[63] Actually, Bryant did not change all that much from his impetuous youthful self when he moved on to Alabama in 1958. The "pit" might have been apocryphal, but the Kill or Be Killed Drill at Alabama in the early 1960s was real: three linemen facing off in a circle to kick, bite, slug, or do whatever else it took to prevail. Bryant built his coaching career at three universities with the fierce and dedicated survivors from his brutal practices.[64]

Bear Bryant was an extreme case, but his coaching style hovered over the football world of the 1950s and early 1960s. One of Bryant's former players and assistant coaches, Charlie Bradshaw, reenacted the Junction Boys when he took over the team at the University of Kentucky in 1962 and proceeded to reduce a squad of eighty-eight to a "Thin Thirty." In a profile of Bradshaw during his first season, *Sports Illustrated* described his system of Total Football as a version of "The New Rage to Win" at any cost, which was coming to define football in the Southeastern Conference in particular.[65] Outside of the SEC, Woody Hayes famously coached at Ohio State with a ferocity that, again according to *Sports Illustrated*, "would make a Marine Corps drill instructor look like Mary playing with her lamb."[66] Closer to home for me, Bert Clark, the coach at nearby Washington State in Pullman, was known for kicking his players as they sprawled on the ground, puking, during the preseason mile run. Across the state at the University of Washington, football practices run by Jim Owens (formerly an assistant under Bryant at Kentucky and Texas A&M) were known as the "death march." Sportswriters—and presumably a large portion of their readers—did not typically regard such coaching tactics as abusive but rather as a harsh corrective to the general "softening" of American youth, or more prosaically as the discipline needed to win football games. The Lexington papers in 1962, for example, defended Bradshaw, denounced *Sports Illustrated*, and denigrated the players who quit.[67]

Bryant's account in *Sports Illustrated* in 1966, a five-part memoir written with John Underwood, began his transformation from a southern icon, frequently vilified outside the region, into a national paragon. Bryant was the most controversial coach in the United States at the time, winner of three national championships but also the subject of two damning articles in the *Saturday Evening Post* in recent years. The first article claimed that he coached his players to injure opponents; the second, that he received inside information from Georgia athletic director Wally Butts before an Alabama-Georgia game. In addition, Bryant had left Texas A&M on probation for his recruiting violations, and at Alabama he coached a segregated team in a segregated conference in continuing defiance of the civil rights movement and the federal government. Bryant lost a shot at the Rose Bowl in 1962 and perhaps a fourth national championship in 1966 because his teams, like his state, resisted integration.

Bryant successfully sued the *Post* for libel over both articles, and *Sports Illustrated* in 1966 was giving him the opportunity to tell his own story.

Bryant explained how his drive to succeed grew out of the humiliating poverty of his Depression-era childhood. He admitted allowing boosters to pay some of his players at Kentucky and Texas A&M, as he might again if he were "a young coach 28 or 30 years old and just starting out . . . if the competition was paying boys and I felt I had to meet the competition." In more or less apologizing for his "mistakes" in running off players at Kentucky and Texas A&M, Bryant did not fail to note how successful his tactics had been—a bit like Arnold Schwarzenegger publicly disavowing the steroids he took as a young bodybuilder, without which there would have been no movie career, let alone two terms in the California governor's mansion.

Bryant was reputedly in the business of building up young men, and former players have offered abundant testimonials over the years to his greatness as a man and a coach. But Bryant built his reputation at Kentucky and Texas A&M as much on those who quit as on those who survived to play fiercely for him. Returning from Junction with 100 out of 111 players, instead of 35, would not have been conducive to myth. And what of those 76 who fled early? Quitters usually don't get to tell their stories.[68] The Cold War cult of toughness found its fullest expression in win-at-all-costs football but also its unacknowledged self-defeat as a tonic for the nation: what value was there in the sort of toughening that drove most away?

Within a year after Bryant's memoirs appeared in *Sports Illustrated*, an athletic revolution was beginning on college campuses. Bryant himself was untouched by the upheavals of the late 1960s, but his style of coaching was not.

COLLEGE FOOTBALL AND THE ATHLETIC REVOLUTION OF THE 1960S

When I arrived at Notre Dame as a freshman in the fall of 1966, the larger world of college football looked something like this: Alabama, Ohio State, Texas, and Southern Cal were the dominant teams in the strongest conferences; Nebraska ruled the Big Eight, but its lumbering farm boys routinely got their butts whipped in bowl games by lean, mean southerners; Penn State won most of its games but played only second-rate eastern teams (essentially competing for the Lambert Trophy, supremacy in the East, not for the national championship); and Miami, Florida, and Florida State did not yet register on the football map. Recruiting in those days was mostly local and regional. Besides the service academies, only Notre Dame truly recruited nationally. Many schools poached in the football hotbeds—Pennsylvania, Ohio, Texas, and California (Florida's ascendancy was many years in the future)—but even there, most of the top high school athletes stayed fairly close to home. I was not recruited to South Bend, but as a Catholic kid with high grades and a fantasy of being a Notre Dame football player I went as a student and was invited to walk onto the team.

I arrived with expectations set by a high school coach from the no-water, rub-some-dirt-on-it school. Instead, I found that Ara Parseghian was no screamer or tyrant but a charismatic, all-seeing god on the high tower at practice and—eventually, after I worked my way into playing time as a junior—a pregame and halftime motivator for whom I would have played my heart out had I not been self-driven. And I was self-driven. Playing football at Notre Dame meant living out a private dream while the country was struggling to awake from a nightmare. To be sure, the troubling outside world that loomed beyond the campus boundaries sometimes intruded on my sheltered world at Notre Dame. In 1966, the year that I graduated from high school and entered college, eleven major and thirty-two minor race riots erupted in American cities; in 1967 there were twenty-five and thirty more, respectively.[69] The surreal 1968 Democratic Convention, the equally bizarre trial of the Chicago Seven that followed, and the killing of Black Panthers Fred Hampton and Mark Clark by city cops all happened just ninety miles away in Chicago, where my roommate and many friends lived. Above all, the war in Vietnam awaited all of us. But while violence was erupting at Columbia, UC Berkeley, San Francisco State, Wisconsin, and other places, Notre Dame's campus remained relatively calm. We demonstrated against recruiting visits by the CIA and Dow Chemical, honored the Vietnam Moratorium in October 1969, and boycotted classes in the spring of 1970 over the invasion of Cambodia. Our campus newspaper regularly editorialized against the war, and nearly one in seven from my graduating class applied for conscientious objector status (a startling figure that I only recently discovered).[70] But we at Notre Dame—many of us, anyway, I cannot speak for all—discovered our political consciences in the sheltered enclave of our small Catholic college.

Our president, Father Theodore Hesburgh, became a hero to the hard-core right for his so-called fifteen-minute rule, a policy he instituted in February 1969 that student protesters could be suspended from the university for not dispersing within fifteen minutes of being warned.

Hesburgh, in fact, was a political liberal on the national scene, a critic of the war and chairman of the Commission on Civil Rights that would issue a damning report that infuriated President Nixon. Hesburgh liberalized dormitory rules during my years at Notre Dame—rules about curfews and girls in the rooms—and brought the university out of its Catholic provincialism into the modern educational world. With his fifteen-minute rule, however, Father Hesburgh seemed reactionary to us (he was among the university leaders of good will and progressive politics for whom the student protests of the 1960s were a wrenching experience). Administrators invoked the fifteen-minute rule for the first time in the fall of my senior year, eventually suspending ten students from among those protesting the presence on campus of recruiters from Dow Chemical and the CIA.

Obviously, not everyone at Notre Dame felt sheltered, but football and the antiwar movement coexisted comfortably. The *Observer*, our campus newspaper, would report a local demonstration on the front page, print an antiwar editorial on page 2, and celebrate our victory over Iowa or Navy on page 8. I knew no one who supported the war, although there must have been some who did, perhaps among my teammates.[71] I also knew no one who boycotted our games on Saturdays because they were fascist or imperialistic. An article in the *Observer*, published a month before my graduation during the student boycott of classes over American troops' invasion of Cambodia, described Notre Dame athletics as a "paradox" by remaining immune to criticism and change. According to the writer, many in the university's "relatively small radical group" despised football's "glorious position" on campus but could find little to complain about in the program itself. Athletic director Moose Krause had apparently once expressed his fear that "the Commies" were infiltrating college athletics, "just as they've gotten into education and religion," but even campus radicals agreed that Krause was a good athletic director. And a spokesman for the radicals denied that there was anything "anti-activist" about sports themselves. As one "long-haired junior" put it: "Hell, I play basketball at the ACC [Athletic and Convocation Center] all the time. . . . But that doesn't mean I believe in Cambodia."[72]

WHILE NOTRE DAME REMAINED relatively sheltered, an "athletic revolution" swept over college football in 1968 and 1969, though it missed most individual football players at the time and more profoundly affected those who followed in the 1970s and after. It is crucial to recognize that the athletic turmoil of the 1960s came from within, from players who were supposedly molded by their football experience into archdefenders of authority and discipline, God and country. In a speech to athletic directors that became famous (or notorious), one of football's shrillest champions in the late '60s, Max Rafferty, the superintendent of public instruction in California under Governor Ronald Reagan, railed against "the kooks, the crum-bums, and the Commies" who were attacking the game in order to undermine the very foundations of the Republic. Rafferty was Francis Wallace in crisis mode. It was not outside agitators, however, but the players themselves—supposedly "above-average, decent, reasonably patriotic Americans," as Rafferty cast them—who were challenging some of the football establishment's most fundamental assumptions. If football had, in fact, been the conservative political and cultural force that its right-wing champions claimed, the protests of the late 1960s could never have happened.[73]

Contrary to their image as defenders of The Establishment against the protesters at UC Berkeley, Penn, and Columbia, football players began launching their own protests in 1967. And the players were usually black. That fall, the president of San Jose State College canceled the season opener against the University of Texas at El Paso (UTEP) out of fear that a protest by black players organized by Harry Edwards (at the beginning of his long career as a sports activist) would lead to violence. Later that season, several black members of UTEP's football team staged a sit-in to protest their subtly racist treatment—proscriptions against interracial dating, preferential treatment for white players in housing and jobs for spouses, "stacking" at certain positions. (There was nothing subtle about the stunning comment made by UTEP's athletic director, George McCarty, in *Sports Illustrated* the following summer, when he attributed the success of "the nigger athlete" in college sports to his being "a little hungrier" than his white teammates. McCarty generously noted that, at UTEP, "we have been blessed with having some real outstanding ones.")[74]

Sport historian David Wiggins has called 1968 "The Year of Awakening" for black athletes in the United States, a year marked chiefly by Muhammad Ali's losing battle with the American justice system and the clenched-fist protest of track stars Tommie Smith and John Carlos at the Mexico City Olympics. Among the thirty-five lesser "black athletic disturbances" on college campuses in 1968 were several in major football programs. In March thirteen blacks at the University of Washington presented their athletic department with four demands, two of which were met: a black assistant coach was hired and an allegedly racist white trainer fired. That spring, after the assassination of Martin Luther King Jr. in April, fourteen black players at UC Berkeley and fifteen at Kansas staged boycotts during spring workouts to protest what they saw as racist practices in athletics or the university as a whole. (At Kansas, one issue was the all-white cheerleading squad.) At Michigan State, whose athletic programs had long been the most integrated in the country, players threatened a boycott over the lack of black coaches, black medical staff, and academic support for black athletes. At Arizona State, football players joined with other athletes in presenting their athletic board with a similar list of grievances. At Washington State, football players returned to spring practice only after school officials apologized for what the players took to be a racial slight from fellow students. At Minnesota, a former player charged coach Murray Warmath's program with discrimination. At Wisconsin, black players boycotted the postseason banquet in protest against an assistant coach, who was shortly fired. At Princeton, five black players quit the team in December after leveling charges of discrimination.[75]

If 1968 was "The Year of Awakening," it was followed by "The Year of Reckoning." The 1969 season marked college football's centennial, an occasion for celebration that turned out to be the sport's most convulsive year ever. Having absorbed one hit after another in 1968, coaches fought back in 1969, empowered by the NCAA convention in January, which authorized the rescinding of scholarships for defiant behavior—a key moment in NCAA history to which I will return. The first major eruptions occurred simultaneously at Oregon State University and the University of Maryland early in the year, well before the season commenced. On the morning of February 25, black students at Oregon State interrupted an address by Linus Pauling, their most distinguished alumnus, to announce a boycott of classes and sporting events after football coach Dee Andros had suspended a black linebacker, Fred Milton, for refusing to shave his beard and mustache.

The protest at Oregon State would play out over several months, but an incident that began at Maryland on the same day would be over in less than two weeks. That evening, after football coach Bob Ward had slapped some players at an off-season workout earlier in the day, nearly the entire team met to draft a petition calling on the athletic director to dismiss him. The players charged Ward with technical incompetence as well as physical and mental abuse, but the latter was the main issue. At a meeting on March 3 with Ward and athletic director Jim Kehoe, player after player rose to voice his complaints, while Ward sat silently. The session finally ended when one player turned to Ward and said, "Coach, how can you want to stay here when nobody wants to play for you?" After Ward resigned on March 5, alumni, parents, and administrators berated Kehoe for "let[ting] the hippies overthrow the coach."[76]

The "Great Football Rebellion" at Maryland was not unprecedented. In 1951 the University of Nebraska's iron-fisted Bill Glassford barely survived a revolt of his players, and in 1956 officials at the University of Washington fired John Cherberg after players complained about abusive treatment. But these were isolated incidents in contexts that conferred on them no broader meaning, not skirmishes in what was beginning to seem like a full-blown war waged by players against their coaches. The Maryland incident proved to be an anomaly, as the battle lines in 1969 were mostly racial (and the players were never again so successful). Following the racial incident at Oregon State, in April sixteen black players at the University of Iowa boycotted the first day of spring practice, prompting Coach Ray Nagel to suspend them for the entire spring. In the fall, incidents at Wyoming, Washington, and Indiana within a three-week period turned the football field into a major battleground in the struggle over civil rights and coaches' authority. At Wyoming, Coach Lloyd Eaton suspended fourteen players after they requested to wear armbands in their game against Brigham Young to protest racial discrimination in the Mormon Church. At Washington, Jim Owens suspended four players after they refused to declare their full commitment to his program. And at Indiana, after fourteen players boycotted practice for unspecified reasons, John Pont invited them to return and then suspended the ten who did not show up the next day. I use the word "suspended" in all of these cases, but Eaton and Pont insisted that the players "dismissed themselves" by their actions.

Football was under siege at campuses around the country, though not at Notre Dame. If my few black teammates were closely following these stories, I did not know it; there were no reverberations on the field or in the locker room. Notre Dame struggled with its own racial issues in the late 1960s, arising from the difficulties facing the few dozen black students among 6,000 undergraduates at an institution just beginning to embrace racial diversity. On two occasions, racial grievances spilled over into athletics, and the second of the two received national attention. In February 1969 five black basketball players issued a statement demanding an apology from their fellow students for their booing at the Michigan State game when the five took the court together. Whether the booing was directed at the five blacks or at their losing coach was unclear, but student body president Richard Rossie issued an apology to the players the next day.[77] The earlier incident involved football. In November 1968 forty members of the university's Afro-American Society marched around the football stadium before our Georgia Tech game to call attention to a list of grievances: low minority enrollment, the tiny number of black professors, the absence of Black Studies courses—the basic concerns of black students at predominantly white universities throughout the country. They also carried a sign directed at our all-white starting backfield. In 1968 the varsity had just three black football players—junior linebacker Larry Schumacher and sophomores Ernie Jackson and Tony Capers (whose football career ended that season with an injury)—a typical situation since Notre Dame had belatedly integrated its football program in 1953. The current freshman class—with Tom Gatewood, Clarence Ellis, Bob Minnix, Clarence Pope, and Herman Hooten—finally began the full integration of Notre Dame football.

Because the protest ended before we took the field, I knew nothing about it until Monday, when I was appalled to read in our campus paper about the shouts from the student section: "Get off the field, you dirty niggers" and "White Power forever!"[78] I knew no one capable of such bigotry, and I have no idea how my black teammates felt about the protest or the students' reaction, because no one on the team brought up the issue at the time. The basketball players the following February could threaten a boycott and demand an apology because they were five among a dozen, and the five best. Austin Carr, Collis Jones, Sid Catlett, Dwight Murphy, and Bob Whitmore brought Notre Dame basketball its first national recognition. What could my three black varsity teammates have done, had they contemplated a similar response? In the spring of 1970, Tom Gatewood, Bob Minnix, and Clarence Ellis, now sophomores and on the varsity, spoke out against the administration's misrepresenting the amount of financial aid provided to black students by including the scholarships for athletes.[79] That spring, the student body also elected its first black president, and the university established a Black Studies program. Notre Dame was changing, and the football team was, too.

But as a member of the football team of 1969, I was never forced to weigh grievances of black teammates against my personal dreams of playing for Notre Dame. Football was being disrupted elsewhere—downstate in Bloomington; out west in Corvallis, Laramie, and Seattle; back east in College Park—but the resulting transformation would play out less contentiously in South Bend, as it did in most locations. Football's turmoil was like a tropical storm forming off the coast that did not quite make it to my mainland. Like most of his coaching colleagues, Ara Parseghian had his rules on personal appearance. One day after practice, we had to file by him, one by one, as he checked for creeping sideburns and hair peeking below our helmets. Ara conducted his inspection in a jokey manner and told a few players that they needed a trim, but nothing came of it. I did not realize at the time that Ara had gone on public record with his scorn of Haight-Ashbury "scum," whose "shiftlessness" represented "the direct opposite of what we strive for in college football."[80] Even had I known he was so openly antihippie, I would not have felt conflicted. In college, through my courses and dormitory bull sessions and simply by living through the times, I had turned against the war and racism, not against my middle-class upbringing.

A NEW ERA

Bob Ward at Maryland coached in the manner of Bear Bryant at Alabama and Woody Hayes at Ohio State, but Bryant and Hayes won national championships in the 1960s while Ward went 0–9 and 2–8 in his two years at Maryland. (Kentucky fired Charlie Bradshaw after the 1968 season after consecutive records of 3–6–1, 2–8, and 3–7.) Coaches who experienced no disruptions in the late 1960s may have been more lucky than enlightened, but the ones who made the necessary adjustments over the next few years proved that they had more than good fortune working for them. The college football establishment, led by the NCAA, officially supported the Vietnam War and opposed student radicalism through the columns of executive director Walter Byers in the NCAA News. In 1969 and 1970 Byers excoriated individuals like Mark Rudd, the leader of the sit-in at Columbia, and groups like the Students for a Democratic Society (SDS), repeatedly warning member institutions of possible SDS conspiracies to undermine college football. He also saluted the "punching style" of ultraconservative vice president Spiro Agnew in his attacks on the liberal press. (Agnew was among those who saw football as a bulwark against radicalism.) In the summer of 1970 and again the following

Christmas, the NCAA sent athletes to Vietnam to boost troop morale and "to give GIs an insight into and a favorable image of campus life."[81]

One of those athletes was Larry DiNardo, Notre Dame's offensive captain in 1970. Larry returned from Vietnam to declare the war "a total waste"—in an interview in the football program for the Purdue game, no less—and promptly found himself receiving requests to speak at rallies. He did not view his position as exceptional, even for a football player; in fact, he considered himself a conservative. "I don't want to be a hero of the New Left," DiNardo told a reporter for *Sports Illustrated*. "I mean, who's *not* against the war?"[82] The following season, some fifty football players at the University of Michigan signed a student petition asking for a halftime show "devoted to antiwar themes." The team's star running back, Billy Taylor, told *Sports Illustrated*, "I don't know anybody who saw it who didn't sign it." Quarterback Tom Slade added, "I'm more conservative than 90 [percent] of the students. I'm pro-Nixon. But I signed with the intention that I'm against the war." Football coach Bo Schembechler simply called the petition a "personal matter," while athletic director Don Canham stated, "I'm not surprised. Who the hell is in favor of the war anymore?"[83]

Either football folk were massively betraying their principles or football's intimate relation with war and conservative politics had been a fantasy in the minds of Francis Wallace, Max Rafferty, and their coreligionists. Likewise, by the 1960s football coaches in general had largely ceased to play a role that still clung to their public image. In the 1920s and 1930s, when coaches first became celebrities, the media often cast them as father figures, whether all-powerful patriarchs or nurturing dads. The latter image persisted into the 1960s, at least in the minds of some old-timers. In the midst of the racial turmoil at the University of Washington in 1969, Royal Brougham (completing his *sixtieth* year at the *Seattle Post-Intelligencer*) advised Jim Owens to "come out of the deep freeze and show a little more warmth toward the players." Brougham expressed admiration for Owens but found him "cold and aloof, lacking the buddy-buddy qualities of many successful leaders. We mean the father-son relationship; the good old arm-around-the-shoulder stuff that unifies team and coaches. Strict discipline? Yes. The coach has to be boss. But this is a new era."[84]

A new era indeed, but the age of football fathers and sons, if it ever existed in more than popular fantasy, had basically ended after World

War II, when the frenzied pursuit of players and profits made college football a more serious business. While kindly old "Pop" disappeared from the sidelines, his iron-fisted alter ego survived into the 1960s in coaches like Bear Bryant, Charlie Bradshaw, Woody Hayes, and Lloyd Eaton, only to be mortally wounded in that decade. (The death throes lasted until 1978 or 1979, when first Hayes imploded on the sidelines of the Gator Bowl and then Frank Kush was fired at Arizona State amid lawsuits and much ugly wrangling.)

The rebellions at Maryland, Oregon State, and Iowa, along with related incidents in other sports at dozens of schools, prompted John Underwood's three-part series for *Sports Illustrated*, "The Desperate Coach," in late August and early September 1969. Underwood cast the coach as the victim of changing times with a new breed of self-indulgent players and craven administrators who failed to support him. That fall, as major incidents wracked the football programs at Wyoming, Washington, and Indiana, the sports pages were filled with opinions on what coaching style could work in this new world.[85] Writing after the University of Washington, without its black players, lost to UCLA, Melvin Durslag of the *Los Angeles Examiner* cited Bruin coach Tommy Prothro's postgame comment that "the problem today isn't as racial as it may seem superficially" but rather that "the relationship is changing between coaches and their players." Durslag agreed. He pointed out that while protesting black athletes acted in blocs, whites remained unorganized, yet "there are countless cases of their becoming disillusioned with college football and dropping quietly from the sport, or remaining in it and comporting themselves in a manner not consistent with the way the coach would like it."[86]

Black players protested collectively and made headlines; white players protested individually and disappeared. In his "Desperate Coach" series, Underwood repeated a story told by Jim Owens about one of his players, a colonel's son, and another by Dee Andros about a number of "good boys—intelligent, first-rate athletes"—on his teams. All were white, and all gave up football. Overnight, it seemed, they became "all the clichés: long dirty hair, slovenly, anti-war, anti-Establishment." "It's frightening," said Owens. "The kid just turned my stomach," said Andros about one of his dropouts.[87]

These were extreme cases, but Durslag's explanation rings true for a more general cultural shift. Durslag saw a changing attitude among college athletes in an "age of sophistication," when "it is becoming increasingly hard to sell them the old oddments, pride, guts, and spirit." Unlike most sportswriters, Durslag blamed not "the kids" but their parents. "We're a material people," he reminded his readers, "and, for all their beautiful philosophy, the kids, God help them, are like us." Amid rising expectations, whether for newly enfranchised blacks or increasingly affluent whites, Americans of all ages were less likely to settle for disappointment. "Dissension and walkouts are rare among college teams going for championships," Durslag pointed out, and they did not occur at all on professional teams, where players received actual salaries "as opposed to the intangible rewards of amateur sports."

Durslag called for a "sharp readjustment" in coaching style at the college level: "The first thing the coach will relinquish is the iron-handed discipline he used to wield. Why should he continue to have this privilege with kids when the rest of us don't? The whole concept of iron-handed discipline is dead anyway. It is dead in our courts, it is dead in our government, it is dead in our homes. Whether this is good or bad is irrelevant. The point is, the coach will have to tailor his methods of handling those in his care."[88]

Such readjustments were already under way. No single coaching style prevailed in 1969 (or in any other year), nor did any particular style guarantee success on the field or peace in the locker room. But Royal Brougham's criticism (and my own experience with Ara Parseghian) notwithstanding, "cold and aloof" was a highly successful model by 1969. In *Meat on the Hoof: The Hidden World of Texas Football* (1972), one of the antifootball books of this era, Gary Shaw described Texas coach Darrell Royal as "the authoritarian father," obsessed with victory, whose relationship to his players was entirely "impersonal." Shaw was a renegade who wrote a football exposé, but loyal players from the Longhorns' 1969 national championship team portrayed Royal in the same way when interviewed more than thirty years later. Former players have described John McKay at USC and Tommy Prothro at UCLA in similar terms.[89]

Old habits of thought die hard, however. In "The Desperate Coach," athletic directors and coaches, along with Underwood himself, repeatedly refer to the players as "kids" and "boys." Underwood did not interview a single player for the series — "kids," after all, are to be seen, not heard. The problem is, if colleges function properly, sometime between arriving at eighteen and departing at twenty-two, "kids" become adults.

Without interviewing All-American center John Didion, Underwood quoted him from the newspaper reports on the incident at Oregon State. Though defending Andros's handling of the issue, Didion tellingly refers to himself and other college players as "men."[90]

Football was supposed to make men out of boys, but some coaches had to learn painfully not to treat their players like children. The protest at Maryland in 1969 was by white athletes, and the players at the University of Florida who organized themselves into the League of Florida Athletes in 1970 were predominantly white.[91] But black athletes in the late 1960s most conspicuously balked at embracing white fathers. The athletic revolution of the 1960s ended by 1972, in part because coaches and administrators, including Ara Parseghian, adjusted with the times. In the spring of 1970, in the midst of Notre Dame's student boycott of classes over the invasion of Cambodia, Ara refused the request of a handful of underclassmen to wear black armbands at the final scrimmage in sympathy with the protest.[92] The next fall, in the words of *Sports Illustrated*'s Jerry Kirshenbaum, Ara gave "a guarded go-ahead to several players who wanted to take part in a campus demonstration." Though making no public pronouncements at the time, Ara himself opposed the war. For him (as for his players), football existed apart from politics.[93]

By this time the country as a whole was turning against the war in Vietnam and toward at least the more superficial elements of the counterculture. And coaches like Ara Parseghian were quietly backing off their insistence on marine-style grooming. Just look at the change in player photos in Notre Dame's football media guides between 1969 and 1971. In 1969 we look like Young Republicans, and the 1970 team looks the same. In 1971 players are sporting facial hair, blacks have moderate Afros, whites have long sideburns and hair below their ears. Neither Notre Dame football nor Western civilization collapsed.

A final personal note. In December 1969 I was one of eleven college football players feted as scholar-athletes by the National Football Foundation at its annual banquet at the Waldorf Astoria. Over a couple of days in New York, we were also treated to dinner at Toots Shor's and a play on Broadway. The head of the foundation had apparently planned to get us tickets for some mainstream musical (it might have been *Hello, Dolly!*—I don't recall for sure), but his wife convinced him that twenty-one-year-old young men might enjoy something a little more up-to-date and youth oriented. We were taken to see *Hair*.

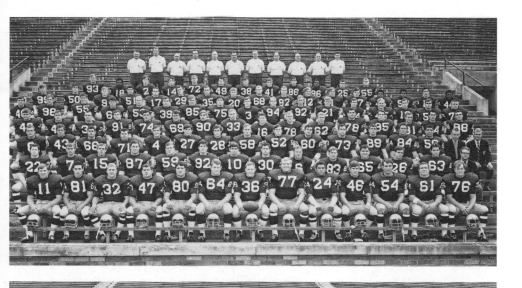

The 1969 (top) and 1971 (bottom) Notre Dame football teams
(Courtesy of the Sports Information Department, University of Notre Dame)

In November 1969 President Nixon, with great fanfare and media coverage, attended the season-ending football game between no. 1 Texas and no. 2 Arkansas. Afterward, he presented a plaque to the winning Longhorns as the "No. 1 college football team in college football's 100th year." The president's flying to Fayetteville was a major national story, made controversial on the sports pages by the snub to undefeated Penn State.

Whether Nixon, a former scrub at Whittier College, was following his genuine passion for football or a strategy for winning support among ordinary football-loving Americans was debated by political commentators at the time. In either case, he became known over the course of his presidency as the nation's number-one football fan, the "Chief Jock."[94] Strategic or not, Nixon's official involvement in football had a long history. As vice president in the 1950s, he was a special guest at several Orange Bowls, attended the opening of Green Bay's Lambeau Field in 1957, and presented the Heisman Trophy to Billy Cannon in 1959. When he visited the New York Giants' locker room before the NFL's 1959 championship game and went around the room greeting the players, he startled them by knowing details of their individual performances that season.[95]

As president-elect at the end of the 1968 season, Nixon attended the Rose Bowl, and as president in 1969, he went to a home Redskins game in addition to the Texas-Arkansas contest. For the Cotton Bowl a few weeks later—Notre Dame's loss to Texas in my own final game—he inaugurated what quickly became an irritating tradition by telephoning the winning locker room afterward. He also called the USC locker room after the Rose Bowl later that afternoon and the Kansas City Chiefs' locker room after the Super Bowl a couple of weeks later. After that, for several years the gesture became as obligatory as kissing babies during election campaigns.

Nixon's involvement with football actually increased over his presidency, sometimes in bizarre ways, as when he set himself up as a sort of unpaid consultant to NFL coaches in 1971 and 1972. He visited a Redskins' practice early in the 1971 season to hearten the players and their coach, his friend George Allen, after back-to-back losses. When the team made the playoffs that season, the president called Allen to suggest a play, which the Redskins eventually ran (for a thirteen-yard loss).

A month later, Miami coach Don Shula wisely declined to use another play offered by Nixon for the Super Bowl. During the 1972 season, the president called Allen so frequently that quarterback Billy Kilmer complained, "He's really hurting us." Nixon was also a longtime friend of Ohio State coach Woody Hayes, a great admirer, and delivered a eulogy at Hayes's memorial service in 1987.

Nixon followed other football-loving presidents—Roosevelt (Teddy, not Franklin), Eisenhower, Kennedy, even LBJ (and he was followed by Gerald Ford, who had played at Michigan in the early 1930s)—but "Nixon's devotion to the game," as Michael MacCambridge puts it, "was at a different order of magnitude than that of his predecessors." More to the point here: Nixon's private presidential passion had a deeper national significance at this historical moment. When journalist Frank Kent wrote his classic *The Great Game of Politics* in 1923, the metaphor already had a long history, but it was during the Nixon presidency that the equating of politics with football became so commonplace, among both politicians and the journalists who covered them, that it became itself a topic for political commentary.[96] Nixon was the "quarterback" of his White House "team," with its "game plans" for reaching the "end zone" of the moment. Pundits wondered whether such metaphors were innocuous, or if they reduced politics and diplomacy to mere sports competitions in some dangerous way. Equating politics with football worked in both directions. Nixon's "sportspeak," as Robert Lipsyte termed it, was a "jocksniffer's" transformation of politics into a game he was never good enough to play. At the same time, sportspeak entangled football in the public's mind ever more intimately with the values of The Establishment. As Larry Merchant, another iconoclastic sportswriter from this period, put it: "Political football has evolved from a shopworn phrase to a disquieting attempt to take over the game by politicians and superpatriots."[97]

While Nixon's passion was real, its manifestations often seemed calculated, as he wrapped football in the American flag at a time when that flag was elsewhere being burned at antiwar rallies. He used football to mark the boundary between radicals and the "silent majority," and between elitists and "regular guys." In addition to his publicized involvement with collegiate and NFL teams, Nixon employed football symbolically on two famous occasions. In November 1969, while several hundred thousand demonstrators occupied the Washington Mall, Nixon signaled his indifference by announcing that he would be watching a college football game on television—casting football as a sport for those who protested against the protesters. That spring, after the invasion of Cambodia that provoked student boycotts at dozens of universities (including Notre Dame), Nixon rose in the middle of the night to make a strange visit to the young people gathering at the Lincoln Memorial for a demonstration the next day. Meeting a group of students from Syracuse University, Nixon startled them by talking about their school's football team. If he intended to find common ground with his young critics, his "language of sport, football small-talk, the parlance of Middle America" only accentuated the gulf between his world and theirs.[98]

The 1960s created "conservative" football fans—not just "traditionalists," who had always been part of the game, but political conservatives for whom football seemed a bulwark against political and social change. In the 1960s football became marked for the radical Left as fascist and imperialist and for the radical Right as superpatriotic. The principal texts in the radical critique became minor classics of the era: Jack Scott's *The Athletic Revolution*, Paul Hoch's *Rip Off the Big Game: The Exploitation of Sports by the Power Elite*, the exposés written by apostate players Dave Meggysey, Chip Oliver, Bernie Parrish, and Gary Shaw—all published between 1970 and 1972.[99] The flag waving for football, on the other hand, became embedded in its routine pageantry, transformed by the times. The national anthem before games took on new meaning, as did color guards of ROTC students and, often, the halftime shows where even the music chosen, Sousa marches or rock 'n' roll, aligned with one side or the other of a gaping generational and political divide.

Although the Super Bowl eventually became our most conspicuous Superpatriot Bowl, the Orange Bowl in Miami preceded it. The game had been inaugurated in the 1930s, along with the Sugar and Cotton Bowls, to compete with the Rose Bowl for winter tourists and national publicity for the host cities. The Orange Bowl in the 1930s sold Florida real estate. The Orange Bowl in the 1960s and 1970s sold God, country, and football.

The impresario of the pregame and halftime shows from 1935 through 1974 was Earnie Seiler, the king of pious and patriotic kitsch. Initially, Seiler simply added more bands, floats, and pretty girls each year to keep the Orange Bowl famous for its pageantry. Over time, he added surprise effects (orange-blossom scent sprayed throughout the stadium, hundreds of balloons released from the field, fake snow or tiny parachutes dropped from the upper deck), and each year he devised a more elaborate way for the queen to pop out of her float for the grand finale of the halftime show. A turning point came in 1965, when moving the game from daytime to prime time brought it to a national audience of 25 million and created unprecedented opportunities for dazzling fireworks and light shows. In 1974, when Seiler turned production of the halftime show over to professionals from Disney World, the Orange Bowl found its natural partner. By this time the Orange Bowl had become a patriotic theme park.

While the emphasis was always on pageantry, a religious and political undercurrent present at least since the 1950s became a tsunami by the late 1960s. The national anthem, without which it now seems unthinkable to begin a football or baseball or basketball game, did not become a staple at American sporting events until World War II. In the postwar years, the Orange Bowl's pregame show always concluded with the anthem played by the combined bands from a nearby marine or navy base and several local high schools. In the 1960s Seiler began adding fireworks and giant flags, and the pregame show acquired its own theme. In 1965 it was "Portrait of an Anthem," with bands depicting the song's birth. In 1966 a huge replica of the flag raising at Iwo Jima featured one of the two surviving GI's from that event. The 1967 pregame show honored Sergeant Robert E. O'Malley, the first marine to win the Medal of Honor in Vietnam. For 1968 there was a sixty-foot replica of the Statue of Liberty; for 1969, a towering Uncle Sam; for 1970, an enormous red, white, and blue pagoda. Christian singer (and later antigay activist) Anita Bryant made her Orange Bowl debut in 1971, singing a special arrangement of the national anthem—as rockets of red, white, and blue shot into the sky—to cap a program of patriotic music with the theme, "Proudly We Hail."[100]

The quieter part of the pregame program was the prayer for peace, apparently begun during World War II. Even this ritual became more elaborately staged, as when the Reverend Billy Graham led the blessing in 1970 with "America the Beautiful" playing softly in the background. (The city of Miami was notorious for what Merchant called "embarrassingly long invocations" before even regular-season Dolphins games.[101])

Prayers for peace and the national anthem, in other words, were Orange Bowl traditions long before the cataclysms of the 1960s, but those once-routine gestures became more highly charged in the new political climate. At the same time, the halftime shows shifted from pure spectacle, with themes like "Oriental Fantasy" or "A Night on Broadway," to celebrations of American traditions and achievements—the space program (1967), country fairs (1968), developments in transportation (1970)—expressions of the American Way under attack elsewhere by hippies and antiwar protesters. In the 1970s Orange Bowl productions became increasingly self-conscious in delivering their political messages. The pregame show in 1973 openly addressed anxieties about American youth, feared to be lost to the counterculture and now Watergate cynicism as well. As a red, white, and blue starburst unfolded on a float, and young people stepped through their routines, a "Voice of Tomorrow" boomed through the stadium: "Hey . . . you there, America . . . look down here . . . I'm the Youth of America. . . . There's always doubt toward any new generation. . . . But look . . . you're too uptight. Relax, for as certain as you and I will grow older, it is also certain that I will mature and become responsible as you have." In 1977 the flag itself was given a voice that struck a more defensive and pleading note: "Some call me the Star-Spangled Banner. Some call me Old Glory. But I don't feel as proud as I used to. . . . When I come marching down your street, salute me, and I promise to wave back to you."[102]

The Orange Bowl eventually reverted to merely overblown pageantry, but for a time, not just in Miami but throughout the country, "The Star-Spangled Banner" became an anthem of division rather than unity. After the 1970s it resumed being a routine gesture at sporting events, until developments such as the recent wars in the Middle East again made it an uncertain challenge: what exactly was the "patriotism" of the moment that it signified—support for a wrong-headed war or for the young men and women sacrificed to it? Under these circumstances, the national anthem could again feel like a crude intrusion on simple athletic contests.

That, too, is a legacy of the 1960s.

COLLEGE FOOTBALL IN BLACK AND WHITE, PART I INTEGRATING THE SOUTHEASTERN CONFERENCE

The Negro is time's intruder.
—Peter Schrag, "Tennessee Lonesome End,"
Harper's, *March 1970*

At the end of the 1960s, football was not yet indelibly black. In 1968 about a quarter of the players in the NFL were African American (about the same as in Major League Baseball, with the National Basketball Association at 50 percent).[1] The college game had marquee black players like O. J. Simpson and Leroy Keyes, to be sure, but after two decades of gradual change, few northern teams were even as integrated as the NFL, and the South had barely begun to desegregate its football programs. But big-time college football was on the verge of a dramatic racial transformation.

While black college football players outside the South were distinctly a minority, even on the most thoroughly integrated teams, they also belonged to the minority leading the assault on American institutions. While the Vietnam War and the antiwar movement dominated headlines between 1968 and 1972, the struggle for civil rights from the 1950s through the 1970s did much more to remake American society. As members of their race, black football players had to feel the exhilaration—and responsibility—of belonging to a political vanguard. As college athletes, however, they were "boys" (like their white teammates) in a world ruled by powerful coaches. To many distraught football fans, the rebellions by black players at Oregon State, Wyoming, Indiana, Washington, Syracuse, and other universities seemed part of a vast conspiracy, but in fact the confrontations between black players and white coaches were a series of local actions, collective but personal, no doubt troubling for many of the coaches but more so for the athletes. And the athletes faced the harshest consequences.

Shocking as it may seem to those who grew up watching Deion

Sanders and Charles Barkley, or Chad Johnson and Terrell Owens, on personality tests given to black and white athletes during the years of black rebellion, black players scored high for orderliness, deference, and "abasement" and low on exhibitionism and "impulsivity."[2] Generations of living under the brutal regime of Jim Crow in the South or the subtler racism in the North reinforced habits for survival that were just beginning to change. To take on the role of integrating an all-white Kentucky or Alabama team, or to take a principled stand against a coach in Wyoming or Oregon, was not to follow deeply ingrained impulses but to defy them. None of these black college football players commanded a national or world stage, as did Muhammad Ali or Tommie Smith and John Carlos. None of them endured the solitary torments of Jackie Robinson. But all of them had more to lose than their peers in the Black Student Union or Black Student Alliance who were leading the broader racial challenge at their universities. Collectively, the black pioneers in the South and the black protesters in the North and West transformed college football for everyone and forever altered the relationship between coaches and athletes. Never again could coaches deal with their players, black or white, simply as "boys."

HISTORY AND MYTH

The racial revolution in college football took place on two major fronts: in the South through the school-by-school breakdown of segregation and in the North through a series of rebellions by black athletes. When the 1960s opened, not one football team in the Atlantic Coast, Southeastern, or Southwest Conferences was integrated (and George Preston Marshall's Washington Redskins were still holding out as the last of the all-white NFL teams). Desegregation in college football crept from the border states southward over the decade—first in the Atlantic Coast Conference, beginning with Maryland in 1963; next in the Southwest Conference, beginning with Southern Methodist and Baylor in 1966; and finally in the Southeastern Conference, beginning with Kentucky in 1967 and ending with Georgia, Louisiana State, and Mississippi in 1972. The SEC's premier team, Bear Bryant's Alabama Crimson Tide, was among the last, lowering the barrier in 1971. A member of Bryant's second integrated recruiting class, Sylvester Croom, became the SEC's first black head football coach in 2004 at Mississippi State. Some changes take a very long time.[3]

On certain occasions, sport has led the country in breaking through barriers to integration and tolerance, most notably on that April day in 1947 when Jackie Robinson first took the field as a Brooklyn Dodger. Football had no such transformative national event because segregation never ruled absolutely, as it did in Major League Baseball from the 1880s into the 1940s. College football outside the South was marginally integrated nearly from the beginning, with William Henry Lewis and William Tecumseh Sherman Jackson lining up for Amherst in 1889. Lewis and Jackson graduated in 1892, Jackson to become an instructor in Greek and Latin at Amherst and Lewis to enroll in Harvard Law School and play so well on the football team there (eligibility rules were loose) that he made Walter Camp's All-America teams in 1892 and 1893 on his way to a distinguished career in law and politics. The comparable histories of several other racial pioneers in college football — men like Paul Robeson (singer, actor, political activist), Fred "Duke" Slater (Chicago judge), and Jerome "Brud" Holland (college president) — leave one dazzled by their achievements as true "scholar-athletes" but also saddened by the realization of what extraordinary character and abilities were required for a young black man to be given a chance just to play football at predominantly white universities. A different kind of black football player began appearing in the 1930s, physically talented but academically ill-prepared, who is unfortunately more familiar.[4] The slow spread of integration was often driven less by progressive principles than by the need to win games. As we have come to know too well, opportunity too often becomes not easily distinguishable from exploitation.

While the NFL remained entirely segregated from 1933 through 1945 due to an unwritten "gentleman's agreement," college football's record of slow and fitful integration is barely less shameful. Yet the symbolism of even just one or two black players on a college football team, itself the most visible symbol of the university, exerted a steady pressure in the broader struggle for civil rights. In the 1960s South, on the other hand, football was nowhere near the vanguard but was merely swept up in the tide of political and social change. College football was not among the first institutions in the South to integrate but one of the last. Richard Pennington has told the story of the integration of the Southwest Conference, beginning with John Westbrook at Baylor and Jerry LeVias at Southern Methodist University in 1966 and ending with Julius Whittier at Texas and Jon Richardson at Arkansas in 1970. Pennington's portrait of LeVias is heart wrenching and appalling: the hate mail and death threats, the spitting and kicks and "nigger" slurs from opponents and even from teammates (directed at blacks on the other team but over-heard by LeVias), the loneliness and bewilderment. Texas newspapers reported none of this at the time.[5]

The same near silence accompanied the integration of the Southeast-ern Conference. While the larger struggle for civil rights was horrifyingly bloody in Alabama and Mississippi, the integration of football in the SEC, as reported by the local press, would appear to have been uneventful. No governor of Mississippi tried to block Ben Williams from donning shoulder pads in 1972 for an Ole Miss steeped in Confederate traditions; no National Guardsman had to escort him into the locker room. The bloody battles that disrupted the lunch-counter sit-ins, Freedom Rides, and voter-registration campaigns of the early 1960s helped make the peaceful integration of SEC football possible and inevitable. College football teams in the Deep South held out longest against integration in part because civil rights activists did not make them a major target. But this is not to say that the integration of "mere" football teams was less threatening to the white southern way of life than blacks voting or going to school with white children. There was nothing "mere" about football in the South. In fact, nothing was closer to the heart of white southern manhood.

Several easily understood desires have conspired to create a myth of football's integration in the Deep South that persists despite regular de-bunking. Following USC's walloping of Alabama in 1970, the story goes, with the Trojans' powerful black fullback Sam Cunningham doing most of the damage, Bear Bryant is said to have brought Cunningham into the Alabama locker room and told his team: "This is Sam Cunningham. This is what a football player looks like." Bryant then went out to find some Sam Cunninghams of his own. Another line is attributed both to USC coach John McKay and, more often, to Bryant assistant Jerry Claiborne: "Sam Cunningham did more to integrate Alabama football in sixty min-utes than Martin Luther King had accomplished in twenty years." The story appeals on several grounds. It gives primary credit to Bryant, the most potent icon in southern football, making him an American, not just southern, hero. It completes the erasure of the controversies that haunted Bryant's career throughout the 1960s—the asterisks in some sportswriters' minds beside Alabama's national championships in 1961, 1964, and 1965 with all-white teams (Bryant likely lost a fourth national championship in 1966—his blemish-free Alabama team losing out to once-tied Notre Dame—due to his failure to integrate) and his reputation for brutality as a young coach at Kentucky, Texas A&M, and initially at Alabama. The myth neatly balances the progressive and the pragmatic: a decision made for football's sake that aligns with democratic principles. And it makes the radical assault on one of the most powerful symbols of racist southern ideology seem a single, tidy, painless event.

There is a vague element of truth in this story, though the basic facts are false. The integration of southern football could not be avoided. Just as Title IX would later mandate gender equity in college athletics, the Civil Rights Act of 1964 led to pressure on southern universities from the U.S. Department of Health, Education, and Welfare—the source of federal education loans—to recruit black athletes.[6] Integration became tolerable for a different reason: the alternative would have struck a more painful blow at southern pride. By the 1960s southern teams could compete for national honors only if they were willing to play integrated northern teams, and when they did, they had to endure northern criticism anyway. Undoubtedly the most hated sportswriter among the white citizens of Alabama in the 1960s was Jim Murray of the *Los Angeles Times*, who wrote a column in 1961 (when Bryant's boys were ranked no. 1 and being considered for the Rose Bowl) in which he described Alabama as a state where "evening dress" meant "bed sheets with eyeholes" and whose all-white football teams were not only un-American but also inhuman.[7]

Nine years later, the Crimson Tide's hosting of USC meant social progress, but Murray made no new southern friends on this occasion. Writing on the eve of the game, he congratulated the "front-of-the-bus champions of the universe, the Alabama varsity," for their willingness to play an integrated team—a sign that the "bedsheet-and-burning-cross conference is coming into the daylight of the 20th century." After USC's decisive victory, Murray declared that Alabama had formally rejoined the Union, having played a football game "against a mixed bag of hostile black and white American citizens without police dogs, tear gas, rubber hoses or fire horses." (Murray added a gratuitous slap in another column four days later with a dictionary of useful terms for travelers in this "foreign country": "'HIRE'—what you part with a comb"; "'SNOW'—what you do while asleep which makes your wife shake you"; and so on.)[8] Murray's columns provoked local reactions such as Jack Doane's attack in the *Montgomery Advertiser* on West Coast "longhairs, yippies, flippies or whatever they call those things in LA and the ultra-liberals" that made up Murray's readership. This was a new Civil War of words.[9]

Whether outsiders' sarcasm stung or infuriated, the greater problem—and the indirect "truth" in the Bryant-Cunningham anecdote—was that competing at the highest level with only white players became increasingly difficult over the 1960s. With Alabama itself slumping badly, Bryant understood well before 1970 that both the political and football worlds were changing. After black students at Alabama threatened a lawsuit, Bryant had allowed five black walk-ons to try out as early as the spring of 1967, but he kept none of them. He also reportedly recruited but failed to sign three black high school stars in 1968, including Frank Dowsing and James Owens, who chose other SEC schools. How hard he tried is questionable; certainly Bryant moved slowly on integration, waiting for other conference schools to bring in black players before taking that step for Alabama. He waited too long for the university's Afro-American Student Association, which finally filed its lawsuit on July 2, 1969, after nearly three years of discussions without results, charging that Alabama "had not recruited black athletes with the same diligence used to recruit white athletes." While the early stages of the legal process were still playing out, in December 1969 Bryant signed Wilbur Jackson as his first black scholarship athlete.[10] Jackson was thus playing on the freshman team when Sam Cunningham ran over the varsity the following September. In short, change was coming to Tuscaloosa long before the storied 1970 USC game. The game itself provided not a catalyst but a rationale for integration, understandable even to Alabama's most racist fans.

Among those most attentive to the complexities of the man and the situation, there are divided views on Bryant's actions, or rather his inaction. One biographer, Keith Dunnavant, casts Bryant as racially progressive—he had wanted to integrate his Kentucky teams in the late 1940s and would have recruited black players to Alabama from the beginning had state law and local custom permitted—but ultimately pragmatic. Dunnavant's Bryant became the "anti-Wallace" not by forcing integration on Alabamians prematurely but by making it work on the field and giving it a powerful symbol in the Crimson Tide football team. In his less hagiographic biography, Allen Barra concludes that Bryant's tardiness in doing "the right thing" was his "greatest failure as a leader." David Halberstam, who reported from the South on the civil rights movement during Bryant's early years at Alabama, also took this more critical view. To Halberstam, Bryant was "the one man in all of Alabama who could go ahead and recruit [black players], and stand up to George Wallace, and bring the culture along with him." But he didn't. In Halberstam's view, Bryant was a great coach but not a great leader, football tough but not strong in the way that mattered most.[11]

TIIE SEC'S BLACK PIONEERS

The story of Bear Bryant and Sam Cunningham distorts the integration of the Southeastern Conference by oversimplifying a far messier history. For the record, these were the black pioneers of SEC football:

- Kentucky (1967): Nat Northington, sophomore defensive back, the first African American to play football in the SEC
- Tennessee (1968): Lester McClain, sophomore receiver, the first to earn a letter
- Auburn (1970): James Owens, sophomore running back
- Florida (1970): Willie Jackson, sophomore receiver; and Leonard George, sophomore running back
- Mississippi State (1970): Frank Dowsing, sophomore defensive back; and Robert Bell, sophomore defensive tackle
- Alabama (1971): John Mitchell, junior defensive end; and Wilbur Jackson, sophomore running back
- Vanderbilt (1971): Taylor Stokes, junior place kicker and receiver; Doug Nettles, sophomore defensive back; and Walter Overton, sophomore receiver
- Georgia (1972): Horace King, sophomore wingback; Chuck Kinnebrew, sophomore defensive lineman; and Larry West, sophomore defensive back
- Louisiana State (1972): Mike Williams, sophomore defensive back
- Mississippi (1972): Robert "Gentle Ben" Williams, freshman defensive tackle

A few footnotes are required. At Kentucky, Northington had a co-pioneer in defensive end Greg Page, until Page broke his neck in a non-contact drill during a preseason practice and died on the eve of the second game. A little over three weeks later, a despondent Northington quit the team and the university, leaving current freshmen Wilbur Hackett and Houston Hogg to complete the integration of Kentucky football the following season. At Tennessee, coaches belatedly signed Lester McClain to be a roommate for highly recruited running back Albert Davis, who then lost his scholarship over an issue of academic qualifications, leaving McClain alone to integrate the program.[12] (Tennessee quickly became the SEC's most conspicuously integrated football team, as those who followed McClain to Knoxville included linebacker Jackie Walker in 1969, twice an All-American and still the NCAA career record holder with five interceptions for touchdowns; and Condredge Holloway in 1972, not just one of the SEC's first two black quarterbacks but also "one of the most popular athletes in Tennessee history."[13]) At Vanderbilt, an injury kept Taylor Stokes from playing as a sophomore, delaying integration by a year. At Alabama, Wilbur Jackson was the first to receive a scholarship, but John Mitchell, a junior-college transfer, the first to see action. The three sophomores at Georgia entered school with two others, but Clarence Pope and Richard Appleby did not play on the varsity until 1973. LSU would have had two black sophomores in 1972, but running back Lora Hinton was redshirted after being injured. And finally, had the NCAA not declared freshmen eligible in 1972, Ben Williams would not have suited up for the Ole Miss varsity until 1973. The University of Mississippi, scene of the bloodiest battles in the larger struggle for school integration and a site of continuing conflict over Confederate symbols into the 1990s, was the very last big-time football power to integrate, not just in the SEC but in the entire country.

By 1972, 8 percent of the football players in the SEC were black. Over the next ten years, their numbers increased to 41 percent, and the all-white conference of just sixteen years earlier was already fading into collective forgetfulness.[14]

Not surprisingly, the SEC's black pioneers were a remarkable group. Lester McClain (despite being recruited only as a roommate), Willie Jackson, Frank Dowsing, John Mitchell, Doug Nettles, Walter Overton, Horace King, Mike Williams, and Ben Williams were at least part-time starters in their first varsity season. Dowsing, Mitchell, both Williamses, and Wilbur Jackson eventually made first-team all-SEC, Dowsing twice and Ben Williams three times (King and Overton made the second team). Dowsing, Mitchell, and the two Williamses became All-Americans; both Williamses, Wilbur Jackson, Doug Nettles, and Horace King all played several years in the NFL.

Dowsing initially was the most remarkable of all, a 9.5 sprinter with a 3.2 grade-point average in premed at Mississippi State, both a football and an academic All-American who was admitted to medical school after his junior year but chose to return for his senior season. Dowsing's coach, Charley Shira, told a reporter that Dowsing was a "prize catch" because "96 percent of the black high-school graduates in the state of Mississippi could not qualify on academic grounds for an athletic scholarship." Southern coaches and athletic directors frequently cited this problem, or "alibi," as a writer in *Ebony* magazine dismissed it. "You know, we've been trying to get outstanding *nigras* on our teams for years," one southern athletic director told *Ebony*'s Lacy Banks. "But there just weren't any down here qualified to pass our academic entrance exams." Banks's response: "So ya'll ended up losing them to UCLA, Harvard, UC Berkeley, Yale and all those other schools up North and on the Coasts?"[15]

Shira's explanation and Banks's mocking disbelief are both credible. Segregated black schools were woefully underfunded, separate but very unequal, and the integration of southern high schools proceeded slowly over the 1960s. On the other hand, football coaches had never recruited only potential dean's-list scholars. Yet southern coaches also had to understand that if their first black players were not exemplary in every way—athletically, academically, socially, emotionally—the fallout could prove disastrous. White southern fans would more readily accept good players who were also "good boys," and the scrutiny of outsiders would be easier to bear if there were no trouble either on or off the field.

READING THE SILENCES

Although the scrutiny within the South must have been intense, there is no record of it. The most striking aspect of the reporting on a major revolution in southern football was how little there was of it. Fans have closer, more intimate contact with basketball players than football players, and the experiences of the SEC's black basketball pioneers from the same era were indeed brutal.[16] Even with their padding and helmets, however, and with the fans at a greater remove, the conference's black football pioneers had to be excruciatingly visible on the field, yet they were nearly invisible in the reporting.[17] As Alexander Wolff wrote in *Sports Illustrated* forty years later, "Trailblazers at major universities all over the South endured on-field cheap shots, racial slurs from fans, and hate mail and abusive phone calls in their dorms. Many fielded death threats."[18] None of that appeared in the contemporary coverage. How could it? In some ways, the integration of southern football was an unwritable story. White southern sportswriters had to recognize, at the very least, the necessity of integration (for the South to compete with the rest of the college football world) and its inevitability (due to legal and political pressure). Progressive sportswriters undoubtedly supported integration more enthusiastically, but even for them, what would have been the story to tell? About the heroic acts of the racial pioneers overcoming generations of bigotry and dispelling racist stereotypes? About the appalling obstacles racist fans and institutions put in their way? About the loneliness and indignities the players endured? Given their predominantly white readership and the necessity and inevitability of integration, white sportswriters had only one way to tell the story: integrated football was working smoothly for all parties and was really no big deal anyway. True or not, that was the story the southern press told over and over.

One might think that a more revealing account could have appeared in a national magazine such as *Sports Illustrated*. But *SI* published only two stories about the integration of the SEC and other southern conferences—the first in 1991, the second in 2005. HBO produced a TV special on the topic in 2008.[19]

Even the schools' own campus newspapers downplayed the revolution taking place. Lester McClain integrated Tennessee football in 1968—and SEC football more generally as well, after Kentucky's aborted beginning the year before—without any particular notice of his race from the *UT Daily Beacon* until the end of his senior year. The *Auburn Plainsman* likewise all but ignored James Owens's race and reported nothing about his experiences.[20] Alabama's *Crimson White* waited until John Mitchell and Wilbur Jackson had completed two seasons to interview them about their experiences (as a junior-college transfer, Mitchell had completed his eligibility, though Jackson had a season remaining). Mitchell had nothing but good to say about the "beautiful relationship" between black and white players. Jackson's comment was less effusive—"For the most part everybody was friendly"—but vague.[21] Georgia's *Red and Black* profiled the school's three pioneers—Horace King, Larry West, and Chuck Kinnebrew—in its preview of the 1972 season, predicting that they "will be remembered as great athletes rather than the first black players." The reporter acknowledged that their initiation "might be a little rough . . . at first. Rough until their ability is recognized and applauded and the only color the fans see is the Red and Black."[22] Whether or how it was rough, the paper did not report as the season played out.

The most surprising near silence came from the black press, not only from local newspapers such as the *Atlanta Daily World* and *Baltimore Afro-American* but also from the national edition of the *Pittsburgh Courier*. Here the explanation must be different. The papers' limited resources had something to do with it, but seemingly more crucial was their primary allegiance to the football at all-black colleges in the South. The sportswriters in the black press understood the mixed blessing of integration: a greater black presence in "major" college football came at the expense of Grambling, Morgan State, Florida A&M, and the rest of the black colleges whose football programs had finally gained national recognition in the 1960s. Grambling became famous for sending more players to the NFL than any other school except Notre Dame; in 1968 NFL clubs drafted eleven players from Jackson State alone.[23] Now these schools were beginning to lose great players to the newly integrated SEC.

To progressive whites in the 1960s, integration was an unalloyed blessing for the nation and for black Americans alike. To black Americans, however, the issue was more complicated. However unequal, separate black institutions—whether academic, economic, or social—were *black*. Integration meant opportunity but also loss. Lora Hinton recalled for an interviewer years later that the black community in Baton Rouge seemed indifferent, if not hostile, to the integration of LSU football. Why didn't Hinton play for all-black Southern University instead, they wondered?[24] According to *Sports Illustrated*'s belated account, this experience was common for the black pioneers, whose friends back home "regarded them as Uncle Toms and wondered why historically black colleges like Grambling, Prairie View and Florida A&M suddenly weren't good enough."[25] The integration of SEC football was more momentous for white southerners than for black, resulting in the loss of a bastion of white southern masculinity but bringing a compensating benefit in the national stature of conference teams through the prowess of black athletes. For some black southerners, the loss felt greater than the gain. And the black press paid relatively little attention.[26]

For a variety of reasons, then, only one story about the integration of SEC football was told as it was playing out, leaving the personal dramas to dribble out in snippets in later interviews, if at all, and leaving analysis to historians, one of whose challenges is to read the silences.

One theme runs through all of the local reporting on the SEC's black pioneers: in a time of "Black Power" and black rage, they were all "good Negroes." The same week in October 1968 that Smith and Carlos raised their clenched fists in Mexico City, Lester McClain had his breakout game for Tennessee. As a starter for the first time due to a teammate's injury, McClain had two touchdown catches in a 24–7 victory over Georgia Tech, the second on a spectacular dive in the end zone. The reporting that week cast McClain as a black Frank Merriwell, that emblem of heroic modesty and sportsmanship created in the 1890s that still defined the country's athletic ideal in the 1960s. McClain told reporters that he dreamed the night before of making great blocks from his wingback position (as opposed to catching touchdowns to the cheers of the crowd). One sportswriter described how, after his diving catch, McClain "jumped up and congratulated his buddies." After the game, he credited his quarterback, Bubba Wyche: "All I did was catch the ball . . . give Bubba the credit." His position coach, Bill Battle, saluted McClain's hard work: "He's the kind who stays after practice, asking you to throw hard-to-catch passes to him. He's worked like the dickens to do this well."[27] At the end of the season, reporters returned to the theme that McClain was Tennessee's hardest worker—after finishing first in the preseason mile run, he consistently won the daily wind sprints in practice—as well as the team's "best blocking wing-back." By the racial stereotypes of the day, these were white traits that complemented McClain's black speed and "relaxed style."[28]

Summing up his experiences under the headline, "Being First SEC Negro Gridder Posed No Problems for McClain," McClain spoke of teammates' fellowship and opponents' sportsmanship. Head coach Doug Dickey complimented him as "a fine football player and a good Christian boy" (!!). After being named SEC player of the week twice that season and having led the team in touchdown receptions, three times catching two in a game, McClain again deferred to Wyche as "a great passer" who "makes the receiver look good. All you have to do is run your pattern and Bubba will drop the ball into your hands."[29]

These were simply the sports clichés of the day, but they resonated powerfully when coming from the mouth of the first black football player in the history of the University of Tennessee and one of three black varsity football players in the entire Southeastern Conference at the time. And the press coverage of McClain's counterparts at other SEC schools stamped them from the same Merriwellian mold. After running back a punt 89 yards for a touchdown as a sophomore, Auburn's James Owens told reporters, "The guys blocked so well all I had to do was run." After touchdown catches of 40 and 53 yards, Florida's Willie Jackson explained that quarterback John Reaves "put it where I could get it." Vanderbilt placekicker Taylor Stokes credited the center and holder with having the tough jobs and gushed, "I've got some good ones. . . . I couldn't get the job done without them." After running back a kickoff 95 yards for a touchdown, Stokes's teammate Doug Nettles told reporters, "The other guys opened up such a big hole that all I had to do was run." Coaches and reporters reinforced this image. Owens was "a very devout Christian" who preached to prison inmates in Montgomery on Sundays. Mississippi State's Frank Dowsing was "genial and a hard worker," a winner of high school oratorical contests, and a member of the Fellowship of Christian Athletes. Alabama's John Mitchell "has a good attitude and works hard." LSU's Mike Williams was "an extremely coachable and dedicated young man." Mississippi's "Gentle Ben" Williams was known for his "easy smile and open friendliness."[30]

There was nothing remarkable about any of these comments in the world of sports journalism in the 1960s. This is how college athletes spoke to reporters and how reporters wrote about college athletes. But the fact that these athletes were black, in the Southeastern Conference, made these words potent. Collectively, they created a single undifferentiated, appealing—and nonthreatening—black figure. For the most part, the athletes disavowed or downplayed their pioneer role. Mitchell admitted wanting to be the first black player at Alabama, but this interview appeared in the *Nashville Banner*, not in an Alabama paper. More typically, when asked how it felt to be Florida's first black player, Willie Jackson claimed that he "never thought about it." After Horace King made racial history at the University of Georgia, the *Athens Banner-Herald* reported, "This business about Horace King being the first black player ever to score a touchdown for Georgia may have been good copy for writers covering the Georgia–North Carolina State game Saturday, but for King himself, it was really no big deal."[31] Whenever asked, the players also insisted that they had experienced no prejudice or discrimination.[32]

Both the formulaic reporting and the players' disclaimers likely helped defuse resistance among SEC fans. For some in the stands, no doubt, a Robert Bell or a John Mitchell was still a "nigger," but at least he was also a "good boy" who still knows his place—his "place" now including Scott Field in Starkville or Denny Stadium in Tuscaloosa. And perhaps integrating SEC football did play out relatively smoothly. Relatively. Bell told a journalist for *Ebony* magazine that SEC football was a relief after "playing in those small hick towns" in high school, "where racial prejudice is at its worst." Bell recalled playing against one guy in high school who kept calling him a "big black nigger." Bell had said nothing in response but just kept hitting him, until they "had to carry him off the field." At Mississippi State, when fans chanted, "Give 'em hell, Robert

Bell," they might not have intended unconditional acceptance, but it was better than "Hey, nigger."[33]

No doubt, the black players who broke down the racial barriers at SEC schools were selected for their "character" as well as their sprinter's speed or giant's strength. No doubt, they spoke and conducted themselves carefully. No doubt, a majority of white teammates and opponents—perhaps after lectures from their coaches—treated them with respect. Nonetheless, what's missing from the contemporary newspaper accounts is the human element: hints of any resistance whatsoever from teammates, classmates, opponents, or the fans and the larger public; and among the black pioneers themselves, a sense of at least occasional feelings of isolation, of the struggle to maintain the "good Negro" posture, of strong feelings—whether fear, anger, frustration, self-pity, determination—that must have been a significant part of their experience. Perry Wallace, the SEC's first black basketball player, described in 1991 the "dual" life he had lived at Vanderbilt, publicly confident, privately brooding. "There was so much at risk that I could have gone one way or another," he told *Sports Illustrated*, "even counting as hard as I fought to come out healthy. When it's over, you have to open up feelings that you had to block out to survive. I could have been consumed by fear and pain, but I fought to overcome that."[34] Many of his fellow pioneers in football must have had similar feelings. By now, accounts of routine racial abuse in the past have become so familiar that they have lost their power to shock. The black pioneers' silence, ironically, can ring louder today by forcing us to imagine what we have not been told.

In November 1969 a sociology professor at the University of Alabama surveyed the views of the school's white students on race and integration, following previous surveys in 1963 and 1966. Students in the 1963 survey had opposed integration by a 5 to 3 margin; six years later, they supported it 3 to 1. Additional details from the latest study were included in a special report published by the campus newspaper in March 1971, late in Wilbur Jackson's freshman year. As the editor of the *Crimson White* reported, "Rapidly increasing acceptance of blacks was found in all four major areas" in the survey. For example, while 56.4 percent of the 676 students polled in 1963 had had no objection to attending classes with blacks, 92.2 percent of 1,039 students felt that way in 1969. Approval of interracial dating increased much more dramatically—from just .9 percent in 1963 to 11.9 percent in 1969. As The *Crimson White* put it, "By 1969, the list of majority-accepted situations included all that were not personally social, but a clear, if decreasing, majority continued to object to rooming with, double dating with, and dating black students."[35]

The *Crimson White* celebrated this progress by titling the story "UA Blacks Today: A New Unification." For Wilbur Jackson (and John Mitchell on his arrival the following semester), the 7.8 percent who still clung to segregation and the 88.1 percent who wanted them to stay away from white female students would not have represented progress but their experience *now*. The fact that their white classmates accepted them—except in matters that were "personally social"—might not have seemed worth celebrating. All of the SEC schools were going through the turmoil of more broadly integrating campus and classroom during the years that the black pioneers were breaking the barrier in football. During Jackson's freshman year at Alabama, the campus paper published a student's letter attacking newly approved Black Studies courses as racist and fraudulent, and a protest by black students escalated into a sit-in in the president's office that led to five arrests.[36] Lester McClain's freshman and sophomore years at Tennessee were marked by a dispute between students and the administration over the institution's refusal to allow Adam Clayton Powell and Dick Gregory to speak on campus.[37] No major racial protest marked James Owens's years at Auburn, but several items in the campus newspaper—a column accusing the university of racism, followed by a flurry of heated responses; a special issue on the racial state of the university that included a story about the Ku Klux Klan's campaign to recruit college students—point to the charged atmosphere within which Owens, like the black pioneers on the rest of the SEC campuses, performed his role as the university's first black football player.[38]

TO TELL, OR NOT TO TELL

After McClain's junior season at Tennessee, Peter Schrag, a journalist for *Harper's*, a liberal national monthly, tried to pry out of him some comments on his experience thus far. Schrag reported hearing shouts of "Hey nigger" and "Hey Leroy," followed by laughter from the Ole Miss stands during a game that fall, but McClain insisted that he had not heard any of this on the field. "Hey Leroy" was shorthand for a local racist joke that also figured in a near incident at the Ole Miss–Kentucky game the previous season, when armed highway patrolmen ringing the field, ostensibly to protect Kentucky's Houston Hogg and Wilbur Hackett from hostile fans, began shouting the lines to each other. As the joke goes, late in a close game between two black schools, the coach tells his quarterback, "Give 'at ball to LeRoy." The quarterback runs to the huddle and calls the play, a handoff to LeRoy, who is buried by the entire defensive line. "Give 'at ball to LeRoy," the coach yells again. Same result. "Give 'at ball to LeRoy," the coach yells a third time. The quarterback turns to the huddle, then after a few moments hollers back to the coach, "LeRoy say he don't want 'at ball." As the burly patrolmen tossed the refrain and punch line back and forth, a furious Hackett yelled at the cops, "Go to hell!," until Kentucky's sports information director calmed him down.[39] None of this was reported at the time.

The joke was still alive at Ole Miss a year later, but McClain claimed not to have heard it. Schrag also wondered what McClain thought about Black Power and black protests on other campuses, but he had to report that "McClain will have nothing to do with the Black Student Union at Tennessee." Schrag asked about the protest by black football players at Wyoming earlier that season; McClain told him that some of the other black athletes at Tennessee have been thinking about it, "but it wouldn't help 'em to say anything." To the obvious frustration of the liberal journalist, McClain was getting by at Tennessee by saying "very little" and keeping to himself. He was at Tennessee for a chance at a better life, not to fight for a cause. Schrag clearly arrived in Knoxville already knowing the story he came to find, only to discover that Lester McClain would not tell it to him. A third time, the white journalist asked the apparently sullen black athlete what he was angry about, still with no answer, until finally McClain mentioned reading Lew Alcindor's comments about racism at UCLA, written after he graduated. McClain admitted to Schrag that "someday I'd like to tell my story the way Alcindor did."[40]

McClain's refusal to tell the white journalist what he wanted to hear has its own eloquence. While he and the other black pioneers might not have felt "free" to tell the truth, we should recognize that their refusals, like their Merriwell poses, also freed them from having to explain themselves to white writers and readers.

Lester McClain did get a chance to tell his story to a campus reporter at the very end of his senior year—to his great regret, it turned out. The early promise of his sophomore season had not been fully realized, as McClain had fewer receptions and touchdowns as a junior and senior. After a four-part series titled "The Black Athlete at UT" appeared in the *Daily Beacon*—in which black members of the track squad criticized the athletic department's treatment of black athletes[41]—a staff writer followed up by asking the school's first black football player for his story. Under the headline "McClain Blasts Athletic Dept," in the first installment of a two-part interview McClain charged his coaches with "deliberately restricting" his career. He claimed that, after recruiting him only to be a roommate for the more talented Albert Davis, the coaches did not want McClain to make them look bad by playing too well. They would not let too many passes be thrown to him, and they pulled him when the offense got close to the end zone in order to limit his opportunities to score. They also undermined his confidence to the point, in McClain's words, that "I actually believed I couldn't catch the ball." The fact that the Chicago Bears had drafted McClain in the ninth round seemed to confirm that he had visible talent not reflected by his declining receptions.

As for his personal experiences, McClain described an incident in which an assistant coach embarrassed him by calling out, "Hey, boy," in a dormitory lobby filled with his teammates, then yelling at him to cut off his moustache. McClain described racial slurs from fans ("Here comes Uncle Tom into the game"; "Look, they got a nigger"), teammates who were nice to him except when their girlfriends were present, and the "cold chill in the air" he felt when he danced with a white girl. He also made it clear that, despite all of his denials to reporters, from the very beginning he had been excruciatingly conscious of his pioneer role and the expectations it entailed. When he considered quitting after being embarrassed over his moustache, he stuck it out because he knew that "too many people had said Blacks in general couldn't make it in the SEC." When a writer for *Ebony* magazine tried to interview him in his junior year, he refused to talk "because of the fear that I would say something [the coaches] didn't want me to say." McClain now criticized the athletic department for "present[ing] a false front to the racial problem." Spokesmen "made up quotes and distributed them to the press without even consulting the athletes they are supposed to be quoting." Even new head coach Bill Battle, who had been McClain's "sympathetic" position coach during the Doug Dickey years, had continued the pattern of "deliberate restriction."[42]

This last charge stung the most, but it ended up stinging McClain rather than Battle. As the local and statewide newspapers picked up the story, Battle publicly expressed his hurt and disappointment that one of his players was dissatisfied. The *Knoxville News-Sentinel* reported that Battle met with McClain and told him that "he had hurt himself more than he had hurt UT, that doors he had worked hard to open were now closed." In a backpedaling response, McClain insisted that he had been quoted out of context, that a two-hour interview mostly on "general" matters had been distorted, that the reporter had ignored the mostly good things that he had said about the UT program. And he vehemently denied that he had said that Bill Battle discriminated against him. To Ben Byrd, sports editor of the *Knoxville Journal*, McClain tried to explain that he was not trying to tear down Tennessee's athletic department but help it see where changes were needed. Having waited so long to speak out, he denied that he was now reversing the position he had expressed throughout his career at Tennessee. He insisted that when he had "told sports reporters in the past that things were fine," he was not lying: "When you say things are fine you're not saying that they're absolutely perfect, you're considering the adjustments you have to make for things to be fine in a predominantly white system."[43]

Just a week earlier, Tom Siler, the sports editor of the *Knoxville News-Sentinel*, had written a valedictory column on McClain, saluting him for his pioneering role. Though not a "great star," McClain had made "a notable contribution" to UT football. He was a young man with "one of the brightest smiles you ever saw," and that smile and attitude, along with his large family, had likely "helped Lester over the rough spots at big, sprawling, impersonal, white-dominated, white-oriented UT." Siler understood that, like Jackie Robinson, McClain in that world had had to "maintain self-control, walk away from trouble. . . . There were slurs, rebuffs, insults. 'I could write a book . . .' says Lester. Instead he held a true course—the college degree, an Orange jersey" (ellipses in the original).[44]

McClain did not write a book, only an introduction to its first chapter in that interview with the *Daily Beacon* a few days later, but instead of providing a release, the experience only confirmed that he had been wise to keep quiet earlier. Having just acknowledged the challenges at a "white-dominated" university (while McClain was still smiling), Siler in a column after the interview dismissed the young black man's complaints as the typical athlete's disgruntlement, made newsworthy only because the athlete happened to be black. Siler was not wholly unsympathetic. He admitted that, when McClain began dropping passes as a junior, "off-the-field problems" might have been a factor; but Siler had no doubt that McClain's performance, not his skin color, had guided his coaches' reactions.[45]

Whether coaches undermined his confidence, as McClain claimed, or they lost confidence in him, as Siler countered, McClain's tentative opening up at the end of his college career exposed the conditions under which all of the black pioneers must have played—and also the reasons for not talking about them. A white sports editor who understood and sympathized with the "good Negro" simply dismissed the malcontent. Being stung once seems to have been enough for Lester McClain. In an interview in 1984, he denied "any trouble with teammates, fans or opponents." Interviewed another eight years later by a graduate student at Tennessee, McClain recalled moments of loneliness and isolation but otherwise insisted that his experience was "one of the smoothest transitions . . . that took place in the South."[46]

Although conditions must have been worse in the deeper South, contemporary accounts provide no glimpse of them. Many years after McClain's first coach, Doug Dickey, had moved on to Florida, where he integrated his second SEC school (with his predecessor's recruits), Dickey acknowledged the "much more significant redneck backlash" in Gainesville than in Knoxville. Rural west Floridians in particular expressed what Dickey termed "a rather nasty level of irritation." No hint of this was reported in 1970 in the *Gainesville Sun*, which instead profiled Willie Jackson as the beneficiary of a white Florida alumnus who arranged for his scholarship and invited him into his home. Jackson himself looked forward to becoming a social worker, in order "to help other people, and very likely kids."[47] More Frank Merriwell stuff.

Hints of other black pioneers' difficult experiences have come out long after the events—but still no more than hints. (Why should black former athletes be any more eager to open themselves to white writers and readers today than they were forty years ago?) In a 1984 interview, Horace King spoke vaguely of "rotten apples" among his teammates at Georgia, particularly the juniors and seniors who "were leaving and didn't have to face it."[48] In 2001 John Mitchell told a reporter, "I wouldn't say everyone accepted me, but Coach Bryant was fair so the players all treated me the same." Mitchell also recalled that when he walked into various establishments in Tuscaloosa, "everybody stopped and looked, then somebody said, 'He's a football player,' and they all went back to what they were doing."[49] An innocuous but telling incident. The young black man was an intruder until recognized as a Bama football player, status that afforded him (limited) privileges. The point is not that breaking racial barriers in the South had to be a wholly bitter experience. It had to be bittersweet, but contemporary coverage left out the bitter altogether.

TRAGEDY IN LEXINGTON

The fullest telling of a black pioneer's story was the first, the integration of Kentucky football by Greg Page and Nat Northington in September 1967, not because it was the most historically significant but because it was overwhelmed by tragedy. Northington was an all-state high school running back in Kentucky, Page an all-state end, both of them recruited not just by the football coach but also by the university president, the governor, and former governor Happy Chandler (who as commissioner had overseen the integration of Major League Baseball by Jackie Robinson in 1947).[50] Page was a not-very-visible lineman, but Northington became an immediate star on the freshman team, averaging six yards per carry; and in his first spring scrimmages with the varsity, he "unreeled touchdown runs of 70, 86 and 90 yards," as sports editor John McGill enthused in the *Lexington Herald*. In describing Northington as "a natural athlete," McGill (no doubt unconsciously) invoked the racial stereotype of the day—as did Kentucky coaches in exclaiming that Northington ran "like an antelope" and "like a race horse" (a real Kentucky thoroughbred).[51] Despite those long touchdowns, however, Northington was switched to defense for his first varsity season, where he was projected as a starter at cornerback. Kentucky was ready for a black football player but perhaps not quite ready for a black offensive hero. (Vanderbilt later moved Walter Ovington from quarterback to receiver, and Georgia shifted Horace King from halfback to wingback, a common experience for black players throughout college football, not just in the South.)

Kentucky was certainly not ready for the death of its other black pioneer. Greg Page broke his neck on the third day of fall practice, was paralyzed from the neck down, and died three weeks later, without leaving the hospital, on the eve of Kentucky's first home game. (In the season opener on the road against Indiana the previous Saturday, Northington had played briefly, running back two punts to officially integrate SEC football.) University officials deferred to the young man's parents to decide whether the game should be played or canceled. As the *Lexington Herald* reported, Robert Page addressed a tearful team in the locker room before the game and told them that his son would want them to play. A memorial service was held in the stadium the next day, followed by the funeral in Middlesboro on Tuesday, which drew not just coaches, teammates, and university officials but even the governor.[52]

The typical reticence, even silence, in the coverage of SEC football's black pioneers was not possible in the face of this tragedy, and the eulogizing of Page, not surprisingly, pushed the "good Negro" to its limits. After the funeral, in a column three times the usual length, John McGill declared that Greg Page had had all of the "requirements of football ability, pride, ambition, and character" and was "a great credit to his university." Page was "liked and respected" by coaches and teammates alike, due in large part to his "outgoing fun-loving personality. He had a big smile which told you immediately that you could be his friend." The young man's parents, who came immediately to Lexington to keep vigil at his bedside, were "sincere, responsible, God-fearing people" who "brought their Bible to the waiting room every day." Page's father attended practice one afternoon while his son lay in his hospital bed and told the team, "All of you boys know Greg is hurt. Don't let that slow you down a bit." Head coach Charlie Bradshaw, a daily visitor at the hospital, considered the Pages "real people." When Greg died, the entire community mourned, and "total strangers offered sympathy."[53]

The eerie casting of Bradshaw as a sort of benevolent Ol' Massa, along with McGill's patronizing of the elder Pages as "sincere, responsible, God-fearing people," make one cringe today. In 1967, however, this language served a purpose. The sudden "freak" blow to the SEC's first experiment with integration—newspaper accounts repeatedly stressed the freakishness of Page's accident, the absence of malice—required a compensating ritual of mutual benevolence. That the terms of such a ritual would derive from plantation myth says much about the conditions under which SEC football was integrated.

The life-and-death drama at Kentucky must be read not simply as a record of what happened but also as a consciously crafted narrative of racial reconciliation required by the extraordinary events. In putting a human face on Greg Page's grieving family, John McGill described the father's growing up "in controversial Mississippi" (a strangely euphemistic adjective in 1967), then serving with the army in the Pacific for four years during World War II (thus a good American)—with no reminder, of course, that the army had still been segregated during the war. Of his childhood, Robert Page told McGill that "there are a lot of good people in Mississippi, like everywhere else." Growing up black in Mississippi left him with no bitterness. As he put it, "A person can be what he wants to be and command respect. You don't have to be like Stokely Carmichael."[54] The father was no militant activist, and he presumably taught his values to his football-playing son. Whether McGill or the senior Page was the principal author of this narrative is impossible to know, but a motive in each case is easily understandable. Robert Page had long experience living as a black man in the Jim Crow South. McGill was something like a midwife at the birth of a new era in SEC football that had gone horribly wrong, and he had to stop the hemorrhaging. As much as black readers needed to be assured that Coach Bradshaw grieved over the loss of Greg Page, white readers needed to be reassured that the young black men invading their cherished world were not Black Power radicals or surly ingrates.

The need to emphasize the freakishness of Greg Page's death was greater for two reasons: because the black community generally viewed the University of Kentucky as a racially hostile place (with basketball coach Adolph Rupp as the most visible symbol of entrenched segregation)[55] and because of Charlie Bradshaw's reputation as a brutal driver in the Bear Bryant mold. This is the same Charlie Bradshaw whose "rage to win" had whittled a squad of eighty-eight to a "Thin Thirty" in 1962. The president of the university initially feared that Page's fatal injury "might have occurred in some sort of punishment drill" and was immensely relieved when an internal investigation confirmed that it was indeed a "freak accident."[56]

Although Bradshaw apparently eased up some after that 1962 season, Phil Thompson, a white teammate of Northington and Page, has described the coach's fundamentally "abusive and sadistic practice methods" continuing into 1967, abetted by two "very cruel and abusive assistants" (one of whom, Charley Pell, went on to head coaching positions at Clemson and Florida). As Thompson vividly remembers, immediately following Greg Page's funeral on Tuesday, the team was bussed back to Lexington and directly to the football field, where Bradshaw conducted a brutal three-hour practice under the lights—no doubt to "get the boys' minds right for football." Three players quit that night; another got into a fistfight with an assistant coach. On Saturday the team traveled to Auburn for its first SEC away game. Thompson recalls standing in the entrance of the stadium, hearing the shouts of fans to "bring on the nigger," asking "where's LeRoy?" and challenging Nat Northington to "come on out, black boy." For the visitors' safety (!) a half dozen Alabama state troopers stood behind the Kentucky bench—with Confederate flags in their holsters alongside their guns and reassurances that they were there "to protect LeRoy." Northington had to leave the game in the second quarter after dislocating his shoulder for the second time that season. (He likely heard more abuse while on the bench than he would have on the field.) The press reported none of this. After the long narrative of racial goodwill and understanding around Greg Page's funeral, Nat Northington's subsequent experiences evoked the more typical near silence.[57]

According to Phil Thompson, a few days later Northington told him, "I can't take this shit anymore," then "slipped out of the football dorm in the middle of the night."[58] Exactly when he left for good is not clear. In the next game, against Virginia Tech, Northington hurt his shoulder again on the first play, and a week later he did not travel with the team to LSU. Although Lexington and Louisville papers did not report his quitting until the following Monday, it appears that he had left the team several days earlier. (The *Lexington Herald* did not list him among the injured players on the Tuesday after the Virginia Tech game.) In a partial reenactment of the original "Thin Thirty," Northington became the eleventh Kentucky player to quit since August and one of fourteen to suffer a major injury. (Besides Page's fatality, a freshman end was paralyzed from another broken neck; the other injuries were less serious.) One player quit because football interfered with his engineering studies and another due to academic difficulties; these were the only details provided by the local papers. The injuries and loss of players seemed just a plague of bad luck, no reflection on Bradshaw's coaching methods.[59]

The dozens who had quit Bradshaw's initial team were disparaged (collectively, not personally) in the Lexington papers, but in 1967 Northington was the only black football player in the entire Southeastern Conference. On this occasion, Coach Bradshaw praised him as "a fine young man with a bright future" who had been undone by unfortunate and uncontrollable events, "principally his shoulder injury which kept him from performing." Northington's own public comments included nothing about his shoulder, Bradshaw's brutal practices, or the Auburn fans' malicious taunts. "I just couldn't make it," he told a reporter. "It's not because of the color thing . . . this was just the wrong one (school), I guess. It's nobody else's fault, but my own. The people are nice, and I like everybody, but it's just that there is something missing. I just couldn't live up to it[.] ... I'm letting a lot of people down, but if I kept going on, I'd just be fooling everybody but my own self" (ellipses in the original).[60]

No one could have anticipated the precise circumstances, but at least one person had foreseen the possibility of such an end. During his recruitment by Kentucky, Northington's mother had written the governor, "If I find that his life is in danger by playing football in the southern states, I will be forced to take action to haul him somewhere else where he won't be abused."[61] A year and a half later, her son indeed left Lexington and enrolled at Western Kentucky (from which he graduated in 1971).

Two black freshmen, Wilbur Hackett and Houston Hogg, stayed at Kentucky despite Page's death and Northington's leaving to complete the integration of Kentucky football the following season. Returning meant not just playing *at* Kentucky, a lonelier place now with Page and Northington gone, but also playing *for* Kentucky in places like Jackson, Mississippi (where they, too, were treated to the "Hey LeRoy" joke). Many years later, Hackett told an interviewer about returning home after Page's funeral to a blunt question from his black friends: "They killed Greg up there, man. What are you still doing up there?" Hackett and Hogg stayed, but they also warned off other potential black recruits.[62]

IRONY IN OXFORD

While the integration of the sec began in tragedy, it concluded in something closer to farce at the University of Mississippi, although that part of the story took place off the field. With its Confederate flags, Rebels nickname, "Dixie" fight song (unofficial), and Colonel Rebel mascot, Ole Miss (itself the slaves' name for Old Master's wife) was more bedecked with the trappings of the plantation myth than any other school, and no football program was more dug in on segregation. The school's most famous and successful coach, John Vaught, refused bowl invitations in the 1950s against integrated opponents, and he remained defiantly committed to all-white football even when rival sec schools began breaking down the color barrier.

In ways both incidental and substantial, football emphatically represented the white South at Ole Miss. The white supremacist governor, Ross Barnett, chose to take his final defiant stand for segregation at the Mississippi-Kentucky football game on September 29, 1962, the day before a riot on campus would leave two dead in a futile effort to prevent

James Meredith from registering for classes under the protection of federal troops. The scene at the stadium of 41,000 Confederate flag–waving fans cheering deliriously and serenading Barnett as he "strutted onto the field" to proclaim, "I love Mississippi! . . . I love her people! . . . I love her customs! I love and respect our heritage!," conjures images from Leni Riefenstahl's Nazi epic, *Triumph of the Will*.[63] The *Saturday Evening Post's* account of the incidents on campus over the next several days described rock-throwing students threatening to kill Meredith and the Yankee soldiers. In a potent juxtaposition, it also included a photograph of smiling, well-groomed Ole Miss students carrying Confederate flags as they boarded a train later that week. The caption explained: "Rebel flags fluttered, but students were social rather than seething when they entrained for Jackson to see Ole Miss play a football game a few days after Meredith's enrollment."[64] As the semester played out, with federal marshals protecting Meredith and federal troops bivouacked on the campus—for a time on the football team's practice field, no less—Coach Vaught kept his players' focus on football, and he was later convinced that his undefeated team "kept Ole Miss from closing its doors."[65] In the fall of 1962, football at the University of Mississippi still meant continuity with the white southern way of life. That would change, though not for ten more years.

A "trickle" of black students followed Meredith to the university until the fall of 1968, when "dozens" began arriving. For them, watching Mississippi play integrated football teams was a painful experience, as they had to listen to the taunts of "Kill that nigger" and "Kill that black SOB" from the stands. They heard the fans shouting "Give 'at ball to LeRoy" when Wilbur Hackett and Houston Hogg came to town with their Kentucky teammates. From their end-zone seats, they cheered for the opposing teams and especially for the opponents' black players, refused to stand for "Dixie" or the Alma Mater, and held up banners that read: "Racist Athletic Department" and "Ole Miss Racism."[66]

This was the University of Mississippi shortly before Ben Williams's arrival in 1972 (Vaught retired as head coach after the 1970 season), exactly ten years after James Meredith integrated the school in the face of violent resistance. Yet Williams's presence on the field was all but ignored in the *Oxford Eagle* and received even less attention in the *Jackson Clarion-Ledger* (one of the South's newspapers known for a rabidly anti-integrationist stance in the 1950s and 1960s). For the SEC, integration may have been old news by 1972, yet the integration of Ole Miss football had to be anything but insignificant. Even the campus newspaper, the *Daily Mississippian*, which marked the tenth anniversary of federally imposed integration with a frank inquiry whether progress or tokenism had followed, barely acknowledged that the football team now had its first black player.[67] Nonetheless, at least one historian of integration at Ole Miss assigns Ben Williams a key role in the successful integration of the university as a whole. By the time Williams left four years later, he was not only a team captain, a three-time All-SEC pick, and an All-American, but he had also, most astonishingly, been elected to the honorific position of Colonel Rebel. The school mascot since 1936, Colonel Rebel (or Colonel Reb), in the words of historian Nadine Cohodas, was "a southern gentleman in the image of a plantation master: flowing white hair, bushy mustache, wearing a long coat nipped at the waist, light pants, dark shoes, and a big broad-brimmed hat." Each year, students elected a Colonel Rebel as a sort of campus king for the campus queen, Miss Ole Miss. Cohodas describes how Williams in his election campaign ignored the fraternities, which had their own candidates, while working the sororities, where "he knew his good looks and boyish charm would go over well with many young women who found him affable, even alluring, like some forbidden fruit."[68]

That the integration of southern football might be sexually charged was not a frequent topic in the (white) press, to say the least. The subject was not taboo, however, for a reporter in *Ebony* in 1970 (no doubt with a copy of Eldridge Cleaver's *Soul on Ice* sitting next to his typewriter), who suggested, "For many Southerners, seeing blacks on a traditionally all-white team is a thrill of a lifetime. Everybody wants to see how that black, super bad, sex machine operates when he runs with the ball or charges from the defensive line." With Shaft and Superfly invading American popular culture in the early 1970s, Williams in his campaign for Colonel Rebel indeed had the invisible support of "brothers" more potent than any fraternity could provide. (The film *Mandingo*, with its theme of forbidden fruit, would be released the following July.) After he won, Williams had to be posed for the yearbook with Miss Ole Miss, a very white Barbara Biggs, presenting the photographer with a distinct challenge: how to suggest the intimacy of the royal consorts without hinting at the ultimate sexual taboo? The solution, as Cohodas describes the photo, was to place the two in an outdoor setting, "standing next to each other, not quite touching," with "a fence between them."[69]

*Colonel Rebel and Miss Ole Miss, University of Mississippi, 1975
(Courtesy of the Southern Media Archive, Special Collections, University of
Mississippi Libraries)*

The entire episode reads today like a script for a *Saturday Night Live* skit, but it had to resonate differently at Ole Miss in 1975. The consternation in the white fraternities over Williams's election must have been considerable, but no greater than that felt by African American students who found a black Colonel Rebel, as Cohodas mildly puts it, "ironic, even disconcerting."[70] The irony is compounded by another Ole Miss historian's widely cited claim that the model for the original Colonel Rebel may have been "Blind Jim" Ivy, an old black man who was the students' unofficial mascot ("dean of the freshman class") from 1896 until his death in 1955.[71] Despite the physical resemblance, it seems doubtful that Ivy was the actual model—and the claim has been disputed—but linking the two accentuates Ben Williams's transfiguration of the image. White students' affection for Blind Jim, matched by Blind Jim's deep loyalty to Ole Miss, reconstituted the benign paternalism of plantation myth. A sexually charged Williams—the football team's best player, not its mascot—was a very different Colonel Rebel.

Should we declare Ben Williams college football's first postmodernist hero or simply recognize his campaign for Colonel Rebel as a brilliant act of black "signifying"? However we read it, Williams's achievement did not quite transform the university overnight. More than other SEC schools, Ole Miss clung to the symbols of its white-supremacist past, refusing to abandon its Rebel mascots and Confederate flags for decades, despite repeated controversies.[72] (Colonel Rebel was not officially retired until 2003.) For his part, Williams went on to play ten years in the NFL, own a construction company in Jackson, serve on the board of directors of his alma mater's foundation, and endow a minority scholarship in his name.[73] An ironic Colonel Rebel indeed.

BLACK QUARTERBACK

The black pioneer of southern football most exposed to public scrutiny was Eddie McAshan. As a sophomore in 1970, McAshan became the first black player at Georgia Tech (an original member of the SEC but an independent since 1964) and, more significantly, the first black quarterback in a major football program in the South. (Freddie Summers had played quarterback for Wake Forest in 1967 and 1968, but the ACC was a distinctly lesser conference in the 1960s. Tennessee's Condredge Holoway and Mississippi State's Melvin Barkum became the SEC's first black quarterbacks in 1972.) As a senior in 1972, McAshan also became the focus of southern football's first headline-grabbing racial protest. Aside from Lester McClain's mild criticism at the end of his senior year, the closest any of the SEC's black pioneers came to controversy was Horace King's admission to a reporter for the *Atlanta Journal* near the end of his sophomore season that he was frustrated over being played at wingback rather than his natural tailback position.[74] (Three days later, King replaced an injured white teammate at tailback, scoring two touchdowns and gaining 78 yards in 19 carries, but the next season found him still at wingback. After he was finally shifted to tailback as a senior, King made all-conference and went on to a nine-year career in the NFL.)

King's public complaint was brief and mild. Perhaps as a quarterback, McAshan could not have avoided controversy. The year McAshan became a starter for Georgia Tech, Holloway was a high school superstar in Huntsville, Alabama. Bear Bryant wanted the extraordinary young athlete—at sixteen, he was picked fourth in the Major League Baseball draft, and John Wooden tried to recruit him to play basketball at UCLA—but Bryant told Holloway up front that Alabama was not ready for a black quarterback. Nor was Vanderbilt in 1971, apparently, when the coaches moved Walter Overton from quarterback to wide receiver for his debut on the varsity. Events proved that Georgia Tech was no more ready in 1970.

The "McAshan Era," as the *Atlanta Journal* repeatedly proclaimed it, had an auspicious beginning, as Eddie was chosen Southeastern Back of the Week after completing 20 passes in 38 attempts for 202 yards in a 23–20 win over South Carolina in his first start. The fact that 14 of those passes and 134 of those yards were to the fullback, mostly on screen plays, and that two of the missed passes were interceptions, should have restrained the celebration; but McAshan led Tech to three more victories before the backlash started. In his fourth game, against Clemson, McAshan was 7 of 18 for 34 yards, with one touchdown and three interceptions, and he was replaced by senior Jack Williams. In the next game, Tech lost for the first time (to Tennessee, 17–6), with McAshan connecting on 23 of 42 passes for 190 yards and a touchdown, as Williams was too sick to play. But four more interceptions raised his total to twelve, a new Tech season record in just five games, and the boos from "a hostile gallery" in Tech's own stadium seemed all directed at him, notwithstanding the five fumbles by his teammates. From this moment on, McAshan's career at Georgia Tech, as a reporter described his first season, "ranged from moments of greatness to downright despair." In that same article, the "quiet, complex individual," photographed in his room decorated with a large peace symbol and a poster of Muhammad Ali, insisted that "he's had no racial problems connected with football, and only a little off the field." The only detail McAshan mentioned was the scrutiny of campus cops when he walked out late at night, making him feel "like I'm in a foreign territory." McAshan insisted that he ignored the boos in the stadium, which had stunned the reporters at the Tennessee game, but he later admitted that they haunted him through his three varsity seasons at Georgia Tech.[75]

McAshan finished his sophomore season with nine touchdown passes and twenty-one interceptions, and the following year offered more of the same, punctuated by a brief suspension in late September. After two "less than impressive" performances in a loss to South Carolina and a narrow win over Michigan State, including five interceptions (and no completions at all against MSU), McAshan lost his starting role for the Army game but came off the bench to complete 17 of 31 passes for 160 yards (and one interception) in a 16–13 loss. Afterward, McAshan told a reporter for the *Atlanta Constitution*, "We didn't come out attacking Army and we certainly were capable of attacking them. In the first quarter, for example, we threw only one pass." McAshan later denied that he intended any criticism of the coaching staff, but Bud Carson suspended him for one practice. This was the low point of a 6–6 season that concluded with a loss in the Peach Bowl, after which Carson was fired. Looking back on this season, after McAshan's own career imploded a year later, Furman Bisher of the *Atlanta Journal* described McAshan as taking "the gaff on occasions for the blunders of a coaching staff that could hardly decide what tie to wear, or how to have its eggs at breakfast."[76]

Each season offers a fresh start, no more so than in 1972 for Georgia Tech, with new coach Bill Fulcher and offensive coordinator Steve Sloan. "Talented but erratic" after two seasons, in the words of *Sports Illustrated*,[77] McAshan was the same in 1972: 239 yards, including a 77-yard touchdown, in an upset of Michigan State that earned him the Associated Press's National Back of the Week honors; followed by 371 yards passing and five touchdowns against Rice the next week (along with five interceptions) in a 36–36 tie. McAshan finished the year as the greatest passer in Georgia Tech history, with seventeen individual school records, including thirty-two touchdown passes but also fifty-two interceptions. And his career ended in what the local press termed a "bizarre" episode, in which three years of simmering frustration finally burst to the surface. Thursday before the concluding annual game with Georgia, McAshan walked out before practice; he then failed to appear on Friday, finally meeting with Coach Fulcher Friday night and into Saturday morning before Fulcher announced that he was suspended for the game.

Telling the press only that the "problems are personal and important and they had nothing to do with my coaches or teammates," McAshan left reporters puzzling over various rumors and denials. Even after Fulcher announced that the suspension would continue through the Liberty Bowl on December 18, McAshan's motives remained mysterious. But the attempts to understand them shed harsh light on the past three seasons. Bisher sympathized with McAshan: "God knows, none of us could even conceive the mental extortion he has been suffered to endure these four years. For his consignment as the first black quarterback at an institution heavy in football and Southern traditions, he required some of Jackie Robinson's features—a hide as tough as a razorback hog and an artist at cheek-turning." Instead, McAshan was a "soft-spoken, gentle, inward young man" who spent three years "in a volatile atmosphere. . . . What came upon him must have been the climax of an accumulation heaped on in the four years spent under a microscope, in severe pressure."[78]

When McAshan finally broke his silence, he basically confirmed Bisher's account. Speaking not to a white sportswriter but to the congregation at a black church, McAshan described how he had been "harassed and heckled," not by opponents but by Tech fans. A seemingly trivial disagreement over getting extra tickets for the Georgia game triggered his walkout, but it had culminated four years of frustration. By this time, McAshan's suspension had provoked a full-scale protest against the Liberty Bowl by civil rights groups in Atlanta, who pressured McAshan's five black teammates to boycott the game. With McAshan's roommate, Greg Horne, as their spokesman, and torn between conflicting loyalties, the five met with their white teammates and announced that they would play. Horne also told reporters that "McAshan was not the only target of harassment" and that "other black members of the team have suffered problems during the season." Given the desire among all parties for an uneventful transition to integrated football, even such mild criticism would never have been made public were it not for McAshan's suspension. The evening of the game, the five black players from Tech and one from Iowa State met with the Reverend Jesse Jackson and agreed to wear black armbands during the game. A reporter for the *Atlanta Journal* offered readers two possible explanations: Jackson claimed that wearing the armbands "was in protest of McAshan's 'racial harassment.' Tech head coach Bill Fulcher said it was in sympathy with the black movement throughout the world."[79]

Only many years later did a fuller account of the experiences of McAshan and his black teammates come out. McAshan described how the tires of his car had been slashed and its windows smashed, and his apartment had been set on fire. His five black teammates reported death threats during the buildup to the Liberty Bowl—not from whites but from the black community. Describing a meeting with black leaders, Greg Horne explained to an interviewer in 1989 what it was like for himself and the others: "All of us were passive people. We were not hellraisers. The blacks [in the community] wanted us to boycott, but we had to make a decision for ourselves. Each of us conferred with our parents. You have to realize that hardly any of our parents had gone to college. To us, getting an education was all that mattered. You also have to understand that we were pawns on the chess board. Not rooks or queens or kings. Pawns were on the front line with no power. We were just 20-year-old kids." Although Jesse Jackson later acknowledged that the five young men "had to worry about being gainfully employed in the future," at the time the black picketers at the Liberty Bowl heckled them and called them Uncle Toms. One of the five described the experience as "heartbreaking." Another said, "It was like a stone in my heart."[80] Greg Horne and his four teammates earned their degrees at Georgia Tech and went on to successful careers outside of football. Eddie McAshan played briefly in the World Football League before returning to Tech for his degree in 1979, but he remained bitter for many years.[81]

Integrating southern football was easy only on paper—or in the papers, to be more precise.

COLLEGE FOOTBALL IN BLACK AND WHITE,
PART II BLACK PROTEST

In the privacy of their offices, over breakfast in strange towns,
wherever two or three coaches get together, they talk about The
Problem.—John Underwood, "The Desperate Coach," Sports
Illustrated, *August 25, 1969*

I missed playing against Eddie McAshan by one year. Georgia
Tech was all-white when Notre Dame played them in 1969, my senior
year, as was Texas in the Cotton Bowl at the end of that season. One of my
teammates in Kansas City in the early 1970s was Warren McVea, the first
African American to play at a major college in Texas (at the University
of Houston in 1965); another was Mike Livingston, a white quarterback
from SMU who had been Jerry LeVias's best friend on the team when
LeVias broke the color barrier in the Southwest Conference in 1966. One
of my roommates and best friends with the Chiefs was Clyde Werner,
a linebacker at the University of Washington when Jim Owens suspended four of his black teammates. Several other teammates—Willie
Lanier, Buck Buchanan, Otis Taylor, Emmitt Thomas, James Marsalis,
Jim Kearny, Marvin Upshaw, Frank Pitts, Gloster Richardson, Robert
Holmes, Willie Frazier—were part of the tidal wave of players from black
colleges that rolled into professional football in the 1960s. Others—Dave
Hill from Auburn, E. J. Holub from Texas Tech, Billy Cannon and Johnny
Robinson from LSU, Jerry Mays from SMU, Jerrell Wilson from Southern Mississippi, Dennis Homan from Alabama—had never had a black
teammate until they left college. I remember another Chiefs player from
the South complaining about one of our black teammates who dated
white women. I was surrounded by football's racial revolution without
fully realizing it.

In rediscovering my own playing days as history, I find in the African
American college players of those years not a group of militant Black
Panthers in shoulder pads, as I expected, but young men often surpris-
ingly like myself, only thrust into a role I never had to play. Like Greg

Horne, they seem generally not to have been "hell-raisers" but "twenty-year-old kids," pursuing an education and a football dream until circumstances forced them to take a stand.

The desegregation of the southern conferences was the quiet phase of college football's racial revolution in the 1960s. The noisy one took place in the supposedly integrated North, and the watershed year was 1969. In the summer of 1968, *Sports Illustrated* ran Jack Olsen's five-part series, "The Black Athlete—A Shameful Story," that became a landmark in the history of sport and race. The revelations of discrimination, exploitation, and outright racism are now familiar, but they severely rattled a sports establishment in 1968 that liked to think of itself as a vanguard of racial progressiveness. The first installment, "The Cruel Deception," exposed college athletic directors who referred to the "nigger athlete," universities that graduated few of their black athletes, and the sort of white fan who could "compartmentalize his attitude about the Negro, to admire his exploits on the field but put him in the back of the bus on the way home." Olsen's story also put white America on alert that a new militancy among black athletes would no longer tolerate such treatment. The second installment, "Pride and Prejudice," examined the cultural clash felt by black athletes on mostly white campuses, debunking the idea that sports were an integrating force. The third, "In an Alien World," a case study of the University of Texas at El Paso, exposed the dark truth behind one of the sports establishment's most cherished stories of racial progress, the victory of all-black UTEP (then known as Texas Western) over all-white Kentucky in the 1966 NCAA basketball championship. Parts IV and V, "In the Back of the Bus" (a broad survey) and "The Anguish of a Team Divided" (a case study of the NFL's St. Louis Cardinals), were equally damning of professional sport.[1]

Insofar as we have a collective memory of black athletic protest in the late 1960s, I suspect that it is vaguely of militant athletes angrily denouncing racism and perhaps hinting at retributive violence. The most indelible image is of the clenched fists of Tommie Smith and John Carlos at the Mexico City Olympics in 1968: an unambiguous symbol of black pride and black defiance that onlookers, whether the thousands at the scene or the millions watching television or seeing the photographs later, cheered or hissed in approval or fury. For the American public, Smith and Carlos disappeared into the symbol they created, which blended with numerous other symbols—from John Kennedy's slumping in his limousine to the writhing ecstatic bodies at Woodstock—to define a convulsive era. The Olympic protests outraged most of the sporting public at the time, a fact conveniently forgotten in recent years as the athletes' principled defiance has been reconstructed as a quintessentially American heroic act.[2]

No protest by black football players imprinted a comparably powerful image in our national memory, but collectively those protests, for those who lived through the era, are likely "remembered" in the same way as the clenched fists of Smith and Carlos. Defiant black players denounced their coaches as racists and demanded change. Depending on one's politics, the players were racial heroes in the struggle for human rights, while the coaches embodied white oppression; or the players mistook discipline for racism, as their coaches vainly tried to stem the tide of anarchy and self-indulgence.

In the contemporary reporting on black protests at Oregon State in the winter and spring of 1969, at Iowa that spring, at Wyoming, Indiana, and Washington that fall, and at Syracuse the following spring and fall, one can glimpse a more complex, more ambiguous, more human struggle playing out behind the public drama. All of the incidents roughly followed a common pattern:

- A group of black players either boycotts practice or is suspended from the team for some infraction of team rules.
- The athletes declare that the issue is discrimination, while the coach insists it is a matter of discipline, in some cases declaring that the players were not kicked off but "dismissed themselves."
- Constituents weigh in—boosters and alumni overwhelmingly for the coach, students and faculty divided, local sports editors and editorial writers for the coach but with varying degrees of sympathy for the players, athletic and institutional administrators publicly for the coach while privately seeking a workable compromise.
- The coach either stands firm or is pressured to compromise, in either case with at least some of the players losing their place on the team. No coach steps down or is forced to resign, but not one of them remains in coaching for more than a few years afterward.

At Oregon State, the incident took place in the off-season and affected all of the school's sports. At Wyoming, whether administrators made any effort to modify their coach's position is uncertain. Otherwise the events at all six schools followed this script.

In stark contrast to the southern press's near silence on integrating the SEC, newspapers in the cities and states where these protests took place covered them fully. Sportswriters tended to take a defensive or conservative stance, as likely did the majority of their readers—defending the coach, the institution, and the community against accusations of racism—but to varying degrees they also expressed bafflement, concern, or ambivalence, again reflecting broader community responses. These local sportswriters wrote the story from a "white" perspective: "they," the black athletes, were making charges against their white coach that also implicated "us." But the handling of the story was not as uniform as in the case of integrating the SEC.

MUCH ADO ABOUT A BEARD IN CORVALLIS, OREGON

By 1969 the frequency of protests and demonstrations made each new incident seem inevitable in retrospect, yet each one also erupted suddenly, as if a random outbreak of a baffling virus. Unlike today, college football players in the 1960s had an actual off-season, the four months from December through March when they rarely saw their coaches. A chance encounter on campus in late February between assistant coach Sam Boghosian and linebacker Fred Milton, who was sporting a mustache and "Van Dyke" goatee, triggered the blowup at Oregon State. With Dee Andros out of town, Boghosian demanded that Milton remove the facial hair, and Andros backed him up when he returned. More than thirty years later, Milton contended that, had Andros been present from the beginning, he would likely have compromised on the issue, but by the time the head coach returned it was already out of hand. Yet as events unfolded, Andros admitted that he and athletic director Jim Barratt had been forewarned that the Black Student Union (BSU) at Oregon State was planning to attack the athletic department, and one local sportswriter reported that Beaver coaches had spoken privately a year earlier about what they would do if their black players rebelled.[3] By his actions and in his public statements, Andros, like Lloyd Eaton later at Wyoming and Jim Owens at Washington, seemed to welcome the opportunity to draw a line in the sand. Milton's neatly trimmed mustache and quarter-inch goatee violated a team rule and seemed to pose a challenge: Will adults or kids make the rules? Do we want discipline or self-indulgence, respect for authority or anarchy?[4]

The junior from Richland, Washington, had been injured in the fall, and there were conflicting reports as the incident played out whether

*Oregon State linebacker Fred Milton and his offending facial hair (*Corvallis Gazette-Times, *February 25, 1969)*

FRED MILTON, Oregon State football player, displays the "Van Dyke" beard which he refused to shave off at the request of OSU Head Football Coach Dee Andros. The Black Student Union at OSU will boycott classes and athletic events in backing Milton.

Milton had already told Andros he would not be returning the following season. In any case, Milton complained that the rule violated his human rights, and he brought the issue to BSU president Mike Smith. Events over the next several weeks proceeded in a remarkably orderly and peaceful manner. On Monday, February 24, the BSU accused the athletic department of racism. On Tuesday, Smith and Rich Harr, a black sophomore defensive back, commandeered the microphone before an address to students by OSU's most distinguished alumnus, Linus Pauling, to announce a boycott of classes and athletic events. President James Jensen, also on stage for the occasion, responded with a pledge "to do what I can to see that there is no discrimination on this campus."[5]

To Andros and the athletic department, the issue was a simple matter of team discipline; for the BSU, it was an issue of human rights and disrespect for black culture. At dual noon rallies on February 26—a reported 4,000 on the main quad to cheer Andros alongside coaches from the other sports, 1,000 in a nearby auditorium to hear a visiting John

Carlos and members of the BSU—sides were clearly drawn. The student senate narrowly endorsed the boycott, with the full support of the student body president, while the faculty senate proceeded more cautiously but eventually ruled that Milton's facial hair was his own business. But community and alumni support for Andros, the hugely popular Great Pumpkin, was overwhelming. (Andros had just backed out of a verbal agreement to leave OSU for the University of Pittsburgh, to the immense relief of the Beaver faithful.) The BSU accused Andros of discrimination on a Monday. On Tuesday, assistant coach Sam Boghosian told boosters at a luncheon that they could either "back us up" or "find yourself another football coaching staff."[6] (This threat was reported in OSU's campus newspaper, the *Daily Barometer*, but not in the *Corvallis Gazette-Times*.) On Friday, "An Open Endorsement" of Andros's action appeared in the *Gazette-Times*, with nearly 900 signatures and a note at the bottom: "SORRY. . . . SPACE LIMITATIONS PREVENT US FROM LISTING THE MANY OTHER CITIZENS WHO HAVE SIGNED THE PETITIONS." The *Gazette-Times* later reported that letters to the athletic department supported Andros 100 to 1.[7]

Due to retire in June, his sunset year suddenly disrupted, President Jensen declined to intervene but charged the existing Committee on Minority Affairs to investigate Milton's case and established a Commission on Human Rights and Responsibilities to resolve the conflict. Angered by Jensen's measured response, Smith and the BSU announced that all black students at OSU would withdraw from school. When the commission finally issued its report in early May, it acknowledged the importance of team discipline but not at the expense of fundamental human rights. In language searching for compromise, the commission declared that facial hair should be regulated only in season and that "human rights should be supported unless they directly interfere with team performance including morale and spirit." That last phrase seemed to open a door for Andros-style discipline, but the commission also less ambiguously declared that "neatly groomed mustaches" should be permitted.[8]

Milton was vindicated, but by this time he had already left Oregon State, along with more than two-thirds of the school's African American students. Of the fifty-six or fifty-seven members of the BSU (accounts differ), only eighteen returned for spring term, including eleven of the seventeen athletes who belonged to the group. (About fifty black African students also remained, as one of them indignantly reminded his white classmates in a letter to the *Daily Barometer*.)[9] When Andros hired his first black assistant at the end of May (a coach and teacher at a local middle school, making an extraordinary leap to the big-time college level), the move seemed forced upon him; but he also declared publicly that no committee could tell him how to run his football program. Of five black football players on the team when the incident began, including one freshman, only two returned for spring practice, and there were no black players in that year's recruiting class. Recruiting black players would remain more difficult for years to come, a factor in the decline of osu football that, beginning in 1971, would continue through twenty-eight straight losing seasons.[10]

While the most outspoken of the black football players was Rich Harr, center John Didion and fullback Bill Enyart, two senior All-Americans, emerged as spokesmen for the white players who chose to take a stand. Didion and nearly sixty others marched to President Jensen's office on the first day of the boycott to present a petition signed by 173 athletes supporting Andros. (It was not reported at the time, but assistant coach Rich Brooks organized the petition, an action by their white teammates that "was the final straw" in alienating the black athletes who decided to leave.[11]) At the rally on the main quad the next day, Didion read a statement calling the conflict "a question of administrative authority and prerogative," not a racial issue. "When a man signs a contract to play a sport here," the statement declared, "he obligates himself to comply with the rules that govern that sport, as set down by his coach."[12] Among those who did not sign the petition, the two singled out in newspaper reports were Enyart and the school's one international star, high jumper Dick Fosbury, whose "flop" style had just won an Olympic gold medal and revolutionized his event.

After the initial reporting on these early rallies, nothing more was said about Enyart and Fosbury in the Corvallis, Salem, or Portland papers. Only the *Eugene Register-Guard*, the voice of rival University of Oregon forty miles to the south, pursued the intriguing fact that Didion and Enyart were friends and roommates who took different sides on an issue tearing apart the football team and athletic department. Only the *Register-Guard* printed Enyart's comments that student-athletes should be governed by "the rules the rest of the students live by." "Times are changing," Enyart told the reporter. "We have to realize this. I think that a successful society is more important than the success of the Oregon State football team." Enyart had no personal grievance and was grateful for what the athletic department had done for him. "But in these times there are things more important than football—although football is pretty important to me. I have great respect for Andros, but he's enforcing white discipline on a black culture."[13] Enyart also wrote or cowrote two letters to the campus paper as the conflict played out.[14]

John Didion spoke for the majority in 1969, but history would take Enyart's side. Looking back at these events that took place during my own college years—when so openly taking either side in such a dispute would have been difficult—I am intrigued by the human dramas only hinted at by the public statements. Because of the timing of the OSU incident, football players had only to declare their loyalties; basketball players had to decide whether to honor the boycott. OSU's black basketball players—Dave Moore and Jim Edmond on the varsity, along with freshman star Freddy Boyd—faced immediate pressure. Moore's comment to a reporter, "I'd like to play but I'll have to go along with the boycott," understated the dilemma of choosing between personal athletic dreams and racial loyalty, between team and black community.

While Moore, Edmond, and Boyd missed the Beavers' final games with Washington State, Washington, and Oregon, a single white player, sophomore guard Tim Perkins, illustrates the dilemma facing the black athletes' conscientious white teammates. On the day of the Washington State game, having obviously agonized over serving both his conscience and his personal desires as a basketball player, Perkins announced at a BSU rally that he was playing the rest of the season "under protest." Perkins acknowledged that protesting but not boycotting might seem "a double standard or a hypocritical stand," but in fact it captures the dilemma perfectly. Perkins was a Pacific-8 basketball player from a Portland suburb, living out his own dream, now finding that dream colliding with the social and political conscience he had likely developed since arriving at college. Like Bill Enyart, he took a public stand at odds with the athletic establishment that had helped form him, but he did not want to cut himself off from it irreparably. His coach, Paul Valenti, would have none of his "protest" and immediately kicked Perkins off the team, only to reinstate him a day later after a private meeting.[15]

I know Tim Perkins—he became one of my first friends when I moved to Corvallis in 1976—and he is the figure through whom I can most easily imagine myself: wanting to do right, but not at the price of martyrdom. However brief his protest, Tim was the sole white athlete to put his own career in jeopardy, and I suspect that he pricked a conscience or two among his teammates. The widespread pricking of consciences, even among those on the sidelines of the struggles, was one of the immediate impacts and enduring legacies of the 1960s.

Of course, the brunt of the OSU protest, as would be repeated in every subsequent incident, was borne by the black athletes. Six of the seventeen participating in various sports did not return for spring term. Of the eleven who did, one football player, Bryce Huddleston, showed up for spring practice with a mustache, was immediately suspended by Andros, and then appealed to the university's newly formed Commission on Human Rights. After missing three days of practice, Huddleston shaved and rejoined the team at the bottom of the depth chart (though he was back on the first team by the fall). At a track meet at the University of Washington in April, sprinters Willie Turner and Ernie Smith (brother of Tommie, who raised his clenched fist at Mexico City) were harassed by UW's Black Student Union (now including Rich Harr after his transfer) for not withdrawing from OSU. Beaver track coach Berny Wagner had the most lenient policy on facial hair in the athletic department, permitting neatly trimmed mustaches long before the Human Rights Commission issued its ruling. Wagner advised Turner and Smith to pass up the meet for their own safety, leaving them bitter toward their fellow blacks in the Washington BSU.[16]

Behind the seismic forces of 1960s social change lay the actions and inactions, the voices and silences of individuals, black and white; some on both sides of the issues guided by principle, others by coercion, each one prodded to look inside and decide whether to take a stand. At OSU, the entire student body and faculty were forced to become involved, if only to honor or ignore the boycott. One instructor in the English Department mocked Andros's code by devising his own rules for personal appearance, requiring his students to wear Indian beads or feathers to class (a joke not appreciated by at least one editorial writer).[17]

The power of the media to shape public opinion in this divisive era was clearly limited. The willingness of nearly 900 individuals to immediately publish their names in support of Dee Andros suggests a lack of deliberation, no thoughtful weighing of opposing arguments to arrive at the wisest position. By February 1969 battle lines had been clearly drawn, and for many onlookers both Andros and Milton instantly assumed familiar roles in the public drama. For some, a football coach represented legitimate authority under any circumstances; for others (not as many), any black protest was a righteous cause. But coverage in the major newspapers in Corvallis, Salem, Eugene, and Portland is nonetheless revealing of the ways the conflict was framed by sports editors and editorial writers and of the disagreements and agonizings within the community reflected in letters to the editor.

While sportswriters and sports columnists adamantly sided with Andros, editorials on the news side expressed more sympathy for the protesting players, though they ultimately endorsed the coach's position, too. Closest to the events, the *Corvallis Gazette-Times* was typical. In small towns with large universities, where the sports editor covers big-time sport for a small-time newspaper, he or she has to deal with a football coach who is the most popular and powerful individual in the community. In his first column on the protest, the *Gazette-Times*'s Jack Rickard explained the competing viewpoints of the white and black players but made his own allegiance clear. The BSU, in his view, had turned an issue of team discipline into a racial matter and in so doing had violated the human rights of fellow blacks who would like to attend classes and play in games. The paper's first editorial a day later was less critical, aligning itself with the numerous "whites in the community, earnestly seeking to understand, to be fair," who were "perplexed by the BSU-called boycott." But the editorial deemed the point of contention to be trivial: "Substantiating the allegations of discrimination in housing and social activities would have served the blacks better."[18]

As events unfolded, the newspaper's editorial stance shifted more decisively toward Andros's side, but that initial statement provides a key to all of the incidents of black protest in college football. The immediate cause—a demand to shave a beard and mustache—was indeed often trivial, but behind it lay a long list of grievances, many of them perhaps trivial, too, but cumulatively weighty and also evoking a long history of racism in the nation. Moreover, "trivial" was in the eye of the beholder. Citing Abraham Lincoln and Mark Twain, another editorial writer challenged the BSU's claim that a beard and mustache were uniquely part of black culture. Yet anyone who was ever an adolescent male trying to coax a few chin whiskers into something resembling a goatee knows that to grow a beard is to be a "man," and in the 1960s young black males were insisting on their manhood. Andros's objection to beards was as trivial as Fred Milton's goatee—except to Andros and his supporters, for whom it signified the authority of the coach and the discipline of the team.

The attack on Milton's beard instantly became a symbol for all the indignities black students had suffered at OSU and in Corvallis, vaguely hinted at in the editorial reference to "allegations of discrimination in housing and social activities." In defense of his department, athletic director Jim Barratt noted the "uphill fight since 1951 in attracting black student-athletes to our campus," due in part to the absence of a black community in Corvallis and of a black-oriented curriculum on campus. A later editorial in the *Gazette-Times*, defending the community against the "unexpected indictment of Corvallis as hostile to blacks and haven of plantation philosophy," acknowledged the existence of prejudice but insisted that it was "disguised and hidden" rather than overt (as if that made it more palatable).[19] Whether the BSU conspired to provoke a confrontation or only seized the opportunity, its members clearly welcomed Andros's action on one level. How can you force attention to "disguised and hidden" discrimination—suspicious glances from shopkeepers, subtle discouragement of interracial dating, and the like—when you are 50 or 60 in a town of 30,000? One answer would be to accuse the man who runs the most powerful source of community pride, the college football team, of racial discrimination.

Letters to the editor create a community portrait (without necessarily representing the community accurately). In Corvallis, the immediate response sounded themes that would be repeated in virtually every subsequent black protest around the country. "Hooray for Dee Andros!" declared the first published letter. "Playing football is a privilege," and "We don't need people like Fred Milton on our football team." "Troublemakers" with their "petty demands" can "follow the same rules everyone else does or get out."[20] The love-it-or-leave-it challenge, more commonly directed at (white) antiwar protesters during these years, is more chilling when thrown at a tiny racial minority. Who were the "people like Fred Milton"—other protesters or other blacks? Most letter writers were more temperate. Belligerent pro-Andros letters ruled for the first several days, then, as would also become the pattern elsewhere, more measured responses followed. One questioned the supposed relationship between personal appearance and "training or ability to play on a disciplined team" and invoked "the rights guaranteed by the Constitution" against "arbitrary rules." Another challenged "middle class white America" to "allow cultural differences for black people."[21] The twenty-nine letters over a two-week period were evenly divided: twelve in various ways supporting Andros, thirteen defending the BSU, four ambiguous or seeking compromise. The two letters from local ministers citing biblical teaching on obedience came down on opposite sides of the issue. The writer who welcomed an unaccustomed dialogue on race in the Corvallis community seemed the only one pleased by the controversy. The black protests of the 1960s provided "teaching moments" for a great many white Americans, as was confirmed by the mostly agonizing rather than pontificating letters from students and faculty to the *Daily Barometer*. (The *Barometer*'s editorials consistently backed President Jensen's handling of the conflict and pleaded against divisiveness.)

Outside the epicenter of Corvallis, coverage in the *Oregon Statesman* (Salem) and *Oregonian* (Portland) was evenhanded on the editorial page and simply pro-Andros in sports. The *Statesman* emphasized the dilemmas confronting both sides: the black athletes "caught in the middle" between their teammates and "their own social groups and friends," the university wishing not "to open the door to other challenges to authority" but also not "to court additional and continuing pressure" through insensitivity on racial issues. *Statesman* sports editor Al Lightner, on the other hand, insisted that the coach had the same right to set rules as any boss for his employees. The *Oregonian* cast the conflict as a dispute between competing "disciplines"—"the discipline administered by the coach and the discipline of solidarity among the black students, with support from some white students and faculty members." Against the editorial writer's desire for compromise, longtime *Oregonian* sports editor L. H. Gregory saw matters more simply: "Either the coach is there to teach football his own successful way, with what he considers the discipline to establish a winning 'team image,' or he isn't."[22]

The exceptions to the pattern of editorial balance and sports-page partisanship were striking: the *Oregon Journal* in Portland was flamingly pro-Andros throughout the paper—its keyword was "discipline"[23]—while, the *Eugene Register-Guard* sided decisively with the players. Besides providing more coverage of the black protesters and their supporters, including the interview with Bill Enyart cited earlier (the scarcity of interviews with the black players in all of the protests is remarkable), the *Register-Guard* also contrasted the handling of similar conflicts at Oregon and Oregon State. Earlier that year, Oregon's acting president, Charles Johnson, overrode an Andros-like demand by the freshman basketball coach that two black players cut their Afro-style hair. An editorial in the *Register-Guard* applauded Johnson for "trying to eliminate legitimate cause for protest and . . . avoid the confrontation that the rabble rousers always seek." Another writer, however, suggested that while OSU's Jensen would in fact have preferred to restrain Andros, he honored the academic principle that departments govern themselves:

"Johnson intervened and got away with it. But there was no guarantee that he would. If the Oregon coach and indeed the whole athletic department had defied him as Andros and the OSU department defied the world, there is no telling who might have won, or at what cost."[24]

The *Register-Guard* alone provided full coverage of an incident barely noted elsewhere and altogether ignored by television broadcasters: a sympathy protest by 350–400 mostly white University of Oregon students before the UO-OSU "Civil War" basketball game in Eugene. Oregon's four black players, two starters and two reserves, had opted not to play the all-white team from Corvallis, and the large group of UO students had received permission to occupy the court while the student body president read a statement and then depart peacefully before tip-off of the televised game. UO coach Steve Belko was furious that the university administration allowed this. More remarkable, neither the demonstration itself nor any comment about it appeared during the telecast of the game. The broadcasters named the players missing from both teams without mentioning that they were black or why they were missing.[25]

The *Register-Guard*'s Jerry Uhrhammer was the only sports editor in the area to side with OSU's black players. What was impossible for a Beaver supporter might have been easy for a Duck, but Uhrhammer waited until March 13 to offer his opinion, when the issue was less inflamed, and what he wrote was thoughtful, not gloating. "No one denies the need for discipline and self-sacrifice in developing an athletic team," Uhrhammer conceded at the outset, but he noted some inconsistencies in applying the rules at OSU. Some white football players had been allowed to grow long sideburns in the off-season, without objection from Andros. And a year earlier, as racial protests were breaking out on other campuses, "members of the football coaching staff were saying privately that they would walk out en masse if they weren't backed up in any confrontation with the blacks." Neither the double standard nor what Uhrhammer called the predetermined "militant, uncompromising posture" of the coaches was reported in other newspapers. "Many people are applauding Andros for it," Uhrhammer continued. "But it is precisely this hard-line stand which makes this a racial controversy and not just a question of whether an athlete should wear a beard during the off-season. It looks to us as if Andros does not understand—or is unwilling to understand—the swift changes taking place in our society. And lack of such understanding prevents him from dealing realistically with the social change as it affects the black athletes he has recruited." Uhrhammer noted that the University of California had just issued a report that noted the "need to determine with more precision the degree of conformity to social rules necessary for team discipline." Uhrhammer concluded that Oregon State needed to do the same because already there were indications that black athletes would be avoiding the school "as a bad place."[26]

ACT TWO: IOWA CITY

In calling for coaches and athletic departments to adjust to the social changes sweeping the country, Uhrhammer spoke for what became college football's future, but many months of turmoil remained before that future would arrive. That April, University of Iowa coach Ray Nagel dismissed sixteen of the team's twenty-two black players for boycotting the first day of spring practice after he had suspended two of their black teammates for "personal problems." Iowa's black athletes had been meeting with athletic department officials for a full year to address what they vaguely called "an intolerable situation." The Board in Control of Athletics had been considering their concerns but had not yet acted on them. After their one-day boycott, the players made public their specific demands for a black counselor and black assistant coach and for extended scholarship support for athletes needing a fifth year to graduate. They also accused Nagel of "ridiculing" the two players that he suspended, issuing an insincere apology, and "lying" to them during the recruiting process.[27]

Nagel remained adamant that the players had "dismissed themselves" by skipping practice, and perhaps because the suspensions disrupted only spring football and not scheduled games in the fall, the conflict was covered by the local paper exclusively in sports, not on the front page, and with little commentary. The sports editor of the *Iowa City Press-Citizen*, Al Grady, wrote just one column on the issue in the spring, in which he defended Nagel's actions as well as the university's history of integration without simply criticizing the actions of the black players, who "stood on principles and ideals, right or wrong." (The *Press-Citizen* provided fewer details, particularly ones that cast Nagel in an unfavorable light, than did the out-of-town *Des Moines Register*. Sportswriters and sports editors at the papers in small college towns could not easily displease the football coach, even through straightforward factual reporting.) After a full summer of simmering, Nagel allowed the suspended players to petition their teammates for reinstatement during an evening meeting on August 27, just before fall practice was to begin. Twelve of the sixteen accepted the offer, but after each player presented his case to his teammates, the team approved only seven of the twelve, two letter-men and five of the seven sophomores. In his column the next day, Grady saluted Nagel for being more tolerant and understanding than he himself would have been. To the big puzzle—why the seven were accepted but not the five—Grady guessed that it was "a question of attitude." "A bad attitude" in 1969, of course, might simply mean self-assertiveness or Black Pride.[28]

The day before the team vote, Grady quoted at length from the first of John Underwood's three articles in "The Desperate Coach" series, which had just appeared in *Sports Illustrated*. He then asked his readers: "How much authority does a coach have? or how much should he have? It's a relevant question—in Iowa City and on every other college campus."[29] The incidents at Iowa and Oregon State were among the dozens cited in the *Sports Illustrated* series, where Underwood blamed everyone but the coaches. He pointed out that coaches were ideal targets for "campus movers and shakers" like the Students for a Democratic Society and Black Students Union "because they make instant headlines." While a new breed of self-indulgent athletes resisted discipline and sacrifice, antiathletic faculty were jealous of the coach's popularity and salary. All of the coach's enemies were abetted by college administrators who, "caught in a crossfire between conservative trustees and alumni on the one hand and radical students and faculty on the other," too often caved in to the latter. Most of Underwood's examples came from small schools and minor sports: one coach fired for confiscating a TV set from four athletes in the off-season, another forced to resign after suspending a player who sat during the national anthem. But several involved big-time football programs.

Underwood did not overtly editorialize, but his sympathies were unambiguous. He interviewed not a single athlete or college administrator, only coaches and athletic directors. The coaches, as he portrayed them, merely tried to play their traditional role of stern fathers, while the kids—Underwood and his interviewees repeatedly called the players "kids" or "boys"—were self-destructively rejecting them. The theme underlying the entire series was expressed by an athletic director: "Athletics are the last stronghold of discipline on the campus. It may be that they are in a life-or-death struggle of their own." Underwood's third and final installment ended in a sort of cliff-hanger: given coaches' discovery that "what seems best and what is happening are often two different things," the issue for coaches now is "authority and the response to authority. How they handle it will be something to see, and there are a lot of concerned people who are watching."[30]

THE AUTUMN OF OUR DISCONTENT

What they saw that fall, within just a three-week period in October and November, was a series of major racial incidents at Wyoming, Indiana, and Washington, all big-time football programs, a nightmare for college football likely worse than even Underwood envisioned. Events at Wyoming were set in motion when the campus Black Student Alliance announced a demonstration for the home game against Brigham Young University on October 18 to protest the Mormon Church's denying the priesthood to blacks. On Thursday before the game, Coach Lloyd Eaton informed Joe Williams, the one black among the team's tricaptains, that any black player who wore an armband at the game to participate in the protest would be dismissed from the team. Friday morning, Williams and his thirteen black teammates arrived at Eaton's office wearing black armbands and asked to talk to him. Refusing to let them speak, Eaton announced, "I can save you fellows a lot of time and a lot of words. You are through."[31]

Not quite two weeks later, on Thursday, October 30, amid rumors of long-simmering discontent, University of Washington coach Jim Owens delayed the start of practice to ask each member of the team, one at a time, to declare if he was fully committed to the program. When four black players gave unsatisfactory answers, Owens suspended them.

The following Tuesday, November 4, as if reenacting the events at the University of Iowa the previous spring, all fourteen black players at Indiana boycotted practice for no clearly stated reason. After Coach John Pont announced that they would not be penalized if they returned on Wednesday, four complied. By their own action, the ten who stayed out were not suspended but had quit.

Owens and Pont were among the coaches portrayed that summer by John Underwood. For Underwood, Owens represented "the compromised coach" after an earlier episode of racial unrest when university officials had forced him to fire a supposedly racist trainer and hire a supposedly under-qualified black assistant coach. Underwood cast Owens as a coach who had achieved peace at the cost of his own dignity and the success of his teams. Pont had fared a little better, according to Underwood, as one of those who had learned how "to cope with the new breed." He "accepts more ideas from his assistants," "concentrates more on nonfootball topics," "tries to tune in to his players' thinking," and "tries to treat every player as an individual."[32] Such compromises, however willing on his part, left Pont a compromised coach, too. (Bear Bryant—who had employed Underwood to help write his memoirs for *Sports Illustrated* a few years earlier and would later have him coauthor his autobiography—represented the ideal of the uncompromised coach.) As Underwood portrayed them, Owens and Pont had already made concessions that should have earned immunity to further protests from their black players.

1. The Wyoming Black 14

This was not true of Lloyd Eaton, an iron-fisted coach from the old school. Eaton did not appear in Underwood's series because his players had never challenged his authority. Simply by coming to his office to ask to wear black armbands, however, the fourteen black athletes violated not one but two team rules. Eaton forbade his players from participating in any way in political protest, whether on the field or in activities entirely removed from football. An approving reporter for the *Laramie Daily Boomerang* explained the coach's oft-stated belief that "no [Wyoming] football player . . . could be a competent student, an excellent athlete and still devote himself to such actions as political and social movements." The players' second offense lay in coming to see the coach collectively rather than individually; Eaton allowed no group actions. There seemed no racial bias in Eaton's response: just a week earlier, he had refused permission to a group of white players who wanted to take part in the national Vietnam moratorium. But he denied the whites permission; he dismissed the blacks from the team. Alerted beforehand to the protest, Eaton had clearly predetermined his extreme response. Then he insulted as well as dismissed his black players. After kicking them off the team, he went on to tell them that if they did not want to play football at Wyoming by his rules they could go on "Negro relief," or play for Grambling or Morgan State, or "go back to picking cotton." (These details came out later.)[33]

Eaton's racial insults transformed a not very politicized group of young football players into a defiant Black 14. Their consciousness had already been raised by the Black Student Alliance on campus, through which they had learned about the Mormon Church's racial policies (a target of periodic black protests in the Western Athletic Conference [WAC] since the spring of 1968), and the veteran players among them could recall racial slurs from BYU players in past games. But Eaton's derogatory comments were the catalyst that dissolved whatever reluctance they might have had to risk their athletic and academic futures.

University of Wyoming president William Carlson immediately convened the board of trustees, who met with the black players Friday night and into the morning, but the young men refused to accept reinstatement if they would still be forbidden to wear the armbands. Eaton's insults could not be retracted as easily as the suspensions. With neither side backing down, the various outsiders who weighed in were equally uncompromising. The trustees, the president, even the governor stood by Eaton, along with, predictably, the Alumni Association and booster clubs. At the BYU game on Saturday, someone in the student section flew a Confederate flag for three-quarters of the contest, as Laramie police declined requests from "at least two students" to have it removed; and in the fourth quarter the Wyoming cheerleaders led fans on both sides of the stadium in chanting, "We Love Eaton" and "E-A-T-O-N." As in Corvallis, "hundreds of calls, telegrams and letters" of support for the coach poured in. The faculty and students initially sided with the black players. The Student Senate held an emergency meeting Saturday morning before the BYU game and voted 15–3 for a resolution opposing Eaton's actions and the trustees' approval. On Sunday, the Faculty Senate convened before a crowd estimated at "upwards of 600 persons" and voted 37–1 to reinstate the fourteen athletes pending a collection of facts from both sides. Seven faculty members, led by Ken Craven of the English department, declared their intent to resign if the players were not reinstated.[34]

Backpeddling commenced immediately. Within days, the Faculty Senate clarified that it had called for an investigation, not an overriding of Eaton's authority. Ninety-six of 111 faculty and 54 of 58 staff members in the School of Agriculture signed a petition backing Eaton. Students in the College of Commerce and Industry questioned the "hasty" action of the Student Senate. In a poll of 1,450 Wyoming students, 69 percent supported Eaton and 65 percent opposed the action taken by their own senate. A student senator who had resisted the stampeding of his impetuous peers was celebrated for his principled stand.[35]

For all of his popular support, Eaton did not have the law on his side. In fact, the previous February, the U.S. Supreme Court in *Tinker v. Des*

Moines School District had specifically ruled that armbands were protected as free speech, and university officials clearly recognized that a blanket denial of football players' right to political protest away from football was outrageous. (The university's weekly student newspaper, the *Branding Iron*, printed a pertinent section of the Supreme Court's ruling on its October 23 editorial page.)[36] Following meetings with President Carlson, Eaton announced that players in the future would be allowed "to participate in student protests or demonstrations at times other than during games or practices," but the new rule would not take effect until the end of the season.[37] For Eaton, having taken an absolute stand, to retreat now would be total defeat. For President Carlson, angering his successful football coach was apparently worse than risking a national reputation for constitutional heresy and racial insensitivity.

While the university community was busy clarifying its positions, there was little disagreement off campus in a state where the love-it-or-leave-it mentality typical of conservatives throughout the country met Wyoming's own Cowboy Way. The Caspar Quarterback Club announced a fund-raising drive "to aid Craven and the other professors" who opposed Eaton "in moving from Laramie." A husband and wife writing to the *Daily Boomerang* echoed this proposal: "As to the matter of Dr. Craven's gracious offer to resign: possibly we should regard it as a golden opportunity and accept it just as graciously." A recent graduate, writing more pompously on the same day, extended the offer to the black players as well: "The 14 in question, and anyone else who entertains the warped precepts of anarchy or public political gymnastics in lieu of good, clean sportsmanship on the gridiron, had best withdraw from the University of Wyoming." With slightly more restraint, the Wyoming High School Activities Association commended Eaton for "refusing to compromise his principles" and chose this occasion to express gratitude for his "constructive and wholesome influence . . . on interscholastic athletics in our state." At year's end, even with the advantage of some hindsight, UPI's broadcasters and journalists declared Lloyd Eaton Wyoming's "Man of the Year."[38]

Against this local media tide stood the student-run *Branding Iron*, or rather its editor, Phil White. In the newspaper's October 23 edition (the first following the suspension of the black players), White wrote an impassioned editorial (presumably his, though unsigned), which opened with devastating irony: "Those who understand are busy trying to understand. Those who know nothing are busy proclaiming their high degree of understanding." The next paragraph was more direct: "For some few white students and almost all black students on this campus, the past week has been not only unbelievable but a cause for despair." White noted the Caspar Quarterback Club's collection for unwanted faculty, as well as the action of six Laramie businesses that "removed their advertisements from this week's newspaper because they believed we would support the Black Fourteen." The young editor also quoted article 1 of the Wyoming Constitution on citizens' freedom from "absolute, arbitrary power" and noted (with '60s-style excess) that the "discipline" asserted by Eaton and his supporters against the right to free speech was one of the foundations of Nazi Germany, too. He concluded with a grim forecast of a possible "war between the races in this country," for which the Confederate flag flown during the BYU game announced the side taken by the citizens of Wyoming.[39]

Letters to the campus paper were overwhelmingly critical of Eaton, possibly because of White's editorial stance rather than general student sentiment. The October 23 edition of the *Branding Iron* also included White's announcement that he was resigning as editor—"bowing to the wishes of most [Wyoming] students who apparently do not want to read anything about racism or the Vietnam War or the urban crisis or drugs or prison abuses or politics." "Admittedly they are rather unpleasant subjects," White stated. "Maybe if the BI doesn't mention them, they will go away." What took place behind the scenes that led to White's resignation, no one explained. White edited one final issue, in which he pleaded with Eaton to reinstate the players without feeling that to do so would mean surrendering, and for the players to accept Coach Eaton in return. But this plea for breaking through the impasse did not sound very hopeful.[40]

Black and white seemed utterly black and white in Wyoming, with no gray areas, yet even this most dramatic and divisive of all the racial incidents had its complicating factors. For one thing, Eaton had an impressive record on integration. As an assistant to Bob Devaney in the early 1960s, he had helped integrate football at the University of Wyoming, and his fourteen black players in 1969, thirteen of them from out of state, might seem a major achievement on behalf of racial diversity in Cowboyland. With unprecedented numbers of black players, Eaton's teams went 10–1 in 1966 and again in 1967 (winning the Sun Bowl, then losing the Sugar Bowl, Wyoming's first major bowl game ever), then turned in a respectable 7–3 in 1968 (while winning a third straight WAC title). The Cowboys entered the BYU game in 1969 with a 4–0 record and talk of being Wyoming's best team ever.

After Eaton suspended the fourteen, local sportswriters contacted the coach's best former black player, Dave Hampton, now with the Green Bay Packers, who declared emphatically, "That man is no racist."[41] Yet at the moment of confrontation, some remarkably stereotypical views of his black players had burst to the surface in the insults he flung at them. The events of October 1969 suggest that, for Eaton, integration was more pragmatic than moral or politically progressive. The relationship between Wyoming's success and black recruiting was by no means coincidental, and it points to the driving force behind the integration of college football more generally—bring in black players and victories followed—despite our natural desire to believe that it was always a matter of good people having the courage to do the right thing.

As events played out, the involvement of "outsiders" led local Eaton supporters to fantasize a vast "black conspiracy."[42] The players' first spokesman after their suspension was Willie Black, chancellor of the university's Black Student Alliance. Once their cause was taken up by William Waterman, a civil rights attorney from Detroit, he became their voice. Having repeatedly insisted that the conflict was over "discipline" and not "race," the Daily Boomerang explicitly acknowledged the racial issue when it announced "Black Hearings" on Waterman's request for an injunction to reinstate the fourteen players, pending the outcome of his lawsuit on their behalf. Judge Erwin T. Kerr ruled against the injunction on the grounds that he had no "supervisory jurisdiction over a verbal directive issued by a football coach, when issued undoubtedly for the best interest and welfare of the team." (Waterman and the black players later lost their lawsuit and the appeals that dragged on until October 31, 1972, on constitutional grounds, though not over the question of an individual's right to engage in political protest. Wyoming's attorney general successfully argued that if the university, a state agency, permitted the wearing of armbands to protest a doctrine of the Mormon Church, it would violate the constitutional guarantee of separation between church and state. The state also raised the question of whether a lawsuit on behalf of the fourteen players, thirteen from out of state, would violate the Eleventh Amendment, which forbids citizens of one state to file suit against any other state. By their own arguments, the University of Wyoming's defense lawyers made it clear that the "outsiders" stirring up trouble on the football team were the black players themselves, lured to Laramie by the football coach's promises.)[43]

Eaton won the battle but lost the war. Following the suspensions, his 4–0 team won its next two games, then dropped the final four. After the Cowboys fell to 1–9 in 1970, "the worst football season for the Pokes since the 1920s,"[44] Eaton was "promoted" to a newly created position as assistant athletic director. He served in that role for a year and then left Wyoming. He became an NFL scout in 1971 then, successively, director of player personnel, scouting director, and scout for the Green Bay Packers over the next several years, but he never coached again. And while support for Eaton was overwhelming within Wyoming in 1969, the coverage of the incident by the national media left a mark on the football program and the university that would take a long time to fade. NBC, CBS, and ABC all sent crews to the Laramie campus for their nightly newscasts (at a time when the three networks had large audiences and their anchormen—Chet Huntley and David Brinkley, Walter Cronkite, and Howard K. Smith and Harry Reasoner, respectively—were voices of authority). An account in *Sports Illustrated* revealed a college president less powerful than his football coach, a coach less reasonable than his players, and civil rights in Wyoming less important than football.[45] Eaton's successors achieved just one winning season in the 1970s, and the University of Wyoming was marked as a racist institution.

The players lost their battle, but most of them survived remarkably well. Three of the fourteen withdrew from the lawsuit, met with Eaton, and played for Wyoming in 1970. Thirteen of the fourteen left Wyoming early, but ten eventually graduated from college. Despite their reputations as "troublemakers," some of them managed to transfer to other football programs, and four even played in the NFL. In the final irony, as BYU became a dominant WAC power in the 1970s but faced continuing outrage over the Mormon Church's racial doctrines, on June 1, 1978, a "revelation" to the president of the church opened the priesthood to African Americans. Fourteen young black football players at the University of Wyoming helped change Mormon theology.

They also changed the University of Wyoming. In December 2002 a sculpture honoring the Black 14, commissioned by the school's United Multicultural Council, was unveiled in the student union. Just one of the fourteen, Mel Hamilton, now an educator and an activist for the National Association for the Advancement of Colored People, returned for the ceremony, intensely proud of the principled stand he and thirteen teammates had taken yet also still bitter after more than thirty years.[46]

2. Loyalty to Whom (at Indiana and Washington)?

The incident at Wyoming is the most famous of the black football protests, and the Black 14 were the only athletes to be christened by the media in the manner of the Hollywood Ten or the Chicago Seven. The Wyoming incident is also the only one that lends itself to a simple morality play: black athletes clearly with the law and basic human rights on their side, victimized by a coach clearly abusing his power and in a manner that was racially abusive as well. In contrast, uncertainties and painful ambiguities marked the incidents at Indiana University and the University of Washington that fall.

At Indiana, the boycott of a Tuesday practice by fourteen black players caught everyone by surprise. Early reports mentioned rumors of discontent about playing time and what would become known as "stacking"—the clustering of blacks at certain positions—and cited a meeting earlier that season between Coach John Pont and his black players to discuss these issues. After the Tuesday boycott, Pont met with the players on Wednesday and gave them a chance to return without penalty. Ten of the fourteen refused and were dismissed from the team (dismissed themselves), though the sophomores and juniors would have another opportunity to reconsider in the spring. On Saturday, the players finally released a list of eight grievances that did little to clarify their position. The coaches were "inconsistent" in treating white and black players' injuries and applying discipline. They indulged in "harassment" and "stereotyping" and made "discouraging and degrading remarks" and "demoralizing suggestions or implications." They created "an atmosphere that is mentally depressing and morally discouraging of blacks." The words were all vague, all abstract. They included no specific incidents or concrete charges that outsiders could clearly grasp.[47]

Unlike Wyoming (but like Washington), Indiana had a black community both on and off campus. Black faculty and staff called for an investigation of Pont's actions, and black cheerleaders and members of the marching band boycotted the game against Iowa that Saturday. The following week, Pont received the inevitable standing ovation from the booster club, but otherwise white responses appeared more troubled and ambivalent than in Laramie. Pont himself initially seemed truly baffled and pained. When asked if the grievances of his black players were valid, Pont answered that "for them they are real, not imagined." He briefly considered resigning. The president and the faculty representative to the NCAA supported Pont but without dismissing the concerns of the players. Edwin Cady, a distinguished literary scholar as well as the faculty representative, expressed pride in the players for conducting themselves "as gentlemen," and he viewed the conflict as part of the necessary social turmoil of the time for which there was no simple answer or solution. The Bloomington and Indianapolis newspapers supported Pont, but in a calm, often pained manner, troubled by the vagueness of the players' grievances and sensitive to the pressures on young black men created by the new "national attitude" that "says to Negroes that if you fail to revolt, to defy, you are letting down your brothers." The sports editor of the campus daily supported Pont for his humane treatment of his players, not for his authority as a coach. The paper's one editorial leveled no charges against Pont but discussed the general problem of "casual racism" that can be more demoralizing than open bigotry. On balance, the letters to the *Bloomington Daily Herald-Telephone* supported Pont, but they tended to express sadness rather than outrage toward the black players—"our guys" as truly as the white players were—and to understand the larger racial context within which the events played out. The few letters to the campus paper were more evenly mixed. What emerges from the coverage of the episode at IU is a sense of mostly conscientious people on all sides struggling to deal with racial and social upheaval in the context of a "game" that had become something much more.[48]

The responses in Seattle were similar. In the middle installment of his series, "The Desperate Coach," John Underwood had focused on three coaches and assigned each a specific role in the morality play of athletic rebellion. Oregon State's Dee Andros was the coach as hero, fearlessly welcoming the confrontation over Fred Milton's beard and mustache, while too many of his coaching colleagues cowered in their offices or blindly waited to be ambushed by the campus BSU or a few spoiled athletes. Maryland's Bob Ward (in an incident with no racial element) was the coach as victim, sacrificed by his university when players complained about his harsh treatment. And the University of Washington's Jim Owens was the coach as whipped dog, a shattered man, the "compromised coach" who survived one black protest but at the cost of his dignity. I cannot help but wonder if Underwood's pitying portrait in September sparked Owens's actions two months later.

Owens survived that earlier uprising in part by hiring a black assistant coach, Carver Gayton, to be his liaison with his black players. Now, in October 1969, after winless Washington played badly in a loss to Oregon but Owens and his staff singled out only black running back Landy Harrell for punishment, black players vented their frustrations in meetings with Gayton and black former UW athletes. Gayton carried their concerns to Owens, who decided to bring the simmering unrest into the open. Apparently advised that he could not require players to sign an actual loyalty oath, Owens instead summoned each squad member, one at a time, before Thursday's practice and asked for a declaration of commitment (whether to the program or to him personally became a matter of dispute). Owens suspended four black players who gave what he considered unacceptable responses, triggering an uproar among blacks on campus and throughout the Seattle area. That Friday, when the team gathered to board buses for Sea-Tac Airport to fly to Los Angeles for the UCLA game, a picket line of black protesters confronted the nine remaining black players on the team. Physically as well as verbally threatened, the nine stayed home on the recommendation of the athletic department.[49]

The sides seemed sharply drawn, but Seattle had a sizable black community and student population and many whites thus had a nuanced understanding of racial matters. In place of the more typically boosterish local sports editors, Georg Meyers of the *Seattle Times* and John Owen of the *Seattle Post-Intelligencer* offered readers probing comments on a complex issue. Meyers pondered the "relentless and contradictory" pressures on the black players who were not suspended—their "loyalty to, or apprehension of, a vocal and incensed black community" pitted against their "personal commitments to their own aspirations as athletes, to teammates, perhaps to coaches." Meyers understood the painful position of Gayton, whose "ominous assignment"—to "bridge the communications gap between the blacks and the rest of the coaching staff"—itself "connotes a gulf" that could prove impassable.[50] (The black assistant coaches at Iowa and Indiana, Frank Gilliam and Trent Walters, must have felt equally torn, but they were barely mentioned as events unfolded there.)

Gayton was the scapegoat for Underwood's displeasure in his account in "The Desperate Coach"—a black assistant forced on the beleaguered

Owens, with "more to say than any four assistant coaches Bud Wilkinson or Bear Bryant ever had," who proceeded to blithely undermine Owens's program. As Underwood put it, "Gayton spoke of a 'relaxing atmosphere,' of a softening of Owens'[s] 'irrational' old standbys like crew cuts and uniform street dress and the 'reaming out' of guys who come late to practice." The results? "'We have good morale,' says Assistant Coach Gayton. What they no longer have, it would appear, is good football," added sportswriter Underwood. As evidence, Underwood noted that Washington's 3-5-2 record in 1968 was Owens's worst in his ten years in Seattle. He did not mention that Owens's teams had won more than six games just once since the Rose Bowl seasons of 1959 and 1960 that made his reputation. Nor did Underwood consider the possibility that racial discord, not the attempts to deal with it, might be a problem. Closer to Gayton and to the events at UW, Seattle sportswriters knew a very different man thrown into a profoundly difficult situation.

The *Post-Intelligencer*'s John Owen also noted the irony that the much-criticized Jim Owens suddenly became more popular after suspending his four black players—"as the one man brave enough to say 'no' to some blacks making unreasonable demands"—than he had been in the past five years. Owen invited those who thought this way to consider the ramifications: "It is well and good to say that Husky football doesn't need the four players. But the practical result of this philosophy would be that the University of Washington would have an all-white football team within a matter of one or two years." Here was the dilemma: the university could not afford "the reputation or the consequences of an all-white football team," yet Owens could not simply be forced "to accept a football program, and a football team, undercut with dissension." Owen concluded that if athletic director Joe Kearney "can solve this one, his next stop should be Paris" (where the United States and North Vietnam were currently trying to negotiate an end to the war in Vietnam).[51]

Kearney himself clearly recognized the dilemma, as he issued a statement supportive of Owens but "also emphasized that any coaching decision entailing far-reaching implications for the total university would be subject to review by the director." Whether because Owens's position was weakened by too many mediocre seasons or because the risk to the university was just too high, UW's administrators forced the coach to reconsider his action. After meeting with each of the four players, Owens reinstated three but sustained the suspension of Harvey Blanks, a talented running back from Chicago whose NFL prospects had vanished with a knee injury the previous spring. It was not reported initially, but apparently Blanks "swore at Owens and challenged him to a fight in front of the team, committing insubordination that wouldn't be overlooked." Owens thus had reason to make the suspension permanent. Meanwhile, Carver Gayton's brother Gary, a Seattle attorney as well as a former UW athlete, had taken on the case of the four dismissed players with the backing of the Black Alumni Association in Seattle. In their different capacities, the Gayton brothers continued to press for Blanks's reinstatement. Failing in this, Carver Gayton resigned from the coaching staff on November 10.[52]

The UW conflict included the ugliest incident of all: on the night the team left for Los Angeles, four young men, two white and two black, forced Owens's seventeen-year-old daughter off the road and hit her in the face. The uproar in Seattle, however, also had the most heartening aftermath. Carver Gayton, whose position between the black players and his fellow coaches proved untenable, went on to a distinguished career at Boeing and in university and public service, including a term as the state's labor commissioner. Of the four players originally suspended, Ralph Bayard was the only one to play again for Owens, but all of them did well after leaving UW. LaMar Mills eventually became an attorney and Greg Alex a minister, both in Seattle, while Bayard became UW's senior associate director for compliance in the athletic department. After playing briefly in the World Football League, Harvey Blanks went into acting. Thirty years after the events of 1969, the four remained close.[53]

REVOLUTIONS, PRIVATE AND PUBLIC

As in John Underwood's articles for *Sports Illustrated*, the principle figures in the press coverage of these incidents were invariably the adults rather than the "kids." Reporters interviewed coaches, athletic directors, chairmen of athletic boards, and university presidents but rarely, or only briefly, the athletes. The players at Wyoming, having been booted off the team without an opportunity to make their case, remained largely invisible in the reporting by the *Laramie Daily Boomerang*. At Indiana, the coverage offered at least a glimpse of the players, as senior defensive end Clarence Price became a spokesman for the black Hoosiers. All of the suspended black athletes wanted to play, Price insisted, and they had friends on the team, but conditions had become intolerable. "Nothing's overt," Price tried to explain. "It's just an attitude. It's a feeling we all have that we are discriminated against."[54] Playing football can entail countless small indignities—impersonal treatment by coaches that feels very personal. If you were black in 1969 and your coach was white, race could easily seem a factor whether it was or not.

The vagueness of the Indiana players' grievances frustrated those who wished to understand, but some tried. One sympathetic university official at Indiana commented that the black players were "trying desperately to find a proper method of presenting their problem." An editorial in the *Bloomington Herald-Telephone* recognized that the conflict was "a collision of consciences" in which all parties were trying to "take not the profitable route but the 'right' one."[55] But it was only the ten black players who forfeited the remainder of their season. Price insisted that the ten held nothing against the four who chose to return to practice. I have a hard time believing that. How could the ten not resent the four? For their part, the four must have felt at least slightly selfish, or guilty, or defeated, or resentful for having been forced to make an uncomfortable decision. The fourteen were among the roughly 300 black students at Indiana, all of them coming of age in the era of Black Power. When consciences collided, bruising resulted. Although the coverage in Bloomington and Indianapolis told a small part of just one of the fourteen stories (Clarence Price's), it acknowledged the people, not just the principles, involved.

According to Price, the protesting ten players had white friends on the team as well as black. The long-standing clichés about team bonds have an element of truth. Looking around the huddle in the fourth quarter of a close game at ten other guys sweating and bleeding like you are, all determined to get that first down or stop the opponents at the goal line, brings out powerful feelings. The bonds of offensive linemen—the grunts who make heroes of the glory boys—or of a linebacking corps or the defensive backs, can also be strong, as can the camaraderie of the locker room and the common suffering of training camp. These bonds have been overromanticized—they are intense but often fragile, ending with the game or the season or the finish to a career—but they are nonetheless real and powerful. When that bond is interracial, it momentarily solves Americans' most difficult and divisive social problem. There are moments during a football game or in a locker room when race truly is irrelevant. There are just two opponents locked in intimate combat, or teammates yoked in a common struggle or sharing in the same insiders' joke. These may be just moments—racial awareness invariably returns—but those moments are momentous in a racially troubled society like ours.

In defying their coaches, the black protesters of the 1960s had to break these bonds with white (and sometimes black) teammates, and no one should underestimate how difficult that could be. Most college football players of the 1960s, black and white, were neither crusading reformers nor impassioned defenders of a system under siege. They were young men in troubled times who did what they felt they had to do, but what some of them had to do if they were black—belonging to a team but also to a minority community on campus—emerged from conflicting needs and desires more complicated than white players faced. The dilemma for white players could come when black teammates protested over a principle in which they also believed, forcing them to choose between that principle and their accustomed allegiances. To opt for principle under those conditions required rare courage. In none of the protests did a single white player quit in sympathy with his black teammates. I certainly cannot condemn them. However agonized I would have been, I cannot imagine that I would have acted differently.

The personal dramas behind the black protests emerged most clearly in the coverage of the incident at the University of Washington. In addition to Carver Gayton—himself not a Hamlet or Lear in the drama but something closer to Horatio or Gloucester, the decent man caught between opposing forces without the power to shape events—some of the "kids" were given human faces. From the very beginning, the *Post-Intelligencer*'s John Owen invited readers to think about the young men, perhaps white as well as black, who escaped their suspended teammates' fate when their coach demanded a profession of loyalty. "You can only guess how many dissatisfied players kept their mouths shut rather than have their athletic careers terminated," Owen commented. Later, he wrote an ironically titled column, "Week in the Life of a Schoolboy," about Lee Brock, the black senior defensive captain who battled valiantly in a loss to Stanford alongside black and white teammates while black students "sat on the 50 yard line hoisting signs of protest against the Husky coach." "It's a difficult position for any man to find himself in," concluded Owen (note that for Owen, Brock was not a "kid" but a "man"). "It's almost an impossible one when you are attempting to be a student, a football player, a counselor, a sociologist and, when you are also attempting to be yourself." After Brock's close friend Harvey Blanks remained suspended and Carver Gayton had resigned, Brock hinted at depths of feeling and long months of frustration: "Sometime, somehow, something good's going to happen around here. I probably won't be around to see it, but it's going to happen."[56]

Perhaps speaking for many of his white teammates, the other captain, white offensive lineman Ken Ballenger, lamented in one of Georg Meyers's columns the passing of "'play it from the heart' football at Washington" and elsewhere—gone, but still cherished "as an ideal." It says much about Lee Brock, but equally much about Washington's white players—and more generally about a large gray area in college football that only seemed black and white at the time—that Brock's teammates voted him most inspirational player at the end of the season.[57]

FOOTBALL TRANSFORMED

Black football players were the "losers" in all of their protests in 1969, as they were in college football's last major one, at Syracuse, the following spring and fall. The incidents at Syracuse were essentially a reprise of those at the University of Iowa: black boycott of practice in the spring after months of simmering resentment, suspension by the coach, protracted and ultimately unsuccessful attempts at reinstatement. Coach Ben Schwartzwalder and his players were of course real people, not actors with a script, so the episode at Syracuse had its own distinct, and distinctly painful, aspects. A single black player did not participate in the boycott, a majority of angry white players opposed reinstating their black teammates, and the chancellor overruled his football coach in a futile attempt to minimize damage to the university. Eventually a thirty-nine-page committee report documented chronic racism in the athletic department with recommendations for change that were largely ignored. The details were likely lost on most of the football public, for whom the black protest at Syracuse would have played out as a too-familiar rerun.[58]

In all of these incidents, the coaches' victories were short-lived or ambiguous. Eaton and Nagel continued coaching only through the 1970 season, Schwartzwalder through 1973, Owens through 1974, and Andros through 1975. Only Pont (who showed the most sympathy for his black players) held another coaching position, leaving Indiana for Northwestern in 1973. Where the coach wielded the iron fist, the cost to his university was greater. Wyoming was deeply branded as a racist place for many years. Andros frankly told John Underwood that his action "has hurt our recruiting of black players."[59] What Andros could not know was that re-cruiting not just black players but black students generally to Oregon State would be more difficult for years to come.

Administrative pressure on Owens to compromise left the University of Washington less scarred, although peace did not immediately settle on the Husky football program. The following fall, three black sopho-mores—Mark Wheeler, Calvin Jones, and Ira Hammon—along with junior Charles Evans, the only other black player on the squad with eli-gibility remaining, quit the team at the end of the season (Wheeler, a month earlier), charging the coaches with racism. The three had come to UW as freshmen in 1969 despite warnings from older black players, only to be confronted by the events of that fall. When they announced a year later that they were leaving the team, they charged that "the racial practices of the University of Washington coaching staff have forced us to the point where we no longer can tolerate the playing conditions im-posed upon us." The players offered no details, but John Owen in the *Seattle Post-Intelligencer* pointed out that Jones and Hammon came to UW because of one man, Carver Gayton, who resigned shortly after they arrived. The *Seattle Times*'s Georg Meyers surmised that the problems were "stacking" and playing time. Meyers also singled out Cal Jones, a "potential All-American" and future NFL pro, as the one who as a star was not personally affected but was giving up the most for the sake of "personal conviction, profound commitment and a lot of sacrifice for his belief that black athletes are mistreated at Washington."[60]

Thirty-five years later, the three players essentially confirmed Meyers's assumptions, telling a reporter for the *Seattle Times* about stacking, a demotion, criticism for not hitting the correct hole despite running 52 yards for a touchdown, being ignored by an assistant coach after scor-ing—the sort of indignities (or perceived slights) that are common to football but could seem (or be) racially charged in 1970. The university responded by hiring two black assistant coaches and a black associate athletic director, actions that persuaded Jones to return—only to face accusations from other black UW students of being an "Uncle Tom."[61] (Jones was good enough to go on to play four years in the NFL.) After going 6–4 in 1970, the Huskies had two 8–3 seasons, then fell to 2–9 in 1973 and 5–6 in 1974, after which Owens was replaced by Don James, who had Washington back atop the conference by 1977.

For the black players at all of the schools, the losses were immedi-ate and in some cases irremediable, yet these young men, whether as willful or reluctant rebels, were agents of change: change in the consciousness of race for coaches, white players, and college football fans and change in the fundamental relationship between coaches and athletes. The major black protests were relatively few, but each one touched other football programs. As Wyoming, Indiana, and Washington played out their schedules without black players in 1969, athletes on opposing teams, as well as their fans, had to wrestle with their own responses. More directly, these uprisings made coaches everywhere contemplate the prospects for disruption of their own programs.

Racial protest was just one element of "The Problem" of youthful rebellion, as John Underwood described it in "The Desperate Coach," but it was the most divisive one on college campuses.[62] The actions of Dee Andros (and his assistants), Ray Nagel, Lloyd Eaton, and Jim Owens all seem predetermined. What Georg Meyers said of Owens—that confronting his players "reflected almost a suicidal impulse"[63]—could have been said about each of these coaches. Owens forced the issue by demanding a declaration of commitment. Andros and his staff had talked about their response a full year before Fred Milton's beard triggered it. In fact, the prospects for a black protest had been on Andros's mind at least since March 1968, when he publicly urged Jim Owens to resist the demands of his black athletes during the initial episode on the Seattle campus. Andros worried that "if he does back down, the Negroes will be making similar demands in Eugene and Corvallis and every other athletic school on the West Coast." When his own time did come, according to Underwood's approving account, Andros "could have ignored the beard or softened his discipline, as many fellow coaches said he should have, but he chose to fight because he was ready to fight." Underwood reported that, just days before, Andros had turned down a coaching offer from the University of Pittsburgh to sign a new five-year contract with Oregon State, which included a memorandum, at his insistence, "stating that Andros alone would set the policies for his football team." Thus armed against gutless administrators, as Underwood reconstructed the events, the coach went to war.[64] Nagel and Eaton likewise suspended their players, without discussion, at the first sign of insubordination, having been forewarned of their discontent several days earlier at Wyoming and several months earlier at Iowa. Whether these coaches were "suicidal" or highly principled, tyrannical or short-sighted, they all acted in a manner that suggested prior planning.

The most embattled coaches in the 1960s were not necessarily the least racially sensitive or most autocratic ones. There is no evidence that Andros, Nagel, Pont, or Owens was overtly or even subtly racist. Testimonies from players who loved Andros—the Great Pumpkin who led his teams onto the field and was renowned for fiery halftime orations and clever postgame country-boy witticisms—poured out as his health failed more than thirty years later. These players included Bill Enyart (the white player who most openly sided with his black teammates), Bryce Huddleston (one of the black players who chose not to transfer), and Fred Milton himself. After leaving Oregon State in 1969, Milton attended Portland State briefly, then transferred to Utah State, where his reputation as a "troublemaker" created more difficulties for him. After Milton graduated, Andros helped him catch on briefly in the Canadian Football League and continued to offer support after Milton settled in Portland. The two became "pretty good friends" in Andros's words in a 2003 interview, while Milton professed deep respect unchanged since he first met Andros. Milton told a reporter that everyone who played for Andros shared this respect, "including the guys who walked off campus with me in 1969."[65] Time and sentiment cannot explain all of this away.

Andros was a decorated veteran of Iwo Jima who as a football coach in the 1960s fervently believed that the lessons of war—the life-and-death necessity of soldiers' complete surrender to their officers' absolute authority—applied to the game of football, too. Ohio State's Woody Hayes and Syracuse's Ben Schwartzwalder, both of whom famously shared this belief, were also combat veterans of World War II, following officer-coaches like "Biff" Jones, Frank Cavanaugh (the "Iron Major"), and General Robert Neyland from earlier generations. Hayes served as a naval lieutenant commander in the Pacific (one of his biographers titled his book *Woody Hayes and the 100-Yard War*). Schwartzwalder earned a Silver Star, Bronze Star, and Purple Heart as a paratrooper in the legendary 82nd Airborne in Europe while rising to the rank of major. While various commentators periodically theorized football's relationship to war, the soldier-coaches put theory into practice, and their beliefs gained wider currency in the hunker-down mood of the Cold War. By the 1960s, however, a generation of young men who had grown up in peace and prosperity were not inclined to "go to war" for their football coach.

Whether Andros was an eager or reluctant combatant in 1969, he misread his black players and the times. He was not alone. The coaches who overreacted to the complaints of their black players seemed to share a belief in a vast black conspiracy targeting intercollegiate athletics that could infect their own programs at any moment. Such think-ing found its way into the *NCAA News*, the official publication sent to the athletic departments of member institutions. In the December 1969 issue, an anonymous writer (presumably under executive director Wal-ter Byers's direction, if not Byers himself) cited "reliable information" that Wyoming had been selected by the Black Panther Party and Black Student Union at a national meeting the previous summer as the site for a protest against the racial politics at Brigham Young. "The evidence is clear," declared the *News*, "that there is operating in this country a hard-core revolutionary force designed to destroy the present governmental and education system of the United States. . . . Intercollegiate athletics is a prime target and vehicle for them because of the publicity value in-herent in sports and the fact that the Negro or black athlete involved in a mild disorder will be a subject of newsprint from coast to coast, whereas the acts of a less-publicized BSU party member may only be reported in the campus newspaper."[66]

Whether or not the football program at the University of Wyoming was targeted in this manner, it was more simply a new racial conscious-ness, rather than an organized conspiracy, that white coaches through-out the country found themselves confronting. At Iowa the statement issued by the black athletes sounded like a lecture by Harry Edwards (who in fact had spoken on campus several months earlier) or class notes from a Black Studies course: the experience of the black athlete reflected "the slave-master relationship"; he was "the gladiator who performs in the arena for the pleasure of the white masses"; he was "brought from the black colony, typically called high school, which is predominantly black," and subjected to the alien standards of the "mother country." And so on.[67] Unsympathetic readers might have heard only the slogans of Black Power rather than the more concrete demand that accompanied the bombast: to address the low graduation rate of black athletes. In my Latin American history course at Notre Dame, I learned about some of the shameful things my country had done to the citizens of other coun-tries. In their newly established Black Studies courses, African American students at Iowa and other universities were learning (or reminded of) what their country did to their own ancestors. On the football field, while my abusive or intolerant coach would seem a jerk, to a black teammate he might seem blood kin to the slave master who lashed his great-great-grandfather, or to the Mississippi sheriff or Chicago cop clubbing his "brothers" on the nightly news. Whether this reaction would be "fair" to the coach was sadly beside the point at this historical moment.

It does not follow that dissent and confrontation were any easier for black football players than they would have been for me. To assume so would be something like subscribing to an older, crueler stereotype: that blacks were impervious to injuries, or at least less susceptible than whites—their thicker skulls, less sensibility to pain, more physical durability (that good ol' slave breeding, you know)—a pernicious idea that could make every injured black athlete a suspected malingerer. For a long time I thought that African Americans of my generation were more "naturally" radical. Afflicted or blessed with what W. E. B. DuBois called "double-consciousness," they would be less ready to submit to the authority of a white man with power. Reading the contemporary accounts of the black protests that forever changed football, I now find what seem to be mostly young men as uncertain and vulnerable as I was, with their own private football dreams not unlike my own, formed by similar football experiences but also racial and economic circumstances quite different from mine. I find these glimpses more compelling than the comments by some of the participants in interviews years later, as the immediacy and groping uncertainty of the moment often disappear from the vantage of retrospect. Like the black pioneers of the Southeastern Conference, most of the black protesters seem to have been reluctant revolutionaries, forced to make hard decisions not demanded of most of us, or caught up in consequences not anticipated in the initial act of defiance.

The world was no more simply black and white for them than it was for me. The black press from that era is a revelation: not full of black anger and routine endorsements of black athletic militancy, as one might expect, but divided over the current racial situation in American sports. While Sam Lacy, the venerable sports editor of the *Baltimore Afro-American*, endorsed the planned boycott of the 1968 Olympics, for example, the *Pittsburgh Courier* downplayed the protest by Tommie Smith and John Carlos as a "trivial" incident that should not tarnish the great victories of black athletes at the games. The *Courier*'s veteran sports columnists, Bill Nunn and Ric Roberts, were thorough integrationists, dismissive of separatist or black supremacist rhetoric and action. They constantly celebrated black athletic prowess and objected to Jack Olsen's attention only to the "dark side" of race and American sport in his "Black

Athlete" series for *Sports Illustrated*. Olsen ignored the "sunny side," the achievements both on and off the field of remarkable men like Paul Robeson, Duke Slater, Charles Drew, and Brud Holland. Roberts ventured that John Henry Johnson, the great Pittsburgh Steelers fullback of the 1950s and 1960s who could not get a coaching job in the NFL (one of Olsen's examples of institutional racism), was passed over by owners because he had been a "'spoiled' prima donna" who had not earned a coaching opportunity.[68] Many white Americans at the time likely viewed blacks as a single mass of militancy, but black America, like white, had its generational divide in the 1960s, as well as its liberals and conservatives, moderates and radicals. The young black athletes caught up in protests wrestled with the conflicting desires and demands of the age.

For all the loud drama of the major black protests, the racial revolution in college football played out more quietly at most institutions. Initially, some coaches backed off recruiting black players—"all but the most outstanding" ones—but such an approach could quickly prove suicidal. As the *New York Times* reported in the midst of the turmoil of the 1969 season, "Much of the problem never comes to the surface publicly. At a number of universities coaches and administrators have quietly met with black players and made concessions." At Kansas, after a two-day boycott of spring drills by fifteen black players in 1968, university officials created a Black History course and appointed a black cheerleader. Michigan State hired a black assistant coach; Wisconsin fired a supposedly racist coach; Stanford dropped BYU from its future schedules; Washington State officials formally apologized for the booing of visiting black students. At Michigan in 1969, first-year coach Bo Schembechler, a hard-nosed screamer in the mold of his mentor, Woody Hayes, relaxed his rules on facial hair at the request of one of his black players. (Hayes himself held out until 1973.)[69] Whether motivated by racial sensitivity or political expediency, universities across the land learned to accommodate black racial consciousness by the 1970s.

The protests of black athletes in the late 1960s hit college football at its heart. While white boys like myself might still respond to fatherly coaches, racially conscious black athletes were less likely to submit to the paternalism of white father figures. Coaches had to become much more sensitive to the economic and cultural backgrounds of their black recruits, and consequently to the individuality of all the players on the team. Likewise, the very ideal of a team—a group of young men who surrender their individual personalities and desires to become a single unit—was challenged by black protesters who claimed that they were different from their white teammates and needed black counselors and assistant coaches who could understand their needs. For decades, African American athletes had had to struggle for the chance to be treated like everyone else, as one player at a time in the 1920s, 1930s, and 1940s slowly integrated college football teams outside the South. Now, with fourteen or sixteen or twenty-two black players on a single team, they were insisting that their special concerns deserved attention. As Gary Gayton, the attorney representing Harvey Blanks, the suspended running back from Chicago, said to Jim Owens, "You're recruiting these kids from the ghetto and you can't treat them the same as the others, like kids out of Puyallup." An unsympathetic columnist in Syracuse complained that the black players had created "a two-platoon squad," not "offense and defense, but black and white." A football "team" became a more complex social organization in the 1960s.[70]

Despite individual defeats, the black protesters won greater personal freedom for all college athletes, black and white; and history, of course, was on their side. In 2002 the University of Wyoming commemorated its Black 14. In 2006 the University of Syracuse awarded Chancellor's Medals to its misnamed Syracuse Eight (there had been nine players, but one was injured) and presented them with letter jackets at halftime of a football game.[71] The broader impact of the black protests has proven more ambiguous. In the wake of the disruptions of the 1960s, coaches lost their cultural authority along with the right to dictate hair length and social behavior, but they retained their fundamental power over the lives of their "student-athletes." Nearly forty years later, we no longer believe that coaches are primarily teachers of life lessons, instillers of discipline and virtue, fathers not just to their own families but to entire teams of young men. In compensation, for fielding championship teams that fill stadiums and luxury suites, coaches now earn millions that would seem obscene for mere professors of football. And a quietly passed piece of NCAA legislation in 1973, making athletic scholarships one-year rather than multiyear grants, gave coaches more control of their players' lives than they had ever had. Football remained the coaches' game that Walter Camp first envisioned, though on quite different terms now. Black athletes sparked a revolution in the late 1960s, but not everything changed.

INTERLUDE 1973: THE NCAA GOES PRO

The history of college football since the 1960s can look like an orderly progression of seasons, each one concluding in conference titles and bowl games, all-conference and All-America teams, a clear or disputed national champion, local bragging rights everywhere settled for another year. Football power shifted during this period from the Midwest to the South, as Miami, Florida, and Florida State rose to the top ranks of football powers, the SEC supplanted the Big Ten as the premier conference, and the state of Florida supplanted Pennsylvania and Ohio as the cradle of football talent. Big games, star players (Archie Griffin, Herschel Walker, Bo Jackson, Peyton Manning, Reggie Bush) and top coaches (Tom Osborne, Bo Schembechler, Bobby Bowden, Joe Paterno) dominated the headlines from week to week, season to season.

I am interested here in a different history: the playing out of the contradiction at the heart of big-time college football since the 1890s, when university presidents first realized that what had begun as an extracurricular activity not many years earlier had become a potentially profitable mass entertainment and a potent vehicle for marketing the university. That history has been marked by a series of academic and ethical crises, set against a backdrop of increasing commercialization, with NCAA and university leaders dealing with the crises as if they were unrelated to the commercialization, which in fact has been an underlying factor.

In this history, the orderly progression of seasons has been repeatedly disrupted by sudden events that set in motion strings of consequences seemingly unrelated to each other or to the developments unfolding each year on the field. An academic scandal is followed by reform legislation at the NCAA convention that provokes protests from black coaches and black-college presidents—an effort to prevent the exploitation of black athletes denounced as racist. After the NCAA loses control over TV rights, televised games proliferate, conferences realign, bowl games are restructured and branded by companies that manufacture garden tools or snack chips—then a coach signs a two-million-dollar contract and college football seems to have been radically changed by market forces beyond anyone's control. An epidemic of arrests for sexual assault, a legal challenge to Title IX, a drug scandal, an investigative report on the excesses of big-time college sports—each erupts without warning, throwing college football into turmoil, an embarrassing though temporary setback in the grand march of seasons. I remember as a kid in grade school learning about the American Revolution: the British soldiers in their neat red uniforms marching precisely down the road, only to be ambushed by ragtag American troops hiding in the trees. Fans who only want to follow their teams on the field must feel like those British soldiers, expecting order but repeatedly surprised by chaos.

I want to connect these events, to find order in that seeming chaos, by spinning out a narrowly focused history of college football since the 1960s. I want to tell a two-part story—one part about tremendous and tremendously uneven financial growth, the other about the experience of the athletes in this new environment. Each of these stories has been repeatedly told and is utterly familiar, but I want to tell them as the intertwined parts of a single story: the playing out of big-time college football's fundamental contradiction. Recognizing their relationship is essential in assessing how well the dual purposes for which college sports purportedly exist—to serve the welfare of both the institutions that stage the games and the "student-athletes" who play them—are served by big-time football today.

What connects this history to the revolutions of the 1960s is the institution of the one-year scholarship in 1973, a crucial event in the history of college football's fundamental contradiction and the foundation for the football world that has developed since then.

A BRIEF HISTORY OF A CONTRADICTION

The historical context for the one-year scholarship begins near the beginning, with the controversies over "commercialism" and "professionalism" that are almost as old as college football itself. "Commercialism" first entered the game in the 1880s, when teams staged their season-ending Thanksgiving Day championship game in New York; and it became rampant by the 1920s as 50,000-seat stadiums sprouted throughout the land. "Professionalism" entered college football openly in the

1890s through the hiring of paid coaches and, surreptitiously, with the recruiting and subsidizing of strapping youths with little interest in, or particular capacity for, higher education. During the sport's formative decades, commercialism made professionalism necessary; professionalism made commercialism possible. College football by the 1920s, with marquee stars such as Red Grange and celebrity coaches such as Knute Rockne, was second only to Major League Baseball in the enthusiasm of the American sporting public, for most of whom the amateur and scholastic standing of the young men on the field mattered very little. Intellectual critics intermittently sniped at the distorted priorities of educational institutions engaged in the mass entertainment business, but with little effect until 1929, when the Carnegie Foundation's famous Bulletin #23 documented the sins of commercialism and professionalism at dozens of institutions. For a brief moment, university leaders faced a decision whether to change course. While a few did, the great majority embraced their contradiction and lurched into the future.

The contradiction has played out in a variety of ways but no more importantly than in the experience of the so-called student-athlete. No Golden Age of fleet and brawny dean's-list scholars ever reigned in college football. Numerous gridiron heroes since the 1920s have undoubtedly been football players who enrolled in classes rather than students who played football, but until 1956 the colleges and universities belonging to the NCAA could profess otherwise. Not until 1956 did the NCAA establish the athletic scholarship that we now take for granted as the foundation of college sports: payment for tuition, room, board, and incidental fees, without consideration of financial need or scholastic merit. For the previous fifty years, since its creation in 1906, the NCAA took the official position that compensating young men for mere athletic prowess would violate the fundamental academic mission of educational institutions and amount to the professionalism that critics decried. This did not mean that football players were not paid. It meant either that they were paid for campus work (sometimes phony jobs of the clock-winding variety) or were subsidized or employed by generous alumni and boosters. Astonishing as it would seem today, in the 1930s alumni financial support of athletes was considered more ethical than institutional support. What justified subsidization from any source was the assumption that participation in athletics did not interfere with the young men's primary purpose in getting a college education. Some claimed more: playing football was itself educational. Sports purportedly developed leadership and built character, supplementing the intellectual training that took place in classrooms. Football did in fact provide working-class and ethnic outsiders with opportunities for a college education and entry into middle-class careers afterward.

Over the 1930s and 1940s, something like a backroom civil war played out in college football, as the major southern conferences moved toward openly subsidizing their athletes while the Big Ten and the old Pacific Coast Conference (PCC) insisted that athletes must be treated like other students, who were able to accept money or employment from alumni or local boosters. The Big Ten and PCC accused the southern schools of professionalism; southerners accused the northern and western schools of hypocrisy for subsidizing their athletes with "jobs" on the order of clearing the snow from the sidewalks at USC. The athletic scholarship finally approved in 1956 resolved this long-festering conflict in the simplest way possible: by making "professionalism" legal.

Almost. The NCAA clung to its fiction of amateurism by designating these institutional subsidies *scholar*ships, not athletic grants, awarded to "scholars" who happened to play football. The NCAA understood this fiction to be just that: executive director Walter Byers promoted the term "student-athlete" expressly to deny the inherent professionalism of students paid to play sports. For Byers, at issue was not some lofty ideal of amateurism but the more pragmatic and dangerous prospect of paid athletes' entitlement to workers' rights.[1] Having subscribed to the fiction, universities then had to live by it. In practical terms, this meant that a football player in the late 1950s and early 1960s could quit the team without forfeiting his scholarship, which was not tied in any way to athletic performance or even to participation. This arrangement enabled NCAA institutions to survive legal claims to workers' compensation in a couple of landmark cases, but it also created a crisis during the athletic revolution of the 1960s. This revolution, in turn, prompted revisions of the athletic scholarship that laid the groundwork for the quieter gradual revolution over the following decades. At its 1967 convention, the NCAA for the first time tied scholarships to continuing participation and good behavior. Two years later, amid signs of apocalypse, it strengthened institutional control over rebellious student-athletes. Then, in 1973, a momentous but quietly passed piece of NCAA legislation—replacing the four-year athletic scholarship with a one-year renewable one—transformed student-athletes into athlete-students without anyone paying much attention.

A SIMPLE MATTER OF TERMINOLOGY

The racial and political protests of the 1960s provoked a new way of talking and thinking about college athletes. During the blowup at Oregon State, President James Jensen invoked "the long tradition of building character by the athletic department" as a justification for not overriding the suspension of Fred Milton. Jensen conceded to Dee Andros the same prerogatives of academic freedom and autonomy in educational matters that belonged to any dean, department head, or member of the faculty. Speaking for the white players who supported Andros, however, John Didion used quite different language. "When a man signs a contract to play a sport here," Didion read from the players' statement, "he obligates himself to comply with the rules that govern that sport, as set down by his coach." Jensen described playing football as a cocurricular experience. Didion described playing football as the athlete's job, at which he "receives nine months pay for four or five months work." According to Didion, the required sacrifices, such as rules for personal grooming, were reasonable on these terms.[2]

The "long tradition" invoked by Jensen was the ground on which universities had justified their sponsorship of what looked from the outside like popular entertainment. If football built character, it served a university's educational mission. Simply hiring young men to play football, on the other hand—with the sort of actual or implicit contract described by Didion—would entail no academic justification. Didion's unsentimental, rights-based explanation spoke to the times as clearly as Milton's protest did. Universities had traditionally served their students *in loco parentis*—in the place of their parents—but Didion declared football players to be "men" who entered contractual relationships with their coaches and colleges. On these terms, instead of having to wrestle with murky questions about what is best for a "boy" on scholarship—team discipline or freedom of self-expression—university administrators would only have to ask what a "man" on scholarship owed his school and what the school owed him in return.

Writers in local newspapers who found this idea attractive picked up on Didion's remarks. An editorial in the *Oregon Journal* wished that the controversy at OSU would "result in a frank discussion of the play-for-pay aspects of college athletics. . . . What nobody is saying is that we have what you might call an employer-employee relationship with your players." In this relationship, you surrender the right to have a beard "when you are employed and your employer (the coach) tells you to shave." Al Lightner in the *Oregon Statesman* put the matter more bluntly: "It's much the same as working for a living. You do what the boss says and live up to his specifications or you suffer the consequences."[3]

The following summer, *Sports Illustrated*'s John Underwood brought this same language to the national discussion. In the first two parts of "The Desperate Coach," Underwood spoke as if from the past, envisioning the ideal coach as one who combined an iron fist with fatherly concern. He saw this ideal surviving mostly in the South, where Bear Bryant ruled (and where not all teams were yet even marginally integrated, Underwood failed to add).[4] Underwood did not mention character building, but it was implicit in the father-son relationship between coaches and players. In the final installment, however, Underwood came out openly for the contractual model, quoting Didion's statement as his starting point. He called on college administrators to abandon the hypocrisy that an athletic grant-in-aid was an *academic* scholarship and to admit that "student-athletes" were athletes first, students second. In return for their athletic efforts on the university's behalf, they were given the opportunity to earn a degree whose "value is unlimited." Wedding the old and new models, Underwood declared the relationship between coaches and players to be "essentially that of employer-employee, with a dash of father-son."[5] Here, in a single phrase, was another perspective on college football's fundamental contradiction, as well as a signal of its imminent unraveling.

Underwood, in turn, was echoed by John Owen of the *Seattle Post-Intelligencer* during the incident at the University of Washington that fall. Owen blamed the quandary in which coaches found themselves — "They feel they have to draw a rigid line someplace, but don't know exactly where" — on the "hypocrisy of intercollegiate athletics." Owen pointed out that, by insisting that students on athletic scholarships were "amateurs," athletic departments could not justify denying them "rights enjoyed by all other students, including the right of protest." If, on the other hand, universities would frankly acknowledge that athletes were employees, "signed to personal service contracts," coaches' demand for "rigid responsibilities to the team and the school" would be justified. The relationship would be mutual and contractual: in accepting a scholarship, the athlete would have "peddled his athletic talents on the open market, in exchange for a college education worth $15,000 or more."[6] Whereas Lightner and Underwood viewed the contract chiefly as a confirmation of coaches' authority, Owen placed greater stress on mutual obligation—a college education in exchange for athletic performance. In Owen's words, playing football was not a "privilege," as the angry opponents of protest insisted, but a job, and players had certain rights, as did workers in any occupation.

The shift from moral or paternalistic to contractual language marked a radical reorientation not apparent at the time and with ramifications that could not have been anticipated. The scholarship-as-employment-contract model solved the knotty conflict between coaches' authority and athletes' prerogatives, but at the cost of the athletes' status as students. And it unintentionally reopened the presumably settled issue of athletes' rights as workers. In 1969 the language of contractual obligation was iconoclastic, a break from the idealistic language of sports during the long reign of the amateur ideal. Assertions of amateur purity were often disingenuous or hypocritical, to be sure, but the adoption of the athletic scholarship in 1956 was the first official break with this ideal. Popular belief in the man-molding and character-building power of amateur college sports did not end with the acceptance of the athletic scholarship, but the contractual language that emerged from the upheavals of the late 1960s—to legitimize the authority of the coach and the obligations of the athlete—unintentionally redefined the "student-athlete" as an "athlete-student." The new contractual model was then institutionalized by the NCAA at its annual convention in 1973.

"DEAD WOOD," BLACK PROTEST, AND THE ONE-YEAR SCHOLARSHIP

The sudden and nearly silent adoption of the one-year scholarship in 1973 has a more immediate history that begins at the NCAA convention in January 1965, the beginning of a movement to shift control of scholarships to coaches and athletic departments. On the convention floor, Earl Sneed, the faculty representative from the University of Oklahoma, proposed replacing the four-year with a one-year scholarship throughout the NCAA, as was already the policy in the Big Eight Conference. (Sneed's proposal would have even permitted scholarships for a single academic term.) Racial and political protests were presumably not yet even imagined; the issue for Sneed was the "boy" (or alternately "lad") who got something for nothing, who could drop his sport without surrendering his scholarship. It may seem odd that universities could not simply cancel the scholarship for an athlete who quit the team, but this was a consequence of the NCAA's fiction that scholarships given to athletes were really academic grants, so as not to admit to "professionalism." The so-called Sanity Code of 1948, the NCAA's first experiment with actual athletic scholarships, explicitly provided that "no athlete shall be deprived of financial aids . . . because of failure to participate in intercollegiate athletics."[7] Despite the collapse of the Sanity Code, subsequent legislation and official interpretations reaffirmed the student-athlete's protection against loss of a scholarship for nonparticipation (or for poor athletic performance, it is important to add).

By 1965, when Sneed proposed to overturn this policy, a seemingly unrelated issue had created a new complication. In 1963 the NCAA had lost a legal appeal by the family of Gary Van Horn, a football player at Cal Poly who had died in a plane crash returning from a game. The family had appealed for compensation to the Industrial Accident Commission in California, which ruled that Van Horn had not been an employee of the university because his funding by a booster group was not dependent on his participation in football. A California district court overruled the commission, however, awarding Van Horn's family what amounted to workers' compensation. With that precedent hovering in the background, the NCAA had to ensure that sanctioned athletic scholarships could not be legally construed as employment contracts. They had to be *academic* grants.[8]

Workers' compensation was an issue for backroom discussion. On the convention floor, Sneed needed to assure his colleagues that his proposal would not lead to abuse by coaches and athletic directors. Sneed explained that in order to compete with schools outside the Big Eight offering four-year scholarships, Oklahoma issued a letter with each one-year grant, assuring the recruit that his scholarship would be renewed if he remained academically eligible, made "an honest effort in athletics," and followed university rules. Sneed also tried to persuade his fellow delegates that coaches would not simply use the one-year scholarship as a "trial" for recruits—one year and out if you're not good enough. "That doesn't happen," Sneed insisted. "I have been with this thing a long, long time, and I think I can say to you that the lad who is honest, the lad who wants to stay, the coaches aren't going to be just ruthless and cut him off. They are teachers, just as we are."[9] Such language in 1965, I should add, sounded familiar, not quaint.

Speaking against the proposal, Father Edmund Joyce of Notre Dame argued that the one-year scholarship would mean "putting the continuance of a grant-in-aid to athletes strictly on the basis of his ability as an athlete," a departure from the NCAA's ideal of students who happen to play sports. It would also, Joyce insisted, surely become a mechanism by which coaches would "try to get rid, under the guise of the rule, of the dead wood of which there is always some."[10]

The formality of the statement belies the hard edge of the issue. The desire to jettison "dead wood" was the true heart of the matter, an open secret in big-time college football. In its profile of Kentucky's Charlie Bradshaw and "The New Rage to Win" that he exemplified, *Sports Illustrated* in 1962 had noted that critics of Bradshaw among his fellow coaches in the SEC believed that he "had deliberately cleared his squad of dead wood." According to one SEC coach, "It's obvious that the practices were made so brutal that untalented players were forced to quit. It's not a new pattern. It's an old one set by Bear Bryant."[11]

What was new in Bradshaw's case that particularly irked some rival SEC coaches was the Kentucky athletic department's leading the players to believe that they had to relinquish their scholarships when they quit. Mississippi's John Vaught was incensed by this, telling the sports editor of the *Louisville Courier-Journal*, "Don't those boys who got chased off the squad know that under the rules they're entitled to four full years of room, board, tuition and books, whether they lay a hand on a football or not?" Vaught was less concerned about the rights of the "boys" than envious of Bradshaw for solving a problem that Vaught and other coaches also faced. The SEC permitted 55 football scholarships per year, but no more than 140 overall for football and basketball combined. According to the sports editor of the *Lexington Herald* (defending Bradshaw and Kentucky), SEC schools typically awarded the full 55 "because the dropout rate is big enough to permit them to do so without going over the maximum." Whether "dropouts" or "dead wood," there were a lot of them, and they could hang onto their scholarships after quitting. In a part of the interview in the *Courier-Journal* not quoted by *Sports Illustrated*, Vaught explained, "If I could dispose of them as easily as Charlie Bradshaw got rid of 30 or 40 boys at Kentucky, you wouldn't see 26 redshirts on my squad."[12]

A little over two years later at the NCAA convention, "dead wood" remained a problem for coaches, who still had no power to rescind the scholarship of an athlete who quit the team, let alone one who turned out not to be very good. The shapers of NCAA policy also clearly understood that the power to terminate a scholarship would violate the fundamental principle that a grant-in-aid was for an education, not for athletic performance, and that the one-year scholarships currently offered by the Big Eight Conference threatened this principle. As Father Joyce pointed out on the convention floor, only recruiting competition from schools offering four-year scholarships pressured Oklahoma and its conference partners to promise annual renewals. If the NCAA adopted the one-year scholarship, coaches everywhere would have the power to eliminate the "dead wood." Despite this prospect, Sneed's proposal was approved by a 131–112 majority, but it failed to gain the two-thirds necessary for adoption.

Act Two. At the 1967 convention, virtually the same proposal, again offered on behalf of the Big Eight Conference by Oklahoma's faculty representative, now David Swank, received a slightly larger majority (138–109) but still not the required two-thirds. Instead, members approved a new interpretation of the current provisions for financial aid to make more explicit universities' right to reduce or cancel scholarships under certain conditions—including nonparticipation and "serious misconduct." This seemingly simple and reasonable provision had two major ramifications: (1) it gave coaches a way to run off the "dead wood" (make their unwanted athletes' lives so miserable that they would quit), and (2) it created the first true *athletic* scholarships. Financial aid was now tied to athletic participation.[13]

Act Three. Two years later, in January 1969, Swank again took the floor to propose a new interpretation of "serious misconduct," which would allow athletic departments to hold athletes to rules that did not govern other students. "Dead wood" was irrelevant this time; racial and political protests were explicitly at issue. The previous summer, the five-part series, "The Black Athlete—a Shameful Story," had appeared in *Sports Illustrated*, and that fall Tommie Smith and John Carlos had raised their clenched fists at the Mexico City Olympics. Black protests against BYU had been erupting on several western campuses since the previous April; black athletes at the University of Texas at El Paso had accused their athletic department of racial discrimination. Throughout the country, in dozens of incidents large and small, smoldering racial unrest was reaching a flash point.

Against this backdrop, on the convention floor the chairman of the NCAA's Eligibility Committee acknowledged receiving questions about the impact of Swank's proposal on athletes wishing to wear sideburns and beards. Representatives from two black colleges, Grambling and

Tuskegee, expressed concern about retaliation against athletes "who refuse to compete with teams from schools where they feel racial discrimination is practiced." They also bluntly asked if the proposed legislation was "the result of articles that appeared in *Sports Illustrated* last summer," and they cited specific problems facing black athletes in segregated or racist communities. Swank admitted that if the coach or athletic director alone were permitted to decide cases of misconduct, "there might be real abuses," but he assured fellow delegates that faculty committees would protect black athletes from improper treatment.[14]

This time, Swank's proposal passed. The principle that athletic departments could establish their own rules was approved 167–79, and reporters covering the convention understood the implications. Under the headline, "College Athletes Who Protest to Face Loss of Financial Aid," Gordon White reported in the *New York Times*: "The intent, according to many persons voting in the majority, is to put an end to financial assistance to students who protest." Or as one of the "desperate coaches" interviewed by Underwood the following summer put it, "We don't have to put up with troublemakers anymore." Little over a month later, Dee Andros would suspend Fred Milton at Oregon State, to be followed by coaches at Iowa, Wyoming, Indiana, and Washington—in each case, under circumstances anticipated by the presidents of Grambling and Tuskegee. Sensitive to the appearance of ruthlessness, not all of the coaches or their universities rescinded the scholarships of their suspended athletes, but they now had the authority to do so.

In 1969 concerns about protesters, particularly black protesters, overrode the qualms about potential abuse by heavy-handed coaches that had blocked similar legislation in 1965 and 1967. NCAA executive director Walter Byers scoffed at the idea that a coach might use his new power "to get rid of his unimpressive athletes, those who fail to make a team." Dead wood. Responding to the suggestion of such a possibility, Byers was more indignant than Sneed back in 1965: "Oh, that's a lot of hogwash. There are no such coaches."[15]

Act Four—the finale. The published proceedings of the 1969 convention record an earnest debate over competing desires to hold college athletes legitimately accountable while preserving their rights as students and citizens and to endorse coaches' legitimate authority but prevent their abusing it. The concerns of representatives from black colleges were seemingly overridden by the paranoia among representatives from predominantly white universities about a black conspiracy threatening college sports. Then, astonishingly, four years later, a proposal to replace the four-year with a one-year scholarship passed by a show of hands, with no debate and scant attention from the press.

The big news of the 1973 convention was the limiting of football scholarships to 30 annually and 105 total, along with the elimination of the so-called 1.6 rule for eligibility that had been established in 1965, a complicated measurement that predicted academic success in college. The new standard would require a 2.0 grade-point average in high school classes. (Contrary to the apparent raising of standards, the new requirements made it easier to recruit academically underqualified athletes.) This was the hot news. The one-year scholarship giving coaches virtually unlimited power over the athletes they recruited was treated by the press as an afterthought. The report in the *New York Times* briefly noted it among the convention's other actions, then explained it more fully in the seventeenth and eighteenth paragraphs of a twenty-one-paragraph article. The Associated Press account in the *Portland Oregonian* did not mention it until the thirteenth of fourteen paragraphs. Even in the *NCAA News*, the one-year scholarship received a couple of sentences and a brief sidebar stating the new rule without comment on its implications.[16] There was no mention anywhere of motives or rationale for the new policy, no mention anywhere of "dead wood."

Was black protest a factor in this decision? The move to give coaches more control preceded the upheavals in athletic departments in the late 1960s, and the final swift approval of the one-year scholarship came after the major upheavals had subsided. The 1969 convention was the only one at which racial protest was explicitly an issue. By January 1973 the turmoil of 1968–70 had passed, coaches had appointed black assistants and relaxed their rules on matters such as grooming; players enjoyed more personal freedom. Perhaps it is noteworthy that Eddie McAshan's suspension by Georgia Tech had played out just a month before the NCAA convention. Coaches everywhere were having to make concessions on matters such as facial hair, adjusting to a new generation more inclined to self-assertion than deference.

Allowing coaches to discard their athletes at will—this is what the one-year scholarship now permitted, though no one was saying it—was seemingly a concession for reducing the number of scholarships, which was a matter of economics. Notre Dame during my years followed Big Ten rules on scholarships (no more than 30 a year), in contrast to the Big Eight with its limit of 45, the Southwest with 50, and the SEC with 55.[17]

The *New York Times* mentioned programs with 200 football players on scholarship at one time. Gary Shaw's *Meat on the Hoof* in 1972 described how the coaches at Texas brought in hordes of scholarship freshmen each fall and ran off the undesirables, "the dead wood of which there is always some," as Father Joyce put it in 1965 with grammatical precision.[18] Before 1967, those who quit could keep their scholarships. After 1967, they automatically surrendered them, so it made (cruel) sense to run off unwanted players. With the one-year scholarship in 1973, coaches could simply clear their forests of dead wood each year for maximum productivity.

The one-year scholarship may have been perversely more humane than abusing unwanted players until they quit, but it is doubtful that humanitarian considerations shifted the votes needed for a super-majority. Economics always drove NCAA policy, and in reducing scholarships, the membership was openly responding to a sense of economic crisis.[19] Coaches undoubtedly complained to their athletic directors and NCAA representatives that, with fewer scholarships, they needed more power to manage them, although the reduction in fact created no competitive disadvantages. Schools with fewer scholarships but more walk-ons had long competed successfully against schools with more scholarships; the new legislation actually put all programs on the same footing for the first time.

Even if the one-year scholarship was a concession to powerful coaches, in approving it the NCAA membership had to be willfully blind, breathtakingly cynical, or spurred by the upheavals of the 1960s. Or some combination of the three. For members to ignore all of the concerns about athletes' rights and possible abuses by coaches that had been expressed on the convention floor between 1965 and 1969, they must have had the recent racial protests on their minds in 1973. Even Swank in 1969 had conceded that, if coaches and athletic directors had complete control, they would abuse it. As he put it, the NCAA would have to "prevent the 'runoff.'" Why the turnabout four years later? The shift was not a landslide; majorities had approved the earlier proposals, just not large enough for passage. "Dead wood" had been a problem since athletic scholarships were first approved. Coaches and athletic directors had wanted more power for years without winning over enough NCAA delegates for the required supermajority.

The case is circumstantial, but the circumstances seem compelling. By 1973 black athletes with "attitude" were becoming the norm. A new model of black masculinity scorned subservience and insisted on black pride. Although confrontations with coaches had ended, all tensions did not suddenly dissolve. In his history of the rivalry between Woody Hayes and Bo Schembechler, Michael Rosenberg mentions an incident in the 1972 season when some of Ohio State's black players met with Hayes to complain that he favored white players.[20] If black college athletes would confront Woody Hayes—Woody Hayes!—they would confront anyone.

Because such incidents were not reported in the press, the tension in the relations between coaches and their black players cannot be documented. But it is doubtful that simple peace and harmony prevailed. In addition, for white Americans, race was becoming a particularly awkward and painful subject—blunt racism no longer permissible and black rights no longer deniable—while open talk of racial matters was a sure way to inflame antagonism. As Byers later admitted in his memoir, "The problems associated with the stepped-up college recruitment of black athletes was a sensitive issue that we preferred not to discuss in public."[21] The silence about race on the convention floor in January 1973, and for that matter in Byers's account of the "Riots of the Sixties" in his memoir more than twenty years later—despite its startling frankness on many other matters—is as telling as the convention debate in 1969.

The alternative explanations are even less flattering: that those who ran college football merely gave in to the cynical exploitation of their athletes or willed themselves not to think about the impact on the athletes of a decision driven solely by economic considerations. If in fact they were simply ignoring the consequences, it would not be the last time.

A NEW FOOTBALL WORLD

The one-year scholarship changed nothing and changed everything. In some ways it seems more symbolic than actual, though powerfully symbolic. By making renewal of scholarships contingent on athletic performance, it absolutely put the lie to all pretenses about the primary importance of *student-athletes*. How can academics be the highest priority if a scholarship is contingent on satisfying the football coach? In practice, coaches could not act as ruthlessly as the one-year scholarship permitted, if for no other reason than that a reputation for ruthlessness would be disastrous for recruiting. The economic expense for universities was also unchanged: a full quota of scholarships cost the same whether the athletes had one-year or four-year grants. I suspect that for a long time after 1973, most college football fans continued to assume that scholarship athletes received four-year "full rides." Many likely still believe that today. Most scholarship athletes have in fact continued to be funded for four years, five when necessary, though how many are not renewed is known only within athletic departments. There has been no federal mandate or public outcry to publish scholarship-renewal stats along with graduation rates.

But the impact of the one-year scholarship was also real and consequential. Most simply and obviously, it allowed coaches to quietly discard their "dead wood" each year. In 1981 Allen Sack surveyed 188 athletes at four Connecticut universities and found that 49 percent of the men feared losing their scholarships "if they did not perform to a coach's expectation."[22] That figure would surely have been at least as high at the football powerhouses around the country. Initially, the one-year scholarship also guaranteed that there would be no more racial protests or resistance to coaches' and athletic-department regulations. But as salaries in the NFL rose dramatically, the likelihood of such protest diminished anyway because the stakes were spectacularly raised for future draftees (as well as those with illusions of pro careers). Over time, in a perfect illustration of the Law of Unintended Consequences, the real significance of the one-year scholarship came in allowing coaches to make increasing demands on their athletes' time, while the athletes were essentially powerless to object. College football players in the early 1960s sometimes quit the team when they saw football interfering with their academic priorities while not delivering enough satisfaction in return. But they kept their scholarships. That changed in 1967; after 1973, they could not even complain, let alone quit. Who would risk losing his scholarship by defying, or even questioning, a coach's authority?

In 1973 the one-year scholarship redefined student-athletes as athlete-students. Within a very short time, then increasingly over the coming years, the implications of this redefinition would become clearer even as its origins were forgotten.

PART II LIVING WITH A CONTRADICTION

REVENUE AND REFORM

The one-year scholarship was part of a package of NCAA legislation in 1972 and 1973 that radically altered college sports.[1] In 1972
the NCAA made freshmen in football and basketball eligible for
varsity competition (as athletes in the "minor" sports had been
since 1968). Then in 1973, as noted earlier, in addition to instituting the one-year scholarship, the organization rescinded the so-
called 1.6 rule, now requiring only that an incoming scholarship freshman have earned a 2.0 grade-point average in his high school courses,
whether physics or wood shop. First approved at the 1965 convention,
the 1.6 rule had used a combination of grades and test scores to predict
a college grade-point average of at least 1.6. To the casual observer, the
2.0 requirement might have looked more rigorous, but in fact it opened
the door to recruiting virtually any athlete the football coach wanted.
Suddenly, with the new 2.0 standard, blue-chip athletes, regardless of
their academic preparation, could be admitted with scholarships; with
freshmen now eligible, they immediately faced the pressures of a ten-
game (and later eleven-, twelve-, thirteen-game) varsity schedule; and
with one-year scholarships, their primary responsibility was to please
their coaches, not their professors. Finally, in a special session in August
1973, the NCAA divided its membership into Divisions I, II, and III. The
schools most committed to big-time football could now begin to legis-
late for themselves.

The consequences should have shocked no one. Some of the news
over the next few years was old, such as the five-part series in the *New
York Times* (the first two installments on the front page) on the "frenzied
'slave market' in recruiting and paying athletes" in order to succeed in a
"win or else" world of "runaway professionalism."[2] But some of the news
was new. Coincidentally(?!), 1972 was also the first year of fully integrated
football, as the last of the Southeastern Conference schools joined the
rest of the football world. The racial transformation of college football

in the 1970s was not accompanied by a comparable academic transformation of the high schools from which the new waves of black football players were coming. Black athletes became disproportionately the beneficiaries of the NCAA's lower admission standards, which therefore disproportionately exploited them. Scandals in college football always seem to come from nowhere, but sometimes they are the predictable effects of distinct causes. Having admitted talented athletes with sixth- or seventh-grade reading, writing, and math skills and made football (or basketball) their top priority, what were universities to do with them in the classroom?

One answer, as the public began to learn within just a few years, was to give athletes credits for courses they did not take or passing grades they did not earn. At several western universities (New Mexico, Utah, Oregon, Oregon State, Arizona State, and San Jose State), athletes maintained their eligibility by enrolling in summer-school classes offered by institutions such as Ottawa University in Kansas and Rocky Mountain College in Billings, Montana, that required neither attendance nor work. During the 1970s, the USC athletic department admitted "330 scholastically deficient athletes," mostly football players, independently of the university's admission process, then kept many of them eligible through devices such as credits for a phony Speech course. At Georgia, the athletic department ran its own laboratory in the university's Developmental Studies Program to circumvent normal academic requirements, several football players remained eligible for a bowl game by receiving credit for a remedial course they failed, and athletes miraculously received good grades in advanced classes after failing remedial course work in the same subjects. When Jan Kemp, an English instructor teaching in Georgia's Developmental Studies Program, protested to the administration, she was fired. Kemp sued, and after the university lost a $1.1 million settlement (reduced from an original award of $2.57 million), the board of trustees commissioned a report that found "a pattern of academic abuse in the admission and advancement of student-athletes at the University of Georgia" due to "pressure from the athletic department" and "with the knowledge of the university's president." Two high-level administrators were fired, and the president resigned.[3]

These are just highlights (or lowlights) from a steady stream of such reports. Bogus credits and unearned grades are just unethical practices until public exposure makes them "scandals." The phony summer-school credits and the lawsuit against Georgia were front-page stories in the *New York Times* and were reported in every major newspaper in the country. The USC mess ran for several days in the sports sections of the *Times* and other papers. *Sports Illustrated* splashed "The Shame of American Education: The Student-Athlete Hoax" across its cover for May 19, 1980, over an image of a brick school building with "Rip Off" scrawled graffiti-style across its face. Inside, John Underwood gathered the dispiriting reports on academic chicanery from recent months into a scathing indictment of the entire system of intercollegiate athletics.[4]

Scandal nullifies the entire purpose of funding a big-time football program to promote the university, and no Division I institution would have welcomed the scrutiny that Georgia and USC received in the early 1980s. The NCAA did not release graduation rates in these years, and for good reason. After minimal admission standards let academically unprepared athletes in, lax eligibility rules too often kept them in school for four years on credits in fluff courses that left many of them not even close to graduating. In the 1982 survey of 188 male and female athletes at four Connecticut universities cited earlier, Allen Sack found that 42 percent felt pressure to major in less-demanding subjects, and 48 percent "said they were encouraged to take easy courses." If this was happening in Connecticut, with no big-time football programs at the time, imagine the situation in the Southeastern Conference or even the Big Ten.[5]

Scandal begets reform—in this case Proposition 48, passed by the NCAA at its convention in January 1983 as a group of college presidents under the auspices of the American Council on Education attempted to reassert academic principles within the NCAA.[6] Prop 48 set requirements for initial eligibility, in effect restoring the principle of the 1.6 rule but with higher standards. To receive a scholarship and be eligible to play as a freshman, a recruit had to have a 2.0 grade-point average in eleven core high school courses (that is, English, math, science, and social studies, not wood shop and welding), as well as a score of at least 700 on the Scholastic Aptitude Test (SAT).

Unfortunately, in the now thoroughly integrated world of college athletics, reform begets charges of racial discrimination. Those most affected by the lower admission requirements had been African American athletes with poor academic backgrounds. Now they were disproportionately affected by the tougher rules. Prominent black basketball coaches and the presidents of several historically black colleges, backed by national leaders such as Jesse Jackson, accused the NCAA of racism in approving Prop 48. At issue was not the core curriculum but the SAT, which had long been challenged for its cultural bias. A front-page story in the *New York Times* reported that less than half of all black high school students, not just athletes, who had taken the SAT in recent years had scored at least 700 (more than 75 percent of white students had achieved that score). Not all black leaders disapproved of raising requirements. Harry Edwards, since 1968 the leading critic of racism in American sports, had for years been charging universities with exploiting their black athletes. Consistent with that campaign, Edwards now approved the NCAA's move and decried the black opposition. To Edwards, the objections to the new rules were "misguided" and "underestimate[d] the intellectual capabilities of black athletes." With three years to go before implementation, black high school athletes had time to prepare, and Edwards believed that as standards went up, black athletes would rise to meet them, resulting in more academic success in college.[7]

Of course Proposition 48 disproportionately affected African American athletes; it was meant to address their disproportionately low graduation rates. Whether the SAT was the proper mechanism was less certain. It is hard to sympathize with university leaders embarrassed by academic fraud in their athletic departments after permitting the conditions that led to the fraud. It is hard *not* to sympathize when their efforts to raise academic standards are condemned as "patently racist," but this was the world of intercollegiate athletics post-1960s, in which opportunity and exploitation had become deeply entangled. Most universities in the late 1960s and early 1970s lowered admission requirements for minority students in general out of the laudable desire to begin correcting for generations of discrimination by creating educational opportunities. The NCAA justified abolishing the 1.6 rule in 1973 on these terms (instead of admitting the actual motives). When scandal hit USC in 1980, the school's president, John Hubbard, defended the athletic department's independent handling of its own admissions as part of the university's "minority access program." Football coach John Robinson declared that not admitting exceptions to the usual entry requirements would be "almost a racial move." From the opposing camp, Joe Paterno insisted that Proposition 48 was not a "race problem. For 15 years we've had a race problem. . . . We've told black kids who bounce balls, run around tracks and catch touchdown passes that that is an end unto itself. . . . We can't afford to do it to another generation." After 1973, whatever the NCAA did or did not do about academic standards most affected the African American athletes who increasingly dominated football and men's basketball.[8]

Lower admission standards in themselves meant neither opportunity nor exploitation. In principle, educational opportunity was real as long as the athlete was capable of seizing it. It turned to exploitation if no amount of remedial course work and tutoring could bring him into the academic mainstream. In practice, the distinction was messier. A professor at USC at the time of that school's scandals determined that 29 percent of the university's black athletes were graduating, compared to 51 percent of all athletes, and that they were channeled into courses such as Special Problems in Speech Communication—taken for varying credits, depending on how many were needed—that kept them eligible but taught them nothing.[9] Bogus credits and doctored grades do not prevent exploitation, they only cover it up. But were all of these students exploited? Malcolm Moran of the *New York Times* interviewed one ex-Trojan who failed to graduate, played two years in the NFL, was now a janitor—and had no regrets. The university had given him what he wanted: an opportunity to play football that got him into the NFL.[10] Had he been a student-athlete, the university would have failed him, but as an athlete-student he might be considered a success. But what about the university itself in this case? What university wants to be known for preparing football players for janitorial service?

CONFLICTING PRIORITIES

Proposition 48 marked the beginning of a reform movement within the NCAA that has lurched into the twenty-first century, yet reform was by no means the only, or primary, business of the organization and its big-time football schools during these years. Sorting through the milestones of the past quarter century can yield parallel timelines (below). The two columns seem unrelated to each other, which is precisely the point, as is the fact that the list on the right is the longer one. With the left hand, as it were, universities with big-time football programs have attempted to raise academic standards and enhance educational experiences (as in the life-skills and student-athlete leadership programs) for the sake of both the athletes and their own institutional integrity (and reputation or "brand"); while with the right hand, they have worked to maximize their revenues in a dramatically changing commercial marketplace. The dilemma not yet squarely faced is the harsh reality that responding to the demands of the marketplace continuously undermines efforts at academic reform.

Ever since college football became a fully commercialized big-time

1976. The College Football Association (CFA) is formed.

1978. After dividing into University and College Divisions in 1968 and Divisions I, II, and III in 1973, the NCAA convention approves splitting 180 Division I schools into Division I-A (105 schools) and I-AA, effective in 1981, to give the big football powers more autonomy.

1981. Not yet satisfied, the College Football Association breaks from the NCAA to sign its own TV contract with CBS and supports a lawsuit filed by the University of Oklahoma and the University of Georgia against the NCAA's TV monopoly.

1982. Jackie Sherrill signs a six-year contract with Texas A&M for more than $1.7 million ($287,000 a year).

1983. Proposition 48 is passed (to go into effect in 1986), requiring a score of 700 on the SAT plus a 2.0 GPA in eleven core high school classes.

1984. The Supreme Court upholds the CFA-backed suit, ending the NCAA's control of television rights.

1987. The USF&G Sugar Bowl (first game played on January 1, 1988) becomes the first major bowl with a corporate sponsor (the Rose Bowl holds out the longest, until 1999). Also, the opening of Georgia's $12 million Heritage Hall begins an "arms race" to build ever more extravagant athletic facilities.

1989. Proposition 42 refines Proposition 48 by forbidding financial aid for "partial qualifiers" (those with the required GPA or SAT score, but not both), who cannot receive scholarships until they are sophomores in good academic standing.

1990. Responding to furious opposition, the NCAA rescinds Proposition 42, allowing partial qualifiers to receive need-based financial aid but not athletic scholarships.

1991. The NCAA's "Reform Convention," led by university presidents, shortens seasons and limits the number of weekly hours coaches can require of their athletes to twenty during the season and eight during the off-season. The Knight Commission on Intercollegiate Athletics also issues its first report, offering specific proposals for reform and more generally calling on presidents to assert greater control. Subsequent reports appear in 1992, 1993, and 2001.

1992. Proposition 16 (amended in 1995, implemented in 1996) modifies Proposition 48 again, this time by creating a sliding scale of SAT scores and GPAs and by increasing the number of required high-school core courses from eleven to thirteen. In response to a new federal requirement, the NCAA releases its first report of graduation rates: 47 percent for all football players, 56

1990. Notre Dame breaks with the CFA to sign its own TV contract with NBC, triggering conference realignments that begin with Penn State's admission to the Big Ten (to begin play in 1995). In 1991 the Big East adds the University of Miami and becomes a football as well as basketball conference. In 1992 the SEC adds Arkansas and South Carolina, and in 1996 the Big Eight adds four teams from the former Southwest Conference (Texas, Texas A&M, Texas Tech, and Baylor) to become the Big 12. In 2003 Miami, Virginia Tech, and Boston College leave the Big East for the ACC and are replaced by Cincinnati, Louisville, and South Florida.

1991. At the same convention, the NCAA also passes cost-cutting measures, including the creation of a "restricted-earnings" coaching position that is challenged in court and leads in May 1998 to an award of $67 million to the affected coaches (with the NCAA settling in March 1999 for $54 million and dropping its appeal).

1992. The Bowl Coalition is created, involving four major bowls (Cotton, Fiesta, Orange, and Sugar) and five major conferences (without the Big Ten and the Pac-10), along with major independents such as Notre Dame, for the purpose of matching the two top-rated teams in a championship game. The Bowl Coalition is replaced by the Bowl Alliance in 1995 (involving four conferences, percent for whites, and 35 percent for blacks

Notre Dame, and three bowls), then by the Bowl Championship Series (BCS) in 1998 (for the first time including the Rose Bowl and the Big Ten and Pac-10 conferences), with a putative national championship game rotating among the Rose, Orange, Sugar, and Fiesta Bowls.

1994. The NCAA and the National Association of Collegiate Directors of Athletics inaugurate the CHAMPS Life Skills Program, and in 1997 they create an offshoot: the NCAA Foundation Student-Athlete Leadership Conference.

1995. Florida State's Bobby Bowden becomes college football's first $1 million coach.

1997. Partial qualifiers are granted four years of eligibility. At the same time, a lawsuit (*Cureton v. NCAA*) is filed on behalf of two African American high school students denied athletic scholarships under Proposition 16. In March 1999 a district court judge rules that Prop 16 is discriminatory because of its "disparate impact" on African Americans, but in December 1999 the Third Circuit Court overturns this ruling on the basis that the NCAA is not a direct recipient of federal funds and thus not subject to Title VI requirements of the Civil Rights Act of 1964.

1997. Florida's Steve Spurrier becomes college football's first $2 million coach.

1998. In the first year of the BCS, the payout to participants in each of the four BCS bowls is $12.5 million; for the eighteen other bowls, payouts range from $750,000 to $3.6 million (thirteen of them paying less than $1.5 million, not enough to cover most teams' expenses).

2001. Twenty-two coaches now have salaries of at least $1 million.

2005. The NCAA institutes the Academic Progress Rate (APR), which measures eligibility and retention, with programs losing scholarships for falling below a minimum score. The first penalties are assessed in 2006, with twenty-three football programs losing scholarships—none of them from BCS conferences.

2005–2006. Under threat of possible congressional action, BCS leaders announce a series of changes that add an additional championship game and increase possible access to BCS bowls for the lesser Division I-A conferences. Oklahoma's Bob Stoops becomes the first $3 million coach.

2006. A presidential task force of the NCAA releases a report urging universities to practice fiscal responsibility and restraint. *USA Today* reports that the average Division I-A coach's salary is $950,000, with at least forty-two coaches earning $1 million and nine earning $2 million or more.

2007. Alabama makes Nick Saban possibly the NCAA's first $4 million coach (reports vary between $3.5 million and $4 million).

2008. Beginning in the fall term, the NCAA requires sixteen core courses for initial eligibility in Division I.

2008. ESPN outbids Fox for the rights to the BCS bowls, increasing Fox's current payment by roughly 50 percent.

---

sport in the 1920s, critics have routinely derided university leaders as hypocrites. It might be more accurate to assume that most of them have been utterly sincere in contradicting themselves. No doubt, the great majority of college presidents have genuinely desired their athletes to earn diplomas and even receive a good education. At the same time, or rather on different occasions, these same leaders have been wholly committed to whatever it takes to produce winning teams and maximize revenues, if for no other reason than to free the institution from having to subsidize athletics. Perhaps they have been guided by the wisdom of Jesus, who enjoined his followers when giving alms to "let not thy left hand know what thy right hand doeth" (Matt. 6:3). Facetiousness aside, university presidents wholly comfortable with the contradiction at the heart of college football have likely been rare.

The fundamental contradiction of an extracurricular activity conducted as mass entertainment has been compounded by the inherent messiness of democratic institutions. The "corruption" of college athletics decried by the Carnegie Foundation in 1929 was most evident in the recruiting and subsidizing of brawny working-class youths who would not otherwise have been in college at all. Calls for academic reform have always addressed the problems raised by athletes who do not "belong" in college. In the 1920s they were the sons of Italian and Polish immigrants who "belonged" in a steel mill or coal mine but, through college football, entered the great American middle class instead. Since the 1960s these outsiders have been the children of African American families struggling to survive in our urban and rural wastelands.

In 1987 the NCAA commissioned its first (and still only) study of the experience of black football and basketball players at Division I institutions. Published in March 1989 by the American Institutes for Research in Palo Alto, the study provided statistical confirmation for what observers of college sports already knew: blacks were overrepresented as athletes (37 percent of football players, compared to 12 percent of the U.S. population and 4 percent of undergraduates at Division I institutions); black football and basketball players arrived at college less academically prepared (58 percent at or below 752 on the SAT, compared to 19 percent of whites, and 61 percent with a high school GPA of B– or below, compared to 31 percent of whites); and they came from lower socioeconomic backgrounds (49 percent in the lowest quartile compared to 13 percent of whites). On overwhelmingly white campuses, more than two-thirds of the black athletes reported feeling different from other students, about a half felt racial isolation and a lack of control over their lives, and a third had experienced at least six incidents of racial discrimination.[11] Division I institutions clearly had not yet figured out how to make black athletes belong at their universities or even help them feel that they belong.

Insofar as the NCAA reacted, its response was to continue a reform movement already under way. After Proposition 48 went into effect for the 1986 season, college football fans learned to count not just the "blue-chippers" in their team's recruiting class but also the "qualifiers" and "nonqualifiers," those who could suit up as freshmen and those who would have to take a detour through junior college or wait a year to compete. A large portion of the nonqualifiers were African American. The next step in raising standards, Proposition 42, denied financial aid to nonqualifiers, who would have to pay their own expenses while becoming eligible. Immediate and furious opposition from black leaders and coaches forced the NCAA to rescind Prop 42, but two years later, Proposition 16 raised the bar again. In addition to increasing the number of required high school core courses to thirteen, Prop 16 created a sliding scale of test scores and grade-point averages. Proposition 48 had required a 700 SAT score and a 2.0 grade-point average in eleven core courses. Under Proposition 16, a student with a 2.0 GPA needed a 1010 SAT to play as a freshman, while an 820 SAT was sufficient if the GPA was at least 2.5. (An 820 was equivalent to a 700 after the Educational Testing Service "recentered" its scores.) On the one hand, Prop 16 responded to the criticism of standardized tests by weighting the SAT less heavily in relation to high school grades. On the other hand, it required more academic course work for incoming freshmen athletes.

A "disparate impact" on African Americans was still obvious. A report from the National Center for Education Statistics calculated that, while 83.2 percent of 1992 college-bound high school seniors—athletes and nonathletes alike—met the requirements of Proposition 48, only 64.7 percent qualified under Proposition 16. Among African Americans, the figure was 46.4 percent, and 42 percent for those at the lowest socioeconomic level.[12] The leaders of the NCAA understood this. In an internal memorandum, the subcommittee working on rules for initial eligibility acknowledged that "African-American and low income student-athletes have been disproportionately impacted by Proposition 16 standards." Enrollment data showed "a drop in the proportion of African-Americans among first-year scholarship athletes in Division I from 23.6 percent to 20.3 percent."[13]

At the same time, graduation rates for black football players were climbing. The six-year graduation rate for African American freshmen entering universities with Division I-A football programs in 1984 (that is, graduating by 1990) was 35 percent. The rate for those entering in 1986, the first year under Proposition 48, was 43 percent—still abysmally low but a significant increase. Over the next nine years, the figure hovered between 42 and 46 percent. For the class entering in 1996, the first year of Proposition 16, it jumped again to 49 percent, where it has more or less stabilized. In each year, black football players graduated at a higher rate than black male students overall (by between 2 and 10 percent). They also continued to graduate at a lower rate than their white teammates—the difference ranging from 12 to 21 percent—and than male students overall by a comparable range. In general, since the entering freshman class in 1986, the graduation rate for black football players has fluctuated between 43 and 50 percent, with an overall rising trend; the rate for white players has stayed mostly between 60 and 62 percent, dropping as low as 55 and rising as high as 67 percent.[14]

All of these figures were calculated by the method mandated by the federal government, which marks schools down for transfers, even those who leave in good academic standing. When the NCAA in 2005 developed its own Graduation Success Rate (GSR) to account for transfers, athletes' performance instantly rose several percentage points in relation to the general student population's. The NCAA, however, did not calculate comparable GSRs for nonathletes, many of whom leave school in good academic standing for personal or financial reasons. Also, the GSR does not downgrade programs, as the federal calculation does, for not renewing an athlete's scholarship—discarding the "dead wood," as they would have said in the 1960s—effectively forcing him to transfer. Whether the federal rate or the GSR is a better measure of a program's academic commitment to student-athletes is not altogether clear.

If we consider just the increase from 35 to 49 or 50 percent in the graduation rates of black football players by the federal method, compared to a rise from 56 to 60 or 62 percent for whites over the same period, academic reform would seem to have had a "disparate impact" on African Americans—to their advantage. Just not disparate enough. The NCAA withstood a legal challenge to Proposition 16—the *Cureton* case, settled in the NCAA's favor in 1999—not on a judgment that it was nondiscriminatory but on a technical ruling that the NCAA as a private organization was not subject to the antidiscriminatory provisions of civil rights law.[15] The court, in effect, left the NCAA to struggle with revising its own legislation. The objections to reliance on standardized test scores remained after *Cureton*, as did the question of what in Prop 48 and Prop 16 mattered, the test scores or the core courses, and the larger issues raised by graduation rates. Claiming credit for graduating black football players at higher rates than black nonathletes begged the question that, given the athletes' financial and academic support, should not their rates have been higher yet? And of course, while black athletes were graduating at increasingly higher rates, they still lagged well behind whites. African Americans were disproportionately the star players and disproportionately the nongraduates; it was the relationship between these two disproportions that remained most troubling.

A MADE-FOR-TV FOOTBALL WORLD

And what was the NCAA up to with its right hand all this time? While university presidents were asserting their control over the reform agenda in the 1990s, they and their athletic departments were also madly scrambling for profits, or just solvency, in an increasingly competitive entertainment market. This latest manifestation was just a continuation of college football's perennial contradiction, but on terms now that exceeded incremental developments to create a strikingly different football world.

Like academic scandals, $3 million coaches' salaries and $50 million athletic budgets do not result from inexorable external forces but from institutional actions. Over the 1960s and 1970s, the major football powers were continually frustrated over the smaller schools' equal power within the NCAA. The separation into two, then three, divisions, and the further separation of Division I-A from I-AA (now the Football Bowl Subdivision and the Football Championship Subdivision, in the marketing language recently adopted by the NCAA), were attempts by the NCAA to placate its most powerful members. Nothing the NCAA could or would do was enough, however, and in December 1976 the major football-playing conferences, with the exceptions of the Big Ten and Pacific-8 (the Pac-10 in 1978), along with the major independents (chiefly Notre Dame, Penn State, Pittsburgh, Florida State, and Miami), created the College Football Association (CFA) for the purpose of controlling their own football world. The absence of the Big Ten and Pac-10 eventually contributed to the demise of the CFA, but not before it had remade college football.[16]

The CFA included the Southeastern, Southwest, and Big Eight Conferences, along with the Atlantic Coast Conference and the Western Athletic Conference (there was no major eastern conference at the time). I say "along with" the ACC and WAC to single them out as the conferences that became "major" with the CFA. The WAC then became instantly "minor" when the CFA collapsed (to be effectively replaced by the Bowl Coalition in 1992, followed by the Bowl Alliance and then the Bowl Championship Series).[17] Joe Kearney, commissioner of the WAC, foresaw this outcome early on. In 1981, after eight of his nine conference teams voted against the CFA's first attempt to sign a television contract independently of the

NCAA, Kearney told reporters that "nobody is kidding us in the W.A.C. We're the nine teams that are the numbers 53 through 61 on the C.F.A. totem pole and when the next cut to an even more elite group of powerful football teams comes, we will be the first lopped off."[18]

Although absent from the announcements of its founding, television revenue was the driving issue for the CFA. As historian John Watterson has reconstructed events, a move in 1974 by the president of Cal State Long Beach, Stephen Horn, to force broader distribution of football TV revenue precipitated the meeting that led to the formation of the CFA.[19] Horn's proposal was defeated, and the big-time football schools continued to receive most of the TV dollars, but as long as the NCAA negotiated television contracts for the entire organization, the football powers would feel vulnerable. When the CFA made its move in 1981, attempting to sign its own contract with NBC, the NCAA managed to block that effort in court. In response, the CFA backed an antitrust lawsuit in the names of the universities of Georgia and Oklahoma, which the Supreme Court ultimately decided in the CFA's favor on June 27, 1984. More than any other single date, this one marks the beginning of the college football world we have today.

Initially, after winning its case, the CFA looked woefully shortsighted. The NCAA had indeed enjoyed a monopoly, and its contracts with ABC, CBS, and ESPN would have paid member schools $73.6 million for the 1984 season. The NCAA had controlled the product, and the networks had paid premium rates for exclusive rights. Now, the CFA had to negotiate its own deal separately from the Big Ten and Pac-10, in a more cluttered, nonexclusive, and regional rather than national TV football marketplace. The CFA signed with ABC and ESPN for a total of $22 million, while the Big Ten and Pac-10 agreed to a joint deal with CBS for $10 million.[20] Individual conferences made additional arrangements with cable networks and local stations for leftover games, with the lesser conferences scrambling for whatever they could get through cable. (Among its corollary effects, the CFA was a boon for cable.)

Once the dust settled, three times as many football games were televised in 1984 as in 1983, but for $25 million less in total revenue.[21] Television income for the Big Eight fell from $6.1 million to $3.8 million; for the SEC, from $11.2 million to $7.5 million. Individual football powers saw comparable declines: for Alabama, from $1.924 million to $764,000; for UCLA, from $1.238 million to $735,317; for Oklahoma, from $1.276 million to $753,208.[22] A televised game was now worth about $300,000 for each team, rather than $700,000; and instead of *The Game of the Week*, Saturdays were now cluttered with five or more games as scarcity instantly gave way to oversaturation.[23] TV ratings for individual games dropped 35 percent from 1981 to 1986, while average attendance dropped as well, from 43,689 in 1982 to 41,170 in 1992, as local teams had to compete with football powerhouses on television.[24] The thirteen or fourteen games now televised (on the West Coast, anyway) from 9:00 in the morning until 10:00 at night on football Saturdays, perhaps one or two of them worth watching, is an expansion of the market unleashed by the CFA.

Less-lucrative overall TV rights continued for several years after the NCAA lost control. In four-year deals for 1987–90, the CFA's contracts with CBS and ESPN paid about $32.5 million per season, while the Big Ten/Pac-10 agreement with ABC was worth about $12.5 million, for a total of $45 million—substantially more than in 1984 but still far short of the NCAA's voided package.[25] In his history of the regulation and deregulation of television rights in college football, Keith Dunnavant estimates that colleges lost at least $200 million over the first ten years of deregulation.[26] Nearly all of the revenue was going to the big-time football conferences, however, fueling the radical division of the NCAA into economic haves and have-nots in the 1990s.

The next stage in creating a new economic order began in January 1990, when Notre Dame broke from the CFA to sign its own contract with NBC. Notre Dame had always gone its own way on certain matters. It became college football's first truly national team in the 1920s out of the necessity of scheduling intersectional opponents due to disdain (and anti-Catholicism) among key Big Ten leaders. With "subway alumni" throughout the country as a result, Notre Dame continued charging no fees for radio rights into the 1940s, long after other schools began seeking their best deal, in order to nourish its national constituency rather than take the small profits. And with the University of Pennsylvania as its only ally, Notre Dame fought a losing battle against the NCAA's initial control of TV rights in the early 1950s. Media rights were just the focal point for an institutional perspective. Notre Dame had risen to prominence as a beacon for despised working-class Catholic immigrants. As bigotry gave way to mere resentment of the school's football dominance in the post–World War II era, Notre Dame came to relish its outsider position.[27]

When I played at Notre Dame in the late 1960s, we were still symbolically the "Christians" taking on the "lions"—the superior athletes at Michigan State and USC. With its own TV contract in 1990, Notre Dame instantly became the lions to a large portion of the college football public. Sportswriters in much of the country vilified the new Notre Dame—arrogant, self-serving, and greedy—for destroying the competitive balance in college football. (With its own TV contract, the Irish would presumably have a recruiting advantage over every other school.) Notre Dame had been the most powerful cohesive force in the CFA; now it was acting entirely in its own interests, because the proposed CFA contract with ABC would have left Notre Dame with too many regional, rather than national, telecasts.[28] Notre Dame's self-interests were not limited to football (the windfall from NBC did not pour into athletics but into the university's general fund, which allocated a portion to the athletic department), but the impact on the CFA was disastrous.

In chronicling the relationship of college football to television, Dunnavant judges Notre Dame's action to have been an inevitable extension of the CFA's initial rebellion. Once universities demanded more autonomy to seek their rightful market share, the CFA coalition could not hold, because CFA members and conferences were not equally marketable. With the end of the NCAA's monopoly in 1984, Notre Dame had in fact been immediately offered its own TV contract but turned it down.[29] The SEC nearly signed a separate television deal in 1987 (with Notre Dame ironically playing the key role in preserving solidarity). Father Joyce, who served as one of the CFA's leading spokesmen from the beginning, set Notre Dame's athletic policy in these years (in consultation with his boss, Father Hesburgh). A new administration in 1990 made a decision that Fathers Joyce and Hesburgh likely would not have endorsed.[30]

Inevitable or not, Notre Dame's break from the CFA in 1990 triggered a "structural upheaval unprecedented in the history of college athletics."[31] Only Notre Dame could command its own television contract; for everyone else, conferences were the key. By June, the *New York Times* was reporting (on the front page) that college football insiders envisioned perhaps three "superconferences," each with its own television network.[32] The *Times* might not have gotten all of the details right, but it accurately predicted the general outline. The SEC and Big Ten were already making plans to expand (Arkansas and South Carolina would begin play in the SEC in 1992, Penn State in the Big Ten in 1995); and in 1996 the Big Eight became the Big 12 by adding four teams (Texas, Texas A&M, Texas Tech, and Baylor) from the suddenly defunct Southwest Conference.

(The other four teams— Rice, Southern Methodist, Texas Christian, and Houston, a recent replacement for Arkansas—instantly dropped from the "major" ranks.) In addition, the Big East, a basketball conference since 1979, became a made-for-TV football conference in 1990, initially with weak football teams but strong TV markets. (The launching of the Big Ten Network in 2007 partially fulfilled another part of the insiders' prediction in 1990, but the SEC in 2008 opted for hugely inflated contracts with CBS and ESPN over creating its own network, too.)

In 1990 Murray Sperber wrote that "intercollegiate athletics has become College Sports Inc., a huge commercial entertainment conglomerate, with operating methods and objectives totally separate from, and mainly opposed to, the educational aims of the schools that house its franchises."[33] And this was before college football was dramatically restructured in the 1990s.

The first real payoff from deregulation, and the fatal stroke to the CFA, came in 1994, when CBS reacted to losing its NFL rights to Fox by offering the SEC $85 million over five years, more than double the conference's take under the expiring CFA contracts. Once the SEC went its own way, the Big 12 ($57.5 million from ABC), ACC ($54 million from ABC), and Big East ($56 million from CBS) followed. Now the WAC, whose Brigham Young had won a (controversial) national championship in 1984, was relegated to cableland along with the rest of the dregs of Division I-A. In the summer of 1997, having unleashed the market forces that now ruled college football but doomed itself, the CFA disbanded.[34]

THE BCS AND COLLEGE FOOTBALL
FOR THE NEW CENTURY

Its legacy remains in the Bowl Championship Series (BCS), the latest arrangement for guaranteeing that the big-time football powers receive all that they are due. From one perspective, the BCS simply consolidated the realignment that began with the CFA and was continued by the Bowl Coalition in 1992, which included the SEC, ACC, Big Eight, Southwest Conference, and Big East but not the WAC. In 1995 the Bowl Coalition was replaced by the Bowl Alliance, without the Southwest Conference now; then in 1998 the BCS for the first time reunited the Big Ten and Pac-10 with the original CFA renegades. In one sense, all three bowl arrangements merely recognized the preexisting inequality within college football, except in the case of the Big East, whose inclusion demonstrated absolutely that television ran the show. While BYU became a "minor" football program (euphemistically called a "mid-major") despite its 60,000-seat stadium, Temple and Rutgers became "major" solely because they resided in valuable TV markets. The power of the BCS to transform the world of college football then became even clearer in 2003, when the defection of Miami, Virginia Tech, and Boston College from the Big East to the ACC made the ACC for the first time the equal of any football conference in the country and worthy of a $258 million, seven-year TV contract. Within three years, the ACC's overall revenue increased 44.5 percent, while the Big East, deprived of its most legitimate football programs, saw revenues increase only 4.8 percent.[35] Nonetheless, the power of the market itself enabled Louisville, West Virginia, Rutgers, and even South Florida to boast top-20 programs by 2007, able to compete for the best high school players by promising the TV and bowl exposure that recruits with NFL dreams expect. The Big East Conference is arguably the single best indicator of how television has changed college football since the 1990s.

The BCS instantly became powerful both as a symbol of the division between the upper and lower regions of Division I-A and as a new instrument for maintaining that boundary. Though purporting to be a system for naming a national champion in the absence of a playoff tournament, the BCS more importantly provided a mechanism for divvying up hugely inflated bowl revenues in this new college football world. With the 1984 Supreme Court decision, the major football powers seized control of television from the NCAA. With the BCS in 1998, television took greater control of college football. The commissioners of the major football conferences created the framework for the BCS, but as Keith Dunnavant puts it, ABC was "the driving force of the new partnership." The network's offer of $500 million for the four BCS bowls over seven years, with average payouts initially of about $12 million per team, elevated the four major bowls above the lesser bowls more dramatically than ever before and made the pursuit of a BCS bowl bid an obsession throughout Division I-A.[36]

According to calculations by *USA Today*, over the first six years of the BCS (1998–2003), the six major conferences took in 93 percent of total BCS revenue and 89 percent of all bowl revenue, while the five mid-majors (Conference USA, Mountain West, Western Athletic, Mid-American, and Big West–Sun Belt[37]) claimed just 4 percent from the BCS (the remaining 3 percent went to Notre Dame and Division I-AA) and 9 percent of the overall total. *USA Today*'s Steve Wieberg pointed out that in 1997, the last pre-BCS season, the major football conferences actually took in a higher percentage of bowl revenue—94 percent.[38] Both before and after the creation of the BCS, the major conferences included all of the football programs most desired by bowl committees and television networks. But the BCS did two things that widened the absolute gap between the major and lesser football conferences. It increased the disparity between the payouts for the top bowls and all the others, while at the same time guaranteeing that the football elite would continue to take home nearly all of this greatly increased revenue. The Sugar Bowl, for example, paid each participating team $3.7 million in 1992 (1991 season). The following year, the first under the Bowl Coalition, the payout rose modestly to $4.15 million, then to $4.45 million in 1994. In 1995, under the new Bowl Alliance, it jumped to $7.8 million. In 1998, under the BCS, it grew to $12.5 million. (The Orange and Fiesta Bowls saw similar increases, as all three finally reached the level of the Rose Bowl, long the most lucrative of the bowls.)[39]

Meanwhile, the Holiday Bowl, to take one typical contrasting example from the mid-range of bowls, increased its payout from $1.3 million in 1991 to $1.8 million in 1998, roughly a 50 percent increase, while the Sugar Bowl's already substantial payout more than tripled.[40] In 1991 the four major bowls (Rose, Orange, Sugar, and Cotton) accounted for roughly a quarter of total bowl payments; from 1998 through 2004, the BCS bowls (Rose, Orange, Sugar, and Fiesta) accounted for over two-thirds of more than twice as much annual revenue.[41] And almost all of it still went to BCS schools, which claim most of the slots in the best-paying non-BCS bowls, too. The payouts from well over half of the thirty-odd bowl games now played each season do not cover the competing schools' expenses. In effect, teams pay a fee of several hundred thousand dollars in exchange for (modest) renown and exposure. Proliferating low-end bowls have become the football equivalent of vanity presses for aspiring but not-very-talented authors.

Initially, the obstacles facing a non-BCS team to win a spot in a BCS bowl were enormous. Undefeated Utah finally broke through in 2004 (the 2005 Fiesta Bowl), only to lose its coach to a BCS team that had slipped from the top ranks. With athletic budgets bleeding red ink, college presidents outside the BCS, led by Tulane president Scott Cowan, then forced those who ran the BCS to add a fifth bowl game, a BCS National Championship Game—and thus two more at-large berths—beginning with the 2006 season. The outsiders won, but not at the expense of the football elite. In 2005–6, when the BCS conferences reclaimed all eight BCS bowl slots, they shared $118.9 million, or 94.4 percent of total BCS revenue. In 2006–7 and 2007–8, when Boise State and Hawaii grabbed BCS bowl slots, the BCS conferences' share dropped to 85 percent, but with the additional BCS bowl, that 85 percent was worth $122–123.5 million. For the 2007–8 bowl season, total revenue from BCS and non-BCS bowls was $221.9 million. Of that amount, the sixty-six BCS teams shared $188.3 million, an average of $2.85 million per school. The fifty-three non-BCS schools shared $31.8 million, an average of $600,000 apiece (but varying widely across conferences).[42] In 2008–9, when Utah became the first outsider to win a second trip to a BCS bowl, the selection of 10–2 and tenth-ranked Ohio State over 12–0 and ninth-ranked Boise State for the final slot maintained the status quo.

Because the additional BCS bowl provides a greater chance for a one-time infusion of revenue into one non-BCS conference at a time, the stakes for a non-BCS team (and its conference) on the verge of a BCS bowl bid are enormous. As *Sports Illustrated* pointed out before Utah played BYU on November 22, 2008, a win would put Utah in a BCS bowl and bring $10 million to the Mountain West Conference. A loss would send the Utes to the Poinsettia Bowl for $750,000.[43] Utah (and the Mountain West) won on this occasion; instead, undefeated Boise State (and the WAC) were relegated to the Poinsettia Bowl. Members of BCS conferences never lose.

The impact of receiving or not receiving a share of BCS bowl dollars varies hugely across the Football Bowl Subdivision (FBS). Consider the average football revenue for each of the BCS conferences in 2006–7 (from the data reported to the U.S. Department of Education):

- SEC: $38.2 million
- Big Ten: $33.7 million
- Big 12: $24.8 million
- Pac-10: $22.9 million
- ACC: $19.5 million
- Big East: $15.2 million

If a BCS bowl payout brings each conference school roughly $1 million, that $1 million represented 2.6 percent of total football revenues for SEC schools, but 6.6 percent for the Big East. Now consider the averages for non-BCS conferences:

- Mountain West: $7.0 million
- Conference USA: $6.9 million
- WAC: $5.2 million
- Sun Belt: $3.8 million
- Mid-American: $3.6 million

Here, if we add a $1 million BCS bowl payout to each conference, it would amount to between 12.5 and 21.7 percent of the new totals.

According to NCAA data, the total net bowl revenue (after deducting participating schools' expenses, that is) for the six BCS conferences in 2007–8 was $126 million, or $21 million per conference. The range was from $14.2 million for the Big East to $29 million for the SEC. For the five non-BCS conferences, the total was $13.4 million, or $2.7 million per conference. But Boise State's BCS bowl berth contributed most of the $7 million in profit for the WAC. The remaining four conferences shared $6.4 million; that's $1.6 million each.[44]

The disparate impact of the BCS is huge within the BCS conferences as well. Within the SEC, a $1 million guaranteed BCS payout was 1.7 percent of Georgia's $59.5 million in football revenue in 2006–7 but 8.3 percent of Mississippi State's $12.1 million. In the ACC, at the lower end of the BCS, that $1 million amounted to 2.5 percent of Virginia Tech's $40.6 million but 11 percent of Duke's $9 million. Year to year, the top teams earning BCS bowl berths come predominantly from a fairly small set of perennial superpowers that earn their rewards by having the strongest football teams. If the issue is fairness, it is hard to complain about them. The distorting impact of the BCS lies elsewhere — not just in the separation of non-BCS from BCS schools but also in the guaranteed BCS payout to the fifty-seven or fifty-eight schools from BCS conferences that do not go to a BCS bowl in any given year. The BCS system rewards mediocrity (and worse) as well as excellence for those with membership in the club. (And the superpowers do not suffer in off years, such as Michigan and Auburn experienced in 2008.) Those outside the club must get lucky, with one of their conference members snagging a rare BCS bowl berth.

The stakes, along with the distorting consequences, were raised in November 2008, when ESPN outbid Fox to televise the BCS bowls beginning in 2011. The cable network, which reaches 16 million fewer homes but receives subscription fees as well as advertising revenue, topped Fox's current payment by 50 percent, raising the likely bowl payout from

$18 million per team to $22 million or $23 million. Those negotiating for the BCS expected complaints from university presidents about putting the games on cable with fewer viewers. Apparently, no one balked.[45]

BIG-TIME COLLEGE FOOTBALL IN
THE TWENTY-FIRST CENTURY

Because of the controversies generated over its method for selecting bowl participants and its success or failure in determining an unambiguous national champion, the BCS is just the most visible part of the intensified commercializing of big-time college football since the 1990s, which also includes the proliferation of televised contests, corporate branding of stadiums and bowl games, institutional contracts with soft drink and shoe companies, huge expansion in the marketing of team-logo merchandise, lavish facilities to lure recruits to campus, and stadiums with luxury suites and seat licenses for the privilege of buying season tickets. Surprisingly, despite these ubiquitous signs of increasing commercialization, the overall economic growth of college athletics and college football actually slowed from the 1980s to the early 2000s. The NCAA has tracked athletic revenues and expenses since 1969 in a series of reports at several-year intervals (with varying degrees of reliability). From 1969 through 1981, the average football revenue (for all teams in whatever was equivalent to Division I-A at the time) increased at an average annual rate of 7.1 percent. From 1981 through 1993, the rate was 12.3 percent; from 1993 through 2003, it was 8.0 percent.[46]

The NCAA's most recent report, for 2004–6, used median rather than average revenues to eliminate the skewing by one-time large gifts from alumni and boosters—Oklahoma State's single gift of $240 million in 2006, for example—and to help university administrators see more clearly their institution's relative position. While the latest report will provide benchmarks for all future ones, it eliminates the possibility of direct comparisons to previous years. The growth of the *median* revenue from 2004 to 2005 was 8.7 percent (from $9.2 million to $10 million); from 2005 to 2006 ($11.6 million), it was 16 percent. The NCAA also refined the reporting methods by distinguishing revenues "generated" by the athletic department from those "allocated" by the state or the institution (in student fees, direct subsidy, or indirect support for maintenance and salaries). The median *generated* football revenue in 2006 was $10.6 million, up from $9.8 million in 2005 and $8.3 million in 2004.[47]

However growth is measured, the unevenness among institutions is what's most significant, with the growth at the high end creating the benchmark for the rest of the subdivision. In 2006 half of the 119 teams in the FBS generated less than $10.6 million in revenue each. The other half generated revenues ranging from $10.6 million to $63.7 million. During the years when the NCAA used averages rather than medians for its calculations, the largest football revenue in 1980 ($6.7 million) was 2.5 times the average revenue for the division ($2.7 million); the largest in 2003 ($52.7 million) was four times the average ($13 million). The latest report simply confirms the strikingly uneven distribution of revenues over this period. In 2006, 30 percent of FBS football programs generated less than $3.7 million in revenues. The next 20 percent generated between $3.7 million and $10.6 million; the next 30 percent, between $10.6 million and $23.2 million; and the top 20 percent, between $23.2 million and $63.7 million.

To break this down by individual institutions, we are dependent on the data reported to the U.S. Department of Education as mandated by the Equity in Athletics Disclosure Act for tracking compliance with Title IX. The NCAA reports only aggregate data (so as not to embarrass institutions whose administrators are being asked to reign in spending). The federal data are for each institution, but as reported by that institution however it sees fit—without the distinctions between "generated" and "allocated" revenues or consistency in reporting on indirect costs, capital expenses, and debt service. Although the numbers for any particular institution are less reliable than the aggregate data from the NCAA, the range across institutions nonetheless can reveal the overall inequality across the subdivision. Tables 1 and 2 rank sixty-six BCS and fifty non-BCS football programs by total football revenue in 2006–7, the most recent year for which data have been published. (Because the service academies are not required to submit reports, only fifty of fifty-three non-BCS schools are ranked.)

Sixty-one of sixty-six BCS teams claimed a profit on football, along with eighteen non-BCS teams. Forty-six BCS and twenty-three non-BCS schools claimed to make money on athletics overall. Knowledgeable observers in recent years have been estimating that, without institutional subsidies, somewhere between two and four dozen athletic departments actually break even or make a profit in any given year.[48] After some earlier partial attempts at greater clarity,[49] the NCAA now claims that fifty-six football programs (rather than seventy-nine) actually produced a profit in 2006; of those fifty-six, just nineteen generated enough to produce

TABLE 1. BCS FOOTBALL PROGRAMS RANKED BY TOTAL FOOTBALL REVENUE, 2006–2007

Institution	Conference	Football Revenue	Football Expenses
Texas	Big 12	$63,798,068	$17,565,006
Notre Dame		$63,675,034	$17,842,288
Georgia	SEC	$59,516,939	$16,372,291
Ohio State	Big Ten	$59,142,071	$32,538,319
Florida	SEC	$58,904,976	$20,691,405
Auburn	SEC	$56,830,516	$22,950,759
Alabama	SEC	$53,182,806	$21,340,593
Michigan	Big Ten	$50,982,629	$14,750,836
LSU	SEC	$48,141,751	$16,408,162
Iowa	Big Ten	$45,335,026	$28,851,512
Penn State	Big Ten	$44,014,052	$14,609,828
Arkansas	SEC	$42,056,467	$22,805,114
South Carolina	SEC	$41,275,362	$12,423,602
Michigan State	Big Ten	$40,795,755	$22,496,400
Virginia Tech	ACC	$40,634,499	$26,179,089
Oklahoma	Big 12	$37,263,255	$18,790,701
Texas A&M	Big 12	$37,123,296	$16,619,256
Wisconsin	Big Ten	$34,105,991	$19,771,064
Washington	Pac-10	$33,694,962	$13,765,662
Clemson	ACC	$32,029,237	$13,880,931
USC	Pac-10	$31,705,207	$18,699,944
Tennessee	SEC	$31,193,706	$13,903,184
Oregon State	Pac-10	$28,299,199	$11,740,804
Nebraska	Big 12	$26,264,849	$13,834,134
California	Pac-10	$26,001,075	$17,283,717
Georgia Tech	ACC	$25,331,130	$9,397,208
West Virginia	Big East	$25,174,217	$13,810,787
Purdue	Big Ten	$25,134,139	$13,680,599
UCLA	Pac-10	$23,539,593	$16,872,615
Arizona State	Pac-10	$23,519,742	$18,629,486
Colorado	Big 12	$23,101,126	$11,449,737
Kentucky	SEC	$21,898,082	$10,155,979
Kansas State	Big 12	$21,730,191	$10,209,079
Oregon	Pac-10	$21,495,626	$12,641,511
Texas Tech	Big 12	$20,827,440	$18,466,180

Football Profit/Loss	Total Revenue	Total Expenses	Overall Profit/Loss
$46,233,062	$105,048,632	$89,313,533	$15,735,099
$45,832,746	$83,586,903	$57,406,114	$26,180,789
$43,144,648	$75,937,460	$61,583,869	$14,353,591
$26,603,752	$109,382,222	$109,197,910	$184,312
$38,213,571	$107,781,004	$92,111,182	$15,669,822
$33,879,757	$89,305,326	$69,834,697	$19,470,629
$31,842,213	$88,869,810	$74,907,732	$13,962,078
$36,231,793	$89,079,982	$68,292,190	$20,787,792
$31,733,589	$76,499,511	$72,232,715	$4,266,796
$16,483,514	$80,203,645	$70,904,103	$9,299,542
$29,404,224	$76,327,504	$71,974,048	$4,353,456
$19,251,353	$63,337,303	$60,090,485	$3,246,818
$28,851,760	$60,544,530	$57,167,414	$3,377,116
$18,299,355	$77,738,746	$62,397,817	$15,340,929
$14,455,410	$65,487,381	$55,949,171	$9,538,210
$18,472,554	$69,430,569	$69,266,317	$164,252
$20,504,040	$69,413,648	$69,413,648	$0
$14,334,927	$82,579,472	$81,401,732	$1,177,740
$19,929,300	$59,648,451	$50,813,075	$8,835,376
$18,148,306	$55,741,548	$48,153,873	$7,587,675
$13,005,263	$76,383,688	$76,383,688	$0
$17,290,522	$95,401,868	$92,557,525	$2,844,343
$16,558,395	$45,409,990	$45,409,990	$0
$12,430,715	$71,121,812	$70,899,239	$222,573
$8,717,358	$60,538,725	$60,538,725	$0
$15,933,922	$49,581,182	$49,169,816	$411,366
$11,363,430	$46,970,708	$42,720,691	$4,250,017
$11,453,540	$62,093,614	$57,056,999	$5,036,615
$6,666,978	$66,088,264	$66,088,264	$0
$4,890,256	$53,473,276	$53,473,276	$0
$11,651,389	$52,631,896	$48,368,260	$4,263,636
$11,742,103	$60,556,515	$59,973,808	$582,707
$11,521,112	$48,346,511	$39,618,000	$8,728,511
$8,854,115	$50,489,771	$49,531,150	$958,621
$2,361,260	$53,561,872	$50,946,286	$2,615,586

Institution	Conference	Football Revenue	Football Expenses
Miami	ACC	$20,769,443	$18,012,074
Illinois	Big Ten	$20,764,472	$9,371,073
Oklahoma State	Big 12	$20,412,787	$9,879,701
Louisville	Big East	$19,023,605	$13,615,991
North Carolina	ACC	$18,147,854	$15,097,818
NC State	ACC	$18,109,836	$7,889,885
Mississippi	SEC	$17,581,209	$7,027,228
Pittsburgh	Big East	$17,545,348	$12,253,716
Arizona	Pac-10	$17,489,510	$9,161,561
Florida State	ACC	$17,457,519	$9,873,264
Boston College	ACC	$17,452,269	$16,176,602
Minnesota	Big Ten	$17,390,376	$8,304,534
Indiana	Big Ten	$17,033,871	$10,180,588
Rutgers	Big East	$15,643,682	$15,643,682
Northwestern	Big Ten	$15,513,675	$11,125,131
Missouri	Big 12	$15,284,731	$9,329,395
Vanderbilt	SEC	$15,219,537	$13,382,699
Syracuse	Big East	$14,866,061	$15,023,146
Virginia	ACC	$14,213,380	$17,145,138
Stanford	Pac-10	$12,927,407	$12,892,487
Wake Forest	ACC	$12,114,647	$10,142,491
Mississippi State	SEC	$12,074,969	$6,419,780
Connecticut	Big East	$11,976,959	$11,726,917
Kansas	Big 12	$11,258,985	$9,869,815
Iowa State	Big 12	$10,807,280	$10,177,360
Washington State	Pac-10	$10,466,370	$7,533,545
Maryland	ACC	$9,290,976	$9,301,052
South Florida	Big East	$9,289,982	$7,611,436
Baylor	Big 12	$9,270,595	$9,170,300
Duke	ACC	$8,966,170	$9,743,924
Cincinnati	Big East	$8,162,664	$7,774,009

Football Profit/Loss	Total Revenue	Total Expenses	Overall Profit/Loss
$2,757,369	$49,219,738	$49,219,738	$0
$11,393,399	$56,804,174	$44,768,059	$12,036,115
$10,533,086	$46,667,284	$41,746,414	$4,920,870
$5,407,614	$53,496,051	$53,146,468	$349,583
$3,050,036	$61,263,269	$61,044,532	$218,737
$10,219,951	$42,634,590	$41,514,272	$1,120,318
$10,553,981	$33,576,473	$33,576,473	$0
$5,291,632	$37,465,582	$37,465,582	$0
$8,327,949	$45,320,053	$41,067,902	$4,252,151
$7,584,255	$42,165,416	$39,945,277	$2,220,139
$1,275,667	$61,203,340	$61,065,308	$138,032
$9,085,842	$64,828,596	$64,828,596	$0
$6,853,283	$44,739,096	$41,527,070	$3,212,026
$0	$44,050,960	$44,050,960	$0
$4,388,544	$40,757,282	$40,757,282	$0
$5,955,336	$48,634,512	$48,634,512	$0
$1,836,838	$39,021,876	$39,021,876	$0
−$157,085	$43,732,382	$43,732,382	$0
−$2,931,758	$64,852,417	$64,852,417	$0
$34,920	$65,480,187	$63,834,193	$1,645,994
$1,972,156	$39,961,624	$39,599,165	$362,459
$5,655,189	$25,842,032	$25,835,258	$6,774
$250,042	$52,811,643	$52,764,644	$46,999
$1,389,170	$65,194,721	$58,046,962	$7,147,759
$629,920	$38,642,013	$38,642,013	$0
$2,932,825	$31,928,453	$29,730,429	$2,198,024
−$10,076	$46,283,648	$46,283,648	$0
$1,678,546	$28,160,631	$27,846,459	$314,172
$100,295	$40,475,819	$40,475,819	$0
−$777,754	$47,507,169	$47,391,264	$115,905
$388,655	$34,172,785	$34,172,785	$0

TABLE 2. NON-BCS FOOTBALL PROGRAMS RANKED BY TOTAL FOOTBALL REVENUE, 2006-2007

Institution	Conference	Football Revenue	Football Expenses
Texas Christian	Mt. West	$13,257,717	$13,257,717
Boise State	WAC	$12,123,981	$8,599,515
Utah	Mt. West	$11,184,198	$8,163,679
Brigham Young	Mt. West	$10,142,975	$9,140,943
Rice	Conf. USA	$9,553,283	$9,123,433
Temple	MAC	$8,717,771	$8,717,771
Southern Methodist	Conf. USA	$8,678,120	$8,678,123
Texas at El Paso	Conf. USA	$8,157,860	$6,479,397
Fresno State	WAC	$7,902,336	$5,905,529
Hawaii	WAC	$7,533,652	$7,033,664
Southern Mississippi	Conf. USA	$7,221,086	$4,460,544
Houston	Conf. USA	$6,925,282	$6,925,282
Tulane	Conf. USA	$6,871,440	$7,535,440
East Carolina	Conf. USA	$6,712,382	$6,975,296
Marshall	Conf. USA	$6,604,877	$5,653,832
Wyoming	Mt. West	$6,598,307	$4,430,217
Florida International	Sun Belt	$6,466,113	$5,905,876
Memphis	Conf. USA	$6,457,912	$6,457,912
Alabama Birmingham	Conf. USA	$6,348,331	$6,201,708
Middle Tennessee	Sun Belt	$5,838,119	$5,838,119
Tulsa	Conf. USA	$5,015,376	$8,670,055
Idaho	WAC	$4,885,021	$3,848,177
Miami University	MAC	$4,819,872	$4,819,872
Eastern Michigan	MAC	$4,653,129	$3,994,892
Buffalo	MAC	$4,551,896	$4,551,896
San Diego State	Mt. West	$4,508,597	$7,523,295
Central Michigan	MAC	$4,465,376	$6,166,514
Nevada-Reno	WAC	$4,446,166	$5,127,316
Ohio University	MAC	$4,445,964	$4,445,964
San Jose State	WAC	$4,308,283	$4,845,310
Central Florida	Conf. USA	$4,293,022	$3,733,457
Bowling Green	MAC	$4,261,871	$3,949,669
Colorado State	Mt. West	$4,106,247	$6,306,241
Troy University	Sun Belt	$3,879,598	$3,790,663
Louisiana at Monroe	Sun Belt	$3,593,026	$2,652,273

Football Profit/Loss	Total Revenue	Total Expenses	Overall Profit/Loss
$0	$39,191,874	$39,191,874	$0
$3,524,466	$21,777,002	$21,608,668	$168,334
$3,020,519	$26,949,005	$26,949,005	$0
$1,002,032	$32,100,899	$31,211,519	$889,380
$429,850	$26,031,598	$26,031,598	$0
$0	$25,836,567	$25,836,567	$0
−$3	$27,708,145	$27,708,145	$0
$1,678,463	$20,831,731	$20,683,906	$147,825
$1,996,807	$25,153,897	$24,379,303	$774,594
$499,988	$26,506,426	$26,416,743	$89,683
$2,760,542	$16,022,899	$15,206,835	$816,064
$0	$28,188,613	$28,188,613	$0
−$664,000	$20,029,935	$20,029,935	$0
−$262,914	$25,080,006	$24,856,277	$223,729
$951,045	$21,340,076	$21,340,076	$0
$2,168,090	$21,031,881	$21,031,881	$0
$560,237	$17,936,027	$17,936,027	$0
$0	$29,335,795	$29,335,795	$0
$146,623	$21,600,512	$21,104,978	$495,534
$0	$17,348,681	$17,348,681	$0
−$3,654,679	$24,276,929	$24,276,929	$0
$1,036,844	$12,730,220	$12,446,569	$283,651
$0	$22,252,089	$22,252,089	$0
$658,237	$19,341,287	$19,298,345	$42,942
$0	$19,724,701	$19,721,763	$2,938
−$3,014,698	$31,106,320	$30,424,823	$681,497
−$1,701,138	$20,434,178	$20,283,634	$150,544
−$681,150	$19,878,194	$19,878,193	$1
$0	$18,671,109	$18,671,109	$0
−$537,027	$16,970,448	$16,948,819	$21,629
$559,565	$29,639,288	$29,639,288	$0
$312,202	$18,087,524	$17,541,569	$545,955
−$2,199,994	$19,777,870	$18,503,237	$1,274,633
$88,935	$13,089,969	$13,089,969	$0
$940,753	$9,122,207	$7,279,426	$1,842,781

Institution	Conference	Football Revenue	Football Expenses
Arkansas State	Sun Belt	$3,576,338	$3,576,338
Northern Illinois	MAC	$3,361,600	$5,494,091
New Mexico	Mt. West	$3,265,057	$5,716,739
Louisiana Tech	WAC	$3,152,397	$3,886,243
Louisiana at Lafayette	Sun Belt	$3,043,713	$3,100,921
Nevada–Las Vegas	Mt. West	$2,768,426	$5,973,689
Kent State	MAC	$2,757,760	$4,253,652
Florida Atlantic	Sun Belt	$2,402,510	$3,615,243
Western Michigan	MAC	$1,841,527	$4,054,783
Ball State	MAC	$1,626,206	$4,652,969
Toledo	MAC	$1,601,476	$4,568,762
Utah State	WAC	$1,442,827	$2,106,989
North Texas	Sun Belt	$1,433,107	$4,219,719
Akron	MAC	$1,331,447	$4,640,002
New Mexico State	WAC	$1,118,277	$4,953,758

Note: Figures for both tables are from "Sports Spending & Gender Equity Database," *Chronicle of Higher Education* online (from the institutional data reported to the U.S. Department of Education's Office for Postsecondary Education, to comply with the Equity in Athletics Disclosure Act of 1994).

a profit for athletics overall (up from eighteen in 2004 and 2005), with an average (not median) net revenue of $4.3 million. (Sixteen athletic departments operated in the black in all three years, just six in all five of the past five years.) The other 100 programs had overall athletics deficits in 2006 averaging $8.9 million, and athletic expenses have increased at a higher rate than revenues.[50] In short, no non-BCS school breaks even on athletics; most lose money on football as well. Most BCS schools make money on football, but less than a third of them make enough to cover the overall athletics budget.

A small handful of athletic departments make enough profit to contribute substantially to other campus programs—an enviable arrangement but a dangerous one, too, as it makes the institution dependent on athletics to achieve its educational mission. For the rest, with expenses outstripping revenues generated by athletics, allocations from the states and the institutions themselves have increasingly had to subsidize the

Football Profit/Loss	Total Revenue	Total Expenses	Overall Profit/Loss
$0	$10,086,859	$10,086,859	$0
−$2,132,491	$16,866,401	$16,381,631	$484,770
−$2,451,682	$26,187,718	$26,187,718	$0
−$733,846	$12,440,515	$12,440,515	$0
−$57,208	$10,107,711	$9,962,308	$145,403
−$3,205,263	$25,166,518	$25,166,518	$0
−$1,495,892	$17,487,695	$16,995,460	$492,235
−$1,212,733	$14,116,774	$13,868,115	$248,659
−$2,213,256	$18,737,921	$18,737,921	$0
−$3,026,763	$15,538,250	$15,538,250	$0
−$2,967,286	$16,980,819	$16,980,819	$0
−$664,162	$13,205,337	$13,205,337	$0
−$2,786,612	$16,787,101	$15,873,899	$913,202
−$3,308,555	$17,792,195	$17,476,590	$315,605
−$3,835,481	$19,434,062	$19,434,062	$0

operation. For the subdivision overall, allocated revenues now make up 26 percent of the total (up from 19 percent in 2004).[51] This is an important number, since it represents millions of dollars that could otherwise be allocated to classroom instructors, new science labs, deferred maintenance on facilities, or any number of other institutional needs.

While the figures for individual institutions are not wholly reliable, the tables nonetheless convey a sense of the range in revenues within and between conferences. If we take the reported numbers at face value, the highest non-BCS football revenue, Texas Christian's, would rank fifty-fifth among BCS schools, after Virginia and before Stanford, making it one of just two non-BCS schools above the median for the Football Bowl Subdivision overall. Forty-three of the fifty non-BCS schools reported football revenues below the bottom team in the BCS. While profits vary widely within the BCS, outside it the range of profits and losses is less than $8 million. Twenty-three non-BCS schools claimed losses ranging from $3 (Southern Methodist) to $3.8 million (New Mexico State); nine broke even on paper, and eighteen claimed profits ranging from $89,000 (Troy) to $3.5 million (Boise State).

Within the BCS, after Texas and Notre Dame at the top, the next nine BCS schools with the largest football profits are from either the SEC (six) or the Big Ten (three), while seven of the nine at the bottom are from the Big East (four) or the ACC (three). Within the major conferences, membership for some schools is like living in the cheapest house in a fancy neighborhood while struggling to pay the property taxes and satisfy all of the covenants. The range of (declared) profit or loss in the Big East was from minus $157,000 (for Syracuse) to $11.4 million (for West Virginia); in the ACC, from minus $3 million (for Virginia) to $18.1 million (for Clemson); in the Pac-10, from $35,000 (for Stanford) to $20 million (for Washington). The Big 12 had a similar range, from Baylor at the bottom ($100,000) up to Texas A&M ($20.5 million), except for Texas off in the stratosphere at $46.2 million. The wider spreads within the wealthiest conferences created more distinct classes. Big Ten football was led in 2006 by Michigan, with a profit of $36.2 million, followed by Penn State ($29.4 million) and Ohio State ($26.6 million). Michigan State ($18.3 million), Iowa ($16.5 million), and Wisconsin ($14.3 million) constituted a sort of middle class, with Purdue ($11.5 million), Illinois ($11.4 million), and Minnesota ($9.1 million) in the lower middle and Indiana ($6.9) and Northwestern ($4.4 million) on the BCS equivalent of food stamps. The SEC had a similar profile, with Vanderbilt ($1.8 million) and Mississippi State ($5.7 million) at the bottom, Mississippi ($10.6 million) and Kentucky ($11.7 million) on the next rung, Tennessee ($17.3 million) and Arkansas ($19.3 million) next, and the remaining six ranging from $28.9 million (South Carolina) up to $43.1 million (Georgia).

As I write, the gaps between major conferences are widening for reasons unrelated to the BCS. In 2007 the Big Ten launched its own TV network (for broadcasting all sports, not just football), which began with payments of about $6 million a year to each school on top of the $9.3 million from CBS and ESPN. The SEC explored the same course before deciding, in August 2008, to renew its contracts with current TV partners CBS and ESPN. First CBS agreed to increase its payments from $30 million a year to an average of $55 million over fifteen years (beginning at $50 million and escalating to $60 million). Then ESPN, currently paying about $21 million, took the SEC's remaining games (again for all sports, not just football) for a jaw-dropping $2.25 billion over fifteen years, an average of $150 million a year. As with the BCS, the greatest beneficiaries are not Georgia, Auburn, and Alabama but Vanderbilt and Mississippi State. Each SEC school is now guaranteed an average of $17 million a year, beginning in 2011.[52]

The BCS creates two distinct classes of football programs; within the BCS, television contracts create subclasses of conferences. Though they are similar in many respects, big-time college football does not depend on television nearly to the extent that the National Football League does (where TV provides $3.7 billion out of roughly $7 billion in total revenue). According to the latest NCAA report on revenues and expenses, ticket sales account for 28 percent of generated revenues in athletics overall, while 30 percent comes from alumni and booster contributions. NCAA and conference distributions (which include television and BCS payouts) amount to 17 percent.[53] For the eighteen or nineteen athletic programs that actually make a profit, the BCS and television are least essential.

Ultimately, the size of the stadium and the demand for tickets determine a football program's financial prospects. Unfortunately, information on individual institutions is meager and scattered, but what we have tells a common story. In his memoir, James Duderstadt, the former president of the University of Michigan, noted that for the 1997 season (pre-BCS), ticket sales amounted to $18.1 million out of $44.2 million of total revenues at Michigan (41 percent), with television and bowl games together contributing less than $10 million.[54] (Michigan broke even that year—though only by not counting $18 million spent to renovate the stadium.) The *Philadelphia Inquirer* reported that $15.7 million of Penn State's $25.4 million in football revenue in 1999 (62 percent) came from ticket sales. With donations from boosters for the right to buy tickets bringing in an additional $8.8 million, $24.5 million out of $33.2 million (nearly 77 percent) in football-related revenue was attributable to stadium seating.[55] This was when Beaver Stadium held a mere 94,000. With its expansion to more than 100,000, Penn State joined Michigan, Ohio State, and Tennessee in college football's most exclusive neighborhood. Five other BCS schools have stadiums seating more than 90,000, eleven others more than 80,000, nine others more than 70,000, and eleven others more than 60,000. Outside the BCS, just BYU and Rice have their own stadiums seating over 60,000, and only BYU fills it.[56]

Filling it is the key. It's not just the 80,000 or 90,000 or 100,000 seats for the top programs that set them apart from others but also the dollars per seat that they can command—the premium pricing for some and the seat licenses or mandatory booster contributions for others. A required donation of $1,000 to buy a $200 season ticket increases gate receipts by a factor of five. Skyboxes or luxury suites—the most anomalous feature of all the strange aspects of education-based college football—add even more. Neither individual nor aggregate figures on stadium suites are consistently reported, but a survey of fund-raising for athletics in 2007–8 by the *Chronicle of Higher Education* found Texas at the top with $16.9 million in gifts for luxury suites (along with $17.6 million for priority seating).[57] Football programs in the major conferences but with smaller stadiums and less demand can at least depend on their guaranteed BCS payout. With perhaps the single exception of BYU, the mid-majors must get by with neither large gate receipts nor BCS bowl money. The disparity in potential revenue, of course, is appropriate for an entertainment business governed by the market. That's how capitalism works. What makes it strange are college football's nonprofit status and claim to a primarily educational purpose.

The Big Ten Network and the SEC's new TV contracts have made the schools at or near the bottom of those conferences less dependent on ticket and seating revenues than the low-revenue programs elsewhere in the BCS. For schools outside the BCS, BCS bowls continue to be the mythical El Dorado, fabled sources of gold that turn out to be fantasies. We live in an age of branding, and some college football brands are simply stronger than others, due not to clever marketing staffs but to decades of football history. The eighteen or nineteen athletic programs that make an actual profit in any given year will mostly be the same ones year after year. The temporary great hoo-ha over a Cinderella Utah or Boise State, or even a South Florida or Rutgers in the BCS, is likely to be no more than that—temporary. The upstart will lose its coach, or its quarterback will leave for the NFL, and the school will return to reality. With its well-established brand, a Nebraska can be down for several years and then rejoin the superelite. A Boise State will have its one dance and then resume scrubbing the floors.

So . . . the more a program needs bowl and TV revenue today, the less likely it is to get it. That's one dilemma. The greater one is that the lesser football powers must make the deepest sacrifices to survive in a marketplace shaped by the interests of the elite. In the scramble for television deals after the breakup of the NCAA's TV monopoly, the mid-major conferences were relegated to cableland, where the rights fees were lowest and the required compromises with academic priorities greatest. With Saturdays glutted, ESPN began offering games on weeknights in 1991. Football used to interfere with class time less than any other sport just Fridays for travel before road games—but by 2004 *Sports Illustrated* could report on a typical November week in which schools from the ACC and three of the mid-majors—the WAC, MAC, and Conference USA—played games on Tuesday, Wednesday, Thursday, and Friday nights in order to appear on ESPN or ESPN2. The ACC (and Big East later) either needed the weeknight games to establish their credentials as major football conferences or just could not turn down the money. For the mid-majors, if they wanted to be on TV at all, they had no choice.

At Northern Illinois University, as *Sports Illustrated* reported in 2004, the president placed an ad in the campus newspaper urging students to attend a Tuesday night game against Toledo to make a good impression on the TV audience, while professors scheduled quizzes in their Tuesday-night classes to prevent them from doing so. Colleges had long left Friday night for high school football games (as they expected the NFL to leave Saturdays to them). Now, a Friday night contest in Fresno on this November date in 2004 conflicted with the local high schools' big rivalry game (and kept the Fresno State coach from watching his own son play in it). A 9:00 A.M. Saturday-morning start for Boise State–San Jose State—wake-up call for the players at 5:30—created no extra academic hardships but made no football sense.[58]

It is worth noting that in the supersaturated world of televised college football, the audiences for these games are small, often tiny. For the 2007 season, the average rating for a game on ABC was 3.9 and on CBS 3.4 (and just 1.9 for Notre Dame on NBC). These compare to average ratings for NFL games of 10.7 on Fox, 10.3 on CBS, and 10.0 on NBC (for *Sunday Night Football*).[59] Ratings on cable are much lower: for a typical week during the 2006 football season, the *highest*-rated college game on ESPN was 1.9 (for Georgia Tech–Clemson), and two others made the network's top 10 for the week, with ratings of 1.7 (West Virginia–Connecticut) and 1.3 (Wisconsin-Purdue). All three games reached 4 percent of the TV-watching audience for their time slots. These were the ratings for ACC, Big East, and Big Ten matchups; no ratings for games between non-BCS schools were reported, but they likely did not reach single digits.[60] (For perspective: in 1969, during the era of the NCAA's television monopoly, the college football "game of the week" — eleven national games and six sets of four or five regional games — had an average Nielsen rating of 26.6 for the season.[61])

Even elite college football does not come close to the ratings for the NFL. When undefeated Big East powers Louisville and West Virginia played on a Thursday night late in the 2006 season, with a spot in the national championship game possibly on the line, the rating of 5.3 was more than 40 percent below the 9.5 rating for ESPN's *Monday Night Football* game that week, which was *Monday Night Football*'s lowest rating thus far that season. Routine NFL games outdraw collegiate "games of the century." Number-one Ohio State versus number-two Michigan on ABC two weeks later earned a rating of 12.9, the highest for any regular-season college game since Notre Dame–Florida State in 1993 but still lower than the 14.6 for CBS's midseason NFL games the next day. The intensely hyped national championship game pitting Florida and Ohio State in January 2007 was only the third-most-watched football game that week, its 17.3 rating coming in behind 20.4 and 19.7 for NFL divisional playoffs. The Super Bowl a few weeks later had a rating of 42.[62]

College football overall has a "mass market": in a 2007 poll, 72.4 percent of Americans identified themselves as fans, behind only the NFL with 76.4 percent and ahead of the National Basketball Association, NCAA basketball, Major League Baseball, and the National Hockey League.[63] But in contrast to the NFL, individual conferences and teams have only "niche" markets, and the lesser conferences and lesser teams have smaller niches. For weeknight games on ESPN and ESPN 2, the revenue is as meager as the ratings: mid-major schools took in about 5.5 percent of total TV dollars for football and basketball combined in 2006[64] — but with each rating point representing over 1 million homes, even a .7 or .5 rating on ESPN means reaching an audience that universities have no other way to target. In the meantime, athletic departments (and college presidents) are skirmishing with professors, as at Northern Illinois, and the athletes are losing no matter who wins.[65] (I will explore the impact on the athletes more fully in chapter 5.)

BCS and non-BCS football teams collectively reported a little over $2 billion in revenue for 2006–7, less than a third of the nearly $7 billion taken in by the thirty-two NFL franchises, but the difference increasingly seems only a matter of scale.[66] Unlike the NFL, however, college football is nonprofit — the entire two-billion-dollar enterprise is subsidized by taxpayer dollars, thanks to a few key parts of the tax code. In 1988

Congress restored a tax deduction for booster donations (including contributions to coaches' salaries) that the IRS had challenged four years earlier; in 1999 the IRS, under pressure from Congress and the White House, extended this deduction to the leases on luxury suites beyond the ticket price for the seats alone. (In the case under review, $143,585 out of $200,000 for a ten-year lease was ruled deductible.) Congress also acted in 1997 to exempt corporate sponsorships (including naming rights for stadiums and bowl games) from taxation. The total cost to taxpayers for all of these deductions, as estimated by the *Philadelphia Inquirer* in September 2000, was $50 million that year.[67] That figure seems low, but the bottom line is that universities pay no taxes on their athletic programs, and much of the money that comes into those programs from both individuals and corporations is tax-deductible for them as well. Congress recently questioned big-time college sport's tax-exempt status but so far has left matters as they are.

Actually, big-time college football differs from the National Football League in more than its tax exemptions. With all of their shared revenue—including close to $4 billion annually from television—NFL clubs can make a profit even when they are lousy on the field or play in half-filled stadiums. NFL clubs do not have to constantly upgrade their facilities in order to attract players. Instead of recruiting wars, NFL clubs take turns selecting the best college players, and they are required to share with all of their players a fixed percentage of their revenues. NFL clubs do not steal each others' coaches, and what they pay their own is not governed by fear of losing him every season that he's successful.

As an entertainment industry, the NFL is much less ruthlessly competitive than big-time college football. And it has no educational mission to complicate its pursuit of profits.

THE NCAA TO THE RESCUE?

Since January 2003 the NCAA has been led for the first time in its history by a former college president. In his first State of the Association Address, Myles Brand announced two agendas: "reform" and "advocacy"—to fix what needs fixing and to remind the public of all that's right with college sports. In his address a year later, Brand announced the principle theme of his presidency to be the distinction between the Collegiate Model ("student-athletes in pursuit of an education") and the Professional Model (athletes as "a labor force in pursuit of a negotiated salary"). The following year, he debunked four "myths" about college sports cherished by cynics: they are "more about sports than college," they are "only about money," the NCAA and its president control them, and "amateurism itself is a myth." In defense of amateurism, Brand elaborated on the Collegiate Model: it "is based on the idea that students come to college to get an education, and some of them—the most gifted and most determined—play sports under the banner of the university for love of the game." Brand then declared, "As old-fashioned as that may sound, I challenge the cynics to survey the 360,000 student-athletes who participate in college sports to see if they don't overwhelmingly say that is exactly why they play." He added, "The work before us now is to recenter college sports, align this enterprise with the academic mission of the university, bring fiscal responsibility to the way in which we manage the business of intercollegiate athletics, especially value-based budgeting, and keep the spotlight focused on the success of the student-athletes."[68]

Brand is a philosopher by training, and he should not be accused of simple intellectual confusion in demanding to "recenter" a system that works for the overwhelming majority, or in advocating for a system that also needs to be reformed. An organization's goals and behavior can be on target but slightly off center, mostly good but still needing improvement. Nonetheless, "reform" and "advocacy," "academic mission" and "fiscal responsibility," touch yet again on the contradiction inherent in big-time college football and also on the long traditions of boosterism and criticism that, due to that contradiction, have attended the sport throughout its history. The "myths" that Brand debunked include the long-standing arguments of big-time football's critics. When he talks about the Collegiate Model thriving, or the vast majority playing for love of the game, he is not talking about football (and men's basketball). When he addresses the need for reform, he is not talking about gymnastics and crew.

Under Brand's leadership, the NCAA in 2005 and 2006 introduced two major initiatives for his reform agenda, one to improve the academic success of "student-athletes" and the other to slow down the spending by Division I athletic departments. The first initiative, the Academic Progress Rate (APR), set a minimum overall score, determined by the retention and academic progress of each athlete, that every team must achieve at the risk of losing scholarships. The second culminated in a report from a fifty-member Presidential Task Force on the Future of Division I Intercollegiate Athletics that called on institutional leaders to engage in "value based budgeting" and to restrain their spending on athletics. (The most recent NCAA report on revenues and expenses, with its distinction between "generated" and "allocated" revenues and its standardized accounting for facilities and support salaries, was an outgrowth of that Presidential Task Force's mission.)

The convolutions of the APR—with its language of "contemporaneous penalties," "10 percent cap," "historically based penalties," and "confidence boundary," along with the fundamental mystery of what the requisite score of 925 actually represents—undoubtedly has blunted its impact on public consciousness. But the penalties at stake—the loss of up to 10 percent of a team's scholarships, with restrictions on recruiting and postseason play for repeated failures—certainly make the APR real and consequential. Had it been implemented immediately in 2005, approximately 30 percent of all Division I football teams (A and AA) would have lost scholarships, but schools were given a one-year grace period. Coaches challenged the APR because, like federally reported graduation rates, it marked down schools for student-athletes who left in good academic standing. Additional tinkering addressed this problem, and in March 2006, when the NCAA announced the first round of penalties, ninety-nine teams (including twenty-one football programs) from sixty-five institutions lost scholarships. Instead of endlessly talking, the NCAA was now doing something about academic standards.[69]

The twenty-one penalized football programs were Alabama A&M, Buffalo, Cal State–Sacramento, Central Connecticut State, Florida A&M, Gardner-Webb, Georgia Southern, Hawaii, Jacksonville State, Middle Tennessee State, Montana State, Murray State, New Mexico State, Nicholls State, Northern Illinois, Prairie View, Stephen F. Austin State, Temple, Tennessee at Chattanooga, Tennessee-Martin, Toledo, and Western Michigan. Conspicuously missing were all of the major programs. Only Buffalo, Hawaii, Middle Tennessee State, New Mexico State, Temple, Toledo, and Western Michigan even belonged to Division I-A.

Good for LSU and Ohio State? Or too bad for the Toledos and Georgia Southerns that lost scholarships while trying to compete in a system created by and for the LSUs and Ohio States? The top football programs have both the luxury of being more selective in recruiting (if they choose) and greater resources for academic support. As with televising midweek games, the system works to the particular disadvantage of the nonelite football programs desperate to rise or just survive. According to the *New York Times*, Division I schools in 2006 were spending $150 million on academic support for athletes—and that figure keeps rising—but as with revenues, the levels of spending are hugely uneven. While programs already losing money cannot afford to lose more, the *Times* reported that usc had 14.5 staff positions and a budget of $1.5 million for academic support of athletics. Georgia's budget for academic tutoring was $1.3 million, "the same amount that the university spends on its centralized campus tutorial program for its 25,000 undergraduate students." By 2008 the *Chronicle of Higher Education* was reporting that Oklahoma's athletic department spent $2.9 million the previous year on academic support, almost $6,000 per athlete. Oklahoma represents an extreme case of a trend: recruit athletes who fail to meet the university's admission requirements—60 percent of Oklahoma's recruits in 2007–8 were "special admits"—then spend enough on tutors, class monitors, and study centers to keep them eligible.[70]

There is a distinct irony in the fact that, in addition to extravagant training and practice facilities, palatial learning centers have become part of the "facilities arms race" for luring recruits. Georgia's cost $7 million; at $15 million, lsu's in 2002 seemed the outer limit of extravagance, until Texas a&m opened its $27 million Alice and Erle Nye '59 Academic Center in 2006. The "biggest jaw-dropper," however, according to the *Chronicle of Higher Education*, is currently the University of Michigan's—but perhaps only until the University of Oregon opens its new facility in 2010, to be built with an undisclosed amount of Phil Knight's Nike money.[71] It would seem perverse to criticize athletic departments for neglecting their athletes' academic welfare, then criticize them for throwing too much money at the solution. Yet with support staffs developing "action plans," monitoring class attendance, and providing tutors for all courses, critics warned that some athletes would never learn to take responsibility for their own academic and postcollege careers. On the other hand, big-time college football was surely more dangerous for academically struggling players in the less well-funded programs, faced with the same athletic pressures but with considerably less support.

The second year of assessing penalties for missing the apr minimum saw similar results, with twelve Division I-A football programs losing scholarships this time, including the first one from a bcs conference, the University of Arizona, which lost four. But the ncaa also made a more ominous announcement: that 40 percent of the football programs across Division I were at risk of losing scholarships in the next round. The threat seemingly produced results. Instead, seventeen teams were penalized in May 2008, two of them this time (Kansas and Washington State) from BCS conferences. (The other fifteen were Akron, Alabama-Birmingham, Buffalo, Central Michigan, Florida Atlantic, Florida International, Hawaii, Idaho, New Mexico State, North Texas, San Diego State, San Jose State, Temple, Toledo, and University of Nevada, Las Vegas.) Washington State lost eight scholarships; San Jose State lost nine. The punishments were serious, but the major football powers continued to escape them, despite the fact that several of them have Graduation Success Rates well below the 60 percent (50 percent by federal accounting) that is supposedly equivalent to a 925 APR. (However challenging for many schools, the APR sets a low bar.) Texas's most recently reported GSR was 50 percent, Georgia's was 48, and Oklahoma's was 46; only two of the penalized schools, Hawaii and Alabama-Birmingham, had GSRs under 50 percent.[72] Such incongruities raised questions about both the fairness and effectiveness of the APR as a tool for genuine academic reform.[73]

With scholarships and postseason play at stake, the APR has certainly increased the pressure on athletic departments, but whether it will benefit students is much less certain. Pressure on instructors to give passing grades to athletes and on tutors to write their papers were a part of college football long before the APR. Following Jan Kemp at Georgia, a handful of other professors and teaching assistants—Linda Bensel-Meyers at Tennessee, Norma McGill at Ohio State, and Caroline Owen at LSU (along with Jan Gangelhoff, for the basketball program at Minnesota)—became nationally famous, and locally vilified, for blowing the whistle on such abuses in their schools' football programs.[74] The APR only raises the stakes.

As if a glimpse of life under the APR, the *New York Times* in the summer of 2006 exposed a situation at Auburn University, where a senior professor of sociology (the chair of the department, no less) had been giving credits (and high grades) to hundreds of students, athletes prominently among them, for directed-reading courses that required little work. Eighteen members of the undefeated, second-ranked 2004 Auburn football team had collectively earned ninety-seven credit hours from this professor, helping Auburn achieve the highest APR score for football among public universities and ranking behind only Stanford, Navy, and Boston College overall. The eighteen athletes averaged a 3.31 grade in their directed-reading classes, compared to 2.14 in the rest of their courses. According to the *Times*, "several" athletes stayed above a

2.0 (and thus kept their eligibility) only through these courses.[75] At the University of Michigan, a psychology professor over a three-year period offered independent studies courses on study skills and time management to 251 athletes, including twenty-two members of the 2007 football team, who received an average grade of 3.62 (compared to 2.57 in their other courses).[76] These arrangements predated the APR, which raises the institutional stakes for academic failure and thus the incentive to avoid it. The more widely publicized cheating uncovered at Florida State in 2007, which kept two dozen players out of a bowl game—athletic department personnel helped athletes with exams and wrote papers for them—may have been more directly APR-related.[77]

Besides increasing the pressure on advisers and tutors to improperly help the weakest students, the APR may also have unintended negative consequences for the capable ones. Because it requires completion of 40 percent of the work toward a specific major in the first two years, the APR makes it riskier to attempt challenging majors such as Engineering and Premed, or to change majors or remain undecided while exploring various intellectual interests—all experiences common throughout any university's student population. Out of a laudable desire to prevent athletes from taking easy courses that lead to no degree, the APR limits the options for capable and motivated students.

Following the announcement of the APR in early 2005, a past president of the National Association of Academic Advisors for Athletics also expressed advisers' concern "that they'll be pressured to place athletes in easier classes and majors." At universities where athletic advisers report to athletic directors instead of provosts or academic vice presidents, pressure could be particularly severe. Again, this is not a new problem. The survey cited earlier, in which Allen Sack found that college athletes in Connecticut were pressured into less-demanding majors, was published in 1982. The difference now is that athletes face an increasingly competitive job market for which their majors must prepare them.[78]

In his State of the Association Address in January 2005, Myles Brand acknowledged "some evidence and considerable anecdote" for cynics' claim "that student-athletes are directed to easy courses, worthless majors and accommodating professors." But he added that there was no "reliable and empirical measurement for the extent of this problem."[79] Just a month later, as part of a series on academics in the new climate of the APR, the *Dallas Morning News* added "some evidence" by reporting that 68 percent of the football players with a declared major at Texas

A&M (according to the team's media guide) were in Agricultural Development, compared to 2 percent of all undergraduates; while 41 percent of the football players at the University of Texas were majoring in Youth and Community Services, compared to .2 percent of all undergrads.[80] In March 2008 a four-day, front-page series in the *Ann Arbor News* reported that 78.4 percent of Michigan's football players with a declared major were in General Studies (compared to 1.6 percent of Michigan students overall).[81]

In November 2008 *USA Today* fully answered Brand's implicit call for an "empirical measurement for the extent of this problem" when it published a survey of the entire Football Bowl Subdivision (along with the major basketball-playing Division I schools) and introduced the general public to the phenomenon of "clustering." A "cluster" was at least 25 percent of the juniors and seniors on a given team majoring in the same subject. An "extreme cluster" was 40 percent in that major. Simply by reviewing the media guides and school websites of 142 schools (identifying majors for 85 percent of the athletes), *USA Today* found widespread clustering. The majors varied by school, from traditional disciplines such as Sociology and Communications to nondisciplinary programs, with names like "General Studies" and "University Studies," or highly specific programs such as Housing and Organizational Management or Apparel, Housing, and Resource Management. Within the Football Bowl Subdivision, *USA Today* found seventy-nine clusters and twenty-eight extreme clusters.[82]

In addition to likely pushing more athletes toward majors unrelated to whatever career aspirations they might have, the APR, as has been the case with every other attempt at academic reform since the 1970s, leaves untouched the intensely competitive, highly commercialized entertainment enterprise within which football players must weigh their academic and athletic priorities. The NCAA's second large initiative under Brand, the report from his Presidential Task Force on fiscal responsibility, was released in October 2006. It warned about runaway spending and urged university presidents "to moderate the growth of athletics budgets so that institutional funds do not increasingly have to cover revenue shortfalls." The task force insisted that there was no financial crisis in college sports but warned that current levels of spending were unsustainable. It proposed requiring institutions to report "detailed financial data, including salaries and expenditures, as a condition of [NCAA] membership." The NCAA, in turn, would publish this data, though only in the aggregate (so that no individual institution would be embarrassed). Most crucially, altering spending habits would be voluntary, as Brand explained at his press conference to unveil the report, if for no other reason than that "dictating expenditure amounts by the NCAA is illegal." (After losing its monopoly on TV contracts for football in 1984, the NCAA attempted to cap the salaries for "restricted-earnings" coaches in 1991, only to lose a second major antitrust lawsuit. Any attempt by the organization to limit salaries or other spending would risk another.)[83]

Mandatory academic reform, via the APR, coupled with *voluntary* restraint in spending—that is the best that the NCAA can offer. In his introduction to the Presidential Task Force's report, Brand mentioned earlier NCAA studies that challenged "conventional wisdom" about benefits from increased spending, and he noted that "these reports were virtually ignored by the intercollegiate athletics community." Why the response to this new report would be any different, he did not say. From his annual addresses, it *is* clear that Myles Brand knows full well what's wrong with big-time college football. Privately, he may well believe that the problems are intractable but that the collapse of the commercial enterprise would cause universities greater harm (as indeed may be the case). In his public statements, however, Brand insists that real progress in academic reform is under way, and that the persistent problems in football (and men's basketball) are overwhelmed by the good in college athletics generally. He also understands the real costs of college athletics beyond the publicly reported profits and losses. But as he put it in his 2007 State of the Association Address, the NCAA can manage academic reform "on a national basis," while "fiscal responsibility is a campus matter."[84] Under Brand's leadership, the NCAA's left and right hands are aware of each other but still cannot clasp.

The great blind spot in the task force's report concerns revenue, not spending. It notes that revenues are rising—partly because "television exposure has proliferated from weekend-only to every-day-of-the-week coverage"—only to make the point that expenditures are increasing equally and threaten to overwhelm a majority of programs. The report calls for more restraint only in spending, however, as if oblivious to the fact that "every-day-of-the-week coverage" might have any impact on the academic reforms that the APR is meant to accomplish. "Fiscal responsibility" requires living within one's means. Absent from the NCAA's current reform movement is any suggestion that the magnitude of the means might itself be a problem.[85]

In its concern for spending but not revenue, the task force followed its leader. In his 2006 convention address, where he articulated the Collegiate Model, Brand self-consciously disavowed any concern about revenue:

> Let me put it provocatively. Athletics, like the university as a whole, seeks to maximize revenues. In this respect, it has an obligation to conduct its revenue-generating activities in a productive and sound businesslike manner. Anything less would be incompetence at best and malfeasance at worst. That is, on the revenue side, the in-put side, athletics, like the university itself, must follow the best business practices. On the expenditure side, the out-put side, as it were, athletics must follow its not-for-profit mission.

Brand cautioned that pursuing the "'business' of college sports" must never "[divert] us from the primary purpose of intercollegiate athletics," the academic experience of the athletes; but he insisted that commercial activity in itself was no obstacle to maintaining that priority. To those who claimed that commercialism "taints the purity of college sports," Brand declared, "Nonsense!" To those who felt "some ambivalence about business issues," he proclaimed, "Let us end the ambivalence and do the best job we can developing revenue for our athletic departments." Sack terms Brand's position "the academic capitalist model of college sports."[86]

In his 2009 address (perhaps his last, delivered in his absence while he was undergoing treatment for pancreatic cancer), Brand returned to the "proper role for commercial activity" as his main theme, the search for the Aristotelian Golden Mean between the extremes of "purity," or "unrealistic idealism," and "crass commercialism" that risks "abridging the values and mission of higher education." According to Brand, "the central stricture on commercial activity concerns the exploitation of student-athletes," but his sense of "exploitation" is limited to improper payments to athletes for endorsements or, more subtly, the use of their images in advertisements for commercial products such as game films or team merchandise. He does not acknowledge that *not* paying the athletes might be exploitive, or that the commercialism itself might contribute in any way to their exploitation.[87]

Brand speaks passionately for the purity of the amateur collegiate athlete, against the misguided notion that college athletics in their entirety should, or could be pure. "Purity" is not the issue, but rather the practical consequences of a "business" in which a few football programs are not easily distinguishable from NFL franchises—except for their more ruthless competitiveness and their athletes' lack of compensation—while others scramble for every leftover dollar irrespective of the impact on "students." For the handful of elite programs, raising more money translates directly into spending more on facilities, coaches' salaries, and the rest of the accoutrements of a "first-class" football program. (NCAA research reveals that programs spend an additional dollar for every new dollar of revenue.) These elite programs, in turn, raise the standards that all of the lesser programs strive—and fail—to meet as they slide deeper into debt. (For them, an additional dollar of spending is not necessarily offset by an additional dollar of revenue.) These programs are the ones that agree to schedule games on Tuesday or Wednesday or Thursday nights, when there is no competition from the SEC or Big Ten but only from lectures and homework. Brand must understand all of this. To say that only spending, not revenue generation, is a problem for intercollegiate athletics must be calculated to put the best spin on behavior that Brand knows the NCAA cannot change.

Whatever he knows to be true, the president of the NCAA cannot openly admit that the financial stakes in today's Football Bowl Subdivision require the players to be athletes first. The persistent problems are no secret among institutional leaders. In its chapter titled "Celebrating the Student-Athlete," the Presidential Task Force report announced "a bold agenda for significant change," specifying issues to be addressed but pointedly offering no recommendations on them. These issues include reviewing the "20-hour rule"—the limit on the hours that coaches can require of their athletes (which is universally ignored)—and its impact on "student-athletes' assimilation into campus life," as well as reconsidering the one-year scholarship (at least to require a "hearing for canceled or reduced athletics aid").[88] This would mean returning in effect to 1973 to reconsider the fundamental relationship of college athletes to their universities; to do so could indeed lead to "significant change." But if the members of the task force could not agree on recommendations on these issues, how will the full NCAA membership ever take "bold" action on them?

For such purposes, the NCAA may be obsolete, as Brand himself and his task force, no doubt unwittingly, imply. The call for voluntary restraint is, in effect, an invitation to pursue alignments outside the NCAA. I will return to that possibility in chapter 6.

OPPORTUNITY, ENTITLEMENT, AND EXPLOITATION

That big-time college football has conflicting priorities is the oldest of old news, but conditions have changed since the 1960s. I now want to focus more directly on the ways that these dual priorities impact the young men who play the game. I begin, then, by returning to the establishment of the one-year scholarship in 1973, which initially was all but ignored by the general public but now seems like a slow-acting virus whose potency has only recently become clear.

A NEW CONTRACT FOR COACHES

As I noted earlier, football initially belonged to the players—beginning in the 1870s, they made the rules and ran the teams—but by the 1920s it had become indisputably a coaches' game. As intercollegiate football spread from the Northeast throughout the rest of the country, the hiring of professional coaches became necessary. And as it was transformed from an extracurricular activity to a commercial spectacle with promotional value for universities, the pressure on coaches to fill stadiums through winning teams ceded them more and more power and financial rewards.

Amos Alonzo Stagg was paid a full professor's salary to start the football program at the new University of Chicago in 1892. With coaches today making millions, to offer a mere professor's salary would be an insult; but consider how remarkable it is that, in order to properly launch a new and ambitious private university (with Rockefeller money), Chicago's first president, William Rainey Harper, made arrangements with a former Yale All-American, two years out of college, to start a football program, agreeing to pay him as much as the school's top professors in order to lure him from the East Coast. By 1892 football was already seen as an agent for building a university and the coach as the key to its success.

In the 1920s, Knute Rockne was far and away the individual at his university best known to the public, and like other top coaches in the 1920s and 1930s, he could supplement his salary with income from football clinics, off-season banquet talks, and magazine articles ("inside dope" either ghostwritten or written "with" a press agent or professional journalist). Magazine articles gave way to TV shows in the 1960s, but the rewards, as well as the pressures, of coaching big-time college football remained relatively constant, or perhaps grew in such small increments that the football public saw little change—until the 1980s.

The NCAA's transformation of student-athletes into athlete-students in 1972 and 1973—making freshmen eligible, dropping the 1.6 rule, and instituting the one-year scholarship—laid the foundation for what followed. Coaches now had unprecedented freedom to recruit and power to manage their rosters, along with a less ambiguous mandate to win games, get to bowls, and get on TV in order to increase revenues in the face of a slumping economy. In redefining the status of student-athletes, the NCAA also changed the coach's implicit contract with his university. As football coach at Oregon State from 1965 through 1975, Dee Andros was also a tenured professor in Physical Education, and such arrangements were common. Giving coaches faculty appointments, usually to teach physical-activity classes or courses on coaching theory, was one of the ways by which universities backed up the claim (or maintained the fiction) that intercollegiate athletics was an extension of its educational mission. When Andros was removed as football coach at the end of the 1975 season, as a tenured professor he had to be reassigned elsewhere in the university (he was bumped up to athletic director, another common practice). Andros was the last football coach hired by Oregon State with faculty status, and many other universities stopped these arrangements around this time. More obviously than before, the purpose of the football team was to win football games, and that was what coaches were paid for.

The salaries of football coaches had provoked occasional controversies since Stagg was first hired at Chicago. When the University of Texas lured Dana Bible away from Nebraska in 1937, the state legislature had to raise the UT president's salary to avoid the appearance of misguided priorities with a football coach earning more than the leader of the entire university. As late as the 1960s and 1970s, the salary of a professorial football coach could not be too far out of line with those earned by deans, if not ordinary faculty. In 1969 Andros made $24,000 at Oregon

State (compared to the president's $34,500 and the dean of education's $29,760), presumably supplemented by some perks that were relatively modest.[1] In the new order that emerged in the 1970s, however, football coaches became free agents in a competitive market. The higher-ed community uttered a collective gasp in 1982 when Texas A&M made Jackie Sherrill the highest-paid university employee in the country by stealing him from Pittsburgh for more than $1.7 million over six years—more than any president, chancellor, or medical-school dean and more than twice the reported $125,000 salary of Michigan's Bo Schembechler, the highest-paid coach in the Big Ten. (That Texas A&M ushered in the era of compensating football coaches at CEO levels had a touch of irony. In 1968 and 1969, *Sports Illustrated* singled out the Aggies as the embodiment of old-style "Boy Scout virtues" amid countercultural and antiwar chaos. Old-school football met greed-is-good economics in Sherrill's signing.)[2]

A ripple effect was inevitable. When universities and conferences won the right to negotiate their own television contracts in 1984, and the competition for market share intensified, coaches were in position to cash in. By 1986, when *USA Today* tried to collect financial data on all major-college football coaches, $150,000 had become the norm at the big football schools, while top coaches were now matching Sherrill's $300,000. (Determining exactly what coaches made was not always easy. For Alabama's Don Perkins, for example, *USA Today* offered a "conservative estimate" of $300,000, calculated from his base salary of $120,000 along with several side deals for "professional or consulting services," "promotions," and radio and TV programs—each worth "$10,000 or more," the highest category on the form that Perkins was required to file with the Alabama Ethics Commission.)[3] Within little more than another decade, some offensive and defensive coordinators would be making such salaries, while head coaches were earning several times as much. Bobby Bowden's $1 million salary in 1995, then Steve Spurrier's $2 million in 1997, did not just raise the standard but obliterated it each time. Competition from an NFL undergoing its own economic transformation in the 1990s was a new driving force, despite the fact that big-name college coaches—including Spurrier, when he left Florida for the NFL in 2002—rarely succeeded at the pro level. For every Super Bowl–winning Jimmy Johnson, there have been several Spurriers (or John McKays, John Robinsons, or Dennis Ericksons) who had little success in the NFL.

By 2001, $1 million was entry level for the upper echelon of college football coaches, with twenty-two millionaires (five each from the SEC and the Big 12, four each from the Big Ten and the Pac-10, three from the ACC, and one from the Big East). Spurrier, Bowden, and Oklahoma's Bob Stoops all topped $2 million. By the end of the 2004 season, at least eight coaches were making $2 million, and the top salary was creeping toward $3 million.[4] In 2006 the senior associate for business affairs at the University of Arizona, whose football program was down but remained the only hope for keeping the athletic department afloat, lamented, "Every time Oklahoma gives Bob Stoops another raise—he's at $3 million now—the rest of us just cringe."[5]

That year, nine coaches made over $2 million, led by Stoops at $3,450,000 (with Joe Paterno and Charlie Weis likely in that club as well but their salaries not reported), and the average salary in Division I-A was $950,000.[6] In 2007 at least four coaches topped $3 million (with Weis also rumored to be in that neighborhood), twelve made more than $2 million, and forty-nine broke $1 million, which was now the average for the subdivision. Although Alabama was widely reported to be paying Nick Saban $4 million, *USA Today* pegged him at $3.5 million.[7] The average of $1 million in 2007 is consistent with the figures recently reported by the NCAA for previous years: a median salary of $582,000 for the Football Bowl Subdivision in 2003 and of $855,000 in 2005.[8] Shortly before the 2008 season opened, *Forbes* magazine put USC's Pete Carroll ahead of everyone at $4.4 million (including $400,000 in benefits and deferred compensation).[9]

While "market forces" drove this inflation, for each upward adjustment of the compensation ceiling, individual athletic directors and university presidents had to make conscious decisions. In 2000 LSU lured Saban from Michigan State, where he was making $697,000, with a deal worth more than $6 million over five years. Because coaches' contracts entail remarkably one-sided obligations, Saban did not remain at that level or stay long. By 2005 he was earning well over $2 million at LSU, when he left for Miami of the NFL—and $5 million—only to be enticed back to the college ranks two years later by Alabama for slightly less (after posting a 15–17 record with the Dolphins).

At each stage, "the market" dictated the going rate for a top coach, and what the NFL paid its coaches was beyond the colleges' control. (NFL coaches' salaries are not made public, but in 2006 Seattle's Mike Holmgren was believed to be the highest-paid, at $7 million, and Chicago's Lovie Smith, at $1.35 million, was widely reported during the run-up to the Super Bowl to be the lowest.[10]) But decisions by university officials repeatedly adjust the market in ways that reverberate throughout college athletics. While officials at Arizona cringe when Bob Stoops gets a raise at Oklahoma, Stoops's coaching colleagues and their agents cheer. "Our deal will help every other coach in America," Saban's agent told reporters when his client signed with LSU in 2000.[11] Some are helped directly, due to contracts that peg their salaries to the current pecking order. Saban's successor at LSU, Les Miles, made $1.8 million in 2007. For winning the SEC championship that season, he was guaranteed the third-highest salary in the conference for 2008—which meant at least $2.85 million when Arkansas signed Bobby Petrino for that amount in December (after Petrino abandoned the NFL's Atlanta Falcons before the season even ended). For going on to win the national championship, Miles was guaranteed the third-highest salary in all of Division I, which happened to be Urban Meyer's $3.4 million from Florida. From these two incentives in his contract, Miles received first a 58 percent raise, then 19 percent on top of that (or 89 percent overall), without even having to renegotiate. He renegotiated anyway—for a salary guaranteed to match the SEC's highest (reported to be Saban's $3.75 million at Alabama), plus $1,000.[12] (What would happen if Saban in turn renegotiated for the highest, plus a thousand? Would the two salaries ratchet up to infinity? Or would neither coach ever be paid because the salary could never be determined? There's a conundrum more challenging than those angels on a pinhead that perplexed medieval theologians.)

The millionaire coaches' club that emerged in the 1990s included not just the traditional superpowers but also climbers like Virginia Tech and Kansas State and, closer to home for me, Oregon State and Oregon. Climbers played a desperate endgame, pouring money into coaches' salaries and athletic facilities in order to stay competitive with their elite rivals. The *Des Moines Register* calculated that the twenty-two coaches in 2001 who averaged $1.2 million in compensation ran football programs with average revenues of $21.7 million, their salaries thus amounting to about 5.6 percent of football revenue. (For comparison, in 2006, when NFL coaches' salaries ranged from $1.35 million to $7 million, clubs averaged $192 million in revenue.) By 2003, when the number of millionaires reached about thirty, the ripple effect meant that June Jones, the coach at the University of Hawaii, with football revenue of roughly $5.6 million, could sign a five-year extension for slightly more than $800,000 a year—over 14 percent of his program's revenue. Jones's salary, in turn, was nearly $300,000 higher than Fresno State's Pat Hill, who ran the most successful program in the conference. By 2006 Hill's salary topped $1.2 million (15.2 percent of his program's revenue). After Jones took Hawaii to a BCS bowl to conclude the 2007 season, the final year of his contract, his school tried to keep him for $1.3 million ($1.6 million in some reports) but lost him to SMU for $2 million (which brought in $8.7 million in revenue in 2006–7, the most recent year for which there are data; $2 million would be 23 percent of that amount). In leaving, Jones slammed Hawaii for its shabby athletic facilities—which perhaps the school could not afford to upgrade because of what it was paying its coach. Such ripples run through every conference and across the entire subdivision.

When the football coach's salary goes up, it also creates ripples within the athletic department. The salaries of coordinators and assistants, of coaches in other sports, and of athletic administrators rise in turn, as do the salaries of NCAA executives. In reporting on Saban's move to LSU, the *Philadelphia Inquirer* noted that NCAA president Cedric Dempsey received $685,000 in cash and benefits in 1998. In 2003–4 Myles Brand made $835,000 (while his successor as Indiana University's president made $261,375). Those charged with maintaining educational priorities in college athletics are indirect beneficiaries when spending spirals out of control.[13]

In October 2006 Representative Bill Thomas, chair of the House Ways and Means Committee, wrote a public letter to Brand questioning the exorbitant salaries paid to coaches by tax-exempt, nonprofit educational institutions. In this spirit, if we take the nonprofit world instead of the decidedly for-profit NFL as our frame of reference, we might be struck by the fact that the average nonprofit CEO's compensation in 2006 was $327,575, with the highest-paid chief executive receiving about $2.5 million (for running the Memorial Sloan-Kettering Cancer Center in New York).[14]

Brand responded to Congressman Thomas by claiming that much of coaches' compensation came from media and apparel deals, not directly from university resources. This is literally true in many cases but practically another fiction like the amateurism of big-time football. A football coach's compensation "package" is akin to the "outside professional activities" permitted to all faculty and staff at a university. A business professor, for example, can consult with a start-up company, a psychology professor can appear as an expert witness in a lawsuit—and they both can be paid well for their expertise. For obvious reasons, the university where I work has rules about such activities: they must be approved by the faculty member's department chair or supervisor, they must not interfere with teaching and other campus responsibilities, and so on. Two of OSU's rules—typical, I assume, for research universities—reflect interestingly on coaches' compensation. One requires that outside activities not "involve use of University property, facilities, equipment, or services, except in limited circumstances when approved by the faculty member's department head/chair and dean or the dean and vice president." The other requires that the faculty member must make it "clear to the outside employer (agency, board, jury, or audience) that he or she is acting in an individual capacity and does not speak, write, or act in the name of the University or directly represent it."[15] The intent of the first rule is to keep faculty members from using publicly owned university resources to enrich themselves beyond their contracted salaries; the intent of the second is to protect the university from liability if a faculty member says or does something outrageous or screws up as a hired "expert."

A football coach *always* acts in the name of the university. A coach has no marketable identity except as the head of the university's football team. The $1 million or $2 million in outside income (much of it tax deductible for whoever provides it) properly belongs to the university as surely as does the $500,000 or $600,000 in official salary. The huge sums from Nike and other apparel companies are particularly bizarre in this regard. Why should the coach, not the university, be paid for having the players wear a certain brand of shoes and uniforms? Regarding this money as somehow "extra," separate from funds controlled by the institution, is a convenient fiction that absolves universities of responsibility for their coaches' millions.

The justification of coaches' salaries on the grounds that they come from outside is akin to the justification of athletic scholarships in the 1930s when they were paid by boosters instead of the institution. Like that system, this one evolved over time, so that it came to seem normal. And the norm was established by the wealthiest programs, which the rest then try desperately to reach.

A NEW CONTRACT FOR ATHLETES, TOO

The ripple effect of rising coaches' salaries has not contaminated the purity of the "student-athlete." Under the new contractual model implicitly established in 1973, coaches were to promote the university's image through winning teams. Their players' implied contract stipulated an education in return for their athletic endeavors. As football then became a full-time, year-round occupation for the players, with the same low chance of a career in the NFL but with less opportunity to be fully engaged students, the logic of the contractual relationship between athletes and universities became increasingly distorted by assumptions persisting from a vanished era. With the cost of their education setting a cap on their compensation, even as the demands on their time expanded, scholarship athletes received in 2008 exactly what they had received in 1968. The dollar value of a scholarship has increased seven- or eightfold since the 1960s, but it still pays for tuition, fees, board and room, and a little extra for incidentals. In a realignment of the ancient contradiction, as college football became increasingly a commercial enterprise for coaches, it remained an extracurricular activity for players. Or as Allen Sack put it, "Socialism for the athletes, free enterprise for everyone else."[16]

In 1973, along with instituting the one-year grants, the NCAA limited the total number of football scholarships to 105. That number was dropped to 95 in 1978 and to 85 in 1994, in each case as a cost-cutting measure. All of the money saved has effectively been redirected to coaches' salaries, not to reducing expenses. If we take the cost of a college scholarship today to be roughly $25,000 per year,[17] then head coaches in top football programs today earn more than the combined scholarships of their entire teams ($25,000 × 85 = $2.1 million). The fact that much of the coach's compensation comes from external sources (boosters, TV shows, and so on) is beside the point. That money could be directed to other needs within the athletic department if the system were different.

Out of the upheavals of the late 1960s, coaches became managers of football teams, not father figures or professors of football and its lessons for life, while players became athletes with annual, renewable contracts who are promised an education in exchange for their athletic services but with major constraints on attaining it. Due to economic circumstances unforeseen in 1973, coaches soon found themselves in a position to cash in on a multimillion-dollar entertainment enterprise. But the players' status did not change. Economist Richard Sheehan calculated the "implicit compensation" of football players in Division I in the mid-1990s as an hourly wage ranging from $3.23 (at an inexpensive state school) to $21.48 (for an expensive private school), for an average of $8.99.[18] Repeating the calculations today would presumably yield similar results. Here in cold numbers we see the bizarre asymmetry of college coaches making CEO salaries while their players earn less than grounds-keepers and secretaries in the front office.

The new contractual model treated the players as professionals but without professionals' compensation or rights. It gave the coach complete power to set the terms of the contract, leaving the players only with a choice of whether to accept or reject it. Comparing the contracts, real or implied, of college and professional football players can be instructive. The standard player contract that I signed with the Kansas City Chiefs in 1970—three one-year contracts, not a three-year contract—bound me to the Chiefs for those three years, plus an "option" year, while allowing the Chiefs to dump me at any time. Once the Chiefs drafted me, I could not negotiate with any other team, and the so-called Rozelle Rule made playing out my option to sign with another club nearly impossible. When NFL players went on strike in 1974 for contractual fairness, we were widely accused of being greedy.

The one-year scholarship established in the same era was only marginally less one-sided. A high school athlete could sign with any college in the country, and he could "play out his option"—transfer to another school—though only by sitting out for a season. And while an NFL coach could release a player even in midseason, a college coach at least had to wait until the end of the school year. NFL players struggled through three failed strikes in 1974, 1982, and 1987 for basic equity in their contracts, with little success until the courts intervened. A series of legal rulings finally resulted in 1993 in free agency for players and empowered them to negotiate a guaranteed collective share of the revenues they produced (roughly 60 percent under the current agreement). College athletes, in the meantime, with no bargaining unit or organization to plead their case, have remained wholly subject to the control of their athletic departments and the NCAA.

The conditions created by the NCAA's rule changes in 1972–73 unsurprisingly spawned an athletes' rights movement, beginning with the Center for Athletes' Rights and Education (CARE) in 1981. At CARE's first press conference, its director, Allen Sack, presented an "athletes' bill of rights," whose preamble declared their right, as students, to "an education similar in quality to other students'" and, as athletes, to "safe working conditions and fair compensation for the money they generate." Sack then ticked off ten specific rights, including "legal assistance and due process in disputes with athletic departments and coaches" and "a multiyear grant-in-aid to help an athlete graduate even if injured." The item that most caught the press's and the public's attention was "the right to form unions and bargain collectively on all issues affecting financial aid and working conditions."[19] To sports fans uncomfortable with even professional athletes bargaining collectively for rights and financial benefits, the idea sounded wildly radical, and such a proposal would likely find little public support even today. Yet if we entertain the heresy that big-time football has become suspiciously like a full-time job, we must recognize that collegians remain bound by a contract whose terms are set by the employer and that only the employer can renew. As the average NFL salary rose from less than $30,000 to close to $2 million over the years since the 1960s, and college coaches enjoyed comparable increases, college football players have not received a raise in more than thirty years.

CARE was short-lived—in part because it lost its funding from the U.S. Department of Education by advocating for a union—but the cause of athletes' rights would be taken up by a state senator in Nebraska in the 1980s and by the Collegiate Athletes Coalition (later the National College Players Association) in 2001, while its basic principles more generally entered the wide-ranging debates about college athletics. Until the adoption of the one-year scholarship, athletes required no rights beyond those enjoyed by all students. As revenues and coaches' salaries soared while the athletes' compensation remained unchanged, a movement to secure athletes' basic rights became unavoidable. Although none of their advocates so far have effected major changes, a legal challenge for athletes' rights is more likely than reform efforts from within the NCAA to transform college athletics in the coming years.

The one-year scholarship is not solely responsible for transforming student-athletes into athlete-students. In addition to the other changes within the NCAA (freshman eligibility, elimination of the 1.6 rule), it was instituted just a few years before the changing economics of professional football and the altered landscape of televised sports began making it less and less likely that scholarship athletes would arrive at college with an education as their own highest priority.

Professional football's status and pay were so low in its early years that many of the best collegians, including Heisman Trophy winners, opted not to play pro ball at all. Into the 1960s, playing college football was less often a career path than an end in itself and a means to a free education. The average salary in the NFL in 1973 was $27,500. By 1984 it had increased to $225,600, then to $462,700 by 1991 and $1,056,300 by 1999.[20] At some point early in that progression, an NFL career obliterated every alternative as the first choice for a talented football player. Who would go even to medical school right out of college if he had a legitimate shot at a million dollars in a few years? At the same time, anyone who came of television-watching age in the 1980s and after grew up in a world in which football in season and sports year-round were on TV twenty-four hours a day, seven days a week. My generation grew up with *The Game of the Week*—collegiate on Saturday, professional on Sunday. My sons' generation grew up with multiple games five or six days (or nights) a week and *SportsCenter* every few hours. The ripple effect was inevitable: what was potentially at stake at the professional level, in both income and celebrity, for college football players increased enormously, as it did for high school players for whom college was the road to the NFL, as it did for middle school and even elementary schoolkids dreaming of NFL glory. In many communities, youth soccer and basketball were more extreme, but football, too, became not a sport kids played in season for fun or self-affirmation but year-round training for the next level and ultimately the NFL.

The system has worked well for those good enough to make it all the way. Of the 54,000 young men playing college football at all levels, about 1,000 sign NFL contracts each year, and about a third of those make their teams. The payoff for all those years of diligent preparation is a salary that now averages close to $2 million. Most of those 330 players won't reach that level, however, as the average salary is distorted by the multiple millions made by superstars. (In 2005, when the average salary was $1.4 million, the median was $569,000.) And less than half of those who make it to the NFL play as many as four seasons. Of course, even a brief stay in the NFL now pays huge dividends. The minimum rookie salary in 2008—what free agents made, not high draft choices with their millions in signing bonuses—was $295,000. Just make the team and you earn more than a quarter of a million dollars right out of college. But those are the ones who make it. The NFL is an all-or-nothing proposition: the college player who is a little bit less talented or lucky than his

NFL-bound teammate receives not a dime. And too many of those who do not make it in the NFL have sacrificed much of their college experience to an unrealized dream.[21]

WHAT COLLEGIATE MODEL?

Comparing college to NFL football is to ignore the essence of the Collegiate Model championed by Myles Brand. So, what about the other end of the bargain, the university's contractual obligation to provide an education in return for athletic service? If the pay for college football players has not risen, and if relatively few of them go on to play professionally, are universities at least still delivering what they offered in 1973?

This is the most urgent question of all, and we lack adequate information for a definitive response, but I fear that the answer is largely no. Aside from missing out on Notre Dame's study-abroad program in Innsbruck, Austria, I played football at Notre Dame in the late 1960s without making a single academic sacrifice. My daily schedule during the season was a Spartan one—classes, practice, dinner and game film, several hours in the library, sleep—but it was manageable (and was facilitated, I should confess, by my lack of a social life in the all-male environment at Notre Dame in those years). When I had no classes until late morning, I slept in after studying late. When a chemistry or physics lab interfered with practice, I went to the lab. Football season ran from late August to Thanksgiving, extending to New Year's only in my senior year, when Notre Dame accepted a bowl bid for the first time since Rockne and the Four Horsemen. (In the not-too-distant past, bowl games were controversial, as an excessive distraction from academic priorities.) In the off-seasons, I lifted weights or ran on most days—workouts were mostly self-regulated—and was less organized because I had more free time. In summers, I returned home to Spokane, where I earned my spending money for the coming year and ran or lifted weights after work.

I left Notre Dame in 1970 not only with the best education the university could offer me but also with a full college experience. I stayed up late (at least in the off-season) for bull sessions—a term that has gone the way of the hula hoop and *Howdy Doody*—with my friends about Vietnam, the Chicago Seven, our favorite novels, what we were learning in our classes. I attended the on-campus screenings of Antonioni's *Blow-Up* and Fellini's *8½* (struggling to think of something intelligent to say about it to my friends afterward). I never missed a visiting writer at the annual week-long Sophomore Literary Festival inaugurated by my class in the spring of 1968. I heard Ralph Ellison read from *Invisible Man* and talk about race in America just days after the assassination of Martin Luther King Jr. I saw the world premier of a Norman Mailer film, *Beyond the Law* (not quite up to Bergman and Fellini, but still an event). I won a drawing in one of my literature classes to attend an evening reception for Joseph Heller, whose *Catch-22* I read annually as my personal rite of spring. Since I had arrived at Notre Dame as a walk-on with a primary focus on my education, I was academically oriented from the outset, but my teammates with football scholarships had the same opportunities whether they took advantage of them or not. We all graduated. The offensive line on which I played as a junior had a collective grade-point average of 3.4.

My fellow Domer Allen Sack (a senior when I was a freshman), who went on to a distinguished academic and sports-activist career, has written about having a slightly different experience from mine. Highly recruited as an all-state quarterback, Allen discovered his intellectual passions as a senior instead of arriving with them as I did. As he has described his experiences, he came to college more focused on football, and he did not fully embrace his academic opportunities until after his final football season ended. But he was able to bloom intellectually because he had worked hard in the classroom as a freshman (when ineligible for the varsity), and because he had always had to take his classes at least semiseriously while pursuing his football dreams. Allen's account of discovering the "life of the mind" as a senior rings true to my own experience; he just found his belatedly.[22] He was no more "typical" than I was, but as a recruited scholarship athlete, he represents the big-time football of our era more directly than I do.

College football has had no golden age. The criticism of distorted priorities that one hears today was also heard thirty years ago—and fifty and eighty years ago. Writing shortly after my own college days, chiefly to celebrate the cultural phenomenon of the Big Game, the faculty representative at Indiana University warned that "the student-athlete has become a specialized product of contemporary culture" and is therefore too easily cut off from the larger life of the campus.[23] But the fact that the criticism remains the same does not mean that the conditions criticized have not changed. Whether or not my experience was the norm in the 1960s, it was available, and I fear that it has become all but impossible in big-time football today.

For reasons noted above that are mostly beyond universities' control, the young men on the football team are more likely to arrive as athletes than as students. Once on campus, the one-year scholarship makes them hired athletes with annual contracts and options for renewal contingent on satisfying the coach. Most players are renewed each year, but they cannot take renewal for granted. In practical terms, this means that they must acquiesce in coaches' increasing demands on their time. While the financial stakes in big-time college football have been soaring, along with the salaries and expectations for coaches, the demands on the athletes have comparably risen—but without compensation.

At the "reform convention" of 1991, the NCAA limited contact hours for varsity sports to twenty a week during the season, but "voluntary" conditioning and film sessions nearly double that in most Football Bowl Subdivision (Division I-A) programs. (In a recent NCAA survey [the Growth, Opportunity, Aspirations, and Learning of Students in College, or GOALS, study], football players in the top subdivision reported spending 44.8 hours per week on their sport, which presumably includes travel time for games.[24]) A former student of mine at Oregon State—not a football player who attended classes but a bright student who played football (and who struggled not always successfully to maintain these priorities)—provided me his daily schedule. It was like mine thirty years earlier, but with the addition of an hour of weight lifting in the morning (stealing from sleep) and a second film meeting in the afternoon before practice.[25] The season itself has been extended, from ten games in my day to eleven, then to twelve (or thirteen under certain circumstances). I wrote term papers for my classes after the season ended; today the season can last beyond final exams. Organized off-season workouts nearly double the eight-hour weekly limit set by NCAA rule—my former student had morning weights and afternoon conditioning and skills practice— while more generally reminding the players of their primary responsibility. Even summers now belong to coaches, who want their athletes in town for "informal" workouts.

For coaches, the extra workouts are essential for individual and team development. How does an athletic director or university president pay his football coach millions of dollars and then tell him, "Oh, by the way, I don't want you getting the boys up too early; remember, their education is our highest priority"? For the athletes, all of the extra time commitments are "voluntary," but if they want to play, they had better volunteer. For those with NFL dreams, the stakes are too high to risk displeasing their coaches (and football is their first priority anyway). For those who come to realize that the NFL is no longer in their future, their coaches have the power to renew or not renew their scholarships. Aside from possible repercussions, anyone good enough to earn a scholarship has been self-driven for a long time in an environment that constantly reinforces the importance of athletic achievement. Slacking off or not meeting expectations might seem like an easy choice, but only for someone who has never made a serious commitment to anything. "Voluntary" workouts are the scandal in college athletics that strangely fails to scandalize.

Ostensibly to make good on their obligation to educate, and to avoid obvious exploitation, the NCAA in 1982 began requiring Division I athletic departments to provide their athletes with necessary academic support. (Just twenty-four universities had formal academic-service programs at the time.[26]) As noted in the previous chapter, palatial academic centers have become recruiting tools for high-revenue programs, but most institutions make do with much less. Whether the building is gaudy or functional, academic-support units at their worst have been sources of academic fraud, keeping athletes eligible by writing their papers or arranging bogus classes. Even at their best, and not by choice but by necessity, they too easily function as little more than eligibility factories.

The previous chapter considered these issues from the perspective of institutional priorities; here I want to think about them in relation to the institution's implicit contract with its athletes. Teams win with great athletes, not great scholars. Success in recruiting means getting the best athletes who can survive academically. It follows inevitably that the highest priority for tutors and academic advisers in athletic departments is to assist the least academically sound or motivated students on the football (and basketball) teams. Highly publicized incidents of academic failure invariably involve marginal students with blue-chip athletic ability, such as when Dexter Manley testified before the U.S. Senate in 1988 that, despite four years at Oklahoma State, he was illiterate. Manley entered college with an ACT score of 8 (the equivalent of less than 400 on the SAT) and a second-grade reading level.[27] He then refused to take remedial reading classes but signed up for easy courses, had a friend do his homework, and cheated on tests. His former academic adviser acknowledged that "we exploited Dexter for four years," then added, "but he exploited us, too. Coaches further their careers with players like Dexter, and players in turn groom themselves for pro ball."[28]

Few athletes arrive at college as ill-prepared as Dexter Manley, but in order to provide educational opportunity, rather than coldly exploit their athletes, athletic departments set up their academic-support systems with their least well-prepared recruits in mind. The primary objective is to maintain their eligibility through academic progress and, ultimately, to graduation, and the recently established APR raises the stakes for failure. Even without the APR, every genuine academic success with these marginal students is a victory over circumstances—sometimes the salvaging of a life from the streets—and conscientious advisers are rightly proud of these triumphs.

The very best students, whether on the football team or in other sports, are more on their own. They can possibly still receive a genuinely good education and graduate with degrees even in Engineering or Premed, though with more academic sacrifices and less of the full college experience than was possible in the 1960s. The heartening story of Florida State's Myron Rolle during the 2008 season would seem to confirm that everything remains possible. The son of Bahamian immigrants and a cornerback good enough to be projected as an early NFL draft pick, Rolle won a Rhodes Scholarship on the day of the Maryland game, then was whisked away to the stadium by private jet and police escort in time for the second half (accompanied by a posse of reporters documenting every moment). Rolle had already graduated in Premed in two-and-a-half years with a 3.75 GPA, conducted biomedical research, and developed a health-education curriculum for elementary students in his summers, and he was now working on a master's degree in public administration as he completed his football eligibility.

Rolle's story is indeed inspiring, but obviously as an exception and not a typical case. He arrived at Florida State with high grades, a high SAT score, and "a bevy of Advanced Placement credits," as well as a ranking by national scouts as "first among college recruits." He succeeded by making sacrifices in both parts of his life. He graduated early with high honors but not without public criticism from an assistant coach "for spending too much time studying." On the other side of campus, one of his professors and academic mentors commented to reporters, "Myron has such a tremendous mind and intellect that it's exciting to think about what he could do if he didn't have all the distractions of football." Rolle proved what's still academically possible for an academic high achiever, but against the system rather than within it.[29]

The capable students, neither marginal nor exceptional, are the ones least well served by the structures set up for student-athletes who are really athlete-students. These are the ones who, were they not athletes, would come to college with no burning intellectual passions and no particular direction but would discover those passions and direction through exposure to the university's intellectual and cultural life. Instead, they are too often steered away from classes and majors that might prove too difficult, then left alone as long as they continue passing their courses. Football players of my generation disproportionately majored in Physical Education, often as preparation for becoming coaches and teachers. Today's athletes often cluster in majors with less clearly defined career paths. "Jock majors" are an old issue but in new circumstances. The point is not that athletes have less-challenging majors than before but that in our more achievement-driven modern universities and national economy, the consequences are potentially graver.

Wrestlers and softball players who are similarly capable but not highly motivated drift along the same path. The "non-revenue" (or "minor," or "Olympic") sports in Division I universities, whether by choice or necessity, operate on the football model (with the added burden of more mid-week competitions). Either the athletic director demands "excellence" from all teams or the athletes and their coaches are themselves committed to excellence. In either case, this means full-time, year-round commitment to the sport, though usually without any possibility (or illusion) of a professional future. Without professional illusions, athletes in these sports are more likely than football or basketball players to come to college as serious students and pursue their own educational opportunities; but those who define themselves as athletes first, students second, make the same sacrifices as the football players do.

For athletic departments and NCAA rules not to acknowledge the different circumstances of those who compete in revenue or nonrevenue sports has unfortunate consequences for both. Big-time football has created the model for sports like wrestling and softball with year-round training and intensified pressure to win. At the same time, football players are treated by the NCAA as if their sport were the same as wrestling or softball and not a multimillion-dollar entertainment business. Big-time college football players today tend to be aware of the millions they generate for their coaches and universities while they receive only access to an education whose full advantages are denied them. I know both from personal conversations and from a public program at Oregon State a few years ago that the more outspoken and thoughtful athletes today speak of college football as a "business" or their "job"—words and ideas that would never have occurred to me when I played. On that NCAA survey in which football players in the top subdivision reported spending 44.8 hours on their sport, many of them claimed that they would like to spend more. Rather than feeling relieved that they do not complain about the demands, educators should be doubly concerned that they have so thoroughly embraced their status as athletes first, students second.

The NCAA's latest effort at academic reform is consistent with a philosophy focused on eligibility rather education. Keeping athletes who are marginal students on track toward graduation to prevent their exploitation is obviously a laudable goal. But all Division I college athletes are governed by the same rules, and all of those with educational aspirations beyond eligibility are not equally well served. The capable but unfocused students are the ones most handicapped by the APR's requirement that 40 percent of degree requirements in a specific major be completed by the end of the sophomore year. The NCAA's own survey of 10,000 college athletes (not just football players), released in January 2007, found that playing their sport prevented roughly 20 percent of them from pursuing a major in "the field of their choice" and 40 percent from taking courses they wanted. Myles Brand was strangely cavalier in responding publicly to these figures, pointing out that athletes are "more suited" for certain majors and that "everyone doesn't get in this world to do everything they want to do." He pointed out that other students often had to make sacrifices because of work. "What we get," Brand declared, "is student-athletes trading off having an athletic scholarship for not having to work 20 or 40 hours a week."[30] Could the president of the NCAA have been implying that playing football was a job?!!

ENTITLED OR EXPLOITED?

Brand also repeatedly insists that the experience of college athletics is itself compensation for the academic sacrifices. Here we desperately need more information. Because the routine rhetoric on college athletics so consistently spins out into extremes of celebration or censure, I have become overly wary of expressing my own beliefs about sport's genuine value. In a famous passage in *A Farewell to Arms*, Hemingway wrote about how words such as "courage" have become meaningless through overuse. I feel the same way about the "discipline," "self-sacrifice," "team commitment," and so on that are supposedly learned in athletics. I believe in them, but I do not believe that they are always learned through sports, and I know that a very different set of distorted values can also be learned.

That said, I assume that a lot of young men make greater academic sacrifices today than I had to make forty years ago but that playing college football is still an invaluable personal experience for them. On an NCAA survey of athletes at eighteen Division I-A institutions in 2006, nearly everyone (97–98 percent) claimed that participation in college sports enhanced their leadership skills, teamwork, work ethic, and ability to take responsibility for themselves. Between 80 and 90 percent believed that athletics contributed to their educational and/or personal development and to their overall university experience in preparing them for life after graduation.[31] Whether life beyond graduation will bear out their optimism is yet to be determined, of course, but we could take these self-assessments at face value while also assuming that a sport that requires twenty hours a week, instead of the forty-five that was reported by football players, could produce the same benefits.

We also know too much about the larger football culture not to believe that there is another side to athletes' experiences not captured in this survey. Athletic experiences are personal, but the possibilities are to some degree shaped by the system, and the current system of big-time college athletics seems programmed to create what *New York Times* columnist William Rhoden has called a sense among athletes of "limitless entitlement" whose "end result is often as evident on the crime blotter as in the sports section." This culture of entitlement too easily fosters dependency, producing star athletes "accustomed to being shepherded through the system without ever having to look out for themselves, from simple perks like not having to stand in line to more serious crutches like being guided through school by tutors and structured study halls." (Rhoden is additionally concerned with how entitlement can "dull racial consciousness and eliminate communal instincts" in African American athletes.)[32] At the same time, despite all of that special treatment, far too many football players leave college without a degree, let alone an education. In other words, the culture of big-time college football has become a decidedly strange mix of entitlement and exploitation. And entitlement itself is an ironic form of exploitation.

Special treatment for college football stars is another very old story. Unethical recruiting practices and illicit payments to athletes began in the 1890s and were widespread by the 1920s, though under circumstances that were radically different from today's. Although the NCAA had no uniform rules or regulatory power until after World War II, universities in those early years were expected to resist "professionalism," which included *any* recruiting by coaches or subsidizing by universities. The ruling fiction was that brawny young men showed up on campus and asked the coach for a chance to try out for the team. The reality was that coaches set up networks of alumni and supporters who scoured the backwoods for prospects to send off to State U with cash in their pockets or promises of jobs when they arrived. Although some boosters got carried away, or the brawny youths they sent to Alma Mater neglected to attend classes, the routine scandals that resulted did not lead to a full-fledged reform movement until the late 1940s. As I noted earlier, although the notion would seem bizarre today, for universities struggling to align their principles with their practices, it was considered more ethical for alumni to provide financial help than for universities themselves to subsidize mere athletic rather than academic ability.

The institutionalization of the athletic scholarship in the 1950s obviously did not put an end to boosters and athletic departments providing extra benefits. A culture of entitlement has been amply documented in the routine reporting on the sports pages, whose incidents have been periodically gathered up into general indictments such as "Athletic Recruiting: A Campus Crisis," or "The Boosters: Growing Problem in College Sports," or some other scandalous aspect of the problem.[33] Between recruiting violations and academic scandals, roughly half of the schools in Division I-A received some sort of NCAA sanction in the 1980s.[34] From January 1954 through August 2008, the NCAA dealt with 185 major infractions for football programs in what became Division I-A, at least one every year except for 1963 and as many as ten (in 1986).[35]

Among the more celebrated cases of the past couple of decades was the one at Auburn in the early 1990s, in which a disgruntled defensive back, Eric Ramsey, secretly taped coaches discussing illegal payments to players, then handed the tapes to NCAA investigators. Auburn's resulting two-year probation in 1993 was the school's sixth.[36] (Auburn subsequently added a seventh major infraction, while Arizona State and Southern Methodist currently lead all schools with eight.) SMU provided the extreme case of boosters run amok in 1987 when it became the only school ever to receive the "death penalty"—shutting down the football program for a full season, which for practical reasons meant two seasons before it could resume—following major infractions in 1958, 1965,

1974, 1976, 1981, and 1985. SMU boosters since the late 1970s had been operating what grew to a $400,000 slush fund for paying athletes, with the cooperation of coaches and the complicity of university presidents and members of the board of governors, including a past and future governor of Texas, Bill Clements. The situation grew so ugly that two players were able to steal the entire under-the-table payroll without repercussion because the coaches feared what the players would tell the media if they were punished in any way.[37] Reading these and other stories, many sports fans must have come to believe that "everyone does it," while only the unlucky ones, or those lacking the top programs' immunity, ever get caught. When a school such as Clemson could leap from mediocrity to a national championship in 1981, be caught cheating, endure its probation, but remain among the football elite, cheating appeared to be a worthwhile risk.

Dishonest football programs are another old story. What was new in the 1980s was the open cynicism of many athletes, evidence of which emerged in the aftermath of the conviction of sports agents Norby Walters and Lloyd Bloom in 1989 for fraud and racketeering. Between 1981 and 1987, Walters and Bloom signed agreements with fifty football players whose eligibility had not expired, from almost three dozen schools, including many of the top programs in the country. Cheating in college athletics usually breaks no state or federal laws, but Walters and Bloom were convicted of defrauding the universities because, as paid professionals, the players they signed were no longer entitled to the scholarship payments they continued to receive.[38] To be sure, Walters and Bloom conducted a sleazy operation, but a sound argument could be made that, as long as universities insisted on treating students as athletes, the athletes had the right to protect their athletic interests by signing with agents. Many of the young men playing college football themselves figured this out. A few months after the verdict, in a survey of 1,182 current or former NFL players conducted by Allen Sack, a third of the players admitted receiving illicit payments while in college, ranging from "money handshakes" (alumni slipping them a few bucks after a game) to $80,000 over a college career. More telling, 53 percent of the respondents—72 percent of the African Americans—"saw nothing wrong with the practice." And the practice continued unchecked by the convictions of Walters and Bloom. In a series titled "College Sports: Out of Bounds" in 1995, the *Boston Globe* reported that sports agents themselves "estimate that three out of four potential first-round draft picks in football and basketball receive cash or gifts either directly from agents and financial planners or from their runners."[39]

Some observers might have taken this news as yet another sign of general moral collapse—consistent with the increasing incidence of plagiarism and other forms of cheating among college students more generally[40]—but an overwhelming majority of the athletes in Sack's survey also claimed that their financial aid was inadequate and that they deserved greater compensation. And anyone who read black criminality into that 72 percent had to ignore the realities of black poverty and black dominance on the field and be blind to the possibility of exploitation. The results of this survey appeared in 1989, before coaches began earning $1 million and $2 million and $3 million, before Division I-A football revenues doubled and then doubled again. None of us at Notre Dame in the 1960s had any idea how much Ara Parseghian made. Players today would have to work hard not to know what their coaches earn and have some sense of what their universities make off football. College athletes might reasonably believe that they are entitled to a fair share.

ENTITLEMENT AND THUGGERY

The idea that star athletes in big-time football programs are exploited might seem laughable to fellow students who resent their lavish facilities and special treatment. This is another old story. When the NCAA at its "reform convention" in 1991 abolished athletic dorms, it eliminated the most conspicuous symbol of athletic extravagance on many campuses, particularly in the South. The first athletic dorms had been built in the 1940s at places like Oklahoma and SMU, and several of them, such as the so-called Bryant Hilton (Paul W. Bryant Hall) at Alabama and Bud House (Bud Wilkinson House) at Oklahoma, over time became famous for their opulence or notorious for their residents' criminal acts. The rash of felonies at Bud House in the late 1980s notwithstanding, the defenders of jock dorms claimed that players bonded and coaches could monitor their behavior and academic progress more effectively when athletes were housed together. Critics argued that isolating football players from the rest of the student body was bad for the athletes.[41]

The NCAA had tried to limit the luxury of athletic dorms several years earlier, but by the time it abolished the dorms altogether (effective in 1996), new "recruiting showpieces" had already emerged to replace them in what *Sports Illustrated* described as "mammoth training complexes, combination indoor practice facilities and weight rooms situated a few steps from the dorms, allowing football players to exist in a sort of hermetic theme park." Georgia's Dawg Mahal (Butts-Mehre Heritage Hall) and Tennessee's Neyland-Thompson Sports Center set the standard in the late 1980s, soon to be rivaled by other football programs competing for the best high school players. College football's facilities-building spree, or "arms race" (or "edifice complex" as the *Philadelphia Inquirer* termed it), was half about generating revenue from remodeled stadiums (through premium seating and luxury suites) and half about making "kids walk into your place and say, 'Wow!,'" as an associate athletic director at Texas put it.[42] *Sports Illustrated*'s preseason issue in 2002 included a photo spread showcasing three examples of "state-of-the-art football": the Lawrence Strength and Conditioning Center at Arizona State, the training table at Vanderbilt (a sumptuous spread of shrimp, crawfish, and other delicacies served daily by chef Majid Noori), and the medical-treatment center at Michigan.[43] No country club or Caribbean resort could have been more lavish. Even the lavish academic-support centers built more recently have, in part, become another substitute for jock dorms.

I must confess that, having worked out for my first couple of years at Notre Dame in a dilapidated field house and never having experienced a facility reserved for athletes, I have had a hard time comprehending that a recruit would choose a school on the basis of its fancy weight room. But context and expectations have changed, and these facilities have become major recruiting tools. At the same time, with tuitions rising and legislative funding for higher education flat or declining, many faculty and students gag at such extravagance—as happened at the University of Oregon in the summer of 2003, when a $3.2 million renovation of the Ducks' locker room left many in the cash-strapped university community wondering yet again about priorities. That story, too, is old. What's relatively new is the bizarre disparity between such extravagance for the care and feeding of football players and their undercompensation relative to the revenues they generate.

What's provided for athletes is, in some ways, what's used to entice all students to the modern university—trendy food courts, country-club-quality fitness facilities, recreation centers—only more exclusive and on a grander scale. Football players at the elite level today experience a sort of lavish servitude, and their status as privileged peons—or is it indentured celebrities?—can have some unsavory consequences. Again the story is not altogether new—remember the Big Man on Campus?—but conditions have grown more extreme. An element of conscious privilege, of athletes believing themselves not bound by the rules that govern the rest of society, seems to lie behind much of the boorish and even criminal behavior that has become a distressingly frequent feature of the college sports news. Jocks drunkenly brawling and groping women at fraternity parties are not recent developments, but either the national media simply began to pay more attention or the degree and scale of misbehavior rose sharply in the late 1980s.

Miami was the first to win notoriety as a football team out of control, with several misdemeanor arrests, a riot in the football dorm, and forty-seven players making $8,346 worth of phone calls through a stolen access number. Miami players reveled in their outlaw image, arriving in Tempe for the 1987 Fiesta Bowl dressed in battle fatigues and taunting opponents on and off the field.[44] In a series of investigative cover stories over the next several years, *Sports Illustrated* exposed Miami's chief rivals for college football's All-Criminal title. In 1989, under the headline "Oklahoma: A Sordid Story: How Barry Switzer's Sooners Terrorized Their Campus," the cover featured quarterback Charles Thompson in handcuffs after his arrest for selling cocaine. Three of Thompson's teammates had recently been arraigned for gang-raping a woman in the football dorm; another had shot a teammate after an argument. Oklahoma's problems, according to *Sports Illustrated*, began with head coach Barry Switzer, who ran his program like a "loose ship."[45]

A companion story described a Colorado football team from which two dozen players over the past three years had been "arrested, for everything from trespassing to serial rape." Eighteen members from the 1987 squad alone had been arrested and sixty-five "contacted" by police. (According to a later *Los Angeles Times* story, police in Boulder began using game programs as mug books to show the victims of certain crimes.[46]) Oklahoma and Colorado were but the most egregious examples of what *Sports Illustrated* termed a more general "American Disgrace" in a special report on dozens of similar incidents at other schools, ranging from assaults (one of them a brawl involving Pitt's Tony Siragusa) to the groping of a sales clerk and striking of a security guard (by Florida State's Deion Sanders). I mention Siragusa and Sanders, future NFL stars and media personalities, to make the point that neither public shame nor career setback necessarily resulted from such incidents.[47]

To Rick Telander, one of *Sports Illustrated*'s reporters on these stories and its senior writer on college football, the game had become simply

The Hundred Yard Lie, the title of the book published later in 1989 in which Telander confessed a visceral revulsion so intense he could no longer bear to cover the sport. Telander was John Underwood's spiritual heir at *Sports Illustrated*, its voice of outrage, with a striking generational difference between the two men in the fact that the coaches who had been for Underwood college football's moral compass were for Telander (who played during the rebellions of the late 1960s) a part of the problem. Underwood's *The Death of an American Game* in 1979 had warned of a "crisis in football" brought about by preventable excesses such as brutality, injuries, and the drugs (amphetamines and painkillers) used to cope with them. Telander's *Hundred Yard Lie* a decade later located ineradicable moral corruption at the very heart of the big-time commercialized game.[48]

Incidents like those at Miami, Oklahoma, and Colorado seemingly erupted everywhere in the 1990s, as sports sections began including brief wire-service reports under headings on the order of "The Police Blotter," and *Sports Illustrated* or a major newspaper periodically totaled the damage. In July 1991 *Sports Illustrated* reported that just since the previous January, two football players at USC, five at Missouri, four at Georgia Tech, three at Syracuse, and two at Purdue had been arrested on various charges, then added, "Space considerations make it impossible to provide a complete list of the schools with a single player arrested." Top programs seemed particularly prone to criminality. Florida State ("Free Shoes University," in the mocking words of rival coach Steve Spurrier) made headlines and a 1994 *Sports Illustrated* cover when several players enjoyed a "shopping spree" at a local Foot Locker. Players at the University of Nebraska were involved in a series of particularly ugly incidents, including sexual assaults committed by running back Lawrence Phillips and defensive lineman Christian Peter. A new rash of incidents at Miami led in 1995 to a cover-story "open letter" in *Sports Illustrated* to the school's president, calling on him to shut down a program that was "broken beyond repair."[49]

The year 1995 was particularly bad for football fans who clung to Frank Merriwell illusions. In addition to the *Sports Illustrated* cover story about Miami, the *Boston Globe* ran a four-part investigative series titled "College Sports: Out of Bounds," which included an installment on athletes' criminal misadventures; and at the end of the year, the *Los Angeles Times* issued a special report, "Crime & Sports '95," based on 252 "police incidents" involving 345 sports figures (127 of them college football players, along with another 40 from the NFL) that occurred between January 1 and December 15 of that single year.[50]

The incidents involving Phillips and Peter at Nebraska were part of the most disturbing new category of athletes' criminality. The *New York Times* reported in 1990 on studies showing that athletes were disproportionately involved in rapes and other sexual assaults, and that they were being shielded by authorities—the incidents were often not reported or were excused (as group sex, for example, rather than gang rape), with the intoxicated female victims receiving the blame. The *Boston Globe*'s "College Sports: Out of Bounds" series reported essentially the same state of affairs: athletes receiving more lenient treatment than nonathletes charged with similar offenses (as well as athletic directors not even reporting athletes' failed drug tests to their university presidents). Of the 252 incidents cited by the *Los Angeles Times*, seventy-seven involved violence against women. A follow-up story in *Sports Illustrated* on the shopping spree at Florida State included additional reports of Seminole players sexually abusing women. In the American heartland, at a Nebraska football program run by a famously straight-arrow coach (Tom Osborne), Phillips and Peter went nearly unpunished, despite their convictions for sexual assault, while the athletic department rescinded the scholarship of one of Phillips's victims, a member of the women's basketball team. With other Cornhuskers arrested for attempted murder, unlawful discharge of a firearm, and theft, Nebraska joined Miami, Oklahoma, and Colorado as an All-Criminal Final Four.[51]

To read in a single issue of the *Los Angeles Times* about 252 criminal acts is overwhelming. To read about them case by case, day to day, is merely numbing, as what once shocked becomes ordinary. Over the 1990s, a general sense of college football players' criminality settled into public consciousness. An ESPN poll in 1996 found that "51% of the 1,019 respondents considered athletes to be involved in crimes against women more often than the general population."[52] The harshest critics contended that so-called student-athletes were acculturated in thuggery and that big-time football programs fostered "rape cultures."

Something was clearly askew in big-time college football, yet the extent of the problem was not as clear as the reporting made it seem. While the specific stories about players such as Peter and Phillips were appalling, the generalizations about football and football players rested on shaky evidence. The *Los Angeles Times*, for example, reached its conclusions, as it explained to readers, after reviewing "more than 2,500 Associated Press and Times articles to find every nationally reported police incident." The total of 252, in other words, did not distinguish between arrests and convictions or between petty and serious crimes. The seventy-seven incidents of violence against women included accusations as well as indictments. Such violent assaults and the telephone calls made by thirty-one athletes at the University of Tennessee on a stolen credit card counted equally as "crimes."

The *Boston Globe* cited a study by researchers at Northeastern University and the University of Massachusetts—presumably, "Male Student-Athletes Reported for Sexual Assault: A Survey of Campus Police Departments and Judicial Affairs Offices," by Todd Crosset, Jeffrey R. Benedict, and Mark A. McDonald—that had been published a few months earlier. According to the *Globe*, this study "reinforces the view that athletes receive special treatment in sexual assault cases," and its researchers found that "varsity athletes at top-ranked Division I schools were significantly more likely to commit on-campus sexual assaults than other male students." The Northeastern-UMass study and the *Globe*'s summary entered public awareness on these terms, yet the researchers were, in fact, much more cautious and tentative. The total number of sexual assaults reported at ten universities over a three-year period was fifty-six, of which thirteen were committed by athletes, "two-thirds" of them (presumably eight or nine, that is) by football and basketball players. Eight or nine assaults at ten institutions over three years does not quite justify describing football programs as "rape cultures." The lead researcher for this study later reconsidered his findings, along with other studies on the subject, and determined that they were inconclusive.[53] But the overstated conclusions from their original report had already entered public consciousness. There were far too many documented cases, but how extensive and representative they were remained unclear. Overstated conclusions based on inadequate data risked discrediting concern about a real problem.

FEELING "SPECIAL"

Whether or not athletes get in more trouble than nonathletes, the pressing question for university administrators should be whether the system itself fosters or discourages antisocial behavior. The recruiting-and-rape scandal at the University of Colorado that broke in February 2004 (from events in December 2001) epitomized how a headline-grabbing incident touches on this larger question. Two young women sued the university for failing to address a known pattern of sexual assaults by football players and recruits, finally settling in December 2007 for $2.85 million.[54] As the case played out, with charges made, disputed, dropped, and repeated, it called attention to recruiting practices more generally. Even where sex was not overtly used to entice coveted high school quarterbacks and linebackers, schools that escorted their prize recruits in private jets and Hummers, gorged them on lobster tails, and set them up with look-but-don't-touch "recruiting hostesses"—the 'Bama Belles at Alabama, the Gator Guides at Florida, the Tiger PAWS at Clemson, and so on—either ran outrageous bait-and-switch scams or initiated their freshman football players into a culture of extreme entitlement. In the wake of the Colorado case, the *Oregonian* acquired the public records on a routine recruiting weekend hosted by the University of Oregon in January 2004. The Ducks spent $140,875.99 on twenty-five recruits, $109,927.64 of it on chartered jets to bring them to campus. The entire experience—including the steaks and lobster tails and tours of the new $3.2 million locker facility—was intended, as coach Mike Belotti put it, to make the young men "feel special."[55]

Too many incidents around the country suggested that continuing to feel special after enrolling might not be healthy for all concerned. One of the most telling comments out of Colorado in 2004 came from a football player who reportedly told his accuser when she first confronted him, "We're Big 12 champs. . . . Why would we need to rape somebody?" The sense of entitlement in that remark is less revealing than the unself-consciousness in making it. The NCAA in August 2004 responded to the Colorado scandal with new recruiting rules to curb what President Brand himself called "this culture of entitlement." Skeptical observers immediately began predicting that coaches would devise new ways to make recruits feel special. And the recruiting process, after all, was just the introduction to the culture of entitlement fostered by lavish facilities, celebrity status, and all the rest.[56]

Part of the entitlement problem is beyond colleges' control. "Blue-chip" recruits can arrive as the product of a youth sports system that has made them feel special since middle school or earlier. Many highly recruited athletes arrive on campus after several years on what William Rhoden calls "the Conveyor Belt," which ushers them from elite youth teams and high school summer camps into and through college, then (for the fortunate few) on to the pros, with everything provided except what really matters.[57] (Basketball is much worse than football in this regard.) The Internet recruiting networks Rivals.com and Scout.com allow high school superstars to track their market worth like pork or beef futures. Television and print media ratcheted up their attention to high school sports around 2005, when Fox Sports Net and ESPN began televising high school football games nationally as well as regionally.[58] In 2006 *Sports Illustrated* introduced its "High School Football Preview," along with weekly power rankings; and the music-video network MTV aired an eight-week reality show chronicling the football season of Hoover High School in Birmingham, Alabama. The series on MTV, according to the *New York Times*, showed "how a coach's ego and a community's zealousness can still corrode what is supposed to be a boys' game." Whether celebratory or critical, print and electronic media shone a brighter light on mere sixteen- and seventeen-year-olds than ever before.[59]

This media attention is troubling in itself, an ironic form of child abuse, but it is also unfortunate for college football programs, whose high school recruits will become even more likely to arrive with a sense of entitlement and perhaps with a belief in their immunity to the rules that govern everyone else. Instead of going to greater lengths to make these young men feel special, universities would serve them better by making them feel ordinary.

Reports from the Police Blotter sometimes seem merely the misbehavior of youth, with expanded possibilities for "misbehavior" since adults gnashed their teeth over juvenile delinquents in the 1950s. Some of the behavior seems just another symptom of what has been called an American "cheating culture" that involves not just college students downloading term papers from Internet sites but also their parents cheating on their income taxes. (*Time* reported in 2004 that 17 percent of Americans consider it okay to do this.[60]) What portion of Americans under twenty-five, or of the general population for that matter, would refuse a super deal from a friend at Foot Locker, or worry if it is legitimate? And some of the reported behavior makes one wonder at the oddly disproportionate outrage over the petty criminality of young "thugs" rather than, say, the more consequential venality of the rich and powerful. But some of this behavior does in fact point to an entitlement culture in big-time football. For a member of the football team, let alone a star, to think of himself as just another student on campus required an impressive sense of perspective by the 1990s, and the obstacles have only risen higher since then.

Yet at the same time that elite athletes have been encouraged to consider themselves special, NCAA rules assure that most of them will be unable to afford any of the extravagance that surrounds them. Lavish expenditures on facilities and amenities benefit less the athlete than the program. Not only do they represent not one dollar of additional compensation for athletes, but they also introduce athletes to unaccustomed extravagance only to jerk it away when their college careers end. Being knocked off the "Conveyor Belt" at any stage can be a wrenching experience, but the longer one rides, the more difficult must be the eventual readjustment. Those who leave college for the "real world" instead of the NFL face a sudden dislocation, and the ones who fail academically may leave with little or nothing as compensation. The sense of dislocation would presumably run deepest for African American athletes who feel alienated in their predominantly white environments despite their privileged treatment.

When the issue is the facilities "arms race" or athletes' "thuggery," critics accuse universities of "coddling" or "pampering"—a problem that is worse at top programs with too much money. When the issue is academic failure or low graduation rates, the charge is "exploitation." Here the problem is worse in financially strapped programs that cannot compete for the best students among the top athletes and that have fewer resources for academic support and more temptation to schedule midweek games. The deeper problem is that the system both pampers and exploits at the same time. What's remarkable is how many college football players manage to keep their bearings.

Hidden behind all of the headlines are most of the actual young men who play on the teams. To counter the negative stories in the media, the NCAA has begun conducting surveys, such as its 2006 "National Study of Student-Athletes Regarding Their Experiences as College Students," which paints a much rosier picture. Seventy percent reported that they were "satisfied" or "completely satisfied" with their educational experiences, 85 percent said that they participated actively in class at least some of the time, 83 percent said that they chose their majors for reasons unrelated to athletics, and so on. The data on African American athletes was less impressive—70 percent said that they chose their majors for nonathletic reasons—but still positive on most issues. Athletes in revenue sports were similarly less enthusiastic than those in nonrevenue sports but still mostly positive. Overall, the great majority of athletes claimed to be having a good educational experience.[61]

How do we reconcile such positive data with graduation rates of 50 to

60 percent in football, as well as the headline-screaming incidents that routinely appear in the sports pages and on *SportsCenter*? Self-reported surveys unfortunately invite a degree of skepticism, and the NCAA's own surveys have inconsistent results. At its convention in January 2008, the NCAA released the results from another survey of 21,000 current athletes. This is the GOALS study cited earlier, which found that those competing in the Football Bowl Subdivision spend 44.8 hours a week on their sport, and that many of them would "like to log more hours if they could." The survey also found that most college athletes "view themselves more as athletes than as students," nearly two-thirds believe that their grades would be higher were they not playing a sport, and "those who viewed themselves primarily as students had higher graduation rates." Where football players as a subgroup stood on these questions was not reported.[62]

The results of the two studies do not mesh. The NCAA's surveys may bring us a little closer to an accurate picture than do the headline-grabbing media stories, but they do not simply settle the issues. We know that the system is full of dangerous pitfalls. To know how well the young men who must navigate that terrain have been faring, we still need more and better information. (The NCAA has promised more reports from its GOALS study.)

LIFELONG BENEFITS?

There is no question that college football has historically provided social and economic mobility for thousands of young men who otherwise would not "belong" in college. Once there was evidence for believing that college football provided lifelong benefits, as sons of mill workers and coal miners entered the great American middle class through their collegiate acculturation and the college degrees they earned by playing football. Former football stars' local celebrity won them jobs with banks and insurance companies. Stars and ordinary participants alike benefited from a widely held belief, shared by prospective employers, that football built character and fostered traits that led to success off the field.

In today's highly competitive, performance-driven job market, has local athletic celebrity become less valuable? It would be good to know. Graduation rates alone—which should be a whole lot higher than 60 percent for a group on which so much academic assistance is lavished— cannot measure the educational success of a college football program.

We need to know what the lives of former players look like five years, ten years, fifteen and twenty years after leaving school, with or without a degree, and what role playing college football had in shaping them. We need to know the impact on their employment but also, however difficult to gauge, the impact of their college experience on the quality of their lives. (Universities are more than trade schools, after all; they have a mission to educate their students for life and citizenship as well as jobs. Athletic programs may be serving those goals well. Or not.)

Whether big-time college football players are ultimately exploited, despite their pampering, can only be determined by the long-term impact of their experience, and we currently lack data to inform an answer. In this entire discussion, we have been considering only the commercialized, big-time version of the sport. In *The Game of Life* (2001) and *Reclaiming the Game* (2003), William Bowen, then president of the Andrew W. Mellon Foundation, and his coauthors (James Shulman for the first book, Sarah Levin for the second) drew on the foundation's database of information on 90,000 students who attended thirty selective colleges and universities in the 1950s, 1970s, and 1990s to demonstrate that distorted priorities can be a problem even at Harvard and Princeton. The chief revelation in Bowen's books was that academic underperformance by athletes and an athletic/academic divide in educational institutions characterize college sports even at Ivy League and other elite universities and colleges. The Ivies and their near relations always stood in public debates for the way intercollegiate athletics ought to be conducted. Bowen and his collaborators presented hard data that challenged that belief.

As their two books showed, the impact of athletics on the institution as a whole, on its values and priorities, was actually greater at small elite schools than at the large public universities that predominate in big-time football because admission is a zero-sum game at the elite schools—each recruited athlete takes a slot that could go to a student with stronger academic credentials—and because the greater proportion of athletes in smaller student bodies (20–30 percent at Yale or Princeton, versus 5 percent at Michigan) has a proportionately greater impact on every aspect of the institution. Athletics also consume a larger portion of institutional funds at small elite schools (which, unlike public universities, can simply raise high tuition even higher to pay for them).[63] Members of the NCAA's Division III, where most of these schools compete, are currently undergoing their own intense self-scrutiny to the point of considering the difficult possibility of creating a new Division IV.[64]

In *The Game of Life*, however, the authors had to wrestle with one bit of data that did not match the otherwise uniform picture of athletes' academic underperformance: former athletes did *better* financially in their later careers than their nonathlete classmates. Those careers, Bowen and Shulman pointed out, tended to be in financial services rather than the presumably nobler professions of law, medicine, and science, and they followed from athletes more likely majoring in the social sciences than in the sciences, the humanities, or the arts. The "athlete culture" on campus, they observed, has "natural affinities" with the "business game," and "games with clear goals and rules, where competitive instincts, team play, and discipline are rewarded, provide a link between the culture of sports and marketplace pursuits."[65]

Bowen and Shulman offered this rationalization with dismay. They were unapologetically elitist in insisting that elite colleges and universities ought not to be in the business of training the merely rich and successful. While this concern touches on larger forces that are transforming our most selective colleges and universities into MBA-prep programs, this is not the nature of the problem in the Football Bowl Subdivision. If the young men who played big-time college football went on to become merely rich and successful, critics could close their laptops and call it a day. Athletic departments and universities would still have to be concerned about ethical and moral standards, as well as threats to their fiscal solvency—no small problems here, of course—but if their athletes, black and white, were undeniably benefiting in their long-term careers, these problems would become amenable to the NCAA's cautious reforms and the universities' own economic exigencies.

The NCAA has begun compiling the sort of data needed to know whether former big-time college football players are helped, hindered, or unaffected in their later lives and careers. Its Study of College Outcomes and Recent Experiences surveyed 8,000 student-athletes who graduated from high school in 1994 to discover "how they regarded their college experience 10 years later and how their lives are progressing." At the NCAA convention in January 2007, the lead researchers presented a preliminary report that 88 percent of the respondents had college degrees, and 94 percent of those "were positive about their overall education."[66] These percentages themselves seem extremely positive about an issue over which there has been grave doubt, to say the least, but how representative were the 8,000 was not explained, nor was there any breakdown by race or sport or elaboration on what "positive" signifies.

The NCAA has promised a fuller report from "the immense amount of information that has been collected." Along with its surveys of current athletes' educational experiences, the NCAA in this study has made a start toward sorting out "opportunity" from "exploitation." But the published reports thus far have not come close to settling the matter.

"OPPORTUNITY," THE COURTS, AND TITLE IX

One final issue, obviously important in itself but seemingly tangential to the present discussion, can also be considered as an aspect of college football's fundamental contradiction and the tangled mix of opportunity, entitlement, and exploitation that results. In 1972, that momentous year when freshmen football players became eligible for varsity competition and a year before the NCAA approved the one-year scholarship, President Richard Nixon signed legislation that included what became known as Title IX. In female college athletes' long legal battle for gender equity that followed, football has always been the enemy. Whether football players have been pampered or exploited, they have received opportunities (through scholarships) and budgeted resources that, before Title IX, were denied to women and that have remained untouchable despite the great challenge to fund the growth of women's sports. Though not always apparent, the conflict between proponents of football and proponents of Title IX has been yet another manifestation of the original contradiction at the heart of college football, playing out in exceedingly ironic ways. The only place where the NCAA and its member institutions have admitted that big-time college football players are actually athletes first and students second has been in court when challenging Title IX's mandate that women receive equal athletic opportunities.

In defending themselves before judges in Title IX lawsuits, university leaders have regularly argued that football should not count in calculating gender equity because it serves a unique marketing function for the university. They have a legitimate point, of course; they just choose not to make that point in other venues, when the issue is appropriate compensation for players, or workers' compensation for injured athletes, or million-dollar coaches' salaries in a nonprofit educational enterprise. As noted earlier, longtime NCAA executive director Walter Byers explained in his memoir that universities adopted the term "student-athlete" in the 1950s expressly to counter legal arguments that scholarship athletes were employees of the university and thus protected as workers. In addition to the appeal by the widow of the Cal Poly player cited earlier, two other obscure cases in the 1950s raised the question of whether injured athletes were entitled to workers' compensation. In one, an injured player at the University of Denver successfully sued for benefits. In the other, the Supreme Court overruled an industrial commission's award of compensation to the widow of a player at Fort Lewis A&M who died from a head injury. With these competing precedents in place, one-year scholarships were particularly vulnerable to appearing as employment contracts that would allow injured players to file claims as disabled workers. Understanding all of this, Byers in the 1960s urged universities that already gave one-year grants to insert a statement about "principles of amateurism, sound academic standards, and financial aid to student-athletes" in the letter sent to recruits.[67]

Following the NCAA's adoption of the one-year scholarship in 1973, member institutions in 1983 successfully argued in two new precedent-setting workers' compensation cases in Indiana and Michigan that, as amateurs and students, the injured parties were not in fact university employees. The NCAA was involved in the Indiana case, which the athlete (Fred Rensing) lost on appeal, and the organization also backed a successful appeal by Texas Christian University in 1997 over compensation for an athlete (Kent Waldrep) who had broken his neck in a game against Alabama way back in 1974.[68] Like most who followed college football in those years, I was oblivious to these rulings, which could have undermined the entire structure of college athletics had the judges ruled differently. The fact that decisions in the Rensing and Waldrep cases initially went against the institutions but were overturned on appeal emphasizes universities' vulnerability on this issue.

Unlike these obscure (but consequential) courtroom decisions, Title IX's transformation of college athletics since the 1980s has been highly publicized, as has its conflict with the football establishment. The tangled legal history is worth summarizing.[69] Title IX was a product of the civil rights and women's movements of the 1960s, originally conceived as an amendment to the landmark Civil Rights Act of 1964 to protect women as well as racial minorities against discrimination. Neither its advocates nor its opponents initially recognized its potential impact on school and college athletics, as it passed easily through Congress and was signed into law by President Nixon in 1972; but by 1974 its implications had become clear, and football seemed most directly threatened. In May 1974 Congress rejected an amendment to exempt revenue-producing sports in determining Title IX compliance, then in

July it approved a more cautiously worded amendment with the same intent—this one requiring "reasonable provisions considering the nature of particular sports." "The nature of particular sports" meant the special requirements of football, with its large number of players, high costs, and significant financial returns. After President Ford, in May 1975, approved the first regulations for compliance as developed by the Department of Health, Education, and Welfare (HEW) and submitted them to Congress for review, in June another attempt to guarantee greater protection for revenue-producing sports failed to get out of committee. In July Congress approved the new regulations.

The NCAA first became officially involved in 1976, when it challenged Title IX's legality after a number of big-name football coaches—including Bear Bryant, Darrell Royal, Bo Schembechler, and Tom Osborne—testified in 1975 that the legislation would be devastating to men's sports.[70] In 1977 yet another bill to exclude revenue-producing sports died in committee. Finally, in 1979 HEW issued its official interpretation of the legislation and established three methods of compliance: through steadily upgrading the status of women athletes; through demonstrating that the needs of women athletes were being met; or through "proportionality," an equitable distribution of resources between men and women on campus. "Proportionality" meant that the percentage of athletic scholarships for women should be the same as the percentage of women in the student body. In 1980 the newly established Department of Education was given oversight of Title IX through its Office for Civil Rights.

Enforcement of Title IX then stalled during the Reagan Era. In 1984 in *Grove City v. Bell*, the Supreme Court limited Title IX's mandate to athletic scholarships only. An athletic department could spend millions on its football program and thousands on all of its women's programs combined and still be in compliance as long as scholarships were equitably divided between men and women. Women's athletics nonetheless made headway at universities where gender equity was understood as an ethical mandate, not just a legal one; then in March 1988, Congress restored the legal obligation by passing the Civil Rights Restoration Act over President Reagan's veto. Four years later, in *Franklin v. Gwinnett County Public Schools*, the Supreme Court raised the stakes for noncompliance by ruling that successful complainants under Title IX could receive monetary damages. Finally, in November 1996 a federal appeals court upheld a lower-court ruling against Brown University, rejecting

Brown's argument that women were less interested in sports than men and therefore entitled to a smaller portion of scholarships. The court also reaffirmed the principle of proportionality as the primary means of demonstrating compliance with Title IX. Under the Equity in Athletics Disclosure Act of 1994 (EADA), Congress required universities to file annual reports on gender equity for tracking compliance. (These EADA reports coincidentally became the principle public source of information on athletic departments' finances.)

No responsible person involved with college athletics could dispute the principle of gender equity in Title IX, but what constituted "equity" and what was required to assure it have defied consensus. For the most part, public debate has focused on simple calculations. If finances were unlimited, the easy solution to achieving proportionality would be to add women's programs until the target numbers of men and women were competing. With limited finances, athletic departments have had to increase revenue in order to add women's programs or reduce expenditures on men's programs (or do both). One of Title IX's unintended consequences has come from its added pressure to commercialize the athletic department in every way possible in order to increase revenues. Dollars raised are dollars quickly spent, however, and eliminating or shrinking men's programs has still been necessary in numerous programs. Since athletic departments have refused to touch their football teams, men's sports such as wrestling, gymnastics, and swimming have borne the brunt of the cuts. While supporters of these "nonrevenue" sports have railed against Title IX, advocates for women's athletics have blamed the overblown football rosters and budgets. The problem has seemed a matter of simple math. Softball can balance baseball, gymnastics offset wrestling, but what women's sport could match football, with its roster of ninety or a hundred players and its budget of several million dollars? The only possible solutions have seemed extreme and have infuriated the opposing side: exempt football, or cut its budget drastically.

I assume that this impasse is utterly familiar, but perhaps not all of its ramifications. The competing arguments for Title IX and for football's exemption from Title IX starkly expose the divided soul of college athletics. Title IX became a political cause of the high-minded, not just for gender equity but also as a corrective to the distorted values in big-time college athletics. More tellingly, it also led athletic administrators to proclaim the truth that they denied everywhere else. As the athletic director at Division 1-AA University of Massachusetts told a reporter for the *New York*

Times in 2001, explaining why a football program that lost $2.5 million the previous year should not be shrunk to comply with Title IX, "Football is a visible sport and one of the few vehicles capable of bringing 10,000 people to campus."[71] Make that 100,000 at Michigan or Tennessee; the argument is similar at all levels. Most universities can no longer claim that football supports the rest of the athletic program—the majority lose money on it—but they can claim that football uniquely markets the university and connects it to its many constituents. Title IX forced administrators to admit that college football is not an extracurricular activity in the way that gymnastics or track is, but a marketing tool.

If so, how can football players be anything but university employees? This is the logical corollary that the NCAA has successfully denied in claims for workers' compensation.

A great absurdity underlies the dispute between football and Title IX, though it cuts both ways. Title IX is concerned with athletic opportunities; big-time football is concerned with marketing and university relations. Title IX is about benefits to student-athletes; football is about benefits to the institution. In its insistence on men's and women's equal rights to collegiate athletic participation and support, Title IX inadvertently focuses attention on the more fundamental issue of what or whom intercollegiate sports are meant to serve, and at what cost. History is a great ironist. In June 1968 Homer Babbidge, the president of the University of Connecticut, gave a talk before the National Association of Collegiate Athletic Directors in which he insisted that the only justification for college athletics was "their value for participants." Babbidge warned that the "need to gratify spectators," the "need for revenues," and the "craving for institutional recognition" risked violating this basic principle. According to Jack Scott, who reprinted Babbidge's talk in his radical critique, *The Athletic Revolution*, "most of the athletic directors reacted to his speech as if they had just had the Communist Manifesto read to them by Fidel Castro!"[72] Yet during the protests of the 1960s, when coaches and athletic directors defended their rules on grooming or political activity by invoking the supreme importance of "discipline," they linked it most openly to the good of the team but also, implicitly, to the good of the individual—the "value for participants" in Babbidge's words. A young man who learned discipline through football supposedly became a better and more successful citizen afterward.

Even as the one-year scholarship put the lie to any pretense that "the value for participants" was the highest priority, the pretense persisted.

Most obviously, it has fueled every honorable effort at academic reform. It has also lain behind every athletic director's or college president's public statements on the value of athletics in an educational setting, and it is Myles Brand's principle theme in advocating for the NCAA and its Collegiate Model today. Yet even Homer Babbidge could not have conceived football in the new millennium when he warned in his 1968 address against serving the alternative "need to gratify spectators," "need for revenues," and "craving for institutional recognition." Football's defenders against Title IX have indirectly acknowledged that "participation," and thus "opportunity," is irrelevant to football, whose true purpose is "institutional recognition." Like the athletic director at UMass, the athletic director at Marshall University spoke for virtually all of his colleagues in explaining why he preferred building up women's programs to reducing his football budget: because football is the chief activity through which alumni remain attached to their university.[73] Again, the logic of this argument would lead to recognizing football players as contracted employees, as athletes for hire, and to compensating them accordingly. If they were truly "student-athletes," as university officials have insisted in other contexts, there would be no justification for exempting them from Title IX calculations.

A different absurdity underlies some of the arguments *for* Title IX, including the one adopted by the courts. While Title IX rightly demands an equal share of athletic "opportunities" for women, the athletic budget from which it demands its rightful share is not determined by opportunity at all. Although concerned specifically with gender equity, Title IX would seem a mandate to return the "value for participants" to the center of college athletics, but Title IX in fact demands "proportionality" within an athletic world driven by football's commercial imperative. The courts have accepted the fiction that college sport is about opportunities for participants and have demanded that women receive their fair share, but they have calculated fairness as if universities still existed in the nineteenth century. The principle of proportionality requires that the gender balance among athletes closely mirror the gender balance of the student body. In the actual world of Division I sports, that idea is nonsensical. The courts' implicit model is the pure amateur sport of a mythical Golden Age, a time when the coach put out a call to all students and made up the team from the best of those who tried out. The reality is that athletes are recruited, and universities with 10,000 or 40,000 students have roughly the same number in each sport. Imagine proportionality on racial terms: the percentage of African American athletes mirroring the percentage of African Americans in the student body. The value of white football (and basketball) players and unathletic black students would soar.

Perhaps the deepest irony in Title IX's mandate for equal opportunity is that the losers in the conflict between football and women's athletics have been not just the nonrevenue men's sports but also male walk-ons more generally. Opponents cannot even agree on the data. A Government Accounting Office report in July 2007 claimed that both men's and women's overall participation in intercollegiate athletics had increased since 1991–92, despite men's sports having been cut at many schools. Looking at a longer time frame, the *New York Times* reported on the thirtieth anniversary of Title IX that, while the number of women competing in college athletics increased from about 30,000 in 1972 to 157,000, the number of male athletes dropped from 248,000 to around 200,000. According to athletics administrators interviewed by the *Times*, besides eliminating some male sports, athletic departments had begun practicing "roster management": capping rosters for male teams by excluding walk-ons while encouraging and recruiting walk-ons for women's teams to offset the huge numbers for football. The problem is that apparently three to four times more males than females try to walk on. "For men, there is a social validation tied to being part of a college team," the female associate athletic director at the University of Wisconsin told the *Times*. Women are less interested in walking on and, if they see little chance of playing, of remaining on the team.[74]

Walk-ons, of course, embody the principles of "participation" and "opportunity." They also come closest to the supposed ideal of pure amateur college athletics: the students who arrive at college, ask the coach to try out, and play for personal motives without financial compensation.

Coaches of wrestling, men's track, and men's gymnastics have blamed Title IX for their loss of teams and athletes. (A number of wrestling groups brought the most recent legal challenge to Title IX, but the Supreme Court in June 2005 refused to hear it.[75]) Supporters of women's sports have blamed football: if the football roster were reduced from, say, ninety to sixty, thirty more wrestlers and runners could compete. The debate over Title IX should be a reminder of the purpose that big-time college athletics supposedly serve. The needs of football created modern college athletics. If not for football, the NCAA would not have contemplated athletic scholarships in the 1950s. As recently as 1972, Big

Ten schools were awarding a total of thirty-four athletic scholarships to all "minor" sports combined when, due to financial difficulties, they cut that number to fifteen, to be spread around as many as forty-five athletes.[76] Division I athletic departments today give hundreds of scholarships, full or partial, in these nonrevenue sports.

With the exceptions of signature sports at certain schools—baseball at Rice and Cal State–Fullerton, for example, or women's soccer at the University of Portland—it is due only to football, through the model it created for other sports (including the sports for women protected by Title IX), that nonrevenue sports are funded so much better at most Division I universities than, say, music, theater, student government, or any other extracurricular activity available to students.

Expenditures on athletics from state or institutional sources are particularly significant—the 25.3 percent of total revenues, reported by the NCAA, that were "allocated" to athletic departments rather than "generated" by them in 2006–7.[77] Funds that go to athletic departments directly from state legislatures might be justified as economic development: recognition of the financial impact on the local community from the 40,000 or 60,000 or 80,000 fans who fill the stadium on Saturday and then eat in local restaurants and stay in local motels. Funds allocated to athletics from the university's general-education budget, on the other hand, are often justified by the argument that they pay for women's teams and other nonrevenue sports, while football takes care of itself but is not able to carry the entire athletic department on its back. These general-ed funds are the dollars that matter most to institutions, and to spend them on athletics rather than on more sections of Spanish or laboratory facilities or any of the university's other pressing needs reveals unstated institutional priorities. (As is often the case, the few universities with the top football programs are sheltered from the dilemmas that face their lesser competitors, in this case because football can fund the entire athletic department without institutional subsidies.)

Universities spend great sums on sports that have little impact on institutional marketing and that originally existed to provide meaningful athletic experiences for students—alongside musical experiences, theatrical experiences, journalistic and literary experiences—but have been recast in the image of big-time football, only on a lower scale. Title IX asserts women's right to a share of that athletic world created by football. By challenging football, Title IX also calls attention to the conflicting purposes of college sports.

6 THINKING ABOUT REFORM

Proposing reforms for big-time college football is a fool's task. Calls for reform have been the background noise against which college football has played out for more than a century. Every now and then, the clamor becomes loud enough to irritate those in charge and their most fervent boosters and to make at least a portion of the broader football public uneasy. But it soon fades into the background again, to be ignored by all but diehard critics.

The indictment has not changed all that much over the years. It is only a slight exaggeration to say that John R. Tunis's "The Great God Football" from 1928 or Reed Harris's *King Football* from 1932 could have been periodically recycled to make the case against big-time football over the years. Consider this charge that football players fail to receive a good education:

> The average man playing football today finds it almost impossible to receive any real benefit from his college course. He must have eight or nine hours of sleep. He must pass hours in learning plays and signals for those plays. Three hours or more a day he must devote to the grueling work on the field. He must appear at certain stated hours for meals and eat prescribed food. Attendance at classes occupies most of the rest of his day, leaving only a short period following supper in which to study. Study, therefore, he can only indulge as an occasional luxury. Coaches and trainers advise him to "live football" during the entire Fall season.

Harris wrote that in 1932, three years after the Carnegie Foundation lambasted universities for operating football as a commercial enterprise instead of an educational one. Harris dated his complaint when he went on to note, "The football season lasts from two or three weeks before the opening of the college year to Thanksgiving Day" and pointed out that "football men are expected to report" for "special Spring practice" as well, as if that were an obvious outrage. While the basic nature of the charges has not changed, Harris could not have conceived of twelve- and thirteen-game seasons with bowl games extending into mid-January, let alone "voluntary" morning weight lifting on top of afternoon practice and film afterward, along with year-round training. Expenditures that Harris found "astounding"—$14,000 for a head coach's salary (roughly $212,000 in 2008 dollars), $3,500–$6,500 for assistants, total budgets ranging from $100,000 to $500,000 (about $1.5–$7.5 million in 2008 dollars)—would be modest today, but again the nature of the complaint has not changed. Underlying the specifics was Harris's more general bafflement: "But what, in heaven's name, has the possession of a winning football team to do with the main business of a college or a university?" This was Reed Harris in 1932. It could be the Knight Commission or the Drake Group or the Coalition on Intercollegiate Athletics in 2008.[1]

Big-time college football survived two major moments of near reform: first, the release of the Carnegie Foundation's famous report in 1929 and then the brief flickering of the so-called Sanity Code after the Second World War. Each potential radical break from business as usual turned out to be a hiccup in the largely uninterrupted process of professionalizing and commercializing college football. After the Carnegie Report, a few schools de-emphasized football—driven by the Depression as much as by reform-minded principles—and the University of Chicago's dropping football altogether after the 1939 season might be seen as a delayed response. But most football programs in the 1930s struggled with the economic fallout from the Depression, not with the accusations in the Carnegie Report. World War II disrupted college football everywhere, and in its immediate aftermath, universities had to decide whether they had the resources for a serious recommitment. Several schools dropped the sport—among other developments, widespread big-time Catholic football (at Fordham, St. Mary's, Georgetown, Gonzaga, and so on) ended here—while others leapt into the feeding frenzy for returning GIs. Football was too deeply embedded in these institutions to be let go.

A perceived need for reform has a long history, then, but according to a later president of the Carnegie Foundation, writing in 1987, "If the situation has changed, it has been for the worse." Ernest Boyer acknowledged that "spectator sports seem to be the best way to build a sense of community" on campus, but he stated this with regret. According to one of our current era's most prominent critics, former Indiana University professor Murray Sperber, the spectator sports providing that sense of community are the "beer and circus" that public institutions offer their students instead of a good education.[2] And not everyone feels membership in that community. Faculty for generations have been stereotyped as antifootball cranks, with a degree of truth in the stereotype. That a major unifying force in American higher education has also been a perennial divisive force among faculty and administrators is one of the many ironies of big-time football, another consequence of its fundamental contradiction.

Everyone who cares about these issues today, not just the critics but also the NCAA's own president, agrees on the current problems. In his 2008 State of the Association address, Myles Brand declared that athletic departments "have the obligation to ensure that those who participate in intercollegiate athletics have a realistic opportunity to receive an excellent education." He called it "exploitive to bring young men or women into college sports when they have little or no chance for academic success." He also acknowledged that nearly all universities subsidize athletics, while insisting that such subsidies were appropriate as long as they "not exceed the benefits that the athletics program generates for the university."[3] Such statements could have come from the Drake Group or the Knight Commission. Disagreements arise only over the severity of the problems and of the reforms needed to address them — say, from incrementally raising academic requirements to eliminating athletic scholarships altogether.

Extreme solutions are the simplest to propose and would obviously have the greatest impact. Universities could put an end to professionalism and embrace true amateurism, as was proposed by John Gerdy, a former associate commissioner in the Southeastern Conference and adviser to the NCAA and the Knight Commission. In a recent book laying out a blueprint for reform, with an apparent expectation that it will actually come to pass, Gerdy traced the beginnings of a "critical mass for change" to 1982 with the call for what became Proposition 48, which was followed in 1984 by the creation of the NCAA Presidents Commission, bringing presidential leadership to bear on subsequent legislation. By Gerdy's account, momentum for reform grew steadily within the NCAA, while being helped from without by the formation of the Knight Commission (whose impact has been "enormous") in 1989, the Drake Group in 1999, the Collegiate Athletes Coalition in 2000, the Coalition on Intercollegiate Athletics in 2002, and the National Institute for Sports Reform in 2003. Gerdy sees in these developments a gathering will to dismantle "departments of professional athletics" altogether: by eliminating athletic scholarships, freshman eligibility, spring practice, off-season workouts, and off-campus recruiting; by reducing coaching staffs, schedules, seasons, and travel; and by tightening institutional control of commercialism, fund-raising, and spending—all of this, by the way, without damaging "the quality of the game."[4] To echo Hemingway's Jake Barnes, isn't it pretty to think so?

Such a program would certainly dissolve the contradiction at the heart of big-time college football, as would proposals from the opposite extreme to openly embrace professionalism by paying full-time, pre-NFL football players what the market dictates in return for their athletic services. Teams could compete in what sportswriter Rick Telander described in *The Hundred Yard Lie* as an Age-Group Professional Football League. (Telander also laid out the radical alternative, along the lines later proposed by Gerdy, for universities not inclined to follow this course.)[5] If we look to perennially warring camps on American foreign policy for analogies, open professionalism would be the "realist" option, as opposed to Gerdy's "idealist" program. Interestingly, Gerdy (like Brand) sees professionalism, not commercialism, as the root problem; in his view, college football could be thoroughly commercial but at the same time truly amateur.

Either extreme course, in principle, could be an honest and honorable one. Universities might justify openly professional college football on either of two grounds: if it produced significant revenue to help meet institutional needs, or if it generated valuable indirect academic benefits through promoting and marketing the university's name. The strange fact that institutions of higher education were engaged in commercial entertainment would still hover over the entire enterprise—why not train competitors for *American Idol*, too?—but at least universities would not be undermining on one side of campus what they were fostering on the other.

The radical alternative, severe de-emphasis or even abolition of football, is more obviously justified on academic grounds and would leave no lingering taint of institutional schizophrenia. Setting aside the most obvious economic obstacle—the millions of dollars of outstanding debt on facilities to be paid off—this move would depend on a crucial premise: that universities indeed no longer need or benefit from the promotional power of their highly visible football programs.

Do they?

As I suggested at the beginning of this book, it is not possible to think in any meaningful way about reforming college football without think- ing also about the nature of the institutions whose football is to be re- formed. Neither football nor organized intercollegiate athletics of any kind existed before the late 1800s, but over the course of the twentieth century, athletics in general and football in particular became not an appendage to American higher education but a constituent element. College presidents in the 1890s and early years of the twentieth century were no doubt amazed to discover that their students' new game could attract thousands of spectators, fevered attention from newspapers, and passionate interest in local business communities. Once they discovered all of this, they quickly set aside their amazement and learned how to exploit it. Many specific cases could be cited in addition to the University of Chicago noted in a previous chapter (its first president immediately hiring Amos Alonzo Stagg to start a football program). Within a decade of Southern Methodist University's 1911 founding, its president, Hiram Boaz (1920–22), authorized the recruiting of "adult special" students to build an instant championship football team, around which Boaz and his successor, Charles Selectman (1922–38), developed mutually benefi- cial partnerships with leading Dallas businessmen. (Dallas civic boost- ers used SMU's appearance in the 1936 Rose Bowl, along with Texas Christian's in the Sugar Bowl on the same day, to promote the following summer's Texas Centennial Exposition before a national audience, a turning point in the growth of Dallas into a national city.)

President Rufus von KleinSmid (1921–47) similarly transformed the University of Southern California through its football team in the 1920s. He helped his coaches stock the team by creating the University Junior College in order to admit students who did not meet academic require- ments, then successfully courted Notre Dame for an annual series, begin- ning in 1926, that attracted over 110,000 fans to Chicago's Soldier Field in 1927 and 1929 and made USC famous as a football school (a reputa- tion it later had to overcome in order to develop into an elite university). The series with Notre Dame could be USC's ticket, of course, because Notre Dame had already become a national phenomenon through its football team. Knute Rockne scheduled teams such as USC on the West Coast and SMU in the Southwest, along with Georgia Tech in the South- east and Nebraska in the heartland—as well as Army, Princeton, and anyone else he could round up within earshot of the New York media— initially because the Big Ten shunned the low-rent Catholic school but soon because ND administrators understood that they could build a real university on their nationally renowned football team.[6]

Notre Dame became *the* American Catholic university in the 1920s and 1930s—instead of, say, Marquette, Villanova, Santa Clara, Holy Cross, Georgetown, or any number of other candidates—because of Rockne, the Four Horsemen, and each season's squad of "Ramblers" (so named for their cross-country schedules before they became the Fighting Irish). Fordham and St. Mary's developed a briefly famous intersectional rivalry in the 1930s, but it was eclipsed by Notre Dame–Army and even Notre Dame–USC in national importance. (Georgetown gave up on big-time football after World War II but became a major university by exploiting its location in the nation's capital instead of its football team.) Elsewhere in Protestant America, while four Methodist schools—USC, SMU, Vanderbilt, and Northwestern—became major universities, others remained small-scale denominational colleges in part because those four played big-time football in major conferences.

Not just sectarian colleges but also public universities acquired local status and national standing through their football programs and conference affiliations. Consider the states with a single flagship university—Ohio, Illinois, Indiana, Nebraska, Louisiana, and so on—and you will find that university in the region's most prestigious football conference. Where "University" and "State University" have more or less equal standing, both play football in major conferences. Michigan State, to cite the most compelling case, became the University of Michigan's peer only after gaining admission to the Big Ten in 1950, replacing the University of Chicago, which had famously dropped big-time football a decade earlier. In our popular understanding of football and failed reform, Chicago president Robert Hutchins's urging the trustees to make this drastic decision was the high-minded road not taken by other equally troubled but less courageous presidents. Chicago more than survived the amputation, as did the Ivy League schools when they "de-emphasized" football in the 1950s, but Chicago, as well as Harvard, Yale, Princeton, and the other Ivies, have long traditions of academic distinction to fall back on, not to mention their huge endowments. (At least one historian of the University of Chicago and its antifootball president concludes that Hutchins temporarily damaged the university by dropping football during this formative period.[7]) Lacking Chicago's Rockefeller millions, had Michigan State dropped football instead of joining the Big Ten, it might be a second-rate agricultural college today instead of one of the nation's leading land-grant universities.

Each American college and university has its own history, and the presence or absence of big-time football does not figure importantly in all of them. But it is nonetheless true that big-time football was a powerful force in shaping American higher education as we know it. The relationship seems at least partly coincidental. Harvard, Yale, and Princeton began playing football games against each other, and taught the game to students at colleges throughout the country, at the very moment that higher education was being transformed by the development of graduate schools and research agendas; by the professionalization of business, law, medicine, the social sciences, and other academic disciplines; and by the expansion of a middle class with sufficient resources and ambition for upward mobility. Over the closing decades of the nineteenth century, the American college ceased being exclusively a seminary for the clergy and a finishing school for the elite and started becoming the training ground for the professions and, more broadly, the pathway to middle- and upper-middle-class success. American higher education was expanding with or without football.

But if football's appearance was an accident of good timing, it nonetheless became an important factor in that expansion. As sleepy state colleges and poorly funded denominational schools began competing for students from the increasingly college-bound population, the publicity generated by the football team became a valuable promotional tool. When local business and community leaders saw that a successful football team could put their city, state, or region "on the map," nonalumni boosters became a major resource (as well as a plague) for college administrators. For students, football became the center of "college life" for nine or ten weeks in the fall—the pep rallies, bonfires, pregame luncheons and postgame dances, along with the games themselves, much of this organized by fraternities and sororities that were themselves closely connected to the football team. Football-mad fraternity brothers and sorority sisters then became the next generation of alumni who returned to campus for Homecoming Weekend and the season-ending Big Game, who maybe chipped in for the new library (SMU built a football stadium in 1926, a library in 1939), and who wrote the president angry letters about the football coach when the team failed for the third year in a row to win the traditional rivalry game. For the broader culture, the Big

Game also brought on-campus and off-campus communities together as no other university events did.

Over the 1920s and succeeding decades, what Douglas Toma calls Football U became an American institution unique in the global world of higher education. With few exceptions, American universities became known outside their own states, if at all, only through their football teams. Even local communities tended to know nothing about the chemistry or English department, or the university president for that matter, but everything about the coach, the quarterback, and the team's prospects for Saturday's game. The result was a decidedly mixed blessing for the institution: the university became well known and had an identity, but only because of its football team. While students charted their career paths by majoring in Premed or Political Science, the source of their passions and bonding was Saturday football games. As alumni, they remained bound to their alma mater—but too often only through football. The community and the state felt connected to their universities—but again only through football. The faculty pursued its research and teaching in the football team's shadow.[8] Not many administrators or faculty members would have chosen to have football play such an important role, yet the gathering of 80,000 or 60,000, or even 40,000 or 30,000, to wildly proclaim their allegiance to Football U was no small thing, and its ramifications were not to be ignored.

For Football U, conferences shaped public perceptions of its academic peers as well as its athletic opponents. When Arizona and Arizona State joined the Pacific-8 Conference to create the Pac-10, they traded Utah, Utah State, New Mexico, and New Mexico State for Stanford, Cal, and UCLA as their "peers." Or consider the Big Ten. Northwestern today ranks among the elite private universities in the country, trailing only seven of the eight Ivies, Stanford, Cal Tech, MIT, Duke, and the University of Chicago in the latest rankings by *U.S. News & World Report*. Membership in the Big Ten for more than 100 years undoubtedly helped Northwestern get there. More telling, all ten public institutions in the conference are ranked among the country's thirty-three best public universities by *U.S. News*. From the Big 12 Conference, by contrast, only recent additions Texas and Texas A&M, with their enormous financial endowments, rank ahead of any of the Big Ten schools. The Big Ten was the first conference to be created (in the 1890s) and remained the premier football conference into the 1970s, while the precursors of the Big 12 (the Big Six, Big Seven, and Big Eight) played football in its shadow. *U.S. News* weighs many factors in its rankings, including retention rates (20 percent), faculty resources (20 percent), and student selectivity (15 percent), but it attributes the highest weight (25 percent) to peer assessment—the opinion of administrators at other institutions. Does the president of Cornell or Florida State know for certain whether Iowa is a better university than Missouri? Or does the president of Cornell or Florida State rank Iowa above Missouri because Iowa has been one of the so-called Public Ivies of the Big Ten since the end of the nineteenth century? (Rankings by *U.S. News* are as controversial among academics as BCS rankings among football fans, but by default they reflect public perception of the country's institutional hierarchy.)

Moving up the *U.S. News* ranking is notoriously difficult.[9] When Penn State joined the Big Ten in 1990, it brought its own institutional resources and reputation to the conference, but its ranking by *U.S. News* went from Quartile Two in 1993 (somewhere between no. 52 and no. 102, though undoubtedly closer to the lower number) to no. 41 in 1995 (and no. 9 among public universities). Was Big Ten membership a factor in its upward assessment? For the conference's longtime members, has association with Michigan (no. 4 among publics), Wisconsin (tied with two others for no. 7), and Illinois (no. 10) kept Iowa (with three others at no. 26), Indiana, and Michigan State (both no. 30 along with two others) consistently above Iowa State, Kansas, and Nebraska (all no. 40) in peer assessments? I pose these questions rather than venture answers because the correlations cannot be proven. And what conclusions should we draw from the fact that, among the top thirty-three public universities as ranked by *U.S. News*, only six—William & Mary, four University of California campuses, and the University of Delaware—do not play in the Football Bowl Subdivision? Of those that do, only Miami of Ohio (no. 26) does not belong to a BCS conference. Membership in the prestigious Association of American Universities (AAU), for public institutions anyway, is likewise heavily weighted toward big-time football schools.[10]

The academic quality of private universities is directly related to their financial resources, most obviously measured by their endowments. (Twenty-two of the twenty-six private universities in the AAU are ranked among the top forty in total endowment.[11]) With enough money, any number of institutions can build a world-class chemistry department and lure a Nobel laureate to join it. Among public universities, Texas and Texas A&M are highly unusual in having huge endowments dropped in their laps (from state-owned oil resources), but Michigan and Virginia (along with the University of California system) are also among the top twenty in endowment (with Minnesota, North Carolina, Pittsburgh, Washington, and Ohio State among the next eleven).[12] The funding-driven quality of public universities is determined by politics, local economies, the social and intellectual cultures in the states—all of the factors that affect every kind of public spending. Football has been another factor, but determining the relationship between football and academic quality among public universities is something of a chicken-and-egg problem—did football prestige attract students and resources, or did institutional prominence build the football program?—or perhaps a temptation to a logical fallacy. (The fact that big-time football preceded academic excellence does not mean that football was necessarily a direct or even indirect cause.) As legislative funding has shrunk in recent years, public colleges and universities of all sizes and qualities have increasingly had to resort to private fund-raising. Larger and better universities for obvious reasons tend to be more successful in fund-raising than smaller and worse ones. Larger and better universities also tend to play big-time football. Is football then a factor in more successful fund-raising? Direct? Indirect? Again, these are questions without obvious answers, yet they are among the most urgent questions for any university president who might contemplate significant changes to the football program.

If every institution has its own history, it is nonetheless safe to repeat the claim I made earlier: big-time college football was an integral part of American higher education as it developed, not something tacked on. And it follows that radically changing, let alone abandoning, high-pressure, highly commercialized big-time football might have serious consequences. If we want a medical metaphor, eliminating football altogether might be closer to removing both kidneys than to amputating a gangrenous foot.

I use "might" instead of "would" because the consequences are uncertain. And which surgical procedures, short of amputation, would be possible without causing chronic complications are not obvious, either. It does seem obvious that college football had a powerful role in the development of American higher education in the twentieth century. Whether it still plays and will continue to play a comparably important role in the twenty-first is not so clear. I know, for example, that successive administrations at Notre Dame since the 1920s built a university on its football team. That university now is highly regarded and very well endowed. As an alumnus who cares as well as a scholar who knows some of the relevant history, I am not at all certain whether Notre Dame still needs a football team competing at the highest level. uc Berkeley, Virginia, UCLA, and Michigan are consistently ranked as the best American public universities, and all of them compete in college football at the highest level. With its 107,000-seat stadium, Michigan also routinely produces one of the largest football revenues. If these first-rate public universities once needed their football teams—did UCLA, the branch campus in Los Angeles, become an academic rival to UC Berkeley at least in part by competing in the Pacific Coast Conference?—do they still need them competing at the same level in order to remain the nation's leading public universities?

Elsewhere in the world of Football U, are the routine athletic deficits at Oregon State and Washington State offset by academic benefits from competing in the Pac-10 with Cal, UCLA, and Stanford as "peers"? Can the enormous revenue-generating football programs at Georgia, Auburn, Alabama, and LSU help these institutions achieve the academic distinction of the best public universities? Will Rice and Tulane slip from their perches in the academic pecking order now that they have fallen from "major" football status? Can Boise State or Fresno State ride football success out of academia's lower tiers? For the great majority of schools, should football, in Douglas Toma's unnerving term, be regarded as "a loss leader in the quest for institutional significance"?[13]

These are again questions that, to varying degrees, lack clear answers. (I would bet that Rice, with its high academic ranking and $4.6 billion endowment, is secure, while everything else is less certain or doubtful.) More important, these questions point to an overriding reality: talk of reforming big-time football, if it is to be meaningful, cannot pretend that one size will fit all. This final chapter actually needs a more cumbersome title, something along the lines of "Thinking about Reform across a Diverse Institutional Landscape."

Most sportswriters and football fans are indifferent to academic memberships and rankings, but those measures of prestige matter a great deal to faculties and administrators (as well as to graduate students and at least the most academically motivated undergrads), and they reflect on questions of educational excellence on which national well-being profoundly depends. (Faculty critics are susceptible to an opposite blindness: a refusal to acknowledge that the academic health of their universities might be in any way dependent on the football team.) No university president would make a decision regarding the football program that he or she knew for certain would harm the academic quality of the institution. The proposals offered by reformers—admit only athletes who are bona fide students, shorten seasons and daily time commitments, and so on—often make such obvious academic sense that anyone who resists them might seem indifferent to educational values. Yet those who resist them include university presidents who were once distinguished faculty scholars, have risen through the administrative ranks, and are now charged with protecting and promoting the best interests of their institutions. Either faculties, trustees (assuming that they are not simply boosters), the members of various state education boards, and even some state governors have all been fooled over and over, or what seems obvious is not.

To reformers, both the problems and the solutions in big-time college football are obvious. To the more thoughtful defenders of the sport, the problems may be obvious but the solutions are not. And the two sides disagree on what's at stake. To reformers, college football is ancillary to the university's purpose, perhaps even antithetical to it. To thoughtful defenders, the football program is essential to achieving the university's true mission—both sides largely agree on what that mission is—or at least they have no assurance that this is no longer the case.

Proposing academic reforms is easy yet pointless if there is little chance that they will be adopted. Would-be reformers should approach the issue from the perspective of what most legitimately concerns those with the power to make change. If a university president is a football booster who loves a championship team for its own sake, or for his or her own reflected glory, no persuasion is possible. But a president who worries about the impact of football on institutional well-being will attend to reason and evidence.

HARD EVIDENCE? HARDLY

In declaring Alabama's Nick Saban the "Most Powerful Coach in Sports" as the 2008 season was about to open, *Forbes* magazine quoted Alabama president Robert Witt on what justified Saban's $4 million salary (actually $5 million, according to *Forbes*, after all of the extras were factored in). Witt cited the 100,000 donors to the university's $500 million capital campaign, for whom football was "a major reason they support us." He also attributed to his new football coach the fact that, in 2007–8, 57 percent of Alabama's freshmen had been in the top quarter of their high school class, up from 54 percent the year before. According to Witt, "Having a coach of his caliber makes it easier to recruit better students and raise more money."[14]

The claims were familiar, but so was the lack of evidence to support them—beyond the coincidence that Nick Saban was the football coach when these things happened. In a paper written in 2004 for the Knight Commission, the distinguished Cornell economist Robert Frank reviewed all of the major studies that had attempted to determine whether football success by some credible measure increases donations to the university and applications from prospective students. (Donations matter when they support the academic mission, not just the athletic program. Applications matter, for most of the institutions that play big-time football, if they come not just from more students but from better ones.) Frank found that the documented evidence for both benefits was meager and inconclusive.

On the relationship of athletic success to the quality of students, one much-cited 1987 study looked at 150 institutions for 1971 and concluded that freshmen entering schools with big-time athletics had 3 percent higher SAT scores, but the methodology did not account for any other characteristics of the universities (such as the fact that big-time football powers tend to be better academic institutions). In trying to correlate SAT scores to athletic success over several years, as measured by won-loss records, the authors of the same study found positive effects, but they were "extremely small" and statistically insignificant. Another study found a "small" correlation between SAT scores and top-twenty football rankings in the 1980s. Another found a "small" impact on applications from better in-conference won-loss percentages. And so on. National football championships were followed by large increases in applications in two cases between 1979 and 1992, but by "modest gains" or even declines in others. Comparing national champions only to their peer institutions, in order to control for nonfootball institutional factors, made a positive relationship even more doubtful. What Frank called "the most careful study to date" was a 2003 report commissioned by the NCAA that I have cited elsewhere. Among their conclusions, the authors of this study "estimate[d] that football winning percentage is positively associated with average incoming SAT scores, but that the effect is small and not significantly different from zero at conventional confidence levels."[15]

The case for fund-raising was equally tenuous, though ultimately unresolved. A study published in *Social Science Quarterly* in 1979 "launched an intense debate" with its claim that "donations are essentially independent of football success." A follow-up study, designed to control for institutional differences, found a mix of positive and negative links between fund-raising and athletic success at different institutions. A third study concluded that gifts to the athletic department but not to the institution as a whole followed from football success. Another found that winning percentages in football over a thirty-year period at one institution actually had a negative correlation with alumni giving. Yet another study found a positive impact from bowl appearances but not from winning records. And yet another found no statistically significant correlations, either positive or negative. The large-scale 2003 NCAA study cited above found only negative correlations, though not of a statistically significant magnitude.

Frank's overall assessment of the empirical evidence is unsurprising: "The most forceful conclusion that can be drawn about the indirect effects of athletic success is that they are small at best when viewed from the perspective of any individual institution. Alumni donations and applications for admission sometimes rise in the wake of conspicuously successful seasons at a small number of institutions, but such increases are likely to be both small and transitory."[16]

Frank's is a reasonable, not definitive, conclusion. Unfortunately, the impact of athletics can be very difficult to measure. Major donors are usually cultivated over time. An unexpected bowl championship might initially draw someone to the university, who then endows a professorship in chemistry ten years later when the team is 3–8. But within the mixed and ultimately inconclusive research results, Frank found confirmation of a basic economic principle. He called college athletics a "winner-take-all-market." Regarding fund-raising, successes in one part of the market are always offset by relative losses in another. Increasing revenue in parts of the market does not benefit the market as a whole but creates a new equilibrium, within which there are still few winners and many losers, most of whom cannot abandon the expectation that one day they will be winners, too. (Frank cited research suggesting that university leaders tend to be as guilelessly optimistic about the future as ordinary citizens.) As the winners' payoffs rise (whether from ticket sales, television, or bowl games), the incentive to become a winner rises, too, despite the fact that a majority will always be losers. Lotteries work the same way.

The other payoff in the football lottery has become popularly known as the "Flutie factor," after Boston College quarterback Doug Flutie's nationally televised and endlessly replayed "Hail Mary" pass to beat Miami in the closing seconds of a game in 1984. Various accounts over the following years claimed that applications to Boston College increased 30, 33, even 40 percent as a result. In this case, claims could be checked against documented figures, as someone at Boston College recently did. Applications to BC did in fact increase 16 percent in 1984 and 12 percent in 1985, but these increases were consistent with the numbers over the previous dozen years, a period in which BC "embarked on a program to build national enrollment using market research, a network of alumni volunteers, strategically allocated financial aid, and improvements to residence halls and academic facilities." In 1978, when the football team went 0–11, applications increased 9 percent. As the game-winning play entered football folklore, however, the Flutie factor entered higher-ed mythology—to be cited by officials at the University of South Florida and the University at Buffalo (formerly SUNY-Buffalo), for example, to explain their strategic decisions to move up to Division I-A.[17]

The mythology was fed by Northwestern's 2,500 new donors to its annual fund (though no new major gifts beyond athletics) after winning the Big Ten championship in 1994 and going to the Rose Bowl. (It was also fed by Gonzaga's increase in freshman enrollment from 549 to 997 between 1997 and 2001 as the Zags became the mid-major darlings of the NCAA basketball tournament.)[18] Perhaps Boise State will experience some Flutie effects following its dramatic victory over Oklahoma in the 2007 Fiesta Bowl. But these are few and isolated cases. And more so than donations, college applications are a zero-sum game: more students applying here means fewer applying there. For higher education as a whole, athletics can have no impact; even if some students choose a particular college for its football team, no students (except for some who play football) go to college because of football who otherwise would not go at all. The same logic more or less governs college admissions within states. Because most students attend in-state public institutions for financial reasons, an increase in enrollment on one campus means a decrease on another and no net gain for the system. Selectivity is also relative. As Frank put it, "It is mathematically impossible for more than ten percent of all schools to be among the ten percent most selective." At the state level, if the better students gravitate to one campus, the losers would be the other public colleges in the state.

Frank's overall conclusion was essentially that big-time football is a closed system, both in terms of the number and relative quality of students who attend the institutions and in terms of economics, since expenditures always rise with additional revenues to create a new equilibrium between a few conspicuous winners and many losers. The occasional success among the perennial have-nots increases the incentive for everyone, but with everyone investing more to achieve that success, the competitive level remains unchanged and the chance of succeeding does not improve. (Frank could have added that when a nonelite team does become spectacularly successful, it usually loses its coach to a more elite team and rarely repeats that success.) Many institutions might well consider whether the desired benefits could more likely be achieved by investing elsewhere. Frank's own primary concern was to make the case for deeply cutting expenditures on big-time college athletics. As he pointed out, if the cuts were uniform, the current balance of power and competitiveness among programs would be unchanged, as would whatever benefits accrued from the programs. For cuts to be uniform, however, all of the participating institutions must agree to them, and the courts must be convinced that the arrangement would not violate antitrust law.

Thus we are back at a familiar dead end, roughly the same one reached by the NCAA in mandating academic reform while leaving financial restraint voluntary. And although the system is closed, acknowledging that fact would not end the fierce competition among individual institutions within the system. If only a few can be winners, everyone wants to be one of the few. Nonetheless, Frank's description of big-time college athletics—more narrowly football for my purposes—as a closed system with few winners and many losers can help focus thinking about the prospects for multilateral rather than systemic reform. Neither the NCAA's mandated reforms nor outsiders' calls for more radical change acknowledge the athletic and academic variability of institutions within the Football Bowl Subdivision. It might be more useful to start with that variability and let thinking about reform flow from there.

DIFFERENTIAL CHALLENGES AND MULTILATERAL REFORM

As Frank's overview makes clear, attempts to demonstrate with hard data whether football success leads to increases in fund-raising or student quality have tended to look at single institutions or groups of institutions that may or may not be generally representative. Studies typically have not distinguished between giving to athletics and giving to academics, nor have they accounted for significant differences among institutions—public or private, BCS or non-BCS, academically high or low ranked—that are crucial factors for understanding whether big-time football benefits the educational enterprise. When reported in the popular media in fifty-word sound bites or press releases, these studies always seem more definitive than they are, but definitively on both sides of the question. One study confirms the Flutie factor; another demonstrates that bowl games have no impact whatsoever on campus fundraising. The only possible consensus on the issue is uncertainty.

In a study published in the *Journal of Sport Management* in early 2007, Jeffrey Stinson and Dennis Howard attempted to account for more of the variables that actually matter for specific institutions—to distinguish between alumni and nonalumni giving to athletic or academic programs at more- and less-prestigious academic institutions. The impact of a BCS bowl might be different for Boise State and Michigan, or for Texas and Baylor within the same conference.

Stinson and Howard found that athletic success in Division I-A was related to a positive increase in fund-raising (with roughly the same impact on giving by alumni and nonalumni), but they qualified that relationship in a crucial way: athletic success increased donations to athletics but not to academics.[19] Drawing on Stinson and Howard's data, the *Chronicle of Higher Education* reported that total giving to the athletic programs for the 119 Division 1-A institutions increased from 14.7 percent of overall giving in 1998 to 26 percent in 2003. More tellingly, between 2000 and 2003 (the most recent year for which data were available), while average donations to athletics increased 75 percent (from $1.2 million to $2.1 million per institution), average nonathletic giving declined slightly (from $6.1 million to $6.0 million). The trend was for giving to athletics at the expense of academics.[20] (One factor in this trend could be the growth of endowments for athletics to fund scholarships or salaries or other expenses from a stable source. Stanford leads the way with $500 million, pursued by other private universities such as Duke and Boston College but also by several state schools.[21])

Stinson and Howard also qualified relative giving to athletics and academics when they factored in the academic reputation of the institutions. Using the rankings of Tier 1, Tier 2, and Tier 3 universities by *U.S. New & World Report*, the researchers found that, the higher the tier, the greater the proportion of overall giving to academics. This correlation makes intuitive sense: universities known for their prestigious academic programs are more likely to attract donations to those programs by alumni and nonalumni alike. It follows, and Stinson and Howard confirmed it, that the Flutie factor more likely operates when a Boise State makes it to a BCS bowl than when a Michigan does.

Stinson and Howard have not settled the question of football's institutional importance once and for all. They could not account for all of the complexities of fund-raising and philanthropy, for the behavior of individual donors, or for the circumstances at individual schools. They also did not address the possible nonfinancial benefits of big-time football or the broader impact of participation at the highest levels, irrespective of season-to-season success. (That is, if it does not matter for institutional fund-raising whether or not Michigan goes to a BCS bowl, does it matter that Michigan continues to have an elite football program that competes in the Big Ten for BCS bowl berths?)

But thinking about the impact of football in relation to different kinds of institutions points in the right direction. Myles Brand and other spokesmen for the NCAA insist that there is no financial crisis in the broad world of college football today. But there are local crises in several parts of that world, or they loom in the near future. The current Football Bowl Subdivision includes 119 schools (with Western Kentucky due to become the 120th in 2009) whose football revenues for the most recently reported year range from barely over $1 million to more than $60 million, whose stadiums have capacities ranging from 16,000 to 107,000,[22] whose institutional endowments (again for the most recently reported year) range from $90 million to $17.2 billion, whose average SAT scores for incoming freshman vary by hundreds of points. Ball State and Louisiana Tech have little in common with Notre Dame and Michigan as institutions. Even within the BCS, and within each of its participating conferences, a Mississippi State or a Baylor differs in fundamental ways from an Alabama or a Texas. The Football Bowl Subdivision has a two-part structure and a single set of rules, but the 119 institutions within it fare very differently under them. The NCAA has been continually reorganizing itself over the past half century, with ever-narrowing divisions to allow the big-time football powers to thrive. But as long as institutions with 30,000-seat stadiums and modest athletic pedigrees try to compete against those with 100,000-seat palaces and long glorious histories, and as long as institutions that admit 60 percent of their applicants compete against ones that accept everyone who applies, neither the current arrangements nor proposals for reform can be equally beneficial or necessary to all.

Table 3 maps BCS and non-BCS institutions' academic profiles over their football profiles. *U.S. News* ranking and AAU membership provide a rough sense of academic status, endowment is a crude measure of institutional resources, and the SAT scores of incoming freshmen (25th and 75th percentiles) are a rough indicator of the academic quality of the student body. (The *U.S. News* rankings for 2009 eliminated Tier 2, placing the top 133 national universities in Tier 1, followed by Tiers 3 and 4. Previously, Tier 1 included only the top fifty schools.) Football revenue and the profit or loss from football—for which we remain dependent on the flawed federal data for individual institutions—along with stadium capacity and average attendance, illustrate the current economic status and potential of the football program. And graduation rates, represented here by the NCAA's most recently reported Graduation Success Rate (GSR) for all players and for African American players,[23] provide a crude measure of the football program's academic success.

The particular circumstances of all 119 institutions in the Football Bowl Subdivision, or even of the 104 in the two parts of Table 3 (fifteen non-BCS institutions are not "national universities" in the *U.S. News* rankings), cannot be represented here, but the table points to four broad categories within which we can imagine administrators weighing the costs and benefits of their football programs. These categories more or less follow Stinson and Howard in mapping football status (BCS or non-BCS) onto academic status (*U.S. News* ranking):

- Elite football (BCS) with elite academics (Tier 1)
- Elite football with nonelite academics (Tiers 3 and 4)
- Nonelite football (non-BCS) with elite academics
- Nonelite football with nonelite academics

There is considerable variability in these categories from top to bottom, as well as a lack of distinct boundaries between the academic tiers. If we rank schools by football revenue, "elite" ranges from $8.2 million to $63.8 million. "Elite" academic institutions range from Stanford and Duke to Kansas State and LSU. (LSU was Tier 3 in 2008, when *U.S. News* ranked the top 130 universities in Tiers 1 and 2, but tied with three others

TABLE 3. FOOTBALL BOWL SUBDIVISION ATHLETIC AND ACADEMIC PROFILES

Institution (BCS)	U.S. News Ranking	SATS (25–75%)	Graduation Rates	SATS 1997
Stanford	Tier 1 #4	1340–1550	93/88	1330–1530
Duke	Tier 1 #8	1340–1540	92/88	1290–1470
Northwestern	Tier 1 #12	1350–1520	92/91	1260–1440
Notre Dame	Tier 1 #18	1300–1510	94/93	1230–1410
Vanderbilt	Tier 1 #18	1300–1480	91/84	1220–1370
California	Tier 1 #21	1220–1470	53/53	1180–1430
Virginia	Tier 1 #23	1200–1420	66/61	1210–1390
UCLA	Tier 1 #25	1180–1430	62/48	1100–1340
Michigan	Tier 1 #26	1220–1380*	70/54	1140–1340
USC	Tier 1 #27	1270–1460	54/55	1070–1310
Wake Forest	Tier 1 #28	1240–1410	83/82	1180–1380
North Carolina	Tier 1 #30	1210–1400	78/70	1120–1330
Boston College	Tier 1 #34	1240–1430	92/86	1200–1370
Georgia Tech	Tier 1 #35	1240–1420	48/36	1240–1410
Wisconsin	Tier 1 #35	1190–1340*	63/58	1110–1300
Illinois	Tier 1 #40	1190–1380*	70/61	1110–1300
Washington	Tier 1 #41	1090–1320	65/53	1020–1260
Penn State	Tier 1 #47	1090–1300	78/77	1080–1280
Texas	Tier 1 #47	1110–1370	50/38	1100–1330
Florida	Tier 1 #49	1140–1360	68/61	1220–1380
Miami	Tier 1 #51	1180–1370	70/61	1030–1260
Syracuse	Tier 1 #53	1110–1330	75/63	1070–1290
Maryland	Tier 1 #53	1170–1380	68/62	1060–1280
Ohio State	Tier 1 #56	1150–1300*	52/41	950–1180
Georgia	Tier 1 #58	1130–1310	48/38	1090–1270
Pittsburgh	Tier 1 #58	1150–1340	67/59	990–1210
Clemson	Tier 1 #61	1130–1320	68/67	1040–1220
Minnesota	Tier 1 #61	1100–1300*	51/40	990–1220
Rutgers	Tier 1 #64	1090–1300	70/70	1060–1290
Texas A&M	Tier 1 #64	1080–1300	56/50	1020–1280
Purdue	Tier 1 #66	1020–1270	63/51	970–1220
Connecticut	Tier 1 #66	1090–1290	77/83	1005–1232
Iowa	Tier 1 #66	1070–1220*	75/69	1030–1220
Indiana	Tier 1 #71	1030–1260	68/59	1100
Michigan State	Tier 1 #71	1070–1220*	51/43	990–1180
Virginia Tech	Tier 1 #71	1100–1300	75/71	1110–1420
Baylor	Tier 1 #76	1110–1310	78/76	1050–1270
Colorado	Tier 1 #77	1070–1260*	75/71	1070–1260
NC State	Tier 1 #83	1070–1260	59/50	1050–1260
Alabama	Tier 1 #83	990–1220*	55/48	950–1180

AAU Member?	Endowment (overall rank)	Football Revenue	Profit/Loss	Stadium Capacity	Attendance (average)
yes (1900)	$17.2 B (3)	$12.9 M	$34,920	50,000	39,332
yes (1938)	$6.1 B (15)	$9.0 M	$100,295	33,941	20,064
yes (1917)	$7.2 B (8)	$15.5 M	$4.4 M	47,129	24,589
no	$6.2 B (13)	$63.7 M	$45.8 M	80,795	80,821
yes (1950)	$3.5 B (23)	$15.2 M	$1.8 M	72,000/39,373[A]	34,629
yes (1900)	$872 M (85)[B]	$26.0 M	$8.7 M	73,347	63,136
yes (1904)	$4.6 B (20)	$14.2 M	($2.9 M)	61,500	59,824
yes (1974)	$1.0 B (72)[B]	$23.5 M	$6.7 M	92,542	76,379
yes (1900)	$7.6 B (7)	$51.0 M	$36.2 M	107,501	110,264
yes (1969)	$3.6 B (22)	$31.7 M	$13.0 M	92,000	87,476
no	$1.2 B (59)	$12.1 M	$2.0 M	31,500	32,595
yes (1922)	$2.4 B (28)	$18.1 M	$3.0 M	60,000	57,417
no	$1.6 B (43)	$17.4 M	$1.3 M	44,500	41,990
no	$1.3 B (54)	$25.3 M	$15.9 M	55,000	50,280
yes (1900)	$1.7 B (38)	$34.1 M	$14.3 M	80,123	81,747
yes (1908)	$1.5 B (48)	$20.8 M	$11.4 M	71,000	54,872
yes (1950)	$2.3 B (30)	$33.7 M	$20.0 M	72,500	67,732
yes (1958)	$1.5 B (46)	$44.0 M	$29.4 M	107,282	108,197
yes (1929)	$16.1 B (5)	$63.8 M	$46.2 M	85,123	85,144
yes (1985)	$1.2 B (60)	$58.9 M	$38.2 M	88,548	90,388
no	$736 M (97)	$20.8 M	$2.8 M	74,476	43,589
yes (1966)	$985 M (71)	$14.9 M	($157,085)	50,000	35,009
yes (1969)	$854 M (89)	$9.3 M	($10,076)	48,055	51,263
yes (1916)	$2.1 B (31)	$59.1 M	$26.6 M	101,568	105,110
no	$593 M (126)	$59.5 M	$43.1 M	92,746	92,746
yes (1974)	$2.3 B (29)	$17.5 M	$5.3 M	65,000	33,315
no	$421 M (158)	$32.0 M	$18.1 M	84,000	81,335
yes (1908)	$2.8 B (24)	$17.4 M	$9.1 M	63,699	51,791
yes (1989)	$640 M (118)	$15.6 M	0	41,500	43,663
yes (2001)	$6.7 B (10)	$37.1 M	$20.5 M	82,600	82,207
yes (1958)	$1.7 B (37)	$25.1 M	$11.4 M	62,500	59,326
no	$328 M (189)	$12.0 M	$250,042	45,000	38,205
yes (1909)	$935 M (80)	$45.3 M	$16.5 M	70,397	70,585
yes (1909)	$1.5 B (45)	$17.0 M	$6.8 M	52,345	37,004
yes (1964)	$1.3 B (56)	$40.8 M	$18.3 M	72,027	70,540
no	$528 M (138)	$40.6 M	$14.4 M	66,233	66,233
no	$1.1 B (70)	$9.3 M	$100,295	50,000	34,378
yes (1966)	$870 M (86)	$23.1 M	$11.6 M	51,808	50,509
no	$545 M (134)	$18.1 M	$10.2 M	53,475	56,356
no	$998 M (78)[C]	$53.2 M	$31.8 M	92,138	92,138

Institution (BCS)	*U.S. News* Ranking	SATS (25–75%)	Graduation Rates	SATS 1997
Iowa State	Tier 1 #89	1030–1220*	55/37	1030–1220
Kansas	Tier 1 #89	1030–1220*	53/47	950–1180
Nebraska	Tier 1 #89	1030–1260*	78/66	950–1180
Auburn	Tier 1 #96	1030–1220*	57/48	990–1180
Arizona	Tier 1 #96	970–1220	41/29	970–1210
Missouri	Tier 1 #96	1070–1260*	59/51	1070–1300
Florida State	Tier 1 #112	1090–1270	69/67	1080–1280
Oklahoma	Tier 1#108	1070–1260*	46/45	990–1220
Oregon	Tier 1 #108	1080–1280	53/42	990–1230
South Carolina	Tier 1 #108	1080–1280	65/63	960–1190
Tennessee	Tier 1 #108	1070–1260*	54/50	990–1180
Kentucky	Tier 1 #116	990–1220*	56/52	1030–1220
Washington St.	Tier 1 #116	1000–1210	68/57	910–1150
Arizona State	Tier 1 #124	960–1220	60/56	960–1200
Arkansas	Tier 1 #125	1070–1300*	52/39	950–1180
Kansas State	Tier 1 #130	990–1260*	67/54	910–1180
LSU	Tier 1 #130	1070–1260*	54/44	950–1180
Cincinnati	Tier 3	990–1220*	73/68	990–1180
Louisville	Tier 3	990–1220*	58/58	870–1110
Mississippi	Tier 3	950–1260*	63/54	950–1140
Mississippi State	Tier 3	950–1220*	63/59	910–1210
Oklahoma State	Tier 3	1030–1220*	62/57	990–1220
Oregon State	Tier 3	950–1190	64/63	949–1195
South Florida	Tier 3	1010–1210	56/46	1000–1220
Texas Tech	Tier 3	980–1190	79/71	960–1170
West Virginia	Tier 3	940–1140	63/56	930–1120

Institution (Non-BCS)	*U.S. News* Ranking	SATS (25–75%)	Graduation Rates	SATS 1997
Rice	Tier 1 #17	1310–1530	82/71	1260–1530
Tulane	Tier 1 #51	1190–1370	67/61	1170–1370
Miami (Ohio)	Tier 1 #66	1110–1260*	83/68	1070–1260
SMU	Tier 1 #66	1130–1330	78/69	1030–1270
Brigham Young	Tier 1 #113	1150–1340*	56/50	1110–1300
Texas Christian	Tier 1 #113	1060–1260	67/62	1020–1220
Ohio U.	Tier 1 #116	990–1190*	81/75	990–1180
Buffalo	Tier 1 #121	1040–1260	61/51	1040–1240
Colorado State	Tier 1 #125	1030–1190*	66/56	1140–1340
Utah	Tier 1 #127	990–1220*	57/45	990–1220

AAU Member?	Endowment (overall rank)	Football Revenue	* Profit/Loss	Stadium Capacity	Attendance (average)
yes (1958)	$569 M (130)	$10.8 M	$629,920	43,000	49,462
yes (1909)	$1.2 B (62)	$11.3 M	$1.4 M	50,250	43,675
yes (1909)	$1.2 B (61)	$26.3 M	$12.4 M	81,067	84,501
no	$423 M (157)	$56.8 M	$33.9 M	87,451	84,689
yes (1985)	$519 M (140)	$17.5 M	$8.3 M	57,803	52,161
yes (1908)	$1. B (75)	$15.3 M	$6.0 M	62,000	60,232
no	$571 M (128)	$17.5 M	$7.6 M	82,300	80,597
no	$1.2 B (63)	$37.3 M	$18.5 M	83,000	84,858
yes (1969)	$471 M (148)	$21.5 M	$8.8 M	54,000	58,845
no	$425 M (156)	$41.3 M	$28.8 M	80,250	78,467
no	$887 M (82)	$31.2 M	$17.3 M	104,079	103,918
no	$909 M (81)	$21.9 M	$11.7 M	67,606	68,824
no	$679 M (106)	$10.5 M	$2.9 M	37,600	33,045
no	$493 M (144)	$23.5 M	$4.9 M	73,379	62,875
no	$856 M (88)	$42.1 M	$19.2 M	72,000/53,727[A]	69,707
no	$346 M (182)	$21.7 M	$11.5 M	52,250	47,383
no	$634 M (119)	$48.1 M	$31.7 M	92,400	92,619
no	$1.1 B (66)	$8.2 M	$388,655	35,000	30,246
no	$794 M (93)	$19.0 M	$5.4 M	42,000	39,881
no	$472 M (147)	$17.6 M	$10.6 M	60,580	49,704
no	$281 M (210)	$12.1 M	$5.70	55,082	49,296
no	$617 M (122)	$20.4 M	$10.5 M	50,616	40,024
no	$428 M (154)	$28.3 M	$16.6 M	45,674	41,374
no	$360 M (174)	$9.3 M	$1.7 M	65,000	53,170
no	$793 M (95)	$20.9 M	$2.4 M	50,500	51,911
no	$430 M (153)	$25.2 M	$11.4 M	63,500	60,400

AAU Member?	Endowment (overall rank)	Football Revenue	Profit/Loss	Stadium Capacity	Attendance (average)
yes	$4.6 B (19)	$9.6 M	$429,850	70,000	13,353
no	$1 B (73)	$6.9 M	($664,000)	64,992	26,112
no	$405 M (160)	$4.8 M	0	30,012	16,186
no	$1.4 B (51)	$8.7 M	($3.00)	32,000	17,171
no	NR	$10.1 M	$1.0 M	65,000	64,497
no	$1.3 B (57)	$13.3 M	0	44,830	30,018
no	$312 M (195)	$4.4 M	0	24,000	16,500
yes	$213 M (247)	$4.6 M	0	30,000	13,568
no	$183 M (265)	$4.1 M	($2.2 M)	30,000	21,794
no	$595 M (125)	$11.2 M	$3,0 M	45,634	42,593

Institution (Non-BCS)	U.S. News Ranking	SATS (25–75%)	Graduation Rates	SATS 1997
Alabama-Birm.	Tier 3	990–1220*	44/43	910–1110
Ball State	Tier 3	940–1130	72/63	870–1100
Bowling Green	Tier 3	910–1110*	75/69	950–1110
Central Florida	Tier 3	1070–1260	49/40	1030–1210
Hawaii	Tier 3	990–1190	42/40	960–1190
Idaho	Tier 3	950–1150*	69/62	950–1180
Kent State	Tier 3	910–1110*	78/69	870–1070
New Mexico	Tier 3	910–1150*	49/42	950–1110
So. Mississippi	Tier 3	910–1110*	80/79	870–1180
Temple	Tier 3	980–1180	49/37	930–1120
Utah State	Tier 3	950–1220*	62/63	780–1180
Western Michigan	Tier 3	950–1150*	58/54	950–1140
Wyoming	Tier 3	990–1190*	54/44	950–1180
Akron	Tier 4	790–950	61/46	910–1110
East Carolina	Tier 4	920–1100	74/70	930–1110
Florida Atlantic	Tier 4	930–1110	51/51	950–1190
Florida Intl.	Tier 4	1060–1220	60/36	1030–1240
Houston	Tier 4	940–1160	53/47	940–1190
La.-Lafayette	Tier 4	950–1110*	67/70	830–1070
Louisiana Tech	Tier 4	950–1150*	64/61	910–1180
Memphis	Tier 4	910–1150*	63/55	870–1220
New Mexico State	Tier 4	830–1070*	54/58	950–1140
UNLV	Tier 4	910–1140	53/49	850–1110
North Texas	Tier 4	990–1200	58/51	900–1120
Northern Illinois	Tier 4	950–1110*	73/65	950–1140
San Diego State	Tier 4	940–1160	56/50	830–1060
Texas at El Paso	Tier 4	919 (?)	57/44	NR
Toledo	Tier 4	910–1150*	63/47	870–1110

Sources: *U.S. News* ranking from *U.S. News and World Report*, "Best Colleges 2009," national universities only (online); SATS (25th–75th percentiles) from *U.S. News and World Report*, "Best Colleges 2009" (online); graduation rates for 2008 (six-year rates for 1998–2001 cohorts) as reported by the NCAA (online); SATS (1997) from *U.S. News & World Report America's Best Colleges* (1997); endowment figures for fiscal year 2008 from "2008 NACUBO Endowment Study"; revenue and profit/loss for 2006–7 from "Sports Spending & Gender Equity Database," *Chronicle of Higher Education* (online); attendance average for 2007 as reported by the NCAA ("NCAA Accumulated Attendance Report," February 4, 2008).

AAU Member?	Endowment (overall rank)	Football Revenue	Profit/loss	Stadium Capacity	Attendance (average)
no	(Alabama system)	$6.3 M	$146,623	71,594	16,706
no	$190 M (259)	$1.6 M	($3.0 M)	21,581	13,085
no	$135 M (317)	$4.3 M	$312,202	30,599	16,080
no	$115 M (344)	$4.3 M	$559,565	70,188	44,018
no	NR	$7.5 M	$499,988	50,000	43,514
no	$176 M (276)	$4.9 M	$1.0 M	16,000	11,479
no	NR	$2.8 M	($1.5 M)	30,520	8,999
no	$343 M (185)	$3.3 M	($2.4 M)	37,700	29,751
no	NR	$7.2 M	$2.8 M	35,169	26,721
no	$237 M (228)	$8.7 M	0	68,532	28,859
no	$146 M (309)	$1.4 M	($664,162)	30,257	13,131
no	$188 M (261)	$1.8 M	($2.2 M)	30,200	19,494
no	$299 M (204)	$6.6 M	$2.2 M	33,500	22,190
no	$178 M (271)	$1.3 M	($3.3 M)	35,202	15,978
no	$95 M (380)	$6.7 M	($262,914)	45,000	41,537
no	$182 M (268)	$2.4 M	($1.2 M)	20,450	15,741
no	$97 M (376)	$6.5 M	$560,237	7,500	7,982
no	$522.4 M (140)	$6.9 M	0	50,000	20,955
no	NR	$3.0 M	($57,208)	31,000	16,651
no	NR	$3.2 M	($733,846)	30,600	18,562
no	$214 M (246)	$6.5 M	0	62,380	29,670
no	$173 M (280)	$1.1 M	($3.8 M)	30,343	14,412
no	NR	$2.8 M	($3.2 M)	40,000	29,281
no	$90 M (391)	$1.4 M	($2.8 M)	30,500	17,734
no	NR	$3.4 M	($2.1 M)	31,000	17,864
no	$115 M (343)	$4.5 M	($3.0 M)	71,400	27,940
no	NR	$8.2 M	$1.7 M	52,000	36,569
no	$176 M (277)	$1.6 M	($3.0 M)	26,248	18,668

ᴬ Vanderbilt and Arkansas have two stadiums.

ᴮ Cal and UCLA are also included in the fourteenth-ranked $6.2 billion endowment for the University of California system.

ᶜ Endowment for the entire University of Alabama system, including the University of Alabama–Birmingham and its medical school.

* ACT scores converted to SAT scores.

at no. 130, the bottom of Tier 1, in 2009). Nonetheless, identifying these four categories can begin to differentiate among the institutions engaged in big-time football.

1. Elite/Elite

In the first category are fifty-seven BCS schools with Tier 1 academic programs, eleven of them private and forty-six public, arranged here by their 2006–7 football revenues (in millions):

#47 Texas ($63.8)

#18 Notre Dame ($63.7)

#58 Georgia ($59.5)

#56 Ohio State ($59.1)

#49 Florida ($58.9)

#96 Auburn ($56.8)

#83 Alabama ($53.2)

#26 Michigan ($51.0)

#130 LSU ($48.1)

#66 Iowa ($45.3)

#47 Penn State ($44.0)

#125 Arkansas ($42.1)

#108 South Carolina ($41.3)

#71 Michigan State ($40.8)

#71 Virginia Tech ($40.6)

#108 Oklahoma ($37.3)

#64 Texas A&M ($37.1)

#35 Wisconsin ($34.1)

#41 Washington ($33.7)

#61 Clemson ($32.0)

#27 USC ($31.7)

#108 Tennessee ($31.2)

#89 Nebraska ($26.3)

#21 California ($26.0)

#35 Georgia Tech ($25.3)

#66 Purdue ($25.1)

#25 UCLA ($23.5)

#124 Arizona State ($23.5)

#77 Colorado ($23.1)

#116 Kentucky ($21.9)

#130 Kansas State ($21.7)

#108 Oregon ($21.5)

#51 Miami ($20.8)

#40 Illinois ($20.8)

#30 North Carolina ($18.1)

#83 N.C. State ($18.1)

#58 Pittsburgh ($17.5)

#96 Arizona ($17.5)

#112 Florida State ($17.5)

#34 Boston College ($17.4)

#61 Minnesota ($17.4)

#71 Indiana ($17.0)

#64 Rutgers ($15.6)

#12 Northwestern ($15.5)

#96 Missouri ($15.3)

#18 Vanderbilt ($15.2)

#53 Syracuse ($14.9)

#23 Virginia ($14.2)

#4 Stanford ($12.9)

#28 Wake Forest ($12.1)

#66 Connecticut ($12.0)

#89 Kansas ($11.3)

#89 Iowa State ($10.8)

#116 Washington State ($10.5)

#53 Maryland ($9.3)

#76 Baylor ($9.3)

#8 Duke ($9.0)

Despite the obvious differences between a Stanford and an LSU, all of these institutions, to varying degrees, share a desire to win football championships and a desire to elevate their academic prestige. All of them below the peerless handful at the very top of Tier 1 identify their own academic "peers" as well as their "aspirational peers," the institutions they resemble and the ones they would like to resemble. For all of these schools, football must somehow serve, or at least not hinder, institutional aspirations.

This group includes the universities most grounded in college football history, ones with institutional cultures shaped for more than a century by major conference affiliations and deep identification with the sport. They have won most of the national championships, produced most of the All-Americans, claimed most of the Heisman Trophies. They also have most of the largest stadiums and the most passionate alumni and boosters (some of whom have periodically let their passions get their universities in trouble with the NCAA). When we think of "big-time football," these are the institutions, for the most part, that most readily come to mind. In theory, the higher an institution's academic ranking, the less it would depend on football for achieving its institutional aspirations, but where football runs deep, it feels essential, foundational.

As long as football serves, or at least does not interfere with, the academic aspirations of these elite institutions, there is little incentive to change it, but within this group are clear divisions. Consider their endowments, a factor in higher education not usually recognized on the sports pages. (The figures in the table were posted before the market collapse in 2008, but the relative reductions have likely been roughly consistent across institutions.) Eight of these universities (Stanford, Texas, Michigan, Northwestern, Texas A&M, Northwestern, Notre Dame, Duke, and Virginia) have endowments over $4 billion that place them among the top twenty in all of American higher education, with Stanford ($17.2 billion) and Texas ($16.1 billion) residing in the endowment stratosphere along with Princeton ($16.3 billion) and behind only Harvard ($36.6 billion) and Yale ($22.9 billion). (The University of California is also over $4 billion, but that is for the system, not the Cal and UCLA campuses alone.) USC and Vanderbilt have endowments over $3 billion; Minnesota, North Carolina, Pittsburgh, Washington, and Ohio State are all over $2 billion. Fifteen of the top thirty-one endowments in the country are represented here (the rest belong to Ivy League and other distinguished private universities). Such endowments would seem to make these universities independent of their football programs for institutional well-being, while all others to varying degrees might worry more about the impact of football on fund-raising. But Texas played championship football in a football-crazed region long before oil money made world-class academic programs possible, and most of these schools have longer football than academic pedigrees. With the nation's nineteenth-largest endowment ($4.6 billion) but no membership in a major conference, Rice University in 2004 demonstrated that football can matter to even the best-endowed schools when it decided, after much soul-searching, against dropping out of Division I-A. But the size of a school's endowment nonetheless might matter in contemplating the potential impact of football on fund-raising.

The fifty-seven institutions in this elite/elite group also have most of the football programs with the highest revenues, but only a third of them actually make a profit or break even on athletics overall according to the latest NCAA report on revenues and expenses. Given the inconsistency in financial reporting, exactly which institutions belong in this class—a total of nineteen according to the report—is not certain, but they are likely among the twenty-two programs that claimed more than $30 million in football revenue in the most recent data submitted to the U.S. Department of Education, from Texas at the top with $63.8 million to Tennessee with $31.2 million.

With profits more or less assured, these institutions have no obvious incentive to reduce spending on football. The rest, to widely varying degrees, must wrestle with their budgets, trying to compete against conference or national rivals without draining essential resources from their academic enterprises, weighing the costs of athletic success against other institutional needs. *SportsBusiness Journal* in 2006 did an in-depth study of athletics at the University of Arizona, where the athletic director felt "caught between trying to compete in an increasingly competitive local entertainment market and defending his program against a growing sense on campus that, as an arm of the university—and one that generates a mere 3 percent of total revenue—it has overstepped its mission."[24] After joining the Big East for football in 2004, the University of Connecticut saw its football revenue rise from $4.8 million to $9 million, but expenses increased from $4.2 million to $10.4 million. (And for the privilege of having a team in a BCS conference, the state of Connecticut had to put up $91 million for a new 40,000-seat off-campus stadium.)[25] Rutgers, another newcomer to big-time football, was struggling in 2008 with the incongruity of a $16.4 million decline in the state's appropriation to the university at the same time the legislature committed $2.25 million over four years to Rutgers athletics.[26] Private institutions can cover shortfalls in athletics with higher tuition; the most elite among them can also draw on huge endowments. Public universities, with their obligation to hold down tuition for the state's citizens, have less flexibility in generating and allocating new resources.

The football superelite face their own challenges, however. They likely have the largest investments in new facilities, whose debt service mandates that there be no slackening in revenues. The bounty of huge revenues can also be a tyrannical boss. The most academically distinguished among the football superelite—Notre Dame, Michigan, and USC most obviously, but Wisconsin, Washington, Texas, Penn State, and Florida are also among the top fifty in Tier 1—might have an additional concern: a reputation as a "football school" could work against their academic reputation. This is a particular issue at Notre Dame, with its unique history, but it also worries at least some faculty and administrators at other football powers, including Michigan—even before the investigative series in the *Ann Arbor News* in March 2008 that revealed the "clustering" of Michigan football players in General Studies.[27] To be both athletically and academically distinguished is not impossible, but it is relatively rare. Just twelve institutions in the top fifty of Tier 1 have football revenues over $20 million.

Regardless of revenues, all of the elite/elite institutions must be concerned about the experience of their "student-athletes." The football superelite must confront the greatest disparity between the wealth generated by football and the meager compensation for the athletes. Those with the largest athletic budgets also likely have the most lavish facilities and the greatest potential for fostering a "culture of entitlement." These programs should also have the best academic-support facilities and services, however, and potentially the highest graduation rates, but that is not always the case. Here is where administrators at many elite/elite institutions should feel most uncomfortable. The most recently tabulated Graduation Success Rate for Division I-A football—for students entering between 1998 and 2001 and graduating within six years—was 66 percent (80 percent for whites and 58 percent for African American players).[28]

A little searching of the NCAA's website turns up the rates at individual institutions included in Table 3, and they make that 66 percent as an average not very meaningful.

Not surprisingly, the most elite private universities had the highest GSRS, with USC a conspicuous exception. The best public universities have a more uneven record. North Carolina and Penn State graduated 78 percent of their football players, with Penn State graduating black players at nearly the same rate. Michigan and Illinois also reached 70 percent, but the University of California at Berkeley, the top public university in the country according to the *U.S. News* rankings, graduated barely half of its football players. Texas and Georgia Tech did worse, and worse yet with their African American players. Among the football superpowers with comparably lousy GSRS were Ohio State, Georgia, Alabama, Tennessee, Auburn, Oklahoma, and LSU. Nebraska, on the other hand, though fallen on hard times in football, graduated 78 percent of its players.

Because the latest reported figures, whether financial or academic, are always slightly dated, it is not possible to correlate, say, LSU's national championship for the 2007 season with a GSR of 54 percent for a cohort whose eligibility expired after 2005. But the fact that the recent national champions with the exception of Florida (68 percent)—that is, USC (54 percent), Texas (50 percent), and Ohio State (52 percent), along with LSU—have low GSRS makes one wonder about the relationship between championship football and graduation rates. Perhaps too many top players simply bailed out after their senior season to train for the NFL draft and the guaranteed millions that go to first-rounders (a reasonable decision by the athletes). But perhaps these schools won with too many great athletes who were marginal or indifferent students. If that was the case, Michigan, Penn State, and Notre Dame must ponder whether they can compete for national championships without doing the same.

With Cal's football fortunes rising since 2001, when the program bottomed out with a 1–10 record, one must wonder if a willingness to admit less-qualified students has helped make that rise possible. Or is the low graduation rate simply due to the upheaval around the coaching change after that 1–10 season? But perhaps Cal has a hard time recruiting athletes who can survive in the school's intense academic climate. By juxtaposing the columns on graduation rates and the SAT scores of incoming freshman, Table 3 highlights a challenge that faces all academically elite universities—and the more elite, the greater the challenge. A limited number of 4.0 high school students have 4.3 speed or athletic skills honed obsessively since middle school. By the NCAA's current rules for initial eligibility, an incoming freshman with a 2.5 high school grade-point average in his core courses must have an SAT score of 820 (or its equivalent on the ACT[29]). On the NCAA's sliding scale, a 2.0 high school GPA requires a 1010 SAT, while 620 is sufficient with a 3.0; and so on, up and down the scale. From bits of NCAA published data, it appears that the average football recruit in Division I arrives at college with an SAT score somewhere between 940 and 1000.[30] The juxtaposed columns in Table 3 suggest how such a young man would fit in at various universities with big-time football programs. In addition to the elite private universities near the top of Tier 1, Cal, Virginia, Michigan, North Carolina, and Georgia Tech have a 25th-percentile score of at least 1200. That is, 75 percent of the students at these schools scored above 1200 on the SAT. (At the elite private institutions, including Rice outside the BCS, that threshold is between 100 and 150 points higher.[31]) An average recruit who might be an academic star in some football programs would likely struggle in this environment, and the academic fit is little better at the majority of BCS institutions. Of the thirty-nine BCS schools ranked no. 83 or above by *U.S. News*, just two have a 25th percentile for incoming freshmen below 1070.

In December 2008 an investigative report in the *Atlanta Journal-Constitution* compared the average SAT scores for football players at fifty-two public universities from BCS conferences with the average SATs for all students. The football players averaged 941, nearly 100 points below the average for athletes overall and 220 points below the full student body. The largest gap was at Florida, where football players' average SAT of 890 (for the freshmen classes of 2002–4) was 346 points below the school's 1236 average. Florida was followed by the most academically elite public universities—UCLA, California, Virginia, North Carolina—which had higher football SATs but also higher overall SATs, resulting in gaps also exceeding 300 points. Georgia Tech's football players had the highest average SAT (1028), but its student body also had the highest average (1344). The smallest gap among all of the schools was 88 points; the average gap was 220.[32]

The point is to imagine how well football recruits fit in academically when they arrive at college. At Alabama, the 25th-percentile score in the latest *U.S. News* ranking is 990. For the incoming classes of 2004–6, the

Atlanta Journal-Constitution data show an average SAT of 1158, compared to 950 for football players. At Texas, the 25th percentile is 1110; the average SAT (2003–5) is 1230 and the average football SAT is 948. At Alabama or Texas, let alone Virginia or California, the average football recruit could easily feel lost in the classroom. At Fresno State, where the 25th percentile is 790 and the 75th percentile is 1050, he might be in the top half of his class. Lower admission standards do not necessarily translate into higher graduation rates — Fresno State's latest GSR was 48 percent — but a higher academic standard for the university either narrows the pool of potential recruits or leaves more of them adrift once they arrive. It should surprise no one that football players "cluster" in certain majors, but the dismal graduation rate at Texas suggests that funneling athletes into Youth and Community Services does not adequately address the problem.

Keep in mind that we have been considering the "average" recruit. Imagine how lost those with 700 or 800 SAT scores might feel. Most big-time football programs take a chance on a handful of these (when they also have 4.3 speed or 320 pounds of muscle, of course). How small or large the handful depends on the program. Athletics administrators know how successful they are with their "high-risk" recruits, but no graduation rates are reported for this particular subset of the class.

By including SAT scores from 1997, Table 3 also reveals the rising academic performance of incoming freshmen at most Tier 1 universities — with the consequently increasing challenge to recruit qualified student-athletes who can fit into the academic environment. As Duke, Northwestern, Notre Dame, and Vanderbilt have become more academically selective, staying competitive in football has become more challenging. (Again, this is a particular issue for Notre Dame, as it persists in its championship-football ambitions.) USC's academic standards have dramatically risen — by 200 points at the 25th percentile and 150 points at the 75th — at the same time that its football program has reclaimed championship status. One must wonder how the experience of USC football players (with their low overall GSA) has been affected. Most state universities in BCS conferences, including football superpowers such as Alabama and Oklahoma, have seen a rise in the SAT scores of incoming freshmen, typically around 50 points, with LSU's climbing by 120 and Ohio State's by 200.

The challenges that follow from this development should be obvious. The better the academic institution, the more selective are its admissions and the smaller is the pool of athletes who can thrive, or even survive, there academically. At the same time, the rationale justifying a highly competitive football program is predicated on its ability to advance indirectly the academic ambitions of the university. Whether the most academically selective universities in the Football Bowl Subdivision, public as well as private, can continue to compete against less-selective "peers" without compromising academic integrity or merely exploiting their athletes—or at the very least relegating them to a jock subculture in which they miss out on much of the college experience (a concern in the Ivy League, too)—is a hard question for academically distinguished (or ambitious) institutions to ask themselves. But most of the less academically selective institutions have also seen rising test scores in their freshmen classes over the past ten years, a period during which the BCS raised the financial stakes for everyone but particularly for institutions struggling to reduce deficits in athletics. Facing an increasingly winner-take-all economy and job market, college-bound high school students have become more competitive about their grades and test scores. Recruiting blue-chip athletes with academic backgrounds that will enable them to succeed in this new environment has become an increasing challenge. The better the school and the more ambitious the football program, the greater the challenge. Rising academic standards and rising financial stakes in football can be a brutal combination.

2. Elite/Nonelite

The second category, for BCS schools with Tier 3 academic status, is much smaller, including just nine institutions (arranged here by their football revenue in millions and without a U.S. News ranking because Tier 3 institutions are not ranked):

Oregon State ($28.3)   Mississippi ($17.6)
West Virginia ($25.2)   Mississippi State ($12.1)
Texas Tech ($20.8)   South Florida ($9.3)
Oklahoma State ($20.4)   Cincinnati ($8.2)
Louisville ($19.0)

This group includes three relative newcomers to the BCS (Louisville, South Florida, and Cincinnati), along with a fourth member of the newest major conference (West Virginia) and five longtime members of major conferences that have achieved only modest or intermittent success on the field (Oregon State, Texas Tech, Oklahoma State, Mississippi, and Mississippi State). Academically, some of these institutions are not easily distinguishable from the bottom third of Tier 1, and they have similar SAT ranges and graduation rates. With the exception of Louisville—whose 25th-percentile SAT score has risen 220 points since 1997—the schools in this group have seen only modest increases compared to many Tier 1 institutions.

All Tier 3 schools aspire to higher academic ranking. (So, too, do those below the top in Tier 1. The president of Florida State, for example, has publicly announced membership in the Association of American Universities to be an institutional goal.) For them, the questions of whether football enhances the university's reputation, creates friends among potential donors for academic programs, and attracts better students are crucial. All of these institutions face the challenges of educating and graduating their athletes that are common, in different ways and with varying degrees of urgency, throughout the Football Bowl Subdivision. They also share with all of those in Tier 1 that lose money on athletics the challenge of determining whether investing in football, rather than in some other part of the institution, most effectively and efficiently serves their institutional aspirations.

The University of South Florida (USF) was founded in 1956 and did not field a football team of any kind until 1997, a move prompted by seeing Miami and Florida State transformed into "national brand names" through their football programs. USF joined Division I-A in 2001 (and Conference USA in 2003), then won the football lottery in 2005: an invitation to join the Big East Conference (selected over the University of Central Florida). With Big East membership (and the accompanying TV and BCS benefits), more than 40,000 students (third most among Florida universities), a location in a major population area in football-mad Florida, and an existing 66,000-seat public facility in which to play (Raymond James Stadium, the Tampa Bay Buccaneers' home field), USF might indeed experience impressive Flutie effects, inspiring other less well-situated institutions to believe they can duplicate its success. But success can bring its own challenges. Whether as petty resentment or another key to instant success, South Florida's rapid rise in the football rankings in the first half of the 2007 season brought accusations that the coach took players who could not get into Florida or Florida State.[33]

And after all of the media fanfare for its 6–0 start in 2007, the Bulls went 3–4 to finish the season (including a loss in a minor bowl game) then followed up with an 8–5 record in 2008 (with a victory in a low-end bowl). Elite status is elusive.

3. Nonelite/Elite

The third category, nonelite football with elite academics, is also small, with ten members (listed this time by their academic rankings, with their football revenue in millions):

#17 Rice ($9.6)	#113 Texas Christian ($13.3)
#51 Tulane ($6.9)	#116 Ohio University ($4.4)
#66 Miami (Ohio) ($4.8)	#121 Buffalo ($4.6)
#66 Southern Methodist ($8.7)	#125 Colorado State ($4.1)
#113 Brigham Young ($10.1)	#127 Utah ($11.2)

This is a disparate institutional mix: Rice, with an academic ranking higher than all but three BCS schools (Stanford, Duke, and Northwestern); SMU and TCU, once high riders in the old Southwest Conference with Doak Walker and Sammy Baugh among their legendary alumni but now relegated to the football boondocks; Tulane, BYU, Colorado State, and Utah, four more universities (two private, two public) demoted in the realignments of the 1990s; Miami of Ohio and Ohio University, two public universities long settled in football's minor leagues; and the University at Buffalo, a school aggressively seeking to rise and hoping that football will provide a boost. The broader breakdown has seven schools struggling to thrive (or survive in Rice's and Tulane's cases, more so for Tulane post-Katrina) after being expelled from the big leagues, one hoping to cash in by upgrading football, and two more or less trying to hold steady in a conference with some of the smallest football budgets in the entire subdivision.

Utah is the recent success story: the school not only cracked the BCS stranglehold on BCS bowls in 2004 and again in 2008 (despite having lost its coach after the first one), but it also rose from Tier 3 to the expanded Tier 1 in the latest *U.S. News* rankings. Whether there is a relationship between the two successes is a question that many college presidents would love to have answered. The school's most recent SAT scores remained unchanged (and unchanged since 1997); its endowment increased by 20 percent from 2006 to 2007 but dropped from 123rd to 124th among all universities (and to 125th in 2008, with a small drop in the fund). Whether football success has changed or will change the institution is not yet evident.

The other institutions in this category certainly long for Utah's success on the field. Tulane considered leaving Division I-A—at the urging of president Scott Cowan, an ad hoc investigative committee of trustees voted 7–1 to do so—but after a massive campaign by boosters and various supporters, the full board decided in 2003 to hold on.[34] Cowan then played a major role in forcing the BCS to add another bowl game in order to increase opportunities for the lesser conferences. Then came Katrina and whatever that catastrophe will mean for Tulane's athletic (as well as institutional) future. (The fact that the incoming SAT scores reported by *U.S. News* dropped from 1220/1425 to 1190/1370 in the latest rankings is not a good sign.)

Rice also weighed dropping or downgrading football, provoking a similar uproar with the same result. The Rice case is particularly interesting because the campus discussion became very public. A Faculty Council Subcommittee on Athletics issued a report in March 2003 that described unprecedented high costs for athletics; routine admission of athletes "who fall far below acceptable standards" (an average SAT 300 points below the average for other students, or 1130 compared to 1426); 60 percent of athletes majoring in three programs—Managerial Studies, Kinesiology, or the noncalculus track in Economics; excessive time pressure on athletes; failure to integrate athletes into the larger university culture; and athletes' disproportionate number of violations of the Honor Code.[35] Versions of these problems face all universities with big-time football programs, but they usually play out without public notice.

A commissioned study by the management consultants McKinsey & Company offered the university four choices: (1) remain in Division I-A and become more competitive, (2) move to Division I-AA, (3) drop football altogether, or (4) move to Division III. After a massive e-mail and letter campaign by alumni and athletics boosters, Rice's board of trustees in 2004 chose the first option—an aggressive recommitment to Rice's athletic traditions of the 1930s, 1940s, and 1950s.[36] With a $4.6 billion endowment (19th largest in the country), Rice can financially afford its choice. Whether it is possible to be "top-tier" in football as well as baseball (a College World Series championship in 2003), with athletes who are also bona fide Rice students, is less certain.

SMU and TCU have less-distinguished academic credentials than

Rice but also more glorious football histories. They do not have to be as academically selective as Rice in recruiting, and any decision to downgrade their football programs would cause even greater uproar among alumni and boosters. All three of these exiles from the old Southwest Conference are ultimately in the same boat, but with differing degrees of buoyancy. SMU is still recovering from the only "Death Penalty" ever imposed by the NCAA for rules violations, which resulted in the suspension of football in 1987 and 1988.[37] The hiring of Hawaii's June Jones with a $2 million salary following the 2007 season raises the intriguing question of whether Jones can duplicate his success at an institution with more selective admissions. (The team went 1–11 in his first season, the same record that SMU posted in 2007.) BYU is more favorably positioned than the three Texas schools, with the bounty from a routinely sold-out, 60,000-seat stadium and its status as the flagship Mormon university with a draw on Mormon high school football players like Notre Dame once had with Catholics. Colorado State reported losing $2 million on football for the most recently documented fiscal year; Ohio University and Miami of Ohio broke even—on paper. All three face the typical budgetary challenges outside the BCS, along with the academic challenges facing the entire subdivision. The University at Buffalo dropped football in 1971, resumed it at the Division III level in 1977, moved to Division I-AA in 1993, then finally rejoined Division I-A in 1999 as a member of the Mid-American Conference. Buffalo was the largest institution in the SUNY system and a member of the Association of American Universities, but without big-time football it was scarcely known outside academic circles. Since 1999 the school has lost most of its football games and millions of dollars on athletics each year, in addition to two football scholarships for failing to meet the APR minimum in May 2008. Its endowment increased 13.2 percent from 2006 to 2007, while higher-ed endowments overall (for 785 institutions) increased 17.2 percent.[38] Despite its invitation to a minor bowl after going 8–5 in 2008 (with a hot young African American coach who is likely to leave soon), what Buffalo has gained from Division I football is not clear.

4. Nonelite/Nonelite

The final category includes most of the Football Bowl Subdivision outside the BCS, with thirteen institutions from Tier 3 and fifteen more from Tier 4 (listed by tier and then by football revenue in millions; Tiers 3 and 4 are both unranked by *U.S. News*):

Tier 3	Tier 4
Temple ($8.7)	Texas-El Paso ($8.2)
Hawaii ($7.5)	Houston ($6.9)
Southern Mississippi ($7.2)	East Carolina ($6.7)
Wyoming ($6.6)	Florida International ($6.5)
Alabama-Birmingham ($6.3)	Memphis ($6.5)
Idaho ($4.9)	San Diego State ($4.5)
Central Florida ($4.3)	Northern Illinois ($3.4)
Bowling Green ($4.3)	Louisiana Tech ($3.2)
New Mexico ($3.3)	Louisiana-Lafayette ($3.0)
Kent State ($2.8)	Nevada-Las Vegas ($2.8)
Western Michigan ($1.8)	Florida Atlantic ($2.4)
Ball State ($1.6)	Toledo ($1.6)
Utah State ($1.4)	North Texas ($1.4)
	Akron ($1.3)
	New Mexico State ($1.1)

Non-BCS schools that are not "national universities"—including football-ambitious Boise State and Fresno State (both in Tier 3, below the top fifty-three, for universities in the West that confer master's degrees)—belong in this category, too.

Here, the overwhelming challenge must be to weigh costs against benefits. Like Utah, Boise State and Hawaii hit the jackpot with BCS bowl appearances after the 2006 and 2007 seasons. As with Utah, it is too soon to know what, if any, institutional payoffs might result. Hawaii is the flagship university in its state, as are the University of Idaho and the University of Wyoming. The others in this group must find their academic niches in the shadows cast by larger or higher-rated institutions (and Idaho has fewer students than Boise State, which draws from a more populous part of the state). Wyoming and Houston have had some football success in the past. Florida Atlantic and Central Florida aspire to South Florida–type success but do not have all of South Florida's favorable circumstances. The fourteen programs with the smallest football revenues in the subdivision are in this group. Most play in small on-campus stadiums, some in large municipal stadiums (with no ties to university traditions) that they cannot come close to filling. The crucial question that all of these schools must ask is: does small-scale, big-time football help in achieving their institutional ambitions, or would expenditures on football achieve better results if directed elsewhere?

The athletes in these programs ostensibly fit in better with the rest of the student body. (Only two schools in this group, Central Florida and Florida International, have a 25th-percentile SAT score above 1000, and few have seen a significant increase in SAT scores since 1997.) But some of these schools are also among the institutions that leap at whatever TV appearances are available, no matter what day of the week or effect on the athletes as students. Apart from these midweek games, these schools place the same demands on their athletes' time that prevail throughout the subdivision, but with some of the smallest budgets most of them also lack the resources for academic support available at the BCS schools. The graduation rates in Table 3, however, suggest that low academic selectivity and small football revenues do not necessarily interfere with academic success. Bowling Green and Kent State from the Mid-American Conference, along with Southern Mississippi and East Carolina from Conference USA, all graduated at least 75 percent of their football players overall and at least 69 percent of their African American players. These numbers put them among the best of the BCS public institutions, while Alabama-Birmingham, Central Florida, Hawaii, New Mexico, Temple, Florida Atlantic, Houston, New Mexico State, and Nevada–Las Vegas ranked among the worst. Kent State ranks near the bottom of the subdivision in football revenue; Temple ranks among the top schools outside the BCS. Campus cultures, or academic cultures within athletics, seem to matter as much as or more than economics in determining academic success.

SURVIVING THE LATEST THREATS TO BUSINESS AS USUAL

Within these four categories (and including the fifteen non-BCS schools that are not national universities) are 119 separate institutions, all of them currently governed by a single set of rules. This arrangement cannot possibly serve all 119 equally well, and from the perspectives of the 119, their presidents and other leaders are responsible only for their own institutions, not the entire system of big-time football. The 119 also have little or no control over the larger football culture. Whatever colleges do, the partly real, greatly delusory lure of the National Football League will remain, its promise of million-dollar salaries and instant celebrity fed by all-day, every-day sports television. Within that larger football culture, universities represent not young athletes' ultimate football dream but a final audition for the NFL dream.

Universities cannot change this entire football world, only their own practices within it. But with so much at stake, whether real or assumed, the impetus for change is overwhelmingly more likely to come from outside than from within. Big-time football has long been vulnerable to external forces on two fronts: economic and legal. As an entertainment business, it is subject to the vagaries of markets and media. Should a handful of television executives or corporate sponsors, or the athletic directors at the leading football powers—or some combination of the above—decide that they can no longer afford to subsidize small-market or low-profile teams, instantly the world of college football would be radically restructured. Alternatively, as a cartel operating a multibillion-dollar entertainment business, the NCAA clings precariously to its tax-exempt, nonprofit status and constantly risks violating antitrust law. The Supreme Court decision in 1984 that ended the NCAA's TV monopoly radically changed college football. The 1998 decision on "restricted-earnings coaches" was less momentous in itself but far-reaching in its implications. Most obviously, it prevents the NCAA from trying to cap the salaries of head coaches, but it also raises the specter of antitrust lawsuits over any attempt to regulate the economics of football. More fundamentally, should the IRS or a congressional subcommittee ever decide that big-time football is more like a business than an educational enterprise, or should a court rule that athletes who generate millions of dollars in revenue are underpaid employees rather than beneficiaries of a free education, college football would be radically changed again.

I am aware of no looming threat of market-driven restructuring, though many institutions are perpetually vulnerable and growing more so. While college football in its entirety has a mass market, individual teams have only niche markets, with larger niches for the perennial powerhouses and the teams in more populous areas. The broadcast and cable networks seem content with current arrangements, but should those arrangements turn unprofitable, what constitutes "major" college football would once again be reconfigured. Weaker teams in the East might fare better than stronger teams in sparsely populated portions of the Midwest, Southwest, and West. Within the major conferences, Mississippi State and Vanderbilt might suddenly belong to a different world from the one inhabited by LSU and Florida. Thinking locally, I have long wondered about the long-term fortunes of Oregon State and Washington State, located in the smallest towns and with the smallest stadiums in the Pac-10 (and without a Daddy Bigbucks, such as Oregon has in Nike's Phil Knight, to compensate). For now, all is relatively calm, but the future is uncertain. Apart from prospects for market-driven restructuring, the current economic downturn could have an impact on college athletics beyond mere belt-tightening. As states cut higher-ed budgets, subsidies to athletics will receive sharper scrutiny (a topic of concern at the 2009 NCAA convention).[39]

Legal threat, on the other hand, has been hovering more ominously over the NCAA for many years, most recently from two distinct directions: Congress and the courts. From one side came the challenge to the NCAA in 2006 from the House Ways and Means Committee and the Senate Finance Committee to justify tax-exempt status for big-time sports programs. As Representative Bill Thomas put it to Myles Brand in his official letter from the House committee, "Why should the federal government subsidize the athletic activities of educational institutions when that subsidy is being used to help pay for escalating coaches' salaries, costly chartered travel, and state-of-the-art athletic facilities?"[40] Good question, but the NCAA has successfully parried such challenges in the past, and a tax-law expert calls its loss of tax-exempt status "a near impossibility under current law." The 2006 elections placed Ways and Means under Democrats' control, with Charles Rangel replacing Bill Thomas as chair, and interest in the issue seems to have dissipated for the time being. But the question will not go away.

From another side has come a sporadic legal battle for "athletes' rights." In recent years, state legislatures in Nebraska, California, Texas, Iowa, and South Carolina have passed or at least considered proposals such as a "Student Athletes Bill of Rights" to compensate college athletes beyond what the NCAA allows. Most recently, Nebraska Legislative Bill 688 was signed into law in 2003, while California Senate Bill 193 died in committee in 2004. States are constrained by federal laws, but these local efforts could be the early stages of a groundswell that in time could reach Congress with sufficient force. A system that pays athletes the equivalent of minimum wage and coaches the equivalent of CEO compensation seems increasingly untenable.

In January 2008 the NCAA escaped its most direct recent challenge: another lawsuit, comparable to worker's compensation cases described earlier, that could have forced institutions to deal with athletes as paid employees. On February 17, 2006, a class-action antitrust lawsuit, *White v. NCAA*, was filed in the names of two former college football players (Jason White from Stanford and Brian Polak from UCLA) and a basketball player (Jovan Harris from the University of San Francisco), challenging the NCAA's cap on financial aid for athletic scholarships. The actual Cost of Attendance (COA) for all students, as calculated by financial-aid officers—for travel and living expenses beyond basic board, room, and books—was about $2,500 more than the NCAA allowed in athletic scholarships. In a letter to the *Denver Post* in 2003, NCAA president Myles Brand himself publicly supported the inclusion of the full COA in scholarships, but the membership would not approve it.[41] Instead, the NCAA voted, effective August 1, 2004, to allow grants and loans up to the full COA but only in cases of demonstrated financial need.[42]

White v. NCAA applied to roughly 20,000 athletes at 144 colleges who would have received around $117 million, which, trebled under antitrust law, would have meant $351 million. And those would have been just the up-front costs for institutions, to be followed by the permanent increase to athletic scholarships. The lawsuit did not ask that universities be required to include the full COA in athletic scholarships, only that they not be prevented from doing so. A victory by the athletes in *White v. NCAA* would have confronted university leaders with an interesting set of choices, to say the least. First would have been the decision whether or not to offer their scholarship football and basketball players the full COA; at $2,500 per athlete, this would amount to $212,500 for eighty-five football players and $32,500 for thirteen basketball players—chump change for major programs but an additional financial burden for those already losing money. Choosing to do so, rather than risk a competitive disadvantage, would then have meant facing the requirements of Title IX—extend the COA to a more or less equal number of female athletes (not to mention wrestlers and baseball players)—or somehow create a different status for athletes in the revenue-generating sports. To do that, however (if legally possible), would have clearly made football and basketball players paid employees, with all of the complications of workers' rights that would come into play.

Moreover, if capping scholarships below the full cost of attendance were declared illegal, it would be a short judicial step to prohibiting any cap on compensation. The third paragraph in the text of the lawsuit opened with this statement: "While big-time college sports have become a huge commercial enterprise generating billions in annual revenues, the NCAA and its member institutions do not allow student athletes the share of the revenues that they would obtain in a more competitive market." The full COA would not do so, either, and the ramifications of *White v. NCAA* might have gone much further. Paragraph no. 44 of the lawsuit stated: "The institutions with major men's football and basketball programs aggressively compete against one another on the field of play, in recruiting student athletes, in seeking to recruit and retain talented coaching staffs, in building athletic facilities that will attract athletes and coaches and in soliciting revenues from television, radio and corporate sponsors. Absent the unlawful GIA [grant-in-aid] cap, the same competitive forces would result in GIAS that covered the full COA."[43] In the absence of any cap on coaches' salaries, facilities, media, and corporate funding, why would the "competitive forces" stop at the COA for athletes? If *White v. NCAA* were successful, how could a Georgia or an Oklahoma be prevented from offering $5,000 or $10,000 to a top recruit, maybe $25,000 for a blue-chip quarterback? In addition, if coaches can make millions from shoe contracts, endorsements, and public appearances, why should the athletes who make their coaches famous be prevented from cutting their own deals? Given the judicial precedents for applying antitrust law to the National Football League and big-time college football's increasingly close resemblance to the NFL as an entertainment industry, once the courts took up these issues, the laws governing the entertainment industry would trump college football traditions. The only uncertainty would be about how many traditional practices would disappear.

As the language quoted from the lawsuit should make clear, the attorneys who filed *White v. NCAA* understood college sports very well. They cited athletes' "30–60 hours per week in practice, team meetings, travel and official games during the season, and many hours per week in athletics-related activities even during the off season," with most of this time commitment made possible by "a large loophole for so-called 'voluntary' workouts that do not count toward the limit and which student athletes understand to be mandatory in the eyes of their coaches." The text of the lawsuit reads like an op-ed piece written by someone from the Drake Group or the Coalition on Intercollegiate Athletics. Given the lawsuit's potential impact, the relative absence of media coverage was remarkable. A profound restructuring of college athletics seemed perhaps imminent.

Instead, in January 2008 the plaintiffs agreed to a settlement with the NCAA. They (and their class in the suit) received $10 million over three years to reimburse their educational expenses, along with easier access for current and future athletes over the next five years to $218 million already provided by the NCAA for educational support. Along with the potential of continuing costs beyond these five years, the NCAA also agreed to allow athletic departments to provide comprehensive health insurance and basic accident insurance at a potential cost of $100,000 for each university. But in return, the NCAA one again escaped a challenge to its basic principle that college athletes are not employees but students entitled only to the cost of their education.[44] The NCAA denied all wrongdoing but agreed to settle "so as to avoid the substantial expense, inconvenience and distraction of continued litigation of the Action." For the plaintiffs, the "Stipulation and Agreement of Settlement" acknowledged that a prolonged legal process would have been expensive and its outcome uncertain.[45]

The NCAA and its members had considerably more at stake than the plaintiffs, and the likelihood of the NCAA's prevailing was considerably less likely, but victory for the plaintiffs throughout the appeals process would indeed have been long and costly. For the NCAA, the settlement was affordable, and what it won was breathing room. The athletes' rights movement will undoubtedly continue along other tracks, and NCAA members will remain vulnerable as nonprofit institutions in a multimillion-dollar entertainment business. But for now, the business of big-time college football (and basketball) can continue as usual.

IMAGINING THE UNTHINKABLE

With *White* safely in the past, and congressional interest in big-time football's tax-exempt status apparently waning, there is currently no urgency for universities to confront their present practices. But the inequality in revenues, benefits, and obstacles to success will not disappear, nor will the enduring conflict between athletic and educational imperatives. The radical shock of an antitrust or athletes' rights lawsuit, a congressional ruling, or a network-driven restructuring remains possible, even plausible. I simply have no idea when or how it might occur.

Here's what I do know (or think I know). College football looked very different fifty years ago. We got here from there not due to uncontrollable outside forces (with the possible exception of Title IX) but by internal responses to shifting conditions. Representatives to the NCAA convention voted to make freshmen eligible and limit scholarships to one year at a time. A group of universities chose to challenge the NCAA's monopoly on

TV rights. One university chose to break the bank for a new coach, and other universities fell in line out of fear of being left out. One university built a $10 million training facility, and others had to have one in order to stay competitive. Saturdays were booked solid, so members of some conferences agreed with ESPN to play games on Tuesday, Wednesday, or Thursday nights rather than be shut out from television altogether. (The temptation of an additional payday has proven too great for even the major conferences to resist; in 2009 the SEC and Big 12 will have games on Thursday nights.) All of these changes in big-time college football have resulted from individuals' choices, not inexorable market forces. And there has been nothing institutionally "strategic" in these decisions, or in many others with lesser impact. Universities today engage endlessly in strategic planning but leave their athletic departments to operate more or less independently, sometimes seeming to lurch along on impulsive reactions to whatever new circumstances arise.

College football will also look very different fifty years from now, but exactly what it will look like and how it will get there—due to cataclysmic action by Congress, courts, or TV networks, or by attrition and adaptation—I have no idea. The NCAA's latest effort at academic reform, the APR, has so far disproportionately (and somewhat mysteriously) penalized nonelite/nonelite programs while also increasing pressure on elite/elite institutions to shelter their athletes from the schools' academic mainstream. Voluntary restraint on spending likely appeals to institutions with small football budgets but is nearly unimaginable for the superpowers, nor would it fit the ambitions of non-BCS programs with dreams of BCS bowl glory and the Flutie effects that might follow.

A hundred years of governance by the NCAA, including six decades of regulatory power and the last twenty-odd years driven by a presidents' agenda, have proven that systemwide reforms inevitably fall short. At the other extreme, unilateral reforms by single institutions are simply too risky—except perhaps for those with the most elite academic programs—if for no other reason than the short-term advantage it could give the most direct institutional rivals in recruitment of students. The problems in big-time football logically push toward neither systemic nor unilateral but *multilateral* reform—institutions determining their own needs, identifying their true "peers" with whom to compete in athletics, then trusting those peers to conduct their football programs in a like manner.

Such a course of action is conceivable—in theory. A university's leaders would have to begin by finding answers to the two key questions: What are the relative benefits and costs to their own institution? And what are the actual benefits for their own athletes? Every institution has the intellectual and financial resources (the latter when the priority is high enough) to make a thorough study of its own football program and its role within the institution. The task would not be easy and the results not free from ambiguity, but that is the state of knowledge within which universities operate anyway. Should the evidence indicate that the athletes and the institution are both well served, the only challenge would be to maintain current practices. Should the evidence dictate necessary changes, possibilities would be readily available on the websites of the Knight Commission, the Drake Group, and the Coalition on Intercollegiate Athletics, among many others.

For this scenario to work, the entire (extended) university community would have to be committed to the effort. After too many years of presidents seeming to ignore what was happening in their own athletic departments, "presidential leadership" has guided reform within the NCAA since 1985, when a forty-four-member Presidents' Commission was formed. A special convention two years later, in July 1987, then offered the sorry spectacle of the NCAA membership, as the *New York Times* put it, "defeating or deferring action on virtually every significant measure sought by a group of university presidents." College presidents seemed at war with their own representatives to the NCAA. "Who's in Charge Here?," the *Times* asked in 1990 after NCAA members rejected a proposal from the Presidents' Commission and after the board of trustees at Michigan State overrode President John DiBiaggio's refusal to make George Perles athletic director as well as football coach. DiBiaggio subsequently resigned . . . as did Paul Hardin from the presidency of SMU, under pressure after reporting the slush fund in his football program to the NCAA . . . as did Bill Atchely from the presidency of Clemson after his board of trustees would not back his attempt to remove his athletic director in the wake of NCAA sanctions. Presidents had their small victories. The "reform convention" of 1991 succeeded, according to the *New York Times*, due to the presence of "a record number of college and university presidents," who adopted a strategy of demanding a record of the votes instead of relying simply on a show of hands. The implication was clear: if they could raise their hands anonymously to be counted, instead of putting themselves on record, athletic directors and faculty representatives might vote contrary to the position of their own presidents.

Instead, the presidents rode their white steeds onto the convention floor and routed the bad guys.[46]

This is not the ideal way to achieve meaningful reform, because presidents at war with their own athletic departments cannot change them without serious collateral damage. Under presidential leadership, the NCAA has arrived at mandatory academic reforms coupled to voluntary restraint on spending, and presidents on their own cannot be expected to do more than this. Moreover, for reformers to demonize the opposition does no good. All champions of reform would do well to follow the advice of Terry Holland to his fellow members of the Drake Group. Holland, the athletic director at East Carolina and former basketball coach at Virginia, wrote a memo in 2006 urging his colleagues to acknowledge "that these people [the NCAA] are well intentioned and are actually honorable, intelligent human beings simply doing their jobs to the best of their abilities. When we attack the job they are doing, they simply become defensive. As we yell louder, they stop listening all together."[47] Meaningful reform cannot come from white-hatted heroes trouncing black-hatted villains. Everyone from athletic-department personnel and faculty on campus to alumni clubs, booster groups, community leaders, and boards of trustees should have the chance to take the high road on behalf of the institution's well-being.

At this point in our little scenario, even with the backing of the entire university community, how could change be implemented? Through the NCAA? The organization is powerless to limit coaches' salaries or dictate other financial restraints. Academic reforms on the order of making freshmen ineligible again or reducing required credit hours in-season would likely get bogged down by rival interests. The constraint of anti-trust law in financial matters is matched by "anti-trust" of a different sort in matters affecting recruiting, eligibility, and everything else involving athletes. The NCAA has been guided, ever since it first took on regulatory powers in the 1940s, by a universal assumption that member schools will cheat. Rules must be so numerous and precise, and enforcement so effective, that cheating will be minimized. The result is an NCAA manual thicker than the Manhattan phone book.

While the overall system is resistant to major changes, any retreat from winning at all costs or competing at the highest level, if pursued alone, would be extraordinarily difficult, if not impossible. (Tulane and Rice acted alone when they contemplated such a course, then backed down.) The alternative to both solo and NCAA-wide solutions would be to decide on a course of action, then identify true "peers," like-minded institutions that can be trusted to embrace the same values.

I have a hard time imagining university presidents voluntarily taking on this challenge, with all of its risks and uncertainties. And I can't imagine the university's full range of athletic and academic constituencies, both on and off campus, embracing the challenge. Yet big-time college football's current financing is likely unsustainable for most universities, and the fiction that the sport exists above all to serve the educational interests of student-athletes grows increasingly ludicrous. Another revolution lies in college football's future, but it remains more likely to be precipitated from without than launched from within. As I write in March 2009, the likely depth and duration of the economic downturn is not yet at all clear. But with state legislatures already announcing cutbacks in their higher-ed budgets, at least in the short term, the allocations to athletics while academic programs are being squeezed will demand more intense scrutiny. My anticipated blow from outside may be gathering force as I write—or this threat, too, may pass as so many others have. But if that outside blow should ever fall, university leaders might find themselves making decisions about their football program that seem impossible now. What initially would seem a catastrophe might even prove to be a godsend.

Notes

ABBREVIATIONS

AAN	*Ann Arbor News*
ABH	*Athens Banner Herald*
AJ	*Atlanta Journal*
AJC	*Atlanta Journal-Constitution*
AP	Associated Press
AUP	*Auburn Plainsman* (Auburn University)
BAA	*Baltimore Afro-American*
BCT	*Bloomington Courier Tribune*
BDHT	*Bloomington Daily Herald-Telephone*
BG	*Boston Globe*
BI	*Branding Iron* (University of Wyoming)
BN	*Birmingham News*
BRMA	*Baton Rouge Morning Advocate*
CGT	*Corvallis Gazette-Times*
CHE	*Chronicle of Higher Education*
CW	*Crimson White* (University of Alabama)
DB	*Daily Barometer* (Oregon State University)
DM	*Daily Mississippian* (University of Mississippi)
DMN	*Dallas Morning News*
DMR	*Des Moines Register*
DP	*Denver Post*
DW	*Daily Worker*
ERG	*Eugene Register-Guard*
GS	*Gainesville Sun*
ICPC	*Iowa City Press-Citizen*
IDS	*Indiana Daily Student* (Indiana University)
IS	*Indianapolis Star*
JSH	*Journal of Sport History*
KJ	*Knoxville Journal*

KNS	*Knoxville News-Sentinel*
LAEHE	*Los Angeles Evening Herald and Examiner*
LAT	*Los Angeles Times*
LCJ	*Louisville Courier-Journal*
LCJT	*Louisville Courier-Journal & Times*
LDB	*Laramie Daily Boomerang*
LH	*Lexington Herald*
LHL	*Lexington Herald-Leader*
MA	*Montgomery Advertiser*
MH	*Miami Herald*
NB	*Nashville Banner*
NOTP	*New Orleans Times-Picayune*
NPC	*New Pittsburgh Courier*
NT	*Nashville Tennessean*
NYDN	*New York Daily News*
NYEJ	*New York Evening Journal*
NYT	*New York Times*
O	*Observer* (University of Notre Dame)
OE	*Oxford Eagle*
OJ	*Oregon Journal*
OS	*Oregon Statesman*
OWH	*Omaha World-Herald*
PI	*Philadelphia Inquirer*
PO	*Portland Oregonian*
PT	*Portland Tribune*
R&B	*Red and Black* (University of Georgia)
SBJ	*SportsBusiness Journal*
SDN	*Starkville Daily News*
SEP	*Saturday Evening Post*
SHA	*Syracuse Herald-American*
SHJ	*Syracuse Herald-Journal*
SI	*Sports Illustrated*
SPI	*Seattle Post-Intelligencer*
ST	*Seattle Times*
TN	*Tuscaloosa News*
UPI	United Press International
UTDB	*Daily Beacon* (University of Tennessee)
WP	*Washington Post*

1. A regrettably ignored and forgotten book by the literary scholar Edwin Cady, *The Big Game: College Sports and American Life* (Knoxville: University of Tennessee Press, 1978), has the most penetrating explanation of this aspect of college football. Warren St. John's *Rammer Jammer, Yellow Hammer: A Road Trip into the Heart of Fan Mania* (New York: Three Rivers Press, 2004) is a journalist's lively account of the tailgating culture at the University of Alabama. Recently reflecting on his own pleasures as a fan and imagining the experience of the 85,000 at Texas or 110,000 at Michigan, longtime critic Murray Sperber realized that those who wish to reform intercollegiate athletics "will have to understand the power that it has over its fans—a significant percentage of the U.S. population—and how deep its roots are in the American psyche." See Murray Sperber, "On Being a Fan," *Chronicle Review*, October 5, 2007.

2. For a more general history of college football, including this era, see in particular John Sayle Watterson, *College Football: History, Spectacle, Controversy* (Baltimore: Johns Hopkins University Press, 2000).

CHAPTER 1

1. In addition to the images of the protesters and antiprotesters (originally published by the staff of the *Columbia Spectator*), see the related photos of the protesters and their "well-groomed adversaries" in *Life* magazine's May 10, 1968, report on the confrontation at Columbia.

2. David Zang, *SportsWars: Athletes in the Age of Aquarius* (Fayetteville: University of Arkansas Press, 2001), p. 78; Charles Wollenberg, *Berkeley, a City in History*, chap. 9, "Heritage of the Sixties" (online at <http://berkeleypubliclibrary.org/system/Chapter9.html>); "Students: Lifting a Siege—and Rethinking a Future," *Time*, May 10, 1968; "The Siege of Columbia," *Ramparts*, June 15, 1968. In the best book on sports in the 1960s, Zang describes several other incidents of jock antiprotests.

3. The Sweeney quote appears in Neil Amdur, *Fifth Down: Democracy and the Football Revolution* (New York: Coward, McCann & Geoghegan, 1971), pp. 29–30; the Babbidge quote appears in Jack Scott, *The Athletic Revolution* (New York: Free Press, 1971), p. 29.

4. AP, "Haircuts Hot Issue of NCAA," *PO*, January 9, 1969; AP, "Racial Tiff at Meeting," *OS*, January 9, 1969.

5. Will Grimsley, "Mod Revolution Continues in Sports," *GS*, November 22, 1970.

6. Alfred Wright, "To the Big Game and to the Barricades," *SI*, January 3, 1966.

7. Abe Peck, *Uncovering the Sixties: The Life and Times of the Underground Press* (New York: Pantheon, 1985), p. 114.

8. Jon Swan, "Football," *Evergreen Review*, October 1968, pp. 37–43; "Jock Lib vs. Big Game," *Berkeley Barb*, November 20–26, 1970. The *Barb* also published a piece about Dave Meggysey, the former NFL player turned radical author. See John Jekabson, "Football Fascists," *Berkeley Barb*, January 14–20, 1972.

9. This was the claim of Richard Morse Hodge in "American College Football," *Outing*, March 1888, p. 483. Regarding American football, Hodge added that "for all its military characteristics it really is a game fit even for Quakers. It has the elements of war without the quarrel, a spirit of encounter with no rancor, discipline and no greater hardship to the players than 'training.'"

10. Walter Camp, *Walter Camp's Book of College Sports* (New York: Century, 1893), p. 98. Daly opened his *American Football* (1921) by declaring the "remarkable similarity . . . between war and football." In *Football and How to Watch It* (1922), Haughton called football "a miniature war game played under somewhat more civilized rules of conduct," in which "most of the combat principles of the field service regulations of the United States Army" are applicable. But football was also likened to chess and to the American corporation (most influentially by Walter Camp), and in a much-told tale, Knute Rockne supposedly found the inspiration for his famous Notre Dame shift by watching the chorus line of the Ziegfeld Follies. Football was like war, but it was also like chess and business, and even like a dance. See Charles D. Daly, *American Football* (New York: Harper & Brothers, 1921), p. 1; and Percy D. Haughton, *Football and How to Watch It* (Boston: Marshall Jones, 1922), p. 145.

11. Peck, *Uncovering the Sixties*, pp. 126, 251.

12. Raymond Mungo, *Famous Long Ago: My Life and Hard Times with Liberation News Service* (Boston: Beacon Press, 1970), p. 127.

13. After quitting the St. Louis Cardinals, Meggysey wrote *Out of Their League* (Berkeley, Calif.: Ramparts Press, 1970), a furious indictment of football at both the college and professional levels. Oliver left the Oakland Raiders to join a hippie commune and write *High for the Game: From Football Gladiator to Hippie* (New York: William Morrow, 1971). And Sauer retired in 1971 from the New York Jets after six seasons because he found the game savage and dehumanizing. Meggysey told a reporter for the *Berkeley Barb* that he "had a lot of support privately" from other players in the NFL following the publication of his book, "but active players cannot support me publicly. That would be the end of their careers." See Jekabson, "Football Fascists."

14. Jerry L. Avorn and others, *Up against the Ivy Wall: A History of the Columbia Crisis* (New York: Atheneum, 1969), pp. 164–65 (see also pp. 96–102, 137, 167–69, 173–74, 178, and 182). Student radicals' accounts in *Rat*, the New York underground newspaper, also identified the opposition as "jocks." See Jeff Shero's "Blockade and Siege" and Jon Moore's "The Bust Comes," both in the May 13–16, 1968, issue (with a "Heil Columbia" cover).

15. April Kimley, "Dramatic Signs of the Failure of Communication," part of "Mutiny at a Great University," *Life*, May 10, 1968.

16. "Profs Inspired Library Blockade," *NYDN*, April 29, 1968.

17. James Simon Kunen, *The Strawberry Statement—Notes of a College Revolutionary* (New York: Random House, 1969), pp. 17, 27–28; "The Siege of Columbia," p. 36; "Profs Inspired Library Blockade."

18. Kenneth J. Heineman, *Put Your Bodies upon the Wheels: Student Revolt in the 1960s* (Chicago: Ivan R. Dee, 2001), p. 141.

19. Stew Albert, "A Difficult Decade to Read," *LAT Book Review*, February 16, 2003.

20. Walter Camp, "Team Play in Football," *Harper's Weekly*, October 31, 1891, p. 845.

21. Walter Camp, "An All-Time All-America Foot-Ball Team," *Century* 79 (February 1910): 594.

22. Robert Cohen, *When the Old Left Was Young: Student Radicals and America's First Mass Student Movement, 1929–1941* (New York: Oxford University Press, 1993), p. 7.

23. Stephen Norwood, *Strikebreaking and Intimidation: Mercenaries and Masculinity in Twentieth-Century America* (Chapel Hill: University of North Carolina Press, 2002), pp. 15–33, 254. The 1903 incident, when football players formed a wedge to break through the strikers' picket line, was anticipated in a short story by Henry K. Webster, "The Wedge," *SEP*, December 28, 1901.

24. Norwood, *Strikebreaking and Intimidation*, pp. 15–18, 22–23, 29.

25. Ibid., pp. 16, 23–24.

26. Ibid., p. 32.

27. By the fall, Harris had expanded his attack into *King Football: The Vulgarization of the American College* (New York: Vanguard Press, 1932), an early example of a familiar genre: the wholesale indictment of college football and the fraudulent educational system that supports it. *King Football* denounced football on the same terms as had John R. Tunis's *Sports Heroics and Hysterics* (New York: The John Day Company, 1928), although it was written by a "radical" rather than a "moderate." Twenty-one years later, *King Football* brought Joe McCarthy down on Harris as evidence of his communist subversion, an attack that in turn was highlighted by Edward R. Murrow in his famous broadcast exposing McCarthy in March 1954 (the centerpiece of George Clooney's 2005 film, *Good Night, and Good Luck*).

28. Cohen, *When the Old Left Was Young*, pp. 56, 64. See also James Wechsler, *Revolt on the Campus* (New York: Covici Friede, 1935), pp. 109–20; and Eileen Eagan, *Class, Culture, and the Classroom: The Student Peace Movement of the 1930s* (Philadelphia: Temple University Press, 1981), pp. 40–56.

29. Cohen, *When the Old Left Was Young*, p. 199; Kai Bird and Martin J. Sherwin, *American Prometheus: The Triumph and Tragedy of J. Robert Oppenheimer* (New York: Knopf, 2005), p. 106; Wechsler, *Revolt on the Campus*, p. 270. Wechsler misidentified Griffith as an end instead of a quarterback. "Heroes," of course, was ironic.

30. Wechsler, *Revolt on the Campus*, pp. 276–78.

31. "Protest Strike at U.C.L.A. Fizzles: Classes Continue," *LAEHE*, November 5, 1934.

32. Cohen, *When the Old Left Was Young*, p. 122; "Berkeley Riot over U.C.L.A. Row," *LAEHE*, November 5, 1934.

33. Bird and Sherwin, *American Prometheus*, p. 118.

34. "Michigan Grid Coach Sends Players into Ford's to Aid Union-Busting," *DW*, November 18, 1937. After Kipke was fired by Michigan, Harry Bennett, Ford's powerful head of security who had arranged the summer work for the football players, now ar-

ranged for his friend Kipke to be appointed to Michigan's Board of Regents, in effect giving the sacked coach "the whip hand over the professors." See John McCarten, "The Little Man in Henry Ford's Basement," *American Mercury*, May 1940, p. 10.

35. McCarten, "The Little Man in Henry Ford's Basement." (I am indebted to Norwood's *Strikebreaking and Intimidation* for this reference.)

36. In a minor incident in May 1935, jocks hooted down a radical speaker at the University of Wisconsin. See Wechsler, *Revolt on the Campus*, p. 331.

37. Edward Cole, "Athletes Aren't So Dumb," *Student Advocate*, February 1936.

38. "Lefty" and "No Holds Barred," *Western Worker*, December 9, 1937.

39. "Stanford Players to Get Bowl Cut," *DW*, December 11, 1940.

40. "Small Subsidies behind Grid Troubles," *DW*, November 8, 1938.

41. Cohen, *When the Old Left Was Young*, p. 122.

42. Cole, "Athletes Aren't So Dumb."

43. Harris, *King Football*, p. 105; Wechsler, *Revolt on Campus*, pp. 294–96; Cole, "Athletes Aren't So Dumb."

44. "Not-So-Red Columbia: The Old Spirit Survives," *NYEJ*, February 20, 1935; quoted in Cole, "Athletes Aren't So Dumb."

45. Brad Austin, "Protecting Athletics and the American Way: Defenses of Intercollegiate Athletics at Ohio State and across the Big Ten during the Great Depression," *JSH* 27 (Summer 2000): 262.

46. Frederick Ware, "We 'Crazy Americans,'" *OWH*, November 8, 1942; Lester Rodney, "On the Scoreboard," *DW*, October 10, 1946.

47. "Our Flag on Wings," *Newsweek*, December 10, 1956; "How the Russians Won All Those Points," *Life*, December 17, 1956. On the United States–USSR athletic rivalry, see Allen Guttman, "The Cold War and the Olympics," *International Journal* 43 (Autumn 1988): 554–68; Joseph Turrini, "'It Was Communism versus the Free World': The USA-USSR Dual Track Meet Series and the Development of Track and Field in the United States, 1958–1985," *JSH* 28 (Fall 2001): 427–71; and Thomas M. Hunt, "American Sport Policy and the Cultural Cold War: The Lyndon B. Johnson Presidential Years," *JSH* 33 (Fall 2006): 273–97.

48. "Soviet Denounces Football Murder," *NYT*, August 11, 1950; "Russians Find U.S. 'Futbol' Rough Game, Designed to Create 'Bandits and Haters,'" *NYT*, November 19, 1952.

49. Dick Hyland, "The Hyland Fling," *LAT*, October 9, 1951. For more temperate writers, the Soviet Union sometimes served as a sort of perverse conscience. When Georgia's governor tried to prevent Georgia Tech from playing in an integrated 1956 Sugar Bowl, an editorial in the *Newark News* worried that this would reinforce Nikita Khrushchev's charges, made on a goodwill tour of southern Asia, that the United States is "an enemy of the colored peoples of the world." Quoted in "Press Taunts Georgia Governor," *BAA*, December 17, 1955.

50. AP, "Halas Defends American Way for Pro Grid Game," *Christian Science Monitor*, August 1, 1957. For this reference, I am indebted to Russell E. Crawford, "Consensus All-American: Sport and the Promotion of the American Way of Life during the Cold War, 1946–1965" (Ph.D. diss, University of Nebraska, May 2004), p. 180.

51. L. H. Gregory, "Greg's Gossip," *PO*, January 31, 1956.

52. "Motion Picture Alliance States Its Principles," *Daily Variety*, February 7, 1944, p. 5.

53. Francis Wallace, *Dementia Pigskin* (New York: Rinehart & Company, 1951), p. 73.

54. Ibid., pp. 225–26.

55. Ibid., pp. 332, 334, 338.

56. Ibid., pp. 242–43.

57. Thomas F. Brady, "Hollywood 'Don'ts'," *NYT*, November 16, 1947.

58. "Stern's Law," *Nation*, November 15, 1958. This is an editorial mocking Stern's views.

59. Wade Thompson, "My Crusade against Football," *Nation*, April 11, 1959. An English professor at Brown, Thompson quoted these coaches as spewers of non-sense—the idea that "Football develops Americanism, Virtue, Godliness, Patriotism and Charity" instead of just wins or losses in games. Like critics in the 1930s, Thompson denounced football for fostering anti-intellectualism, not ideological conservatism.

60. Allison Danzig, "Men with Missions," *NYT*, February 28, 1958; "Eisenhower Receives Award from Football Hall Here before 2,000," *NYT*, October 29, 1958. A forthcoming book from the University of Illinois Press, *Cold War Football* by Kurt Kemper, develops this topic fully.

61. "Is College Football in Trouble?," *SEP*, October 11, 1958. The comment accompanied a profile of Oklahoma coach Bud Wilkinson.

62. John F. Kennedy, "The Soft American," *SI*, December 26, 1960; Tim Cohane, "Football Is Violence," *Look*, August 28, 1962. Kennedy also chose the most prominent football coach of the time, Oklahoma's Bud Wilkinson, to chair his President's Council on Physical Fitness. See also Donald J. Mrozek, "The Cult and Ritual of Toughness in Cold War America," in *Rituals and Ceremonies in Popular Culture*, ed. Ray B. Browne (Bowling Green Ohio: Bowling Green State University Press, 1980), pp. 178–91; Robert L. Griswold, "The 'Flabby American,' the Body, and the Cold War," in *A Shared Experience: Men, Women, and the History of Gender*, ed. Laura McCall and Donald Yacavone (New York: New York University Press, 1998), pp. 328–48; and Jeffrey Montez de Oca, "The 'Muscle Gap': Physical Education and U.S. Fears of a Depleted Masculinity, 1954–1963," in *East Plays West: Sport and the Cold War*, ed. Stephen Wagg and David L. Andrews (New York: Routledge, 2007), pp. 123–48. De Oca identified hundreds of articles on a "muscle gap" published in newspapers and magazines in this period.

63. Paul Bryant and John Underwood, "A Run-in with Rupp and Trouble down in Texas," *SI*, August 22, 1966. This is part 2 of the series "I'll Tell You about Football," which ran in the magazine from August 15 through September 12. And see Jim Dent and Gene Stallings, *The Junction Boys: How Ten Days in Hell with Bear Bryant Forged a Championship Team* (New York: St. Martin's, 1999). Dent reported that it was actually 35, not 27, who survived out of 111 players.

64. Mark Kriegel, *Namath: A Biography* (New York: Viking, 2004), p. 81.

65. Morton Sharnik and Robert Creamer, "The New Rage to Win," *SI*, October

8, 1962; and Shannon Ragland, *The Thin Thirty: The Untold Story of Brutality, Scandal, and Redemption for Charlie Bradshaw's 1962 Kentucky Football Team* (Louisville, Ky.: Set Shot Press, 2007). *The Thin Thirty* is self-published and, at times, laughably grammar- and diction-impaired, but the interviews with quitters and nonquitters alike convincingly flesh out the basic story told by *SI*.

66. Roy Terrell, "You Love Woody or Hate Him," *SI*, September 24, 1962.

67. In a series of remarkable columns leading up to the 1962 season opener with Florida State, *Lexington Herald* sports editor Ed Ashford (September 7, 13, 18, 22) and assistant sports editor Billy Thompson (September 7, 21, 22) not only excused but endorsed Bradshaw's tactics (as well as those of his mentor, Bear Bryant, in his notorious first season at Texas A&M) and dismissed the fifty-odd players who quit as "boys" unwilling to "pay the price." In one of Thompson's columns (September 21), the team doctor (with the concurrence of two other local physicians, all of them former college football players) declared football to be "a hard, tough sport that requires hard, tough conditioning. . . . The boys who quit football at Kentucky this year probably shouldn't have been there in the first place." On October 4, Ashford denounced *Sports Illustrated*'s "hatchet job" on Bradshaw (based on the magazine's press release), then ignored the article when it appeared shortly after.

68. Someone has told the stories of the quitters (as well as those who stuck it out) under Charlie Bradshaw at Kentucky in 1962. See Ragland, *Thin Thirty*. While Ragland honors both groups, those who quit seem more self-determined and principled.

69. Maurice Isserman and Michael Kazin, *America Divided: The Civil War of the 1960s*, 2nd ed. (New York: Oxford University Press, 2004), p. 207.

70. See Jerry Kirshenbaum, "The Greening of Notre Dame," *SI*, December 14, 1970.

71. Allen Sack, who graduated from Notre Dame in 1967 and went on to become a professor and sports activist, writes in his memoir of sports in the 1960s— generalizing about the nation as a whole—that "the vast majority of athletes were among the [antiwar] movement's most outspoken critics" (*Counterfeit Amateurs: An Athlete's Journey through the Sixties to the Age of Academic Capitalism* [University Park: Penn State University Press, 2008], p. 64). Following Sack at Notre Dame by just three years, my own sense is that, by 1969 or 1970, college athletes were part of the student mainstream—not politically "radical" but opposed to the war. We both rely on our own sense of the times on a subject where no statistical or documentary evidence exists.

72. Frank Vatterott, "ND Athletics—Are They a Paradox?," *O*, May 20, 1970.

73. Max Rafferty, "Interscholastic Athletics: The Gathering Storm," in Scott, *Athletic Revolution*, pp. 20–21.

74. Jack Olsen, "The Black Athlete: The Cruel Deception," *SI*, July 1, 1968. This is the first in Olsen's landmark five-part series. UTEP was Texas Western in 1966, when its all-black basketball team beat all-white Kentucky for the NCAA championship in a game that became immortalized as the mortal blow against racism, a stark allegory of black and white (literally). The 2006 feel-good film about the episode, *Glory Road*, ignored the on-campus racism reported in *Sports Illustrated*.

75. David K. Wiggins, "'The Year of Awakening': Black Athletes, Racial Unrest, and the Civil Rights Movement of 1968," in *Glory Bound: Black Athletes in White America* (Syracuse, N.Y.: Syracuse University Press, 1997), pp. 104–22; "On the Campus, Protest at Washington," *Life*, March 15, 1968 (one of several brief reports on racial problems in sports); "Negro Athletes Threaten Boycott at Major Colleges," *NYT*, May 19, 1968; "All-American Problem," *SI*, May 6, 1968; Anthony Ripley, "Irate Black Athletes Stir Campus Tension," *NYT*, November 16, 1969; George Vecsey, "New Princeton Coach Is With It," *NYT*, February 6, 1969.

76. Zang, *SportsWars*, pp. 119–39 (quotations from 133 and 135).

77. "Black Players Protest Booing," *O*, February 13, 1969; "Rossie Apologizes to Players," *O*, February 14, 1969.

78. "Blacks Demonstrate at Game," *O*, November 18, 1968.

79. "Black Athletes Dissatisfied with Publicity on Black Aid," *O*, April 23, 1970.

80. John Underwood, "Shave Off That Thing!," *SI*, September 1, 1969.

81. Walter Byers, "A Personal Viewpoint . . . Phony Plebiscites," *NCAA News*, October 1969; Walter Byers, "A Personal Viewpoint . . . Freedom Fighters," *NCAA News*, April 1970; Walter Byers, "A Personal Viewpoint . . . Lessons in Learning," *NCAA News*, July 1970; "Student-Athletes Will Visit Vietnam," *NCAA News*, June 1970; "Athletes Go to Vietnam for Holidays," *NCAA News*, December 15, 1970.

82. Amdur, *Fifth Down*, pp. 143–44; Kirschbaum, "The Greening of Notre Dame."

83. "Scoreboard," *SI*, November 1, 1971; Michael Rosenberg, *War as They Knew It: Woody Hayes, Bo Schembechler, and America in a Time of Unrest* (New York and Boston: Grand Central, 2008), p. 95.

84. Royal Brougham, "Advice (for Free) from R.B.," *SPI*, November 8, 1969.

85. See, for example, Marty Ralbovski (Newspaper Enterprise Association), "No Room for Radicalism," *LDB*, October 30, 1969; AP, "Racial Unrest in College Football Puzzling," *BDHT*, November 16, 1969; and UPI, "Player-Coach Rapport Key," *SPI*, November 4, 1969. Similar surveys of coaching methods appeared the following season. See Anthony Ripley (New York Times Service), "Black Athletes Join Militants," *Minneapolis Tribune*, November 17, 1969; and AP, "College Football Faces Unpredictable Decade," *SHA*, September 6, 1970.

86. Melvin Durslag, "Durslag Says: Days of Iron Hand Dead," *SPI*, November 6, 1969.

87. John Underwood, "The Desperate Coach," *SI*, August 25, 1969; Douglas Hartmann, *Race, Culture, and the Revolt of the Black Athlete* (Chicago: University of Chicago Press, 2003), pp. 180–81.

88. Durslag, "Durslag Says: Days of Iron Hand Dead."

89. Gary Shaw, *Meat on the Hoof: The Hidden World of Texas Football* (New York: St. Martin's, 1972), pp. 196–97; Terry Frei, *Horns, Hogs, and Nixon Coming: Texas vs. Arkansas in Dixie's Last Stand* (New York: Simon & Schuster, 2002), pp. 18–27. A current colleague of mine, who played for Prothro, and my first roommate with the Chiefs, who played for McKay, both described their coaches to me as fundamentally "cold and aloof."

90. John Underwood, "Concessions—and Lies," *SI*, September 8, 1969.

91. See Amdur, *Fifth Down*, pp. 64–67.

92. A handful of underclassmen on the team asked me as a graduating senior and captain to speak to Ara about the matter, but he denied my request on their behalf, and I recall that they did not press the issue. In his memoir, Allen Sack (three years ahead of me at Notre Dame) reports that seven players approached Ara on their own about missing a spring practice to attend a demonstration and were denied. After some of them skipped the practice anyway, Ara suspended no one; he only required them to spend a day picking up trash in the stadium. See Sack, *Counterfeit Amateurs*, p. 62.

93. Ibid., p. 63.

94. Bud Collins, "Hail the New Head Coach," *BG*, August 14, 1974.

95. For the incidents in this and the following two paragraphs, see Michael Mac-Cambridge, *America's Game: The Epic Story of How Pro Football Captured a Nation* (New York: Random House, 2004), pp. 159–60; Richard M. Collins, "Richard M. Nixon: The Psychic, Political, and Moral Uses of Sport," *JSH* 10 (Summer 1983): 77–84; Dave Anderson, "Political Football," *NYT*, July 1, 1973; and Rosenberg, *War as They Knew It*, p. 318 and passim. See also "The Nixon and Sports Website" at <http://www.sarantakes.com>.

96. See, for example, Ike Balbus, "Politics as Sports: The Political Ascendancy of the Sports Metaphor in America," *Monthly Review*, March 1975, pp. 26–39.

97. Robert Lipsyte, *SportsWorld: An American Dreamland* (New York: Quadrangle/NYT, 1975), pp. 13–14; Larry Merchant, *And Every Day You Take Another Bite* (Garden City, N.Y.: Doubleday, 1971), p. 23.

98. Collins, "Richard M. Nixon," p. 82.

99. Scott, *Athletic Revolution*; Paul Hoch, *Rip Off the Big Game: The Exploitation of Sports by the Power Elite* (Garden City, N.Y.: Doubleday, 1972); Meggysey, *Out of Their League*; Oliver, *High for the Game*; Bernie Parrish, *They Call It a Game* (New York: Dial Press, 1971); Shaw, *Meat on the Hoof*.

100. All details from the *Miami Herald* published the day after the games.

101. Merchant, *And Every Day You Take Another Bite*, p. 36.

102. Details again from the *Miami Herald*.

CHAPTER 2

1. Jack Olsen, *The Black Athlete: A Shameful Story* (New York: Time-Life, 1968), p. 170.

2. Harry Edwards, *Sociology of Sport* (Homewood, Ill.: Dorsey Press, 1973), p. 225.

3. Among major southern independents, the University of Miami had its first black varsity player in 1968 (Ray Bellamy), Florida State in 1969 (Calvin Peterson), and Georgia Tech in 1970 (Eddie McAshan). Peterson was miserable at Florida State and flunked out after the season. In 1972 he shot himself in the stomach and bled to death. Alexander Wolff recaps this story in "Ground Breakers," *SI*, November 7, 2005.

4. David K. Wiggins, "Prized Performers, but Frequently Overlooked Students: The Involvement of Black Athletes in Intercollegiate Sports on Predominantly

White University Campuses, 1890–1972," *Research Quarterly for Exercise and Sport* 62 (June 1991): 170.

5. Richard Pennington, *Breaking the Ice: The Racial Integration of Southwest Conference Football* (Jefferson, N.C.: McFarland, 1987).

6. Wesley Pruden Jr., "Black Stars Fire Mississippi State Hopes," *National Observer*, October 19, 1970. At Florida, for example, a report in 1968 that the university was not in compliance with the Civil Rights Act led directly to the recruiting of the first black athlete in 1968 and of the first black football players the following year. See "Integration and Athletics at the University of Florida," <http://www.clas.ufl.edu/users/brundage/website/sports.html>.

7. Jim Murray, "Bedsheets and 'Bama," *LAT*, November 20, 1961.

8. Jim Murray, "End of a Charade," *LAT*, September 11, 1970; Jim Murray, "Hatred Shut out as Alabama Finally Joins the Union," *LAT*, September 13, 1970; Jim Murray, "Language of Alabama," *LAT*, September 17, 1970.

9. Jack Doane, "Just the Facts, Ma'am," *MA*, September 17, 1970. Also see Jack Doane, "Jim Murray at It Again," *MA*, September 30, 1970 (on Murray's ridicule of southern accents); and Charles Land, "No Insults at All," *TN*, September 14, 1970 (responding to another West Coast writer on the topic of football and race). The following season, a similar exchange followed the LSU-Wisconsin game, when the *Baton Rouge Morning Advertiser* published excerpts from a column in the *Madison Capital Times* that basically portrayed the LSU contingent as a bunch of racist rednecks. See Bernell Ballard, "Sports Front," *BRMA*, October 4, 1971, along with Ballard's column on October 11, where he printed some readers' letters in response.

10. John David Briley, *Career in Crisis: Paul "Bear" Brant and the 1971 Season of Change* (Macon, Ga.: Macon University Press, 2006), pp. 20–33.

11. Keith Dunnavant, *Coach: The Life of Paul "Bear" Bryant* (New York: Simon & Schuster, 1996), pp. 249–56; Allen Barra, *The Last Coach: A Life of "Bear" Bryant* (New York: W. W. Norton, 2005), p. xxv; David Halberstam, "Just a Coach, Not a Leader," ESPN.com, December 20, 2002 (<http://espn.go.com/page2/s/halberstam/021220.html>). See also Brent Wellborn, in "Coach Paul Bryant and the Integration of the University of Alabama Football Team," *Southern Historian* 18 (1997): 66–80.

12. A controversy over his SAT score—a suspicion that someone took the test for him—cost Davis his scholarship. After attending Tennessee State instead and then playing pro football, Davis later earned a master's degree at Tennessee and became a school administrator. See Robert Thomas Epling, "Seasons of Change: Football Desegregation at the University of Tennessee and the Transformation of the Southeastern Conference, 1963–1967" (Ph.D. diss., University of Tennessee, 1994), p. 11.

13. Russ Bebb, *Vols: Three Decades of Big Orange Football, 1964–1993* (Champaign, Ill.: Sagamore, 1994), p. 90. Despite his achievements, Walker must have felt doubly estranged at times as an African American player who was also gay. Apparently, his sexual orientation came out only after his career ended—and kept him from receiving later honors, such as induction into his hometown's hall of fame—but his secret must have compounded his sense of difference from his teammates. Walker died of AIDS in 2002. See Chris Wohlwend, "Long in the Shadows, a Player's Legacy Is Restored," *NYT*, April 18, 2008.

14. Epling, "Seasons of Change," p. 124.

15. Pruden, "Black Stars Fire Mississippi State Hopes"; Lacy J. Banks, "Black Football Players in the White South," *Ebony*, December 1970, p. 132.

16. For details on each of the black basketball pioneers in the SEC, and the ACC as well, see Barry Jacobs, *Across the Line: Profiles in Basketball Courage: Tales of the First Black Players in the ACC and SEC* (Guilford, Conn.: Lyons Press, 2008); and William F. Reed, "Culture Shock in Dixieland," *SI*, August 12, 1991. SEC basketball was integrated during the same years as football, beginning with Vanderbilt in 1967–68 (Perry Wallace) and completed by Mississippi State in 1972–73 (Jerry Jenkins and Larry Fry).

17. No one could have been less visible than Darryl Hill, who integrated Maryland's football team in 1963 but was left out of the school yearbook entirely, even in the team photo. (A yearbook staff member substituted the 1962 team photo for the 1963 photo in order to erase evidence of Hall.) See Wolff, "Ground Breakers."

18. Ibid.

19. Reed, "Culture Shock in Dixieland"; Wolff, "Ground Breakers"; *Breaking the Huddle: The Integration of College Football* (HBO, 2008). HBO focused on Darryl Hill, the pioneer at Maryland, Jerry LeVias at SMU, and Wilbur Hackett at Kentucky, while also crediting Bear Bryant with making the decisive blow against segregation.

20. When Owens was a senior, the paper included a cursory story on Auburn's black athletes in an issue assessing racial progress at the university. See Roy Summerford, "Black Athletes Have Broken Race Barrier," *AUP*, October 5, 1972.

21. Nathan Turner, "Blacks Discuss Football Careers," *CW*, January 18, 1973.

22. Bill Lee, "The First Time," *R&B*, August 9, 1972. The paper did not avoid other controversial issues, such as gay rights, the athletic department's loosening of its rules on athletes' grooming, and the Black Student Union's demand for a cultural center.

23. On Jackson State, see Wolff, "Ground Breakers."

24. Interview with Lora Hinton, September 1, 1993, LSU Libraries Special Collections, #4700.0327, p. 59.

25. Wolff, "Ground Breakers."

26. *New York Times* columnist William Rhoden judges the integration of sports to have been a disaster for black institutions and black people generally, enriching individuals while estranging them from their history and their communities. For the white sports establishment, the acquisition of black muscle and black showmanship was all gain. See William Rhoden, *Forty Million Dollar Slaves: The Rise, Fall, and Redemption of the Black Athlete* (New York: Crown, 2006), pp. 135–37.

27. Marvin West, "Vols Swat Jackets in 'Good' Workout, 24–7," *KNS*, October 13, 1968; Tom Siler, "McClain Has 'His' Day," *KNS*, October 13, 1968; Marvin West, "Huffing, Puffing Kiner Jars Jackets," *KNS*, October 14, 1968; George Leonard, "Overtime Pays Off (2 TDs) for Lester McClain," *NB*, October 14, 1968.

28. Roland Julian, "Vols' Fired-Up McClain Eager for Vandy," *KNS*, November 27, 1968.

29. AP, "Being First SEC Negro Gridder Posed No Problems for McClain," *NB*, November 28, 1968.

30. Ben Cook, "'Atta Way to Go, Big O," *BN*, November 1, 1970; Joe Halberstein, "Coaches, Players Worked Things Out," *GS*, September 20, 1970; Roy Neel, "Stokes' Kicking Surprise to Many, but Not Taylor," *NB*, September 15, 1971; Jimmy Davy, "Tide, Defense Concern Vandy," *NT*, October 4, 1971; "Mike Williams: LSU Supersoph," *BRMA*, September 28, 1972; Don Foster, "Bulldogs Must Beat Dixie's Best to Brighten 1970 Grid Fortunes," *SDN*, September 2, 1970; Clyde Bolton, "James Owens: Fast Pioneer on the Plain," *BN*, September 2, 1971; "Dowsing Keeps Bulldog Fans Dizzy," *SDN*, September 25, 1970; Delbert Reed, "Reading Read," *TN*, September 2, 1971; Harvey Faust, "Mark 'Gentle Ben' Williams as Future Rebel Standout," *OE*, November 24, 1972.

31. Edgar Allen, "Sidelines," *NB*, October 9, 1971; Ray Crawford, "Jackson: Runs in Blur, Blends with Gators," *MH*, September 20, 1970; Benjy Anderson, "Horace King Places Value on Performance, Not Firsts," *ABH*, October 1, 1972.

32. "Being First SEC Negro Gridder Posed No Problems for McClain"; Crawford, "Jackson: Runs in Blur, Blends with Gators"; Faust, "Mark 'Gentle Ben' Williams as Future Rebel Standout."

33. Banks, "Black Football Players in the White South," p. 136.

34. Reed, "Culture Shock in Dixieland."

35. Pete Cobun, "UA Blacks Today: A New Unification," *CW*, March 1, 1971.

36. Mike Thompson, "Black Studies Added," *CW*, September 21, 1970; Despina Vodantis, "Blacks Anxious to Belong Even in 'Racist' University," *CW*, October 19, 1970; "Letters," *CW*, October 19, 1970, and October 26, 1970; Pete Cobun, "Blacks Occupy President's Office; 5 Arrested in Wednesday Protests," *CW*, April 22, 1971; Pete Cobun, "UA Blacks Continue Protests in Second-Week Demonstrations," *CW*, April 29, 1971.

37. For a summary, see "1968–69: UT's Year of Changes," *UTDB*, September 25, 1969.

38. See Chuck Taylor, "Auburn—a Study in Institutional Racism," *AUP*, January 29, 1970; "Readers Dispute Taylor's Charge," *AUP*, February 5, 1970; Jerry Moore, "Black Students Concerned with 'Racism,'" *AUP*, February 19, 1970; Nancy Henley, "Officials Dispute Taylor Column," *AUP*, February 19, 1970; Anthony Copeland, "Racial Injustices Must Be Corrected," *AUP*, February 19, 1970; Linda Parham, "AU Admission Policy Questioned, Explained," *AUP*, February 26, 1970; Greg Lisby, "Ku Klux Klan Recruits Young Americans," *AUP*, October 5, 1972; "Black Students Want Areas of Improvement," *AUP*, October 5, 1972; Greg Lisby, "Black Criticizes Klan Story, Reiterates Complaints," *AUP*, October 12, 1972; Jimmy Doctrie, "Blacks Disturbed by Story," *AUP*, October 12, 1972.

39. Raymond Hughes, "Desegregating the Holy Day: Football, Blacks, and the Southeastern Conference" (Ph.D. diss., Ohio State University, 1991), pp. 78–82.

40. Schrag, "Tennessee Lonesome End."

41. Bob Raissman, "'If You Want to Be a Pioneer . . . ,'" *UTDB*, May 18, 1971; Bob Raissman, "'Tennessee . . . a Nightmare to Me,'" *UTDB*, May 20, 1971; Bob Raissman,

"'They Say It's in Our Minds,'" *UTDB*, May 22, 1971; Bob Raissman, "'The White Man Has to Change and Accept Us . . . ,'" *UTDB*, May 26, 1971.

42. Rob Christenson, "McClain Blasts Athletic Dept," *UTDB*, May 27, 1971; "McClain Says Bill Battle Discriminated," *UTDB*, May 28, 1971.

43. "McClain Unhappy with His Career as a Vol," *KNS*, May 28, 1971; "Lester Visits Coach," *KNS*, June 1, 1971; Ben Byrd, "Lester's Story—'Trying to Help, Not Hurt, UT,'" *KJ*, May 29, 1971.

44. Tom Siler, "A Long Look . . . Backward," *KNS*, May 23, 1971.

45. Tom Siler, "'Hey, Coach, Put Me In,'" *KNS*, June 2, 1971.

46. Pennington, *Breaking the Ice*, p. 149; Epling, "Seasons of Change," pp. 109, 111, 112–14.

47. Ralph Mueller, "Willie Jackson's Gator Career Reads Determination," *GS*, September 10, 1970.

48. Pennington, *Breaking the Ice*, pp. 149–50.

49. Hannah Gordon, "Football Finds Pioneer with John Mitchell," *Daily Bruin* (online), August 27, 2001.

50. Details beyond what was reported at the time were provided by Phil Thompson, a teammate of Northington and Page and another all-state player at one of Kentucky's most integrated high schools, who was solicited by the governor to help recruit Northington and Page and then became their roommate. Thompson shared his experiences and relevant items from his scrapbook with me in November 2007.

51. John McGill, "Time Out," *LHL*, August 20, 1967. (The *Herald-Leader* was the combined Sunday edition for the city's two papers. McGill was sports editor of the *Lexington Herald*.)

52. Rick Bailey, "Football Injury Fatal to Page," *LH*, September 30, 1967; John McGill, "Mourners Bestow Respect at Greg Page's Funeral," *LH*, October 4, 1967.

53. John McGill, "Time Out," *LH*, October 4, 1967; "Page's Father Speaks to Team," *LH*, August 25, 1967.

54. McGill, "Time Out," *LH*, October 4, 1967.

55. On Rupp and Kentucky, see Jacobs, *Across the Line*, pp. 182–87. At the team banquet after Kentucky lost the NCAA championship to all-black Texas Western in 1966, the sports editor of the *Lexington Herald*, Billy Thompson, serving as master of ceremonies, told the team and their supporters, "At least we're still America's number one white team." See Frank Fitzpatrick, *And the Walls Came Tumbling Down: Kentucky, Texas Western, and the Game That Changed American Sports* (New York: Simon & Schuster, 1999), p. 221 (quoted in Jacobs, *Across the Line*, p. 186). John McGill succeeded Thompson as the *Herald*'s sports editor.

56. Fitzpatrick, *And the Walls Came Tumbling Down*, p. 142. Away from football, Bradshaw was a devout Christian whose mourning for Page was likely genuine and profound. In the story titled "The New Rage to Win" (*SI*, October 8, 1962), Bradshaw's most brutal assistant told the reporters, "We teach the word of Christ," making the poor boy "rich in useful experiences. This is his salvation." Football's tyrants could be complex men.

57. Phil Thompson's recollections come from his response to the blog of the

Louisville Courier-Journal's Eric Crawford (regarding *The Thin Thirty*), posted on October 4, 2007; from personal e-mails to me from Thompson on November 19, 2007, and November 21, 2007; and from an unpublished letter sent by Thompson on December 31, 2005, to Wendell Barnhouse of the *Dallas Morning News* (provided to me by Thompson). No hint of any of this appears in John McGill's account of the game, "Auburn Air Game Bombs Kentucky to Third Straight Defeat, 48–7," *LHL*, October 8, 1967.

58. Thompson e-mail, November 19, 2007.

59. John McGill, "Time Out," *LH*, October 29, 1967; Johnny Carrico, "Squad of 74 down to 59," *LCJT*, undated (from Phil Thompson).

60. Rick Bailey, "Northington Quits UK, Football Team," *LH*, October 23, 1967; Billy Reed, "Nat Northington Quits Kentucky Football Team," *LCJ*, October 23, 1967.

61. Quoted by Betty Boles Ellison in *Kentucky's Domain of Power, Greed, and Corruption* (San Jose, New York, and Lincoln: Writers Club Press, 2001), p. 64. This is a self-published book, written by a graduate student at the University of Kentucky, whose account of the experience describes a battle with university officials over access to the presidential papers. Such circumstances raise questions about reliability, but the direct quotation from an archival letter, on an issue tangential to the author's main story, would seem to be credible.

62. Wolff, "Ground Breakers."

63. William Doyle, *An American Insurrection: The Battle of Oxford, Mississippi, 1962* (New York: Doubleday, 2001), pp. 112–13. Two days before the game, *Lexington Herald* sports editor Ed Ashford speculated on the consequences for Ole Miss and SEC football should Governor Barnett follow through in his threat to close the university rather than admit a Negro student. In Ashford's remarkable column, there was nothing at stake more important than the fate of John Vaught's championship football team and the finances of its SEC rivals who might be deprived of their lucrative scheduled games with the Rebels. Whatever should happen in the confrontation between Barnett and the Kennedy White House, Ashford regretted it would be too late to spare Kentucky's undermanned ("thin thirty") football team a whipping on Saturday. For some southerners, football was indeed more important than segregation. See Ed Ashford, "It Says Here," *LH*, September 27, 1962.

64. Robert Massie, "What Next in Mississippi?," *SEP*, November 10, 1962.

65. Nadine Cohodas, *The Band Played Dixie: Race and the Liberal Conscience at Ole Miss* (New York: Free Press, 1997), pp. 161–69.

66. Ibid.

67. Burnice Morris, "Integration: Progress or Tokenism?," *DM*, September 29, 1972; Dudley Marble, "Redemption: Rebel Defense Assumes Unfamiliar Hero's Role," *DM*, September 25, 1972.

68. Cohodas, *The Band Played Dixie*, p. 185.

69. Ibid.

70. Ibid.

71. David G. Sansing, *The University of Mississippi: A Sesquicentennial History* (Jackson: University Press of Mississippi, 1999), p. 276. William Faulkner presumably

modeled Deacon in *The Sound and the Fury* loosely on Blind Jim. Also see Joshua I. Newman, "Army of Whiteness? Colonel Reb and the Sporting South's Cultural and Corporate Symbolic," *Journal of Sport and Social Issues* 31 (November 2007): 315–39 (Newman quotes Sansing on page 322).

72. William F. Reed, "Culture Shock in Dixieland," *SI*, August 12, 1991; William Nack, "Look Away, Dixie Land," *SI*, November 3, 1997.

73. Information from the University of Mississippi website announcing the Robert "Ben" Williams Minority Scholarship.

74. Norman Arey, ". . . Runner, Not Receiver, Says Georgia's Horace King," *AJ*, November 29, 1972.

75. Ed Shearer (AP), "McAshan Ignores Boos at Georgia Tech," *GS*, November 12, 1970.

76. Jim Hunter, "McAshan May Face Disciplinary Action," *AJ*, September 28, 1971; Jim Hunter, "McAshan Rejoins Team," *AJ*, September 29, 1971; Furman Bisher, "Return of a Conqueror," *AJ*, September 29, 1972.

77. "The Independents," *SI*, September 11, 1972.

78. Furman Bisher, "Eddie McAshan, in Passing," *AJ*, December 14, 1972.

79. AP, "Georgia Tech Board Upholds Ban of McAshan from Liberty Bowl," *NOTP*, December 16, 1972; John Head, "McAshan Absent as Groups Air Bowl Protest Scheme," *AJC*, December 17, 1972; Jim Hunter, "Tech Blacks Say They Will Play," *AJC*, December 17, 1972; Jim Hunter, "Georgia Tech's Blacks Torn between Two Strong Loyalties," *AJ*, December 19, 1972.

80. Hughes, "Desegregating the Holy Day," pp. 126–31.

81. Ibid., 134–38.

CHAPTER 3

1. Jack Olsen, "The Black Athlete—A Shameful Story," *SI*, July 1–29, 1968.

2. See Douglas Hartmann, *Race, Culture, and the Revolt of the Black Athlete* (Chicago: University of Chicago Press, 2003); Amy Bass, *Not the Triumph but the Struggle: The 1968 Olympics and the Making of the Black Athlete* (Minneapolis: University of Minnesota Press, 2002); and Kenny Moore, "A Courageous Stand," *SI*, August 5, 1991.

3. "Andros Rolls with Punch, Predicts No More Problems," *PO*, March 8, 1969; Jerry Uhrhammer, "Beard Affair," *ERG*, March 13, 1969. All of the contemporary reporting, and the accounts based on it, said that the chance encounter was between Milton and Andros, not between Milton and Boghosian. A long retrospective on an ailing Andros in 2003 set the record straight and included Milton's generous account. See Kerry Eggers, "Mustache Incident Led to Decline in Beaver Football," *PT*, August 29, 2003.

4. David K. Wiggins reconstructs the incident at Oregon State, as well as incidents at Cal (involving the basketball team) and Syracuse (football), in *Glory Bound: Black Athletes in a White America* (Syracuse: Syracuse University Press, 1997), pp. 123–51 (reprinting Wiggins's 1988 essay in the *Journal of Sport History*). See also John Sayle Watterson, *College Football: History, Spectacle, Controversy* (Baltimore: Johns Hopkins University Press, 2000), pp. 320–26.

5. Jack Rickard, "Black Students Plan Boycott at OSU," *CGT*, February 25, 1969.

6. "Boycott Draws Comments," *DB*, February 26, 1969.

7. "An Open Endorsement," *CGT*, February 28, 1969; "Barratt Outlines Athletic Department Stand," *CGT*, March 7, 1969.

8. Tom Brown, "OSU Coaches Told to Modify Rules to Permit Mustaches," *CGT*, May 8, 1969.

9. Brown, "OSU Coaches Told to Modify Rules"; Herbert Wanyanga, "Not All Gone" (letter to *DB*, March 12, 1969).

10. From 1965 through 1968, Andros's teams won twenty-six games, lost thirteen, and tied one, placing second in the Pac-8 conference in all but the first year and gaining renown as "Giant Killers" in 1967 by upsetting no. 2 Purdue, new no. 2 UCLA, and no. 1 USC within a four-week span. From 1969 through 1975, their record would be 25-51: 6-4 in 1969 and 6-5 in 1970, then 5-6 in 1971 to begin a long skid into oblivion. OSU would not have another winning season until 1999.

11. Eggers, "Mustache Incident."

12. Jack Rickard, "Majority of Athletes Support Coaches; Black Hoopers Practice," *CGT*, February 26, 1969; "Didion Asks Student Backing for Policies," *CGT*, February 27, 1969.

13. Neil Cawood, "OSU's Enyart, Didion Split on Black Boycott," *ERG*, February 27, 1969.

14. "Two Cultures," *DB*, February 28, 1969; and "Voices of Sanity" (with four co-signers), *DB*, March 4, 1969.

15. "Perkins Dismissed from Squad for Protest Move," *CGT*, March 1, 1969; "Perkins Back on Team," *CGT*, March 3, 1969.

16. Wiggins, *Glory Bound*, p. 143.

17. "Playing—And Paying," *OJ*, March 8, 1969.

18. Jack Rickard, "Rick's Ramblings," *CGT*, February 26, 1969; "Confrontation on Campus," *CGT*, February 27, 1969.

19. "Barratt Outlines Athletic Department Stand," *CGT*, March 7, 1969; "Racial Prejudice in Corvallis," *CGT*, March 19, 1969.

20. "Hooray for Andros," *CGT*, February 28, 1969.

21. "Individual Rights" and "Express Culture," *CGT*, March 4, 1969. Pro-Andros letters appeared on March 1 and March 3 (no edition on March 2, a Sunday).

22. "'Harmony' at OSU," *PO*, March 7, 1969; L. H. Gregory, "Greg's Gossip," *PO*, March 6, 1969.

23. See editorials on February 27 and March 8; see also George Pasero's column in sports, "Pasero Says," on February 27 and March 11.

24. "'Meditation' at Notre Dame," *ERG*, March 4, 1969; Don Robinson, "Academic Freedom Defeats OSU Blacks, Frustrates Jensen," *ERG*, March 6, 1969.

25. Mike Stahlberg, "Mac Court Walkout Backs OSU Blacks," *ERG*, March 9, 1969; Jack Rickard, "Rick's Ramblings," *CGT*, March 10, 1969.

26. Uhrhammer, "Beard Affair."

27. Jim Martz, "2 Starters out of Iowa Drills," *DMR*, April 3, 1969; Ron Maly, "Iowa Drops 16 Negro Gridders," *DMR*, April 19, 1969; Ron Maly, "Boycotting Blacks at

Iowa Charge 'Intolerable Situation,'" *DMR*, April 21, 1969; "Our Problem Is Nagel—He Lied: Allison," *DMR*, April 25, 1969.

28. "Return of Blacks up to Squad: Nagel," *DMR*, May 9, 1969; Al Grady, "Al Grady's Column," *ICPC*, April 21, 1969; "UI Football Squad Will Vote Tonight on Black Athletes," *ICPC*, August 27, 1969; "7 Blacks Rejoin Squad for UI Grid Drills," *ICPC*, August 28, 1969; Al Grady, "Al Grady's Column," *ICPC*, August 27, 1969.

29. Al Grady, "Al Grady's Column," *ICPC*, August 26, 1969.

30. John Underwood, "The Desperate Coach," *SI*, August 25, 1969; and John Underwood, "Concessions—and Lies," *SI*, September 8, 1969. The middle installment was "Shave Off That Thing!," September 1, 1969.

31. "Fourteen Black Athletes Remain Suspended," *BI*, October 23, 1969.

32. Underwood, "Concessions—and Lies." Owens is profiled in "Shave Off That Thing!" For the earlier incident at the University of Washington, see "A Negro Boycott of UW Sports?," *SPI*, March 2, 1968; "Statement from Black Athletes," *SPI*, March 3, 1968; Phil Taylor, "UW Negroes List Demands as Athletes," *SPI*, March 12, 1968; and John Owen, "UW, Negroes in 'Tentative Truce,'" *SPI*, April 17, 1968.

33. Pete Fetsco, "Negro Athletes out for Failure to Abide by Athletic Department Rules," *LDB*, October 19, 1969; "Eaton Isn't Quitting," *LDB*, October 21, 1969. For Eaton's racial insults, see *The Black 14*, video documentary produced by Mike McElreath and Adeniyi Coker Jr., University of Wyoming, Laramie, Wyoming (1997).

34. "Fourteen Black Athletes Remain Suspended"; Pete Fetsco, "Negro Athletes out for Failure to Abide by Athletic Department Rules," *LDB*, October 19, 1969; "Faculty Senate Seeks Query," *LDB*, October 21, 1969. The *Daily Boomerang* reported the student senate vote to be 17-1, but the campus paper printed the senate resolution along with the 15-3 vote in its October 31 edition (the *Branding Iron* was a weekly paper) and in general seems the more reliable source for the initial events.

35. "Ag Faculty, Staff Back Eaton in Player Episode," *LDB*, October 22, 1969; "C & I Students Question Hasty Action," *LDB*, October 22, 1969; "Eaton Has Big Support from University Students," *LDB*, October 25, 1969. The faculty senate's 37-1 vote was termed a "small plurality" in a pro-Eaton column by sports editor Jim Graham in the *Denver Post* ("Eaton Took Right Stand," reprinted in the *Daily Boomerang* on October 23, 1969). Coincidentally, the *Branding Iron* for October 23 reprinted an editorial from the *Denver Post* expressing "outrage" over Eaton's depriving fourteen athletes of their constitutional rights. The different views on the sports pages and the editorial page of the *Denver Post* were similar to, though more extreme than, the responses in Oregon papers to the incident at Oregon State.

36. The Supreme Court ruling was also noted by the attorney who represented the black players; see Richard L. McCall, "Waterman Says State Cannot Be Grid Power and Be Isolationist," *LDB*, October 29, 1969.

37. Carolyn Pratt, "Football Rule Modified Some," *LDB*, October 24, 1969.

38. "Faculty Senate Seeks Query"; "They Will Be Heard" (editorial), *LDB*, October 21, 1969; "Long Interest in School" and "Collective Courage" (letters), *LDB*, October 22, 1969; "WHSAA Commends Lloyd Eaton," *LDB*, October 23, 1969; "Eaton Named Man of Year," *LDB*, December 31, 1969.

39. "Editorial Commentary," *BI*, October 23, 1969.

40. Pembroke Woodhink, "Phil White Resigns as BI Editor," *BI*, October 23, 1969; "We Are Pleading," *BI*, October 31, 1969. In this final issue, White also printed on the editorial page, without comment, a passage from the *Book of Mormon* in which the Lord punishes a people for their iniquities by turning their white skin ("they were white, and exceeding fair and delightsome") black and cursing their seed and the seed of whoever shall mix with their seed. An outraged letter from more than two dozen LDS students in the November 7 edition of the *Branding Iron* denounced White's abridgement of the passage and explained that the passage about the cursed people, the Lamanites of the sixth century B.C., "has absolutely nothing to do with the Black man or Negro," nor with "the Mormon position regarding the Black man and the Priesthood, nor is it any basis for accusing Mormons of racism."

41. "They Will Be Heard"; and "Five Black Players Charge White Athletes Are Favored," *LDB*, October 22, 1969.

42. "Waterman Denies Any Part in 'Conspiracy,'" *LDB*, October 31, 1969.

43. "Black Hearings Begin; Kerr Will Rule within One Week," *LDB*, November 11, 1969; "Kerr Refuses Reinstatement," *LDB*, November 18, 1969; "Motion Filed to Dismiss Suit against UW," *LDB*, November 21, 1969; James E. Barrett, "The Black 14: Williams v. Eaton, a Personal Recollection," *Wyoming History Journal* 68 (Summer 1996): 2–7. Barrett was the attorney general who represented Eaton.

44. Ben Pacheco, "Eaton Steps Up, Shurmur Is New Coach," *BI*, December 11, 1970. Both President Carlson and Eaton insisted that the decision had been made in December 1968 and had nothing to do with the Black 14 incident or the dismal season just completed.

45. Pat Putnam, "No Defeats, Loads of Trouble," *SI*, November 3, 1969. The presence of the network news teams was reported in the *Branding Iron* ("Fourteen Black Athletes Remain Suspended").

46. Clifford A. Bullock, "Fired by Conscience: The Black 14 Incident at the University of Wyoming and Black Protest in the Western Athletic Conference" (online at <http://uwacadweb.uwyo.edu/RobertsHistory/fired_by_conscience.htm>); "Black 14 Member Says Racism Still out There," *Call* (Kansas City), December 20, 2002; *Black Fourteen* video.

47. "14 Negroes Boycott I.U. Practice," *IS*, November 5, 1969; Max Stultz, "10 Negroes off I.U. Team Forever," *IS*, November 6, 1969; *BCT*, November 9, 1969;

48. Stan Sutton, "Pont Considers, Nixes Resigning, Will Stand on Week's Decisions," *BCT*, November 9, 1969; Larry Moran, "Blacks Seek Investigation; Pont Considered Resigning," *BDHT*, November 9, 1969; Bob Hammel, "DQs Stand, Cheer Pont," *BDHT*, November 12, 1969; Bob Collins, "5 I.U. Players Can Return in Spring," *IS*, November 7, 1969; Max Stultz, "Surprise Party Hits Both Sides," *IS*, November 7, 1969; Art Berke, "A Vote for Pont," *IDS*, November 11, 1969; "Casual Racism," *IDS*, November 12, 1969. Seven letters to the *Herald-Telephone* appeared on November 8, 10, 11, 12, 13, 14, 17. Five letters to the *Indiana Daily Student* appeared on November 11 (two), November 14, November 15, and November 20, in addition to a longer "As I See It" column by a student on November 13.

49. Phil Taylor, "Owens Suspends 4 Huskies for Season," *SPI*, October 31, 1969; John Owen, "Owens Suspends 4 Husky Gridders," *SPI*, October 31, 1969; Phil Taylor, "Blacks Refuse to Make Trip," *SPI*, November 1, 1969; Frank Herbert, "We're Not Going, Man, We'd Have to Come Back," *SPI*, November 1, 1969; John Owen, "Dissension Rips UW Squad Following Suspensions," *SPI*, November 1, 1969; Dan Raley, "Apple Cup '69: Right Is Right," *SPI*, November 17, 1999.

50. Georg N. Meyers, "The Sporting Thing," *ST*, November 2, 1969; John Owen, "A 'Second Chance,' but for Whom?," *SPI*, November 7, 1969.

51. Owen, "A 'Second Chance.'"

52. Phil Taylor, "New Hearing for 4 Huskies," *SPI*, November 7, 1969; John Owen, "The Real Cause of 'The Crisis,'" *SPI*, November 2, 1969; "Owens Wanted Boycott—Gayton," *SPI*, November 4, 1969. Blanks's defiance of Owens was reported by Dan Raley in "Apple Cup '69."

53. "Owens Girl Stopped by 4; Hit in Face," *SPI*, November 1, 1969; Raley, "Apple Cup '69."

54. Larry Incollingo, "Boycott Explained to IU Blacks," *BDHT*, November 7, 1969.

55. Ibid.; "When Consciences Conflict," *BDHT*, November 7, 1969.

56. Owen, "The Real Cause of 'The Crisis'"; John Owen, "Week in the Life of a Schoolboy," *SPI*, November 9, 1969; Phil Taylor, "Gayton Resigns UW Post," *SPI*, November 11, 1969.

57. Georg N. Meyers, "The Sporting Thing," *ST*, November 10, 1969; "3 UW Gridders Honored," *SPI*, November 21, 1969.

58. Wiggins, *Glory Bound*, pp. 130–34; Neil Amdur, *Fifth Down: Democracy and the Football Revolution* (New York: Coward, McCann & Geoghegan, 1971), pp. 108–22; and see the *Syracuse Herald-Journal* for April 19 and April 30, 1970, and beginning August 23, 1970. There was another sequel in late October 1970, at Idaho State in Pocatello, where the coach suspended fourteen black players for skipping a mid-week practice, but Idaho State did not register importantly in the world of college football. (See the *Idaho State Journal*, beginning October 22, 1970.)

59. Underwood, "Shave Off That Thing!," p. 23.

60. "Mark Wheeler Dropped from Husky Squad," *ST*, October 23, 1970; Bob Schwarzmann, "Wheeler Won't Say Why," *ST*, October 27, 1970; "Blacks Quit Husky Football," *ST*, November 23, 1970; Georg N. Meyers, "The Profound Commitment of Cal Jones," *ST*, November 24, 1970; John Owen, "And Then There Were None," *SPI*, November 24, 1970. See also the *Post-Intelligencer*'s coverage for November 24–26.

61. Greg Bishop, "At Long Last, Peace," *ST*, November 6, 2006.

62. Underwood, "The Desperate Coach," p. 70.

63. Meyers, "The Sporting Thing," *ST*, November 2, 1969.

64. UPI, "Andros Urges Owens to Resist Negro Demands," *SPI*, March 15, 1968; Underwood, "Shave Off That Thing!," p. 23.

65. Eggers, "Mustache Incident." See also the extensive front-page coverage in both the *Portland Oregonian* and the *Corvallis Gazette-Times* for October 23, 2003, following Andros's death after a long illness.

66. "Militant Groups Doing Great Disservice to Black College Athletes," *NCAA News*, December 1969.

67. "Black Athletes' Statement: Main Point Is Graduation," *ICPC*, April 21, 1969. Ray Nagel blamed Edwards's visit to the Iowa campus for the rebellion that followed. See "Hawkeyes, Gophers Have Had Woes Too," *BCT*, November 5, 1969.

68. See Sam Lacy, "Pro and Cons on Olympic Boycott," *BAA*, December 9, 1967; Ric Roberts, "Racism in Sports," *NPC*, August 3, 1968; Roberts, "JHJ Is 'Burning,'" *NPC*, August 10, 1968; Bill Nunn Jr., "Change of Pace," *NPC*, October 26, 1968; "Olympic Committee Quits 'Making Ado' about Balled Fists," *NPC*, November 1, 1968.

69. "Negro Athletes Threaten Boycott at Major Colleges," *NYT*, May 19, 1968; Anthony Ripley, "Irate Black Students Stir Campus Tension," *NYT*, November 16, 1969; Michael Rosenberg, *War as They Knew It: Woody Hayes, Bo Schembechler, and America in a Time of Unrest* (New York and Boston: Grand Central, 2008), pp. 59, 145.

70. Raley, "Apple Cup '69"; Arnie Burdick, "Orange Togetherness," *SHJ*, April 30, 1970.

71. William Kates (AP), "Thirty-six Years Later, School Honors Players' Anti-Racism Stand," *Newsday* (online), October 21, 2006; Matt Eagan, "Belated Award in Fight for Fair Play," *Hartford Courant* (online), October 21, 2006. The eight of nine players who returned to Syracuse for the awards had impressive post-college credentials: a regional manager of an insurance company, an account executive, a vice president of asset management, a vice president of a development firm, a manager for a state department of juvenile justice, an adjunct professor and adult-education teacher, an executive director of a housing commission, and a special-education teacher. See the transcript of the "Syracuse Eight" press conference on the Syracuse athletics website (<http://www.suathletics.com/Sports/Football/2006/syracuse8presser.asp>).

INTERLUDE

1. Walter Byers explained this in his controversial memoir, in which the notoriously hard-nosed and high-handed executive director repudiated much of what he had fought for over his long career. See *Unsportsmanlike Conduct: Exploiting College Athletes* (Ann Arbor: University of Michigan Press, 1995), p. 69. Allen Sack and Ellen Staurowsky in *College Athletes for Hire: The Evolution and Legacy of the NCAA's Amateur Myth* (Westport, Conn.: Praeger, 1998) and Murray Sperber in *Onward to Victory: The Crises That Shaped College Sports* (New York: Henry Holt, 1998) emphasize the conscious hypocrisy of Byers's term.

2. "5,000 Turn Out for Rallies on Campus," *CGT*, February 27, 1969; "Didion Asks Student Backing for Policies," *CGT*, February 27, 1969.

3. Al Lightner, "Sportslightner," *OS*, March 2, 1969; "Playing—And Paying," *OJ*, March 8, 1969.

4. John Underwood, "Shave Off That Thing!," *SI*, September 1, 1969.

5. John Underwood, "Concessions—and Lies," *SI*, September 8, 1969.

6. John Owen, "Athletics and the Black, Clenched Fist," *SPI*, November 17, 1969.

7. Quoted in Sack and Staurowsky, *College Athletes for Hire*, p. 44.

8. Ibid., pp. 80–81.

9. *1964–1965 Yearbook of the National Collegiate Athletic Association Containing the Association's Year-End Reports and the Proceedings of the Fifty-ninth Annual Convention at Chicago Illinois*, January 11–13, 1965, pp. 298–307.

10. Ibid.

11. Morton Sharnik and Robert Creamer, "The New Rage to Win," *SI*, October 8, 1962.

12. Ibid.; Earl Ruby, "What'll NCAA Say about Boys U. K. 'Bumped,'" *LCJ*, September 4, 1962; Ed Ashford, "It Says Here," *LH*, September 7, 1962. In another column (September 8), Ashford informed his readers, "Most schools figure to lose 50 per cent or more of their freshman crop each year." In his account of Kentucky's "Thin Thirty," Shannon Ragland describes at length how players who quit were tricked into signing waivers relinquishing their scholarships, not knowing that they had a right to keep them. See Shannon Ragland, *The Thin Thirty: The Untold Story of Brutality, Scandal, and Redemption for Charlie Bradshaw's 1962 Kentucky Football Team* (Louisville, Ky.: Set Shot Press, 2007), pp. 166–72.

13. National Collegiate Athletic Association, *Proceedings of the 61st Annual Convention*, Houston, Texas, January 9–11, 1967, pp. 121–28.

14. National Collegiate Athletic Association, *Proceedings of the 63rd Annual Convention*, Los Angeles, California, January 6–8, 1969, pp. 99–105.

15. Gordon S. White Jr., "College Athletes Who Protest to Face Loss of Financial Aid," *NYT*, January 9, 1969; Underwood, "Concessions—and Lies," p. 31.

16. National Collegiate Athletic Association, *Proceedings of the 67th Annual Convention*, Chicago, Illinois, January 11–13, 1973, p. 123; Gordon S. White, "N.C.A.A. Scraps 1.6 for a Scholastic Ruling," *NYT*, January 14, 1973; "NCAA Ends 1.6 Rule, Limits Scholarships," *PO*, January 14, 1973; "Convention Delegates Adopt Numbers, Kill 1.6 Rules" and "Financial Aid Limits, Awards Explained," *NCAA News*, February 1, 1973.

17. John Sayle Watterson, *College Football: History, Spectacle, Controversy* (Baltimore: Johns Hopkins University Press, 2000), p. 303. Watterson mentions a limit of forty for the SEC, not the fifty-five openly acknowledged in 1962.

18. White, "N.C.A.A. Scraps 1.6"; Gary Shaw, *Meat on the Hoof: The Hidden World of Texas Football* (New York: St. Martin's Press, 1972); Terry Frei, *Horns, Hogs, and Nixon Coming: Texas vs. Arkansas in Dixie's Last Stand* (New York: Simon & Schuster, 2002), p. 20.

19. Watterson, *College Football*, pp. 303–5.

20. Michael Rosenberg, *War as They Knew It: Woody Hayes, Bo Schembechler, and America in a Time of Unrest* (New York and Boston: Grand Central, 2008), p. 116.

21. Byers, *Unsportsmanlike Conduct*, p. 155.

22. Reported in Neil Amdur, "Problems Are Mounting in N.C.A.A.," *NYT*, March 21, 1982.

CHAPTER 4

1. I follow Allen Sack (*College Athletes for Hire: The Evolution and Legacy of the NCAA's Amateur Myth* [Westport, Conn.: Praeger, 1998], written with Ellen J. Staurowsky; and *Counterfeit Amateurs: An Athlete's Journey through the Sixties to the Age of Academic Capitalism* [University Park: Penn State University Press, 2008]) in tracing the current state of college athletics to the NCAA conventions of 1972 and 1973. The literature critical of priorities in college athletics is enormous. Among the major scholarly studies in addition to these are John Thelin's *Games Colleges Play: Scandal and Reform in Intercollegiate Athletics* (Baltimore: Johns Hopkins University Press, 1994); Murray Sperber's *College Sports, Inc.: The Athletic Department vs. the University* (New York: Henry Holt, 1990), *Onward to Victory: The Crises That Shaped College Sports* (New York: Henry Holt, 1998), and *Beer and Circus: How Big-Time College Sports Is Crippling Undergraduate Education* (New York: Henry Holt, 2000); and Andrew Zimablist's *Unpaid Professionals: Commercialism and Conflict in Big-Time College Sports* (Princeton: Princeton University Press, 1999). Sportswriters' polemics, such as John Underwood's *The Death of an American Game: The Crisis in Football* (Boston: Little, Brown, 1979) and Rick Telander's *The Hundred Yard Lie: The Corruption of College Football and What We Can Do to Stop It* (New York: Simon & Schuster, 1989), have also contributed to this literature.

2. Joseph Durso, "Athletic Recruiting: A Campus Crisis," *NYT*, March 10, 1974. Subsequent installments appeared on March 11 (front page), 12, 13, and 14.

3. Philip Taubman, "Faking of College Credits for Athletes Is under Inquiry," *NYT*, January 9, 1980; Gordon S. White, "Preferred Admissions Reported at U.S.C.," *NYT*, October 15, 1980; Dudley Clendinen, "State Survey of Georgia U. Cites Preferential Grading for Athletes," *NYT*, April 4, 1986. And see John Sayle Watterson, *College Football: History, Spectacle, Controversy* (Baltimore: John Hopkins University Press, 2000), pp. 326–31.

4. John Underwood, "The Writing Is on the Wall," *SI*, May 19, 1980.

5. Sack's study was reported in Neil Amdur, "Problems Are Mounting in N.C.A.A.," *NYT*, March 21, 1982.

6. Sack calls Prop 48 "a masterpiece of public relations" by the NCAA to "salvage its image as a defender of academic integrity." It is possible to grant NCAA members a less cynical motive, while still recognizing the wrongheadedness of a system built on undermining academic standards, then belatedly (and inadequately) trying to clean up the mess. See Sack, *Counterfeit Amateurs*, p. 119.

7. Gordon S. White Jr., "Black Colleges Threaten to Leave N.C.A.A. over Academic Policy," *NYT*, January 13, 1983.

8. Malcolm Moran, "Former U.S.C. President Defends Policies," *NYT*, October 17, 1980; Malcolm Moran, "At U.S.C. Issue Is Responsibility," *NYT*, October 26, 1980; White, "Black Colleges Threaten to Leave."

9. Moran, "At U.S.C., Issue Is Responsibility."

10. Ibid.

11. "Studies of Intercollegiate Athletics, Report No. 3: The Experience of Black Intercollegiate Athletes at Division I Institutions," Center for the Study of Athletics, American Institutes for Research, Palo Alto, Calif., March 1989, pp. 13–23.

12. Jeffrey A. Owings and Marilyn M. McMillen, *Who Can Play? An Examination of NCAA's Proposition 16* (Washington, D.C.: National Center for Education Statistics, 1995).

13. Quoted in a press release from the Trial Lawyers for Public Justice, the group that represented the two student-athletes suing the NCAA, October 9, 1998.

14. Data for the incoming freshmen classes from 1984 through 2001 are available on the NCAA website.

15. "Third Circuit Holds NCAA Not Subject to Title VI," *You Make the Call* (National Sports Law Institute, Marquette University Law School) 2, no. 3 (Winter 2000), online.

16. On the College Football Association, see Watterson, *College Football*, pp. 332–52. On the CFA and television, see Ronald A. Smith, *Play-by-Play: Radio, Television, and Big-Time College Sport* (Baltimore: Johns Hopkins University Press, 2001), pp. 152–69.

17. The WAC schools affected were BYU, Colorado State, Wyoming, Utah, Hawaii, New Mexico, UTEP, San Diego State, and Air Force.

18. Gordon S. White Jr., "TV Issue Dividing Football Colleges," *NYT*, August 23, 1981.

19. Watterson, *College Football*, pp. 334–36.

20. Gordon S. White Jr., "Colleges May Find TV's Golden Egg Is Tarnished," *NYT*, August 26, 1984.

21. Keith Dunnavant, *The Fifty-Year Seduction: How Television Manipulated College Football, from the Birth of the Modern NCAA to the Creation of the BCS* (New York: Thomas Dunne Books, 2004), p. 173. Citing the testimony before a Senate committee, Ronald Smith reports (*Play-by-Play*, p. 170) the total figure for the CFA as $35 million (down just $4 million but for twice as many games). This figure conflicts with other published figures on the CFA overall and its conferences individually, and Smith nonetheless concludes that CFA schools lost television revenue for a decade after the ruling (p. 168).

22. Dunnavant, *Fifty-Year Seduction*, p. 174.

23. White, "Colleges May Find TV's Golden Egg Is Tarnished."

24. Walter Byers, *Unsportsmanlike Conduct: Exploiting College Athletes* (Ann Arbor: University of Michigan Press, 1995), p. 293.

25. Rudy Martzke, "CBS, CFA Team up for $60 M," *USA Today*, September 19, 1986.

26. Dunnavant, *Fifty-Year Seduction*, p. 180.

27. Murray Sperber tells this story in *Shake Down the Thunder: The Creation of Notre Dame Football* (New York: Henry Holt, 1993) and *Onward to Victory*.

28. Michael Goodwin, "When the Cash Register Is the Scoreboard," *NYT*, June 8, 1986; Dunnavant, *Fifty-Year Seduction*, p. 180.

29. Smith, *Play-by-Play*, p. 169.

30. Sack, *Counterfeit Amateurs*, pp. 130–33.

31. Dunnavant, *Fifty-Year Seduction*, pp. 218–19, 241.

32. William C. Rhodes, "Big College Football Leagues Are Trying to Get Bigger Still," *NYT*, June 23, 1990.

33. Sperber, *College Sports, Inc.*, p. xi.

34. Dunnavant, *Fifty-Year Seduction*, pp. 239–45. See also Richard Sandomir, "CBS Gets Football, College Variety," *NYT*, February 12, 1994; "A.C.C. Signs Network Deal," *NYT*, February 15, 1994; "CBS Gets Deal with Big East," *NYT*, February 16, 1994.

35. "Major Conferences before and after Realignment," *SBJ*, December 8–14, 2008.

36. Dunnavant, *Fifty-Year Seduction*, p. 256.

37. The Big West folded in 2000, in effect to be replaced by the Sun Belt in 2001.

38. Steve Wieberg, "Utah on Verge of Big Play Day, Huge Payday," *USA Today*, December 2, 2004.

39. Figures from the bowls' websites and Rodney D. Fort, *Sports Economics* (Upper Saddle River, N.J.: Prentice Hall, 2003), p. 470.

40. The Peach Bowl's payout increased from $900,000 in 1991 to $1.6 million in 1998, and the Gator Bowl's from $1 million to $1.65 million; the Sun Bowl's payout stayed virtually unchanged.

41. Figures from the bowls' websites.

42. "Bowl Championship Series: Five-Year Summary of Revenue Distribution, 2003–2007," and "2007–08 Postseason Football Analysis of Excess Bowl Revenue and Expense by Conference" (both online at www.ncaa.org).

43. "Stewart Mandel's Three-Point Stance," *SI*, November 24, 2008.

44. "2007–08 Postseason Football Analysis of Excess Bowl Revenue and Expense by Conference."

45. Michael Smith and John Ourand, "How ESPN Bid Bowled Over BCS," *SBJ*, November 24–30, 2008; Richard Sandomir, "Assets and Subscriber Revenue Give ESPN an Edge in Rights Bidding," *NYT*, November 25, 2008.

46. Mitchell H. Raiborn, "An Analysis of Revenues, Expenses and Management Accounting Practices of Intercollegiate Athletic Programs," National Collegiate Athletic Association, May 11, 1970; Mitchell H. Raiborn, "Revenues and Expenses of Intercollegiate Athletic Programs: Analysis of Financial Trends and Relationships 1978–1981," National Collegiate Athletic Association, September 1982; Daniel L. Fulks, "2002–03 NCAA Revenues and Expenses of Divisions I and II Intercollegiate Athletics Programs Report," National Collegiate Athletic Association, February 2005. I used Raiborn's and Fulks's figures to calculate average annual increases, taking compounding into account. The other reports were compiled by Raiborn in 1978, 1986, and 1989 and by Fulks in 1994, 1996, and 1998.

47. Daniel L. Fulks, "2004–06 NCAA Revenues and Expenses of Division I Intercollegiate Athletics Programs Report," National Collegiate Athletic Association, March 2008; Gary Brown, "Refined Reporting Shines Brighter Light on Spending," *NCAA News* (online), April 17, 2008. The new accounting procedures did not eliminate all controversy. Following the release of the report, an official at Maryland called attention to its failure to account adequately for parking and concessions, and officials at Texas pointed out that, while student fees were counted as "allocated" resources, the athletics department received no credit for the free seats

provided for students. Institutions' different methods of spending and reporting money continued to make a completely accurate report impossible. See Eric Kelderman, "Athletic Directors Cry Foul over NCAA's Data," *CHE*, May 30, 2008.

48. Richard G. Sheehan, *Keeping Score: The Economics of Big-Time Sports* (South Bend, Ind.: Diamond Communications, 1996), pp. 277, 306; Zimbalist, *Unpaid Professionals*, p. 264; Fort, *Sport Economics*, p. 263. In his 1996 book, Sheehan calculated in one chapter that forty-one Division I-A football schools made money; in another chapter, he estimated that the number was "about thirty." Zimbalist, in 1999, suggested that "perhaps a dozen top schools" regularly generate surpluses, while another two or three dozen occasionally do. And Fort most recently calculated that 35 percent of Division I-A (roughly forty schools) made a profit in 2001.

49. In his 2002–3 report on revenues and expenses, Fulks calculated that, without direct institutional support, the average athletics profit of $2.2 million for Division I-A in 2002–3 ($29.4 million in revenue, $27.2 million in expenses) was actually an average loss of $600,000. A separate report by Jonathan M. and Peter R. Orszag factored in the costs of owning athletic facilities, which never appear in the reported data, concluding that, on top of the average of $27.2 million in expenses, schools were not accounting for $24 million in annual capital costs (of which $10.6 million was for football, obliterating the reported average profit of $5.9 million). The authors looked at a sample of only eight schools, however. See "The Physical Capital Stock Used in Collegiate Athletics," commissioned by the National Collegiate Athletic Association, April 2005.

50. See Fulks, "2004–06 NCAA Revenues and Expenses." From 2004 to 2006, median total generated revenue for the entire subdivision increased 16 percent, from $28.2 million to $35.4 million, while expenses increased 23 percent, from $28.9 million to $35.8 million. In making the point that generating new revenues does not reduce deficits, Fulks confirmed the earlier report by Robert E. Litan, Jonathan M. Orszag, and Peter R. Orszag, "The Empirical Effects of Intercollegiate Athletics: An Interim Report," National Collegiate Athletic Association, August 2003. Myles Brand made the statement about just six profitable programs in all of the past five years in his 2009 "State of the Association" address, available on the NCAA website.

51. Chloe White, "UT Will Explore Generating More Money for Education from Athletics," *KNS*, January 17, 2008; Fulks, "2004–06 NCAA Revenues and Expenses," p. 7.

52. John Ourand and Michael Smith, "Networks Make Their Case to SEC," *SBJ*, June 2–8, 2008; John Ourand and Michael Smith, "CBS to Pay SEC Average of $55 Million Annually," *SBJ*, August 18–24, 2008; Michael Smith and John Ourand, "ESPN Pays $2.25B for SEC Rights," *SBJ*, August 25–31, 2008; John Ourand, "Focused on Making the Numbers Work," *SBJ*, January 5–11, 2009.

53. "2004–06 NCAA Revenues and Expenses." In Fulks's 2002–3 study, 27 percent came from ticket sales, 18 percent from alumni and boosters, 9 percent from the NCAA and conferences, 7 percent from radio/television, and 2 percent from bowl games as a separate line. The importance of bowl games and television was increas-

ing—the total of 18 percent from bowls, TV, and distributions from conferences and the NCAA in 2002–3 was up from 14 percent in Fulks's 1996–97 study—but gate receipts were still the lifeblood of college football.

54. James J. Duderstadt, *Intercollegiate Athletics and the American University: A University President's Perspective* (Ann Arbor: University of Michigan Press, 2000), pp. 130, 136.

55. Gilbert M. Gaul and Frank Fitzpatrick, "Rise of the Athletic Empires," *PI*, September 10, 2000.

56. For stadium capacities and average attendance, see Table 3 in chapter 6. Some non-BCS schools play in enormous municipal stadiums but don't come close to filling them. Tulane, for example, used to play in its own large stadium (the Sugar Bowl) but now plays in the 65,000-seat New Orleans Superdome, averaging 26,112 in 2007. Alabama-Birmingham plays at 83,000-seat Legion Field (71,000 as reported by the NCAA) and averaged 16,706. Rice has its own 70,000-seat stadium but averaged 13,353 in 2007.

57. "Fund-Raising for Athletics in 6 Major Conferences," *CHE*, January 23 2009.

58. Austin Murphy, "Tuesday Night Lights," *SI*, November 22, 2004.

59. "College Football Regular Season Ratings," *SBJ*, September 8–14, 2008; "NFL Ratings Trends," *SBJ*, September 1–7, 2008.

60. "Nielsen Weekly Sports Ranking," *SBJ*, November 6–12, 2006. The 2006 season was the last for which the *SBJ* published weekly ratings as part of its "Media Tracker."

61. "25 Million Viewed Each Grid Telecast in 1969," *NCAA News*, February 1970. Each set of regional games was assigned an overall Nielsen rating.

62. All of these ratings are from the weekly "Nielsen Weekly Sports Ranking" published in the *SportsBusiness Journal*.

63. From an ESPN sports poll reported in *SBJ*, September 8–14, 2008.

64. "National Football and Basketball TV Rights Deals for Division I-A Conferences," *SBJ*, September 11–17, 2006.

65. When the Big Ten announced the creation of its own cable TV network in 2006, it must have seemed a boon to the minor or nonrevenue sports, which would receive two-thirds of the programming. This could only mean that the volleyball and wrestling teams would likely end up competing more often on weekdays, so as not to compete with football or basketball on weekends. The TV-made football world was hard on nonfootball athletes, too.

66. After many years of annually ranking the financial value of NFL franchises, *Forbes* magazine in December 2006 began doing the same for college football. *Forbes* valued fifteen programs between $51 million and $97 million, with Notre Dame at the top. The following year, *Forbes* expanded the list to twenty programs, ranging from Wisconsin at $43 million to Notre Dame at $101 million. The average NFL franchise was worth ten times as much as Notre Dame's football program, with the Dallas Cowboys and the Washington Redskins leading the way at more than $1.5 billion. Though the scale of the collegiate game is much smaller, for one of the leaders of the financial press to now be treating the NFL and big-time college

football as similar enterprises marked another symbolic milestone. See Jack Gage and Peter J. Schwartz, "The Most Valuable College Football Teams," *Forbes* (online), December 22, 2006; Peter Schwartz, "The Most Valuable College Football Teams," *Forbes* (online), November 20, 2007; Kurt Badenhausen, Michael K. Ozanian, and Christina Settimi, "The Richest Game," *Forbes* (online), September 11, 2008.

67. Gilbert M. Gaul and Frank Fitzpatrick, "Athletic Empires Depend on Taxpayer Dollars," *PI*, September 13, 2000. This was part of a series titled "The Price of Winning: The Business of College Sports," which ran on the front page from September 10 through September 14.

68. Myles Brand, "State of the Association Speech," January 2003; Myles Brand, "State of the Association Speech," January 11, 2004; Myles Brand, "NCAA President Calls for Value-Based Budgeting for Intercollegiate Athletics Programs," January 8, 2005. All are available on the NCAA website.

69. AP, "N.C.A.A. Passes First Phase of Its Academic Reform Package," *NYT*, January 11, 2005; Eric Prisbell, "Coaches Say New NCAA Academic Plan Is Flawed," *WP*, July 20, 2005; Brad Wolverton, "NCAA Rescinds Scholarships at 65 Colleges," *CHE*, March 10, 2006.

70. Pete Thamel, "Athletes Get New College Pitch: Check Out Our Tutoring Center," *NYT*, November 4, 2006; Brad Wolverton, "Spending Plenty So Athletes Can Make the Grade," *CHE*, September 5, 2008.

71. Wolverton, "Spending Plenty."

72. GSRs are for students entering college from 1998 through 2001 and graduating within six years. Data available on the NCAA website.

73. Brad Wolverton, "NCAA Penalizes 112 Teams for Failing to Meet Its Academic-Progress Requirements," *CHE*, May 3, 2007; "APR Data Show Improvement, Challenges," *NCAA News* (online), May 2, 2007; Pete Thamel, "Smaller Programs Are among Hardest Hit in N.C.A.A. Academic Report," *NYT*, May 7, 2008. The seventeen penalized Division I-A teams were listed on Rivals.com as a sidebar to Steve Megargee, "It's Academic: NCAA Reveals APR Sanctions."

74. Tom Farrey, "Defining Bravery in College Sports," ESPN.com, October 7, 2003; Jeff Miller, "Unpopular Belief," *DMN*, February 22, 2005.

75. Pete Thamel, "Top Grades and No Class Time for Auburn Players," *NYT*, July 14, 2006; Pete Thamel, "Changes in Auburn's Policies Outlined," *NYT*, July 22, 2006; Pete Thamel, "More Questions at Auburn after Audit Reveals Grade Change Helped Athlete Graduate," *NYT*, December 10, 2006; Pete Thamel, "Professor at Center of Academic Investigation by Auburn Is Suspended," *NYT*, December 23, 2006; Paula Wasley, "Auburn U. Settles with Professor Who Offered Easy Grades to Athletes and Other Students," *CHE*, July 30, 2007.

76. Jim Carty, John Heuser, and Nathan Fenno, "Athletes Steered to Prof," *AAN*, March 16, 2008.

77. Ray Glier, "F.S.U. to Bar as Many as 25 Players from Bowl," *NYT*, December 19, 2007.

78. Jeff Miller, "Stress Test," *DMN*, February 20, 2005 (this is the first in a four-part series); Thamel, "Athletes Get New College Pitch"; Amdur, "Problems Are Mounting in N.C.A.A."

79. Brand, "NCAA President Calls for Value-Based Budgeting for Intercollegiate Athletics Programs."

80. Jeff Miller, "One Major Issue: Do Athletes Get Easy Ride?," *DMN*, February 20, 2005.

81. John Heuser and Jim Carty, "Kinesiology Reserves Slots for Athletes," *AAN*, March 17, 2008. The series ran March 16–19.

82. Jill Lieber Steeg, Jodi Upton, Patrick Bohn, and Steve Berkowitz, "Athletes Guided toward 'Beating the System,'" *USA Today* (online), November 19, 2008. A link to a drop-down table allows readers to see every program with a cluster, listed by sport.

83. "'The Second-Century Imperatives: Presidential Leadership—Institutional Accountability," A Report from the Presidential Task Force on the Future of Division I Intercollegiate Athletics; and Myles Brand, "National Press Club," October 30, 2006. Both the report and Brand's talk to the National Press Club about it are available on the NCAA website. And see Brad Wolverton, "College Presidents Call for Increased Disclosure of Athletics Spending," *CHE*, November 10, 2006.

84. Myles Brand, "In All, Fairness," 2007 NCAA Convention State of the Association, January 5, 2007 (available on NCAA website).

85. "Second-Century Imperatives," p. 10.

86. Myles Brand, "2006 NCAA State of the Association Address," January 7, 2006 (available on NCAA website); Sack, *Counterfeit Amateurs*, p. 161.

87. Myles Brand, "The 2009 State of the Association Speech" (available on NCAA website).

88. "Second-Century Imperatives," pp. 50–52.

CHAPTER 5

1. I am grateful to OSU staff archivist Karl McCreary for this information.

2. Myron Cope, "The Proudest Squares," *SI*, November 18, 1968, pp. 98–110; "Scorecard," *SI*, June 16, 1969, pp. 13–14. Al Grady reflected on the example of A&M, implicitly so unlike Iowa, in his "Al Grady's Column," *ICPC*, June 21, 1969. The *Ann Arbor News* reported that Texas A&M first offered Schembechler $250,000, but he turned it down for Michigan's counteroffer of half that amount. See Michael Rosenberg, *War as They Knew It: Woody Hayes, Bo Schembechler, and America in a Time of Unrest* (New York and Boston: Grand Central, 2008), pp. 307–8.

3. A list by state appears in *USA Today*, September 24, 1986; see also, Mark Mayfield, "Perkins CEO of 'Bama's Big Business," *USA Today*, September 25, 1986.

4. Pete Thamel, "To Keep Coaches, Universities Must Dig Down Deep," *NYT*, January 2, 2005.

5. Bruce Schoenfeld, "Tough Times in Tucson," *SBJ*, June 19–25, 2006. The number of millionaire coaches in 2006 is cited in the class-action lawsuit *White v. NCAA*, filed on behalf of football and basketball players denied a reasonable share of the revenues they generate.

6. "Compensation for Div. I-A College Football Coaches" (<http://i.usatoday.net/sports/graphics/coaches_contracts07/flash.swf>). This is a database compiled by *USA Today*, listing all coaches' salaries and other compensation, with the exception

of those at Notre Dame, Penn State, and nine other universities, mostly private, which did not share information—thus the supposition about Paterno and Weis without the confirmation. *USA Today* updates its database each year.

7. Jodi Upton and Steve Wieberg, "Million-Dollar Coaches Move into Mainstream," *USA Today*, November 16, 2005; "Compensation for Div. I-A College Football Coaches."

8. Daniel L. Fulks, "2004–06 NCAA Revenues and Expenses of Division I Intercollegiate Athletics Programs Report," National Collegiate Athletic Association, March 2008. Fiscal year 2004 is 2003–4, which means the 2003 season.

9. Peter J. Schwartz, "The Best (and Worst) College Football Coaches for the Buck," *Forbes* (online), August 13, 2008. The *Chronicle of Higher Education* confirmed Carroll's $4.4 million (which made him the highest-paid employee in private higher education). See Jeffrey Brainard, "The Biggest Campus Paycheck May Not Be the President's," CHE, February 27, 2009.

10. Gerry Dulac, "The Money Question: It's Not Everything, But It Is Something," *Pittsburgh Post-Gazette* (online), December 31, 2006; "Agent: Smith Negotiations at a Stalemate," AP online (available on the *Washington Post*'s website), February 22, 2007.

11. Gilbert M. Gaul and Frank Fitzpatrick, "Coaches in the Big Time Can Break the Bank," *PI*, September 11, 2000.

12. Mike Knobler, "LSU's Miles Scores with Bowl Bonus," *PO*, December 25, 2007; AP, "L.S.U.'s Miles Signs New Contract," *NYT*, March 14, 2008; and "Compensation for Div. I-A College Football Coaches."

13. Gaul and Fitzpatrick, "Coaches in the Big Time Can Break the Bank"; Mark Alesia, "Brand's $835,000 Salary Receives Support of NCAA," *USA Today*, March 25, 2005. The salary for IU's president is from the survey published by the *Chronicle of Higher Education* in its November 14, 2003, issue.

14. Noelle Barton, Maria DeMento, and Alvin P. Sanoff, "Top Nonprofit Executives See Healthy Pay Raises," *Chronicle of Philanthropy*, September 28, 2006.

15. "Outside Employment," from Oregon State University's faculty handbook (<http://oregonstate.edu/facultystaff/handbook/outsideemp.html>).

16. Allen Sack, *Counterfeit Amateurs: An Athlete's Journey through the Sixties to the Age of Academic Capitalism* (University Park: Penn State University Press, 2008), p. 116.

17. In the NCAA's latest report on revenues and expenses, the average cost of an in-state grant-in-aid at a public institution was $19,700; for an out-of-state student in 2005–6, it was $29,100. I use $25,000 to approximate the mix of recruits. For private schools, the cost was considerably higher, of course—an average of $39,600.

18. Richard G. Sheehan, *Keeping Score: The Economics of Big-Time Sports* (South Bend, Ind.: Diamond Communications, 1996), pp. 296–98. Sheehan's calculations factored in graduation rates and the benefits of a degree, as well as direct benefits such as tuition dollars.

19. Sack, *Counterfeit Amateurs*, p. 89. For Sack's full account of CARE, see pp. 84–97.

20. M. J. Duberstein, "NFL Economics Primer 2002, National Football League Players Association, April 2002."

21. Ibid.; "2004 Pre-Season Salary Averages & Signing Trends," National Football League Players Association, September 2004; Bob Glauber, "Cheering Stops, Trouble Starts," *Newsday*, January 12, 1997.

22. Sack, *Counterfeit Amateurs*, pp. 43–45.

23. Edwin H. Cady, *The Big Game: College Sports and American Life* (Knoxville: University of Tennessee Press, 1978), p. 144. In another account from our era, sportswriter Rick Telander, who played at Northwestern during the same years that I was at Notre Dame (he graduated one year after me), expressed regret that he had missed out on much that Northwestern offered him—"the clubs, the intramurals, the discussion groups, the little things that happen while a football player is at practice or pumping iron or studying a wide receiver's moves." See Rick Telander, *The Hundred Yard Lie: The Corruption of College Football and What We Can Do to Stop It* (New York: Simon & Schuster, 1989), p. 69.

24. Brad Wolverton, "Athletes' Hours Renew Debate over College Sports," *CHE*, January 25, 2008.

25. Weight lifting during the season is simply part of the advanced knowledge about conditioning and nutrition since I played. We did jumping jacks before practices and games, ate thick steaks for pregame meals (which we digested about the time the game was ending), and lifted weights only in the off-season.

26. Andrew Zimbalist, *Unpaid Professionals: Commercialism and Conflict in Big-Time College Sports* (Princeton, N.J.: Princeton University Press, 1999), p. 43.

27. The lowest ACT score I can find on a conversion table for the old SAT, before "recentering," is 9, which is equivalent to 400 on the SAT.

28. Dexter Manley and Tom Friend, *Educating Dexter* (Nashville, Tenn.: Rutledge Hill, 1992), pp. 81, 88.

29. Sara Lipka, "2 Victories for a Scholar-Athlete—and Florida State," *CHE*, December 5, 2008; Pete Thamel, "For Florida State Player and Scholar, Game Day Is Different, *NYT*, November 20, 2008.

30. Brad Wolverton, "Athletics Participation Prevents Many Players from Choosing Majors They Want," *CHE*, January 8, 2007.

31. Josephine R. Potuto and James O'Hanlon, "National Study of Student-Athletes Regarding Their Experiences as College Students," September 2006, available at NCAA.org.

32. William C. Rhoden, *Forty Million Dollar Slaves: The Rise, Fall, and Redemption of the Black Athlete* (New York: Crown, 2006), p. 177.

33. See "Athletic Recruiting: A Campus Crisis," *NYT*, March 10–15, 1974 (all on the front page, by several writers); and Neil Amdur, "The Boosters: Growing Problem in College Sports," *NYT*, March 29–31, 1981 (only the first installment on the front page); as well as "College Sports: Have the Schools Lost Control?," *NYT*, March 21–24, 1982 (again, various writers).

34. John Sayle Watterson, *College Football: History, Spectacle, Controversy* (Baltimore: Johns Hopkins University Press, 2000), pp. 353–54.

35. The complete list is available on the NCAA Legislative Service Database (at <http://web1.ncaa.org/LSDBi/exec/miSearch>).

36. Robert McG. Thomas Jr., "Tapes Bring Auburn Penalties," *NYT*, August 19, 1993.

37. For a detailed discussion of the SMU mess, see Watterson, *College Football*, pp. 353–78.

38. William E. Schmidt, "3 Agents and Player Charged in Fraud of Colleges," *NYT*, August 25, 1988; Steve Fiffer, "Crime Figure Testifies to Link with Sports Agent," *NYT*, March 15, 1989; Steve Fiffer, "Two Sports Agents Convicted of Fraud and Racketeering," *NYT*, April 14, 1989. All of these appeared on the front page.

39. Robert McG. Thomas Jr., "Illicit Pay in Wide Use, Study Contends," *NYT*, November 17, 1989; Daniel Golden, "Agents of Deceit," *BG*, September 10, 1995 (the series continued through September 13).

40. In a 2001 survey of 4,500 college students by Donald McCabe of Rutgers, 74 percent admitted cheating. See Ginny McCormick, "Whose Idea Was That?," *Stanford Magazine*, September/October 2003, p. 68.

41. Alexander Wolff, "Upstairs Downstairs," *SI*, October 14, 1991.

42. Gilbert M. Gaul and Frank Fitzgerald, "On Campus, an Edifice Complex," *PI*, September 12, 2000.

43. "Welcome to the Big Time," *SI*, August 12, 2002; Bill King, "Race for Recruits," *SBJ*, December 5–11, 2005.

44. Robert Sullivan, "Time to Play Foote Ball?," *SI*, December 21, 1987.

45. Rick Telander and Robert Sullivan, "You Reap What You Sow," *SI*, February 27, 1989. After OU president Frank Horton resigned, the acting president in 1989 was none other than David Swank, the former faculty representative who had worked to push through the one-year scholarship in the late 1960s. Oklahoma and Georgia (another scandal-ridden school in the 1980s) were also the lead litigants in challenging the NCAA's TV monopoly in 1981, the initial act that led to the financial free-for-all in college football. The title of the article, "You Reap What You Sow," had a layer of irony unintended by authors and editors.

46. Elliott Almond, "It Was No Game," *LAT*, December 27, 1995.

47. Telander and Sullivan, "You Reap What You Sow"; Rick Reilly, "What Price Glory?," *SI*, February 27, 1989; Jerry Kirshenbaum, "An American Disgrace," *SI*, February 27, 1989.

48. John Underwood, *The Death of an American Game: The Crisis in Football* (Boston: Little, Brown, 1979); Telander, *The Hundred Yard Lie*.

49. Austin Murphy, "Unsportsmanlike Conduct," *SI*, July 1, 1991; Sonja Steptoe and E. M. Swift, "Anatomy of a Scandal," *SI*, May 16, 1994; Michael Farber and Shelley Smith, "Coach and Jury," *SI*, September 25, 1995; Almond, "It Was No Game"; Nobles, "Miami's Patton Indicted in Theft of Credit Card," *NYT*, December 18, 1991; "Cash Bounties Reported at Miami," *NYT*, May 21, 1994; "12th Miami Player in Trouble," *NYT*, July 4, 1996 (the headline said "12th," while the story said "11th"); Alexander Wolff, "Broken beyond Repair," *SI*, June 12, 1995. According to Michael MacCambridge, *Sports Illustrated*'s 1995 cover appeared during a competition for the managing editor's position, its sensationalism undoubtedly an effort by one of

the candidates to promote himself. See MacCambridge, *The Franchise: A History of Sports Illustrated Magazine* (New York: Hyperion, 1997), p. 369.

50. "College Sports: Out of Bounds," *BG*, September 10–13, 1995 (including Daniel Golden, "It's a Crime," September 11, 1995); Elliott Almond and others, "Crime & Sports '95," *LAT*, December 27, 1995.

51. Gerald Eskanazi, "The Male Athlete and Sexual Assault," *NYT*, June 3, 1990; Golden, "It's a Crime"; Julie Cart, "Sex and Violence," *LAT*, December 27, 1995; Douglas S. Looney and John Walters, "Seminole Shame," *SI*, June 6, 1994; Jack McCallum and Kostya Kennedy, "Nebraska's Double Standard," *SI*, April 29, 1996.

52. Todd Crosset, "Male Athletes' Violence against Women: A Critical Assessment of the Athletic Affiliation, Violence against Women Debate," *Quest* 51 (August 1999): 245.

53. Todd W. Crosset, Jeffrey R. Benedict, and Mark A. McDonald, "Male Student-Athletes Reported for Sexual Assault: A Survey of Campus Police Departments and Judicial Affairs Offices," *Journal of Sport and Social Issues* 2 (May 1995): 126–40; Crosset, "Male Athletes' Violence against Women," 244–57.

54. Howard Pankratz, "$2.8 Million Deal in CU Rape Case," *DP* (online), December 5, 2007.

55. Kelli Anderson and George Dohrmann, "Out of Control?," *SI*, February 23, 2004; Kelley King, "Doing the Legwork" (in "Scorecard"), *SI*, January 27, 2003; Ken Goe, "In Wake of Colorado Recruiting Scandal, Recruiting Visits Need Restructuring," *PO*, February 23, 2004; Ryan White, "The High Price of Recruiting," *PO*, April 19, 2004.

56. Anderson and Dohrmann, "Out of Control?"; Wendell Barnhouse, "Cheaters Will Just Overlook New Rules," *CGT*, August 9, 2004.

57. Rhoden, *Forty Million Dollar Slaves*, pp. 171–95.

58. FSN began offering regional games in the mid-1990s, adding national contests in 2005. In 2006 it offered eight national games, along with 85–100 regional ones. The ESPN networks televised four high school games in 2005, then twelve in 2006.

59. Erik Spanberg, "Prep Football Sees More Action," *SBJ*, August 21–27, 2006; Joe Drape, "High School Football, under Prime-Time Lights," *NYT*, September 17, 2006; Christopher Lawlor, "Football Teams, Communities across USA Thrilled for National Exposure," *USA Today*, September 1, 2006.

60. David Callahan, *The Cheating Culture: Why More Americans Are Doing Wrong to Get Ahead* (New York: Harcourt, 2004); "Numbers," *Time*, March 22, 2004, p. 19.

61. Potuto and O'Hanlon, "National Study of Student-Athletes Regarding Their Experiences as College Students."

62. Wolverton, "Athletes' Hours Renew Debate over College Sports."

63. James L. Shulman and William G. Bowen, *The Game of Life: College Sports and Educational Values* (Princeton, N.J.: Princeton University Press, 2001); William G. Bowen and Sarah A. Levin, *Reclaiming the Game: College Sports and Educational Values* (Princeton, N.J.: Princeton University Press, 2003).

64. Bill Pennington, "Division III Seeks Harmony between Field and Classroom," *NYT*, February 13, 2007.

65. Shulman and Bowen, *The Game of Life*, pp. 273–74.

66. "Research Studies Highlight Convention Menu Sessions," *NCAA News*, January 6, 2007.

67. Walter Byers, *Unsportsmanlike Conduct: Exploiting College Athletes* (Ann Arbor: University of Michigan Press, 1995), pp. 69–71, 74–75; Allen J. Sack and Ellen J. Staurowsky, *College Athletes for Hire: The Evolution and Legacy of the NCAA's Amateur Myth* (Westport, Conn.: Praeger, 1998), pp. 80–82.

68. Sack and Staurowsky, *College Athletes for Hire*, pp. 85–87; Sack, *Counterfeit Amateurs*, pp. 111–14, 145–50.

69. The most comprehensive accounts of Title IX are Linda Jean Carpenter and R. Vivian Acosta, *Title IX* (Champaign, Ill.: Human Kinetics, 2005); and Welch Suggs, *A Place on the Team: The Triumph and Tragedy of Title IX* (Princeton, N.J.: Princeton University Press, 2005. (Carpenter and Acosta's volume is a comprehensive legal primer on Title IX. The "tragedy" in Suggs's title is women athletes' loss of an alternative to the NCAA's big-time-sports model with the collapse of the Association for Intercollegiate Athletics for Women.) A "Title IX Legislative Chronology" is provided on the website of the Women's Sports Foundation. In my account, I follow this timeline, which draws on the University of Iowa's "History of Title IX Legislation, Regulation and Policy Interpretation." The most fully elaborated argument against Title IX (as a case of feminist excess) is Jessica Gavora, *Tilting the Playing Field: Schools, Sports, Sex, and Title IX* (San Francisco: Encounter Books, 2002).

70. Kathryn Jay, *More Than Just a Game: Sports in American Life since 1945* (New York: Columbia University Press, 2004), p. 166.

71. Bill Pennington, "More Men's Teams Benched as Colleges Level the Field," *NYT*, May 9, 2002.

72. Jack Scott, *The Athletic Revolution* (New York: Free Press, 1971), pp. 23–34.

73. Robert Lipsyte, "Title IX Debate Is about Football," *NYT*, May 12, 2002.

74 "Intercollegiate Athletics: Recent Trends in Teams and Participants in National Collegiate Athletic Association Sports," U.S. Government Accountability Office, Report to Congressional Addressees, July 2007; Sara Lipka, "GAO Examines Effects of Title IX," *CHE*, July 27, 2007; Pennington, "More Men's Teams Benched"; Bill Pennington, "Want to Try Out for College Sports? Forget It," *NYT*, September 22, 2002.

75. "Supreme Court Refuses to Hear Title IX Lawsuit," *WP*, June 7, 2005.

76. "Big Ten Cuts Back Some Scholarships," *NYT*, May 28, 1972.

77. Fulks, "2004–06 NCAA Revenues and Expenses of Division I Intercollegiate Athletics Programs Report."

CHAPTER 6

1. Reed Harris, *King Football: The Vulgarization of the American College* (New York: Vanguard Press, 1932), pp. 89, 30.

2. Ernest L. Boyer, *College: The Undergraduate Experience in America* (for the Carnegie Foundation for the Advancement of Teaching; New York: Harper & Row, 1987), p. 182; Murray Sperber, *Beer and Circus: How Big-Time College Sports Is Crip-*

pling American Undergraduate Education (New York: Henry Holt, 2000). In addition to *Beer and Circus* and *College Sports, Inc.: The Athletic Department vs. the University* (New York: Henry Holt, 1990), Sperber's most direct critiques of big-time college sports, his *Shake Down the Thunder: The Creation of Notre Dame Football* (New York: Henry Holt, 1993) and *Onward to Victory: The Crises That Shaped College Sports* (New York: Henry Holt, 1998) are histories of college football (with particular attention to Notre Dame) in which issues of distorted priorities inevitably arise.

3. Myles Brand, "Leadership and Challenges: The Roles of Intercollegiate Athletics in the University," State of the Association Speech, January 12, 2008 (on NCAA website).

4. John R. Gerdy, *Air Ball: American Education's Failed Experiment with Elite Athletics* (Jackson: University Press of Mississippi, 2006), pp. 119–55.

5. Rick Telander, *The Hundred Yard Lie: The Corruption of College Football and What We Can Do to Stop It* (New York: Simon & Schuster, 1989). Telander summarized his views in "Something Must Be Done," *SI*, October 2, 1989.

6. On Rainey and Stagg, see Robin Lester, *Stagg's University: The Rise, Decline, and Fall of Big-Time Football at Chicago* (Urbana: University of Illinois Press, 1995). On Notre Dame's rise, see Sperber, *Shake Down the Thunder*. On the others, see my own *King Football: Sport and Spectacle in the Golden Age of Radio & Newsreels, Movies & Magazines, the Weekly & the Daily Press* (Chapel Hill: University of North Carolina Press, 2001), pp. 79–85 (other sources are cited there).

7. William McNeill, *Hutchins' University: A Memoir of the University of Chicago, 1929–1950* (Chicago: University of Chicago Press,), p. 97.

8. J. Douglas Toma, *Football U.: Spectator Sports in the Life of the American University* (Ann Arbor: University of Michigan Press, 2003). Toma's definition of a "Football U.": "They are places where football matters in several ways: in the expression of institutional culture on campus; in the national reputation of what are essentially local institutions; in the support by local communities needed to build institutions; in the ways people related to and identify with institutions; in the development of institutions as brand names; and in external relations and institutional advancement" (p. 19). Toma cites the Carnegie Foundation's 1990 study, *Campus Life: In Search of Community*, and foundation president Ernest Boyer's 1987 book, *College: The Undergraduate Experience in America*—using the quotation cited in note 2 of this chapter as an epigraph to one of his chapters—to make the case for football's community-building power. As a college professor, Toma is surprisingly sanguine that the "collegiate experience" of sports and partying is more important to students than "the intellectual life of institutions, which is of paramount interest only to faculty, graduate students, and a relative few administrators" (83). This is the basis of Murray Sperber's indictment of American higher education in *Beer and Circus*. Reading Sperber against Toma can provide a clear sense of the immense divide over big-time college sports within the academy.

9. Recent research has found that movement is most difficult for national universities, particularly for the better ones. Increasing selectivity in admissions has the greatest likelihood of improving a school's ranking, followed by improving

graduation rates. See Peter Schmidt, "Most Colleges Chase Prestige on a Treadmill, Researchers Find," *CHE*, November 10, 2008.

10. Sixty universities belong to the Association for American Universities on the basis of various indicators of academic excellence. Twenty-nine of the thirty-four public institutions play Division I-A football, with only the State University of New York at Buffalo outside the BCS; the others are four UC campuses and another SUNY campus. Just seven of the twenty-six private universities play Division I-A football: Northwestern, Rice, Stanford, Syracuse, Tulane, USC, and Vanderbilt, with Rice and Tulane outside the BCS.

11. "2007 NACUBO Endowment Study Results," National Association of College and University Business Officers (available online).

12. Ibid.

13. Toma, *Football U.*, p. 119.

14. Monte Burke, "The Most Powerful Coach in Sports," *Forbes*, September 1, 2008. With estimates ranging from $3.5 million to $5 million, Saban's salary is a moving target for reporters.

15. This is the study by Robert E. Litan, Jonathan M. Orszag, and Peter R. Orszag, "The Empirical Effects of Collegiate Athletics: An Interim Report," National Collegiate Athletic Association, August 2003.

16. Robert H. Frank, "Challenging the Myth: A Review of the Links among College Athletic Success, Student Quality, and Donations," Knight Foundation Commission on Intercollegiate Athletics," May 2004.

17. Bill McDonald, "Phenomenology," *Boston College Magazine*, Spring 2003.

18. Toma, *Football U.*, pp. 225–26; McDonald, "Phenomenology."

19. Jeffrey L. Stinson and Dennis R. Howard, "Athletic Success and Private Giving to Athletic and Academic Programs at NCAA Institutions," *Journal of Sport Management* 21 (January 2007): 235–64.

20. Brad Wolverton, "Sharp Growth in Athletics Fund Raising Leads to Decline in Academic Donations on Some Campuses," *CHE*, September 25, 2007. I calculated nonathletic giving from the *Chronicle*'s table of "Trends in Giving to Athletic Programs," which charts average athletics donations per institution and the proportion of total gifts going to athletics for each year from 1998 through 2003. If an average athletics donation of $858,613 in 1998, for example, was 14.7 percent of total gifts, that total would be $5,840,905, meaning that $4,982,292 was nonathletic giving (and so on, for each successive year).

21. Brad Wolverton, "For Athletics, a Billion Dollar Goal Line," *CHE*, January 23, 2009.

22. Florida International currently has a stadium seating 7,500, but construction is under way for a facility seating 18,000 (with plans for eventually reaching 45,000).

23. As noted earlier, the Graduation Success Rate (GSR) is the NCAA's revision of the graduation rate used by the federal government, which penalizes schools for transfers. The GSR is thus higher than the federally reported rate; a GSR of 60 percent is roughly equivalent to 50 percent by the federal calculation.

24. Bruce Schoenfeld, "Tough Times in Tucson" and "Hope Rests on Football, Basketball," *SBJ*, June 19–25, 2006.

25. Erik Spanberg, "Snap Decision or Good Strategy?," *SBJ*, September 10–16, 2007. Financial data for all years are from the Department of Education.

26. Katie Thomas, "Rising Criticism as Rutgers Invests in Athletics," *NYT*, October 18, 2008.

27. Toma, *Football U.*, pp. 206–9, 259. The series in the *Ann Arbor News*, cited in chapter 4, ran from March 16 through March 19, 2008. The *News* reported that Michigan football players were overwhelmingly admitted to the university in kinesiology, because of its lower standards, then transferred after two years into general studies, where they could pad their schedules with independent studies and courses in such subjects as the Ojibwe language (whose former students, interviewed for the report, could not remember a single word).

28. "NCAA Student-Athletes Graduating at Highest Rates Ever," October 14, 2008 (news release on NCAA website).

29. Minimum ACT scores required by the NCAA are the sum of the scores in math, science, English, and reading. The ACT scores listed by *U.S. News* are composites. The NCAA minimum 68 on the ACT (with a 2.5 GPA) is equivalent to a composite score of 17 and an SAT score of 830. It is less confusing to convert ACT to SAT scores for comparing institutions.

30. In 2001 the NCAA published a report in which the average SAT score of prospective student athletes in the revenue sports (football and basketball) was 1009 (compared to 1083 for Division I athletes in all sports). See "NCAA Research Report 99–03: Academic Characteristics by Sport Group of Division I Recruits in the 1997 and 1998 NCAA Initial-Eligibility Clearinghouse," National Collegiate Athletic Association, May 2001. In his "State of the Association" address in January 2007, Myles Brand reported that the most recent data on entering student athletes for all of Division I showed an average SAT of 1059 (Brand's point was to compare that score to the 1026 for all students). I assume from the earlier data (on *prospective*, not actual, recruits) that the SAT score for football recruits was below the 1059 for all athletes. Both the report and the address are available at ncaa.org. In December 2008 the *Atlanta Journal-Constitution* reported the average SAT score for football players at fifty-two public universities in BCS conferences (along with Memphis and Hawaii) to be 941. The SAT scores were taken from public documents filed by the universities as part of an NCAA accreditation process required every ten years. The data thus ranged from as early as 1997 to as late as 2007 (depending on when the school went through the accreditation process), making direct comparisons difficult. Were the private BCS universities included—their reports are not public documents—the SAT scores at Stanford, Duke, Northwestern, Notre Dame, and other academically selective schools would presumably raise that 941 average by several points. See Mike Knobler, "AJC Investigation: Many Athletes Lag Far behind on SAT Scores," *AJC* (online), December 28, 2008 (with accompanying tables and online database).

31. In a 2005 interview with Allen Sack, the director of admissions at Notre Dame stated that the average SAT for a football recruit was 1048, or 242 points below

the 25th percentile and 452 points below the 75th percentile. See Sack, *Counterfeit Amateurs: An Athlete's Journey through the Sixties to the Age of Academic Capitalism* (University Park: Penn State University Press, 2008), p. 140.

32. Knobler, "AJC Investigation."

33. Bob Ford, "Intruder Joins BCS's Cozy Table; South Fla. Becomes a Title Threat," *PI*, October 17, 2007.

34. William M. Chace recounts this episode in his memoir, *100 Semesters: My Adventures as a Student, Professor, and University President, and What I Learned along the Way* (Princeton, N.J.: Princeton University Press, 2006), pp. 309–40. Also see Ray Glier, "Tulane Board Votes to Keep Football in Division I-A," *NYT*, June 11, 2003.

35. "Athletics at Rice: A Report to the Faculty Council," by the Subcommittee on Athletics, March 21, 2003.

36. Welch Suggs, "Rice U. Considers Major Changes in Athletics as Report Identifies Host of Problems," *CHE*, May 6, 2004; Welch Suggs, "Rice U. Backs away from Major Changes in Sports," *CHE*, June 4, 2004.

37. Eric Prisbell, "'Death Penalty' a Relic of the Past," *WP*, October 10, 2007.

38. Buffalo's endowment in 2006 was $194 million, 239th overall (compared to $220 million in 2007, for 248th). For 2006, see "2006 NACUBO Endowment Study Results," National Association of College and University Business Officers (online). For the growth from 2006 to 2007, see "NACUBO Press Release and Fact Sheet on 2007 Endowment Study Results," January 24, 2008 (online). For 2008, Buffalo's endowment of $213 million was ranked 247th.

39. Libby Sander, "Athletics Programs Scramble to Streamline Budgets in Difficult Times," *CHE*, January 30, 2009.

40. Paul Fain, "Congressman's Letter Grills NCAA on Tax-Exempt Status of College Sports," *CHE*, October 13, 2006; Brad Wolverton, "NCAA Defends Tax-Exempt Status as Congressional Scrutiny of Colleges Increases," *CHE*, November 24, 2006; John D. Colombo, "The NCAA, Tax Exemption, and College Athletics," Illinois Public Law Research Paper No. 08-08, February 19, 2009, p. 27.

41. Brand's most important predecessor, Walter Byers, executive director from 1951 to 1988 and virtually the creator of the modern NCAA, fought very effectively against this idea for more than thirty years, both in court and within the NCAA; he then decided in his postretirement book, *Unsportsmanlike Conduct: Exploiting College Athletes* (Ann Arbor: University of Michigan Press, 1995), that athletes should be paid.

42. Tom Farrey, "NCAA Might Face Damages in Hundreds of Millions," *ESPN The Magazine* (online), February 21, 2006; Myles Brand, "Welfare of Student-Athletes NCAA's Top Priority" (letter to the editor), *DP*, August 17, 2003.

43. The text of the lawsuit is available as the "Second Amended Complaint" under "Court Documents" on the *White v. NCAA* class action website (<http://www.ncaaclassaction.com/court.php3>).

44. Michelle Brutlag Hosick, "NCAA Agrees to Settlement," *NCAA News*, January 30, 2008; Brad Wolverton, "NCAA Will Pay Big to Settle Antitrust Lawsuit," *CHE*, February 8, 2008.

45. "Stipulation and Agreement of Settlement between White and NCAA," on NCAA website (the quoted statement is on p. 5).

46. Gordon S. White Jr., "Clemson Head Says He Quit over Lack of Support," *NYT*, March 7, 1985; Michael Goodwin, "N.C.A.A. Session Rebuffs Presidents," *NYT*, July 1, 1987; William C. Rhoden, "Who's in Charge Here?," *NYT*, February 4, 1990; William C. Rhoden, "N.C.A.A. Agrees to Reduce Coaching Staffs," *NYT*, January 9, 1991.

47. Quoted in Sack, *Counterfeit Amateurs*, pp. 159–60.

Index

Carlson, William, 106, 107

Carnegie Foundation, 4, 129, 154, 233, 234

Carroll, Pete, 194

Carson, Bud, 86

Cavanaugh, Frank, 121

Center for Athletes' Rights and Education (CARE), 199–200

Central Connecticut State University, 183

Chandler, Albert "Happy," 76

Cherberg, John, 44

Chicago Bears (NFL), 31

Chronicle of Higher Education, 178, 184, 249

Claiborne, Jerry, 60

Clark, Bert, 38

Clements, William, 211

Clemson University, 78, 85, 176, 179, 211, 218, 278

Coalition on Intercollegiate Athletics (COIA), 234, 235, 275, 278

Cohane, Tim, 36

Cohodas, Nadine, 82, 84

Cole, Edward, 29

College football: media relations to, 1, 4, 7, 22; contradiction at heart of, 1–2, 127, 128–30, 153, 198, 224, 235, 236; conflicting priorities in, 2, 9, 127–28, 149–53, 178–79, 188–90, 202–13, 233–36, 243–44, 276–77; racial protests in, 2, 42–44, 89–125; problems and scandals in, 2–3, 127–28, 146–47, 185–86, 210–12, 214–17, 219; economics of, 2–3, 8–9, 128, 157–81, 183–84, 188–90, 191 202, 234; history of, 3, 21–22; commercialism in, 3, 24, 127, 128–29, 150–53, 157–60, 166, 188–90, 234; "professionalism" in, 4–5, 22, 128–29, 134, 145, 210, 234, 236; reform of, 4–5, 127, 147–57, 181–90, 233–36, 248–49, 276–80; and 1960s radicalism, 5–6, 15–21, 39–46; as media-made public drama, 6–7; as entertainment, 7, 127, 129,

272, 275, 276; institutional benefits from, 8, 9, 229, 237–48; as source of community, 8, 23, 234–35, 239–40; as fundamental to American higher education, 9, 237–44; and politics, 15–18, 20–21, 23–30, 31–34, 41, 46–47; and the counterculture, 17–18, 20, 36; as war, 18, 22, 284 (n. 10); integration of, 59; racial transformation of, 118–25; as education, 129–30, 131; as work, 131–33, 197–202, 207–8, 224–25; television revenues for, 158–60, 161, 176–77, 178, 188–89, 231, 243; television ratings for, 159, 179–80; bowl revenues in, 162–64; non-BCS programs in, 162–66, 167, 172–76, 178–79, 180–81, 251, 254–57, 267–71; BCS programs in, 162–66, 167–71, 174–81, 251–54, 258–67; revenues from, 166–80, 260–61; attendance at, 177; fund-raising for, 178; market for, 180; nonprofit status of, 180–81, 272, 273; facilities "arms race" in, 184, 213; resemblance of to National Football League, 190; relation of to "nonrevenue" sports, 207; and "college life," 239; as marketing tool, 239; relation of to institutional fund-raising, 239, 244, 245–46, 248, 249–50; relationship of to institutional endowments, 241–42, 249, 259–60, 268; relationship of to recruiting students, 244–45, 247–48; in relation to institutional differences, 250–71; legal threats to, 272, 273–76; economic threats to, 272–73; future prospects for, 272–73, 276–80; financial values of top programs in, 307–8 (n. 66). *See also* College football coaches; College football players; Football; Football Bowl Subdivision; "student-athletes"; National Collegiate Athletic Association

College Football Association (CFA), 5, 150, 151, 157–58, 159, 160, 161

Georgia Tech, 6, 67, 89, 179, 215, 237; integration of football team at, 84–88, 138, 290 (n. 3); football and academics at, 262, 263

Gerdy, John, 235–36

Gilliam, Frank, 113

Glassford, Bill, 44

Gonzaga University, 234, 247

Graduation Success Rate (GSR), 10, 156, 185, 261–62

Grady, Al, 102, 103

Graham, Rev. Billy, 55

Grambling State College, 67, 136

Grange, Red, 129

Green Bay Packers (NFL), 109, 110

Gregory, L. H., 100

Griffin, Archie, 127

Griffith, Homer, 26

Griffith, John L., 29

Grimsley, Will, 17

Grove City v. Bell, 226

Hackett, Wilbur, 63, 71, 72, 80, 81

Hair (Broadway show), 15, 50

Halas, George, 31

Halberstam, David, 62–63

Hamilton, Mel, 110–11

Hammon, Ira, 119

Hampton, Dave, 109

Harden, Paul, 278

Harper, William Rainey, 191

Harper's magazine, 57, 71–72

Harr, Rich, 93, 95, 97

Harrell, Landy, 113

Harris, Jovan, 274

Harris, Reed, 26, 27, 29, 233–34, 285 (n. 27)

Harvard University, 21, 22, 24, 28, 238

Haughton, Percy, 18

Hayes, Woody, 33, 38, 46, 48, 53, 121, 124, 140

Hearst, William Randolph, 29

Hesburgh, Rev. Theodore, 40, 41, 160

Hill, Darryl, 292 (n. 17)

Hill, Dave, 89

Hill, Pat, 196

Hinton, Lora, 64, 67

Hoch, Paul, 54

Hogg, Houston, 63, 71, 80, 81

Holiday Bowl, 163

Holland, Jerome "Brud," 59, 124

Holland, Terry, 279

Holloway, Condredge, 64, 84, 85

Holmes, Robert, 89

Holmgren, Mike, 194

Holub, E. J., 89

Holy Cross University, 238

Homan, Dennis, 89

Hooten, Herman, 45

Horn, Stephen, 158

Horne, Greg, 87, 88, 89–90

Howard, Dennis, 249, 250, 251

Hubbard, John, 148

Huddleston, Bryce, 97, 121

Hundred Yard Lie, The (Telander), 215, 236

Huntley, Chet, 110

Hutchins, Robert, 238

Hyland, Dick, 31

Indiana University, 76, 176, 196, 203, 225, 234; football racial protest at, 6, 44, 48, 57, 91, 104–5, 111–12, 113, 118, 120; football finances at, 176; football and academics at, 241

Iowa City Press-Citizen, 102

Iowa State University, 87, 241

Ivy, "Blind Jim," 84

Jackson, Bo, 127

Jackson, Ernie, 45

Jackson, Jesse, 87–88

Jackson, Wilbur, 62, 63, 64, 66, 70, 71

Jackson, William Tecumseh Sherman, 59

Jackson, Willie, 63, 64

Jackson Clarion-Ledger, 81

Jackson State University, 67

Jacksonville State University, 183
James, Don, 119
Jenkins, Charley, 30
Jensen, James, 93, 94, 131
Johnson, Chad, 58
Johnson, Charles, 100
Johnson, Jimmy, 193
Johnson, John Henry, 124
Johnson, Lyndon Baines, 53
Jones, Calvin, 119
Jones, June, 195–96, 269
Jones, Lawrence "Biff," 121
Joyce, Rev. Edmund, 134–35, 136, 160

Kansas City Chiefs (NFL), 6, 17, 52, 89
Kansas State University, 195
Kearney, Joe, 114, 157, 158
Kearny, Jim, 89
Kehoe, Jim, 44
Kemp, Jan, 146, 185
Kennedy, John F., 2, 5, 36, 53
Kennedy, Robert, 2
Kent, Frank, 53
Kent State University, 271
Kerr, Erwin T., 109
Keyes, Leroy, 57
Kilmer, Billy, 53
King, Horace, 63, 64, 66, 69, 75, 85
King, Martin Luther, Jr., 2, 5, 43
King Football (Harris), 233–34
Kinnebrew, Chuck, 63, 66
Kipke, Harry, 27, 285–86 (n. 34)
Kirschenbaum, Jerry, 50
Knight, Phil, 273
Knight Commission on Intercollegiate
   Athletics, 234, 235, 245, 278
Knoxville Journal, 74
Knoxville News-Sentinel, 74
Krause, Edward "Moose," 41
Kunen, James Simon, 21
Kush, Frank, 48

Lacy, Sam, 123
Lanier, Willie, 89

Laramie Daily Boomerang, 105, 107, 109,
   115
LaRouche, Chester, 35
LeVias, Jerry, 59–60, 89
Levin, Sarah, 222
Lewis, William Henry, 59
Lexington Herald, 76, 79, 135
Liberation News Service, 20
Liberty Bowl, 86, 87–88
Life magazine, 2, 21
Lightner, Al, 100, 132
Lipsyte, Robert, 53
Livingston, Mike, 89
Look magazine, 36
Los Angeles Examiner, 48
Los Angeles Evening Herald, 26–27
Los Angeles Rams (NFL), 33
Los Angeles Times, 31, 61, 214, 215–16,
   216–17
Louisiana State University (LSU), 28,
   89, 243, 259, 272; integration of
   football team at, 58, 63, 64, 67, 69,
   79; football finances at, 184, 194, 195;
   football scandal at, 185; football and
   academics at, 262, 264
Louisiana Tech, 250
Louisville Courier-Journal, 135

Major League Baseball, 180; integra-
   tion of, 57, 59, 76
Manley, Dexter, 205
Manning, Peyton, 127
Marquette University, 238
Marsalis, James, 89
Marshall, George Preston, 58
Marshall University, 229
Massachusetts Institute of Technology
   (MIT), 240
Mays, Jerry, 89
McAshan, Eddie, 84–88, 89, 138
McCarty, George, 42
McClain, Lester, 63, 64, 66, 67–68,
   71–75, 85
McDonald, Mark A., 217

NCAA News, 46, 122, 138
Nettles, Doug, 63, 64
New Mexico State University, 176, 183, 240, 271
New Pittsburgh Courier, 66, 123–24
New York Daily News, 21
New York Evening Journal, 29
New York Times, 35, 124, 137, 138, 147, 148, 149, 160, 183–84, 185, 209, 216, 219, 227–28, 230, 278New York University, 28
Newsweek, 30
Neyland, Robert, 121
Nicholls State University, 183
Nixon, Richard, 2, 6, 224; as "Chief Jock," 52–54
Northern Illinois University, 179, 183
Northington, Nat, 63, 76–80
Northwestern University, 24, 118, 176, 259; role of football in institutional history of, 238; football and academics at, 240; and "Flutie factor," 247; football and academics at, 264, 267
Norwood, Stephen, 24, 25
Nunn, Bill, 123

Observer (University of Notre Dame), 41
Ohio State University, 33, 38, 39, 46, 53, 121, 180, 242, 259; football finances at, 176, 177; academic scandal at, 185; football and academics at, 262, 264
Ohio University, 267
Oklahoma State University, 166, 266
Oliver, Chip, 20, 54, 284 (n. 13)
Olsen, Jack, 90, 123–24
Olympic Games, 30, 95; racial protest at, 42, 90, 123, 136
Omaha World-Herald, 29
Orange Bowl, 52, 151, 152, 163; as Superpatriot Bowl, 54–56
Oregon Journal (Portland), 100, 131–32
Oregon Statesman (Salem), 100, 131
Oregon State University, 192–93, 195, 207, 243, 266; football racial protest

at, 6, 48, 50, 57, 91, 92–102, 112, 119, 121, 131; football scandal at, 146; football and academics at, 204; football finances at, 272–73
Osborne, Tom, 127, 216, 226
Ottawa University, 146
Overton, Walter, 63, 64, 85
Owen, Caroline, 185
Owen, John, 113, 114, 117, 119, 132–33
Owens, James, 63, 66, 68, 71
Owens, Jim, 38, 44, 47, 89, 92, 104–5, 112–15, 118, 120, 121, 125
Owens, Terrell, 58
Oxford Eagle, 81

Pacific Coast Conference, 4, 130, 243
Pacific-8 Conference, 157
Pac-10 Conference, 151, 157, 159; finances of, 161, 164, 176, 194, 273
Page, Greg, 63, 76–78
Page, Robert, 76–78
Parrish, Bernie, 54
Parseghian, Ara, 17, 20, 40, 46, 50, 212
Paterno, Joe, 127, 148, 194
Peach Bowl, 86
Pell, Charley, 78
Pennington, Bill, 59
Pennsylvania State University, 39, 52, 151, 157, 160; football finances at, 176, 177; football and academics at, 241, 261, 262
Perkins, Don, 193
Perles, George, 278
Peter, Christian, 215, 216
Peterson, Calvin, 290 (n. 3)
Petrino, Bobby, 195
Philadelphia Inquirer, 177, 181, 196
Phillips, Lawrence, 215, 216
Pitts, Frank, 89
Pittsburgh Courier. See New Pittsburgh Courier.
Poinsettia Bowl, 164
Polak, Brian, 274
Pont, John, 104, 105, 111–12, 118, 121
Pope, Clarence, 45, 64

UT Daily Beacon (University of Tennessee), 66, 72–73, 74
Utah State University, 121, 240

Valenti, Paul, 96
Vanderbilt University, 213, 238, 259, 272; integration of football team at, 63, 64, 68; integration of basketball team at, 70; football and finances at, 176, 177; football and academics at, 264
Van Horn, Gary, 134
Vaught, John, 80, 81, 135
Vilardi, Paul, 21
Villanova University, 238
Virginia Tech, 79, 151, 162, 165, 195
Von Kleinsmid, Rufus, 237

Wagner, Berny, 97
Wake Forest University, 84
Waldrep, Kent, 225
Walker, Doak, 267
Walker, Jackie, 64, 291 (n. 13)
Wallace, Francis, 31–34, 42, 47
Wallace, George, 63
Wallace, Perry, 70
Walters, Norby, 211
Walters, Trent, 113
Ward, Bob, 43–44, 46, 112
Warmath, Murray, 43
Washington Redskins (NFL), integration of, 58
Washington State University, 15, 38, 98; football racial protest at, 43, 124; APR penalty for, 185; football finances at, 243, 272–73

Waterman, William, 109
Watterson, John, 158
Wechsler, James, 29
Weis, Charlie, 194
Werner, Clyde, 89
Wesleyan University, 24
West, Larry, 63, 66
Westbrook, John, 59
Western Athletic Conference (WAC), 106, 110, 157, 161, 162, 165, 179
Western Kentucky University, 250
Western Michigan University, 183
West Virginia University, 176, 179, 180, 265
Wheeler, Mark, 119
White, Gordon, 137
White, Jason, 274
White, Phil, 107–8
White v. NCAA, 273–76
Whittier, Julius, 59
Whitwell, Buck, 24
Wieberg, Steve, 162
Wiggins, David, 42
Williams, Jack, 85
Williams, Joe, 104
Williams, Mike, 63, 64, 69
Williams, Robert "Gentle Ben," 63, 64, 69
Wilson, Jerrell, 89
Witt, Robert, 244
Wolff, Alexander, 65
Wyche, Bubba, 68

Yale University, 21, 22, 25, 238